Education, Employment and Human Resource Development

Education, Employment and Human Resource Development

Editor

DR. DIGUMARTI BHASKARA RAO
M.Sc., M.A., M.A., M.Ed., Ph.D.
R.V.R. College of Education
D–43, S.V.N. Colony
Guntur–522006 (A.P.)
India

DISCOVERY PUBLISHING HOUSE
NEW DELHI-110002

First Published-2003
Reprinted-2010
ISBN 81-7141-681-0

Published by
DISCOVERY PUBLISHING HOUSE
4831/24, Ansari Road, Prahlad Street,
Darya Ganj, New Delhi-110002 (India)
Phone: 23279245 • Fax: 91-11-23253475
E-mail:dphtemp@indiatimes.com

Printed at:
Arora Offset Press
Laxmi Nagar, Delhi 110 092.

Preface

Education, Employment and Human Resource Development are closely connected with each other. One influences much the other and one supports the other in its effectiveness. Proper education provided to people helps them in getting appropriate employment and in excelling in it. The in-service education programmes enhance the efficiency of employees and contribute to the purposeful human resource development. Any deficiency in education leads to the production of inefficient human resources, and these resources do not adequately meet the employment opportunities. So, the educational programmes and human resource development activities should consider the requirements of employment avenues. If these trio are monitored effectively, the products of employment will be upto the expectations of the clientele.

This book on 'education, employment and human resource development' provides the worldwide expertise. This book will help the teachers, administrators and planners in planning their programmes effectively and suitably.

I am thankful to Prof. Gudmund Hernes, Director of the International Institute for Educational Planning, UNESCO, Paris, France for his kind co-operation in all of my academic endeavours.

Bhaskara Rao Digumarti

Acknowledgements

I am thankful to Prof. Gudmund Hernes, Director, International Institute for Educational Planning, UNESCO, Paris, France for granting me permission to reproduce all the articles appeared in this book from the publications of IIEP, Paris.

The articles in this book are reproduced from the Report of Intensive Training Course in Education Employment and Work, New Delhi, India, 1987; Report of an Intensive Training Course on Education Employment and Work, Gabarone, Botswana, 1989; Report of an Intensive Training Course on Education, Employment and Human Resource Development, Bangkok, Thailand, 1990; Report of Sub-regional Intensive Training course on Education, Employment and Human Resource Development, Buea, Cameroon, 1991; Report of Sub-regional Workshop on Education, Employment and Human Resource Development, Seol, Republic of Korea, 1992; Report of Sub-regional workshop on Education, Employment and Human Resource Development, Quatre Bornes, Republic of Mauritius, 1992; Report of Sub-regional Workshop on Education, Employment and Human Resource Development, Suva, Fiji, 1993; and Report of Sub-regional Workshop on Education, Employment and Human Resource Development in Central and Western Asia, Tashkent, Republic of Uzbekistan, 1993. I am thankful to the editors of those reports and contributors to those courses and workshops.

I am also thankful to the UNESCO's International Institute of Educational Planning, Paris; UNESCO's Principal Regional Office for Asia and the Pacific, Bangkok; UNESCO-BREDA, Senegal; University of the South Pacific, Fiji; Commonwealth

Fund for Technical Cooperation; Ministry of Education and Science, Mauritius; Korean Educational Development Institute; Ministry of Higher Education Computer Services and Scientific Research, Cameroon; National Institute of Development Research and Documentation, University of Botswana, Botswana; and National Institute of Educational Planning and Administration, New Delhi, India.

I am also thankful to Mr. Ian Denison and Mrs. Rachelle Recher for the kind correspondence and cooperation in preparing this publication.

Dr. Digumarti Bhaskara Rao
Sai Soudha, Guntur

CONTENTS

1

Education and Employment

N.V. Varghese

The education and employment concept is divided into two sections: *(i)* a global development scenario which explains the context in which education and employment are to be analyzed; and *(ii)* basic concepts which introduces some of the essential concepts useful in understanding and analyzing education and employment situation in any country.

1. Global Development Scenario

In the context of education employment relations, education is essentially seen in its economic dimensions—its impact on the productive labour force as a key instrument in promoting economic and social development. The attempt is to identify the forces which affect the relationship between patterns of educational distribution in occupations by sectors of economic activity and expected outputs of school and training programmes.

1.1 Role of Education

The role of education in promoting and sustaining economic development can be convincingly illustrated from the growth patterns of many of the countries. For example in Japan advancement in technology, industrial rationalization and productivity growth depended on the introduction of professional skill in the areas of science and technology. Korea's prominence in export of quality controlled manufactured goods is, to a very large extent, due to its exceptional reserve of qualified school graduates. China's gradual industrialization and technical progress were due to the importance given to adapting emerging local know-how to modern criteria. In all the three cases it can be said that education, employment and training were inter woven into general fabric.

1.2 The Sectoral Shifts

The sectoral composition in developing countries over the last two decades has shown certain shifts. First, the share of agriculture in GDP has declined and correspondingly that of the industry and services has increased. Second, the proportion of labour force engaged in agriculture has declined and correspondingly its proportion in industry and services has gone up. Third, there has been more improvement in productivity (measured in terms of GDP divided by labour force in each sector) in industry than in agriculture. Thus, it is not only that the share of labour force in industry that has increased but that its productivity has also increased. Industry, slowly but steadily, is emerging as a prominent sector in the developing countries.

1.3 Role of Technology

Industrial development depends on technological development. Technological development may be indigenous or as a result of imported technology. Technology import results in dependency on the developed nations. Therefore the attempt in the developing countries is to develop technology indigenously rather than resorting to a policy of technology import. This follows from the belief in the primacy of indigenous technology to facilitate self-sustaining economic growth. Needless to say that education has a tremendous role in technological development.

The "application of practical and theoretical knowledge to production through a sequential succession of techniques" is the essence of technological change. Such technological changes can exist if prior research and testing have taken place. Thus technological development in intrinsically associated with the extent of Research and Development (R&D) activities prevailing in any economy. As the present day technological development is the result of past R&D activities, the future technological development depends on the present ventures in R&D. The role of research becomes crucial in this context as it determines the potential technological developments.

The global pattern of development has shown that over the years disparities between the developed and less developed economies, have widened. These could be attributed to the disparities in the rates of technical changes witnessed in these two groups. Such disparities have led to polarization of development and underscore the necessity of technological developments in developing countries. In this sense, technological development has become a survival question for the developing world.

1.4 The Challenge

The challenge before the developing world is to make a rational choice between technological development for long term and self sustained growth on the one hand and amelioration of poverty which is immediate and imminent on the other. Where technology is a must for survival, education and training policies become key areas of intervention to prepare people and society for new technological culture and to ensure more flexible labour force. Given the fact that technological developments are often labour displacing, it adds another dimension to the challenges of the developing countries.

Unemployment is persisting in all the developing countries and is increasing over the years. Therefore any policy to adopt labour displacing techniques of production (which is inherent in technological developments), adds to the already aggravated situation of unemployment. Moreover, unemployment and poverty are associated factors. Direct attack on poverty which has to be immediate, implies generation of employment. On the other hand embarking upon a policy of technological change, while essential and unavoidable, will result in short term unemployment. The governments of the developing nations, in this sense, are faced with the duality inherent in growth objectives and have to make the crucial choice. This is the challenge for the developing nations in the present day context.

1.5 The Option

The challenge of technology requires changes in basic curricula and provision of a broad-based work-related education for young people. In addition, vocational and professional training should have proximity with a production place. Many a government may not have adequate resource to meet these two educational objectives. Therefore governments have to increasingly seek the financial and professional involvement of production sectors in training of the nations' future scientific technological and industrial cadres. Such a widening of participation will give the government an opportunity to spend their resources on the education of the masses without compromising with the need for R&D which is so crucial for the survival and sustenance of these countries.

2. Basic Concepts

There are various concepts essential in analyzing education and employment. Since the definitions tend to vary, a discussion on some of the basic concepts becomes necessary to facilitate communication in the workshop.

2.1. Labour Force

Labour force comprises of all economically active population. It includes both employed and unemployed. Labour Force Participation Rate (LFPR) is the percentage of total labour force to total population. Generally population aged ten and above is considered for calculating LFPR. Labour force participation rates exhibit certain general pattern:

(a) LFPR of men and women below the age of 25 declines with increase in access to higher education;

(b) LFPR of men and women above the age of sixty decline with increase of old age benefits and other social security provisions; and

(c) LFPR of females varies accordingly to cultural traditions. It is also quite sensitive to total income of the family.

2.2 *Employment*

Employed persons are those who are working and receiving a wage. Employment has three aspects: income, output and recognition. Very often distinctions are also made between employment, work and self employment. Wage becomes an important criterion to distinguish employment. Work is a broader concept which is more related to the social roles of an individual and it does not necessarily imply a wage; *i.e.*, the criterion of 'being paid' cannot be applied in the case of work. Self-employment is different from wage employment. The self-employed engage themselves in productive activities and make an earning.

Employment can be classified according to economic activities and occupational categories. In general, with economic development the proportion of labour force engaged in primary sector comes down and that in the secondary and tertiary sectors go up. Thus the pattern of distribution of workers in a country indicates the level of economic development achieved by an economy.

Related to employment are the notions of under-employment and unemployment. Under employment exists when persons in employment are not working full time and are willing and able to work for a longer duration. Under-employment is of two types—visible and invisible. Visible under-employment means working less than the normal hours of work. Invisible under-employment exists if more people are engaged in an activity than would be needed to produce the output which they produce. Earnings of invisible under-employment will be low and they are utilized less than their full capacity.

2.3 *Unemployment*

Unemployment is a state of not working. Unemployment can be voluntary or involuntary. Involuntarily unemployed are those who are not working but seeking employment at the on going wage rate. Unemployment in general refers to the involuntarily unemployed. Based on the factors affecting it, unemployment is categorized into frictional, structural, cyclical, seasonal etc. Disguised unemployment is very common in less developed economies. Disguised unemployment exists when withdrawal of a part of the labour force from the traditional field of production would leave the total output unchanged. In technical terms it means marginal productivity of labour is zero.

2.4 Labour Market

Employment and unemployment will be reflected in the labour market. Labour market was traditionally considered to decide the wages which is the price for labour. However, in the latter explanations wages are fixed to jobs and therefore main function of the labour market is to adjust between men and jobs and wages are automatically determined. The radical explanations consider labour markets as divided into primary and secondary labour market. Some of the versions further subdivide the primary into several segments. Primary segments of the labour market are characterized by high wage, employment stability, better promotion possibilities etc., whereas secondary labour markets are characterized by low wage, with no stability in employment. Labour turn over is high in the secondary labour market.

Labour mobility is the movement of labour. Labour mobility can be between different regions (spatial) or from one employment status to another (vertical) or from one occupation to another (horizontal).

2.5 Wages

Wage in the wider sense is the reward for the factor of production namely labour. In its narrow and more commonly used sense wages refer to payment to workers and employed persons.

Two important bases for wage determinants are: *(i)* payment by time; and *(ii)* payment by results. Salary paid to the employees is perhaps the best example of payment by time. Payment by result is related to the actual work done. The work done can be measured in terms of: *(a)* piece work; *(b)* time allowances. In the former payment is according to the number of output he has produced *i.e.* output is priced as the criterion for payment. And in the latter the output is fixed and he is paid as per the normal time than actual time taken to finish the output.

2

Education and Employment: Some Basic Concepts

N.V. Varghese

1. Introduction

The attempt in this paper is to introduce the readers to some of the basic and elementary concepts useful in diagnosing education and employment situation in a country. The concepts discussed in this note are classified under different headings. Section 2 introduces the concepts of GNP and GDP. Section 3 introduces the concept of labour force and work force. Section 4 deals with the concepts of employment and work. It also deals with industrial and occupational classification of employment. Section 5 elaborates on the concept of unemployment. Section 6 deals with labour market. Section 7 introduces the concept of wage. Section 8 deals with labour mobility and the final section is on education.

2. GNP and GDP

Gross National Product (GNP) measures the total domestic and foreign output claimed by residents and is calculated without making deductions for depreciation. It comprises of gross domestic product adjusted by net factor income from abroad, *i.e.*, is the income residents receive from abroad for factor services (labour and capital) less similar payments made to non-residents who contributed to the domestic economy (World Bank: 1987).

GNP per capita is arrived at by dividing gross national product by population of the country. For purposes of international comparisons the World Bank converts GNP to US dollars. This procedure of conversion generally uses three year average of the official exchange rate.

Gross Domestic Product (GDP) measures the total final output of goods and services produced by an economy—that is, by residents and non-residents—regardless of the allocation to domestic and foreign claims. It is calculated without making deductions for depreciation (World Bank: 1987).

GDP by industrial origin is measured at producer prices or at purchaser values. GDP at producer prices is equal to GDP at purchaser values less import duties. GDP at producer prices is referred to as GDP at factor cost and GDP at purchaser values is referred to as GDP at market prices.

The economy is broadly divided into three sectors—agriculture, industry and services. These three sectors are some time referred to as Primary, Secondary and Tertiary Sectors. Agricultural Sector comprises of agriculture, forestry, hunting and fishing, Industry comprises of mining, manufacturing, construction and electricity gas and water. All other branches of economic activity are categorized as Services. GDP share from each of these three sectors is taken as an index of level of development of the economy. With advances in economic development the share of agriculture in GDP comes down and correspondingly the shares of other sectors increase.

3. Labour Force

The total population of a country can be divided into those who are economically active and those who are not. Economically active means all persons, who furnish the potential supply of labour for production of economic goods and services. Labour force comprises of all economically active persons aged ten and above. It includes the number of persons employed and unemployed but excludes economically inactive population (World Bank: 1987).

International classification by status categorizes the economically active population under the following headings:

(a) ***Employer:*** A person who operates his or her own economic enterprise or engages independently in a profession or trade and hires one or more employees.

(b) ***Own account worker:*** A person who operates his or her own economic enterprise or engages independently in a profession or trade and hires no employees.

(c) ***Employee:*** A person who works for a public or private employer and receives remuneration in wages, salary, commission, tips, piece-rates or pay in kind.

(d) ***Unpaid family worker:*** A person who works a specified minimum amount of time (at least one-third of normal working hours) without pay, in economic enterprises operated by a related person living in the same household.

(e) ***Member of Producer's co-operative:*** A person who is an active member of producer's co-operatives regardless of the industry in which it is established.

(f) ***Persons not classified by status:*** Experienced workers with status unknown or inadequately described and unemployed persons not previously established.

Labour Force Participation Rate (LFPR) is the percentage of total labour force to the total population aged ten and above *i.e.*, total number of persons employed plus unemployed divided by total population aged ten and above multiplied by a hundred.[1]

Labour force is to be distinguished from workers[2] and work force. Workers denote those who are participating in any economically productive activity. This participation can be physical or mental, direct or indirect involvement (supervision etc.) in work. Sum total of the workers constitutes work force. Work force participation rate is the percentage of workers to the relevant age group population (ten years and above).

Sometimes a distinction is drawn between labour force, work force and supply of labour. As mentioned earlier, labour force includes employed and unemployed persons: work force includes only employed, *i.e.*, labour force minus unemployed gives work force. Supply of labour on the other hand includes hours worked and intensity of working effort (Uthoff and Pernia: 1986).

Historical behaviour of labour force participation rates exhibits certain discernable pattern (Uthoff and Pernia: 1986).

(a) LFPR of men and women below the age of 25 tend to decline over a period of time as a result of access to higher education;

(b) LFPR of men and women above sixty decline because of old age benefits and social security system;

(c) Male LFPR between 25 and 55 years of age show only marginal declining trend;

(d) Female LFPR vary between geographical areas depending upon cultural traditions and agricultural structure. Women are mainly engaged in primary sector activities. Female LFPR is sensitive to total income of the family.

4. Employment

Employment and work are sometimes used interchangeably. However, a distinction need to be drawn between the two. Perhaps, wage is the criterion on which these two can be distinguished.

Productive activities which directly take place in the realm of market forces are treated as employment. Market denotes exchange and in this sense work which has a direct exchange value is employment. In other words, when work is directly exchanged for a wage, it becomes employment. Work, on the other hand, does not necessarily mean earning a wage. For example, those who are engaged in household economic activities may not be receiving a wage as a direct payment for the work they perform; but they may be receiving or sharing the profit borne out of the output that they produce and market.

Sen (1975) notes that the concept of employment is vague in any economy in which wage system is weak and self-employment and unpaid family labour are common because the criterion of 'being paid a wage' cannot be reliably applied.

Accordingly, this vagueness was a problem confined to less developed economies where market system is less developed.

Employment has three aspects (Sen: 1975):

(a) It gives an income to the employed;

(b) It yields an output;

(c) It gives a person the recognition of being engaged in something worth while.

Of recent the concept of work and employment and distinctions between the two assumed a different dimension even in the well developed market economies primarily resulting from the changing technological conditions of production. During the industrial stage employment was organised in a central place, say in a factory, all people had uniform working hours and uniform frequency in the payment of wages. In the post industrial phase, 'contractual systems of employment' emerged (Watts: 1983). Now work need not necessarily be organised in a central place. At present, with the revolution in the communication and information net work, work can be very easily organised in the households itself. Therefore, people undertake contractual work and locate themselves away from the bureaucratic set up and industrial concerns. They finish the job and receive the payment. And this payment is not the same as wages. This is different from conventional type of employment.

Self employment means working for oneself. This is different from wage employment. That is to say when one works for others for a fixed wage it becomes wage-employment and when one is working for oneself it becomes self-employment. Self employment is increasing rather fast in many of the less developed economies. And many a time it is suggested to re-orient educational systems to equip individuals to be self-employed.

Another term which is very often used in literature on employment is under-employment. Under-employment exists when persons in employment who are not working full time would be able and willing to do more work than they are actually performing at present (ILO: 1984). Under-employment is of two types—visible and invisible. Visible under-employment means working less than a certain number of hours per year. This number of hours be either the number of hours desired or the number of hours considered normal or appropriate. People are invisibly under-employed if more of them are engaged in a certain activity than would be needed to produce the output which they produce. (Monly and Costa: 1981). Their earnings are abnormally low, and their jobs do not permit full use of their capacities or skills. Under-employment of the educated is a serious problem in many of the developing economies.

4.1 *Classification of the employed*

Employment is very often discussed in terms of industrial classification and occupational classification. Industrial classification denotes the distribution of the employed by sectors of activity. According to the International Standard Industrial Classification of Economic Activities, the major divisions of industries are:

(a) Agriculture, hunting, forestry and fishing

(b) Mining and quarrying

(c) Manufacturing

(d) Electricity, gas and water

(e) Construction

(f) Wholesale and retail trade, restaurants and hotels

(g) Transport, storage and communication

(h) Financing, insurance, real estate and business services

(i) Community, social and personal services

(j) Activities not adequately defined.

It is generally believed that the relative distribution of workers between sectors is an indicator of the level of economic development achieved by any economy. Process of economic development is associated with a gradual shift of the work force from primary to secondary and further to tertiary sector. Thus the least developed economy will have the highest proportion of its work force engaged in primary sector activities and the most developed economy will have the highest proportion of its work force engaged in the tertiary sector activities. It is to be noted here that, of late this shift is not stage wise—from primary to secondary to tertiary—in many of the less developed countries tertiary sector is growing faster than secondary sector. This is primarily due to the growth of service sectors in the tertiary sector due to the increased welfare measures adopted by the public authorities. In India too more proportion of work force is employed in tertiary sector than in secondary sector.[3]

Occupational classification denotes distribution of employment between different occupational divisions. Till the seventies data on employment were collected as per International Classification of Occupations (ISCO) adopted by ILO in 1958. In 1968 ILO revised the occupational classification. As per the revised classification there are 8 major occupational groups, 83 minor occupational groups, 284 unit groups and 1,506 occupational categories. Because of this change in the occupational classification data are not strictly comparable over a period of time.[4]

The International Standard Classification of Occupations gives the following major groups of occupations.

- 1. Professional, technical and related workers.
- 2. Administrative and managerial workers.
- 3. Clerical and related workers.
- 4. Sales workers.
- 5. Service workers.
- 6. Agriculture, animal husbandry and forestry workers, fishermen and hunters.
- 7/8/9. Production and related workers, transport equipment operators and labourers.
- 10. Workers not classifiable by occupation and members of the armed forces.

5. Unemployment

Unemployment is the state of not working. Unemployment can be voluntary and involuntary. Those who are not working and not seeking an employment are treated as voluntarily unemployed. They do not come under the category of economically active population. Involuntarily unemployed are those who are not at work but are seeking work or available for work at the on-going wage rate. This category is important from the economic point of view. In discussions, unemployment unless otherwise qualified, refers to those who are involuntarily unemployed. Unemployment rate refers to the percentage of total unemployed population to the total labour force.

The general definition used by the ILO for unemployment includes all persons above a specified age who, on the specified day or for a specified week, came into one of the following categories:

(a) workers available for employment whose contract of employment had been terminated or temporarily suspended and who were without a job and seeking work for pay or profit;

(b) persons who were available for work (except for minor iliness) during the specified period and were seeking work for pay or profit, who were never previously employed or whose most recent status was other than that of employee (*i.e.*, former employers, etc.) or who had been in retirement;

(c) persons without a job and currently available for work who had made arrangements to start a new job at a date subsequent to the specified period;

(d) persons on temporary or indefinite lay-off without pay.

The following categories of persons are not considered by the ILO to be unemployed:

(a) persons intending to establish their own business or farm, but who had not yet arranged to do so, who were not seeking work or pay for profit;

(*b*) former unpaid family workers not at work and not seeking work for pay or profit.

Unemployment is, very often, categorized into various types. Frictional unemployment denotes unemployment caused by industrial friction such as immobility of labour, ignorance of job opportunities; shortage of raw materials, break down of the machinery or plant etc. Seasonal unemployment refers to unemployment which is due to seasonal variations. Those employed in agricultural activities are subjected to seasonal unemployment if they do not plan for their employment in the off seasons in agriculture.

Structural unemployment refers to unemployment arising out of structural changes in the economy. Technological changes will result in structural changes in the production process. It may displace labour and result in structural unemployment.

Cyclical unemployment refers to unemployment resulting from the business cycles in the economy. During periods of depression many people are thrown out of employment and they are referred to as cyclically unemployed.

Perhaps the most important and most commonly discussed type of unemployment is disguised unemployment. Disguised unemployment means that a withdrawal of a part of the labour force from the traditional field of production would leave the total output unchanged (Sen: 1975). "In technical terms this will mean marginal productivity of labour, over a wide range, is zero" (Nurkse: 1953). Disguised unemployment is very common in all agriculture based labour surplus economies. A distinction is to be made between incidence and duration of unemployment. Incidence of unemployment is the percentage of unemployed in a given population group. It is the unemployment rate.[5] Duration of unemployment denotes mean years or months unemployed since graduation (Sanyal: 1985).

6. Labour Market

Labour market is the institution which mediates between demand for and supply of labour. It used to be believed that the price of labour—wage—is determined in the labour market depending upon the relative supply of and demand for labour.

The classical economists assumed full employment and hence the primary function of labour market is considered to be to ascertain the price of labour services at a given point of time. Given the assumptions of homogeneity of labour units and flexibility of wages, equilibrium in the labour market was a general case and dis-equilibrium was only a temporary aberration. The neo-classicals, though did not subscribe to the classical assumption of homogeneity of labour units too considered that the primary function of labour market is to allocate and rationally adjust labour skills and labour demands so as to establish equilibriating wage rates.

From the educational point of view different economists have emphasized different aspects of education which is given premium in the labour market. As per human capital version it is the cognitive skills (Shultz: 1981), to Arrow (1973) it is the filtering or screening role, to Spence (1973) it is the signalling role of education which the employers consider dear in their recruitment. To Thurow (1972) Fields (1974) and Bhagawati and Srinivasan (1977) it is the hiring practice which is very important. To the radicals labour market is segmented (Reich, *et. al.*: 1973).

As per the segmentation theory labour markets are divided into two: *(i)* primary and *(ii)* secondary labour markets. Primary labour market is characterized by employment stability, high wages, better working conditions and internal labour market. Secondary labour markets are characterized by low skill requirements, low wages, poor working conditions and high labour turn over and no promotion avenues.

Some versions of the segmentation theory further divides the primary segment into two—upper and lower tiers. Jobs in the upper tier require decision making abilities where as those in the lower tier involve routinized activities. However, educational qualifications become a requisite for entry into the primary sector where as they are not so essential in the secondary sector of the labour market.

A mention about internal and external labour market is in order. Internal labour markets refers to the Labour Market internal to an organisation primarily for promotion into higher posts.

External labour market is the useful recruitment place for any job. In internal labour market only employees of the same organisation are candidates where as the external labour market is primarily for the unemployed though employed also may be part of it to improve their jobs prospects.

7. Wages

Wage, in the wider sense, is the reward for the factor of production namely labour and hence includes any payment for work whether it is work done for an employer or that of a self-employed person. In a narrow and more commonly used sense wages refer to payment to employed persons. Wage rate is the stated amount at which a person is hired.

Some times a distinction is drawn between wages and salaries. Wages are associated with lower level manual workers paid on hourly, daily or weekly basis where as salaries refer to monthly or annual payments preferably for white collar employees.

Two important bases for wage payment or wage determination are: *(i)* payment by time; *(ii)* payment by results. (Robertson: 1961). Payment by time means deciding and paying a fixed amount of money to an individual with given and known characteristics for a certain specified period of time. Salary is the most common payment based on time. Salary is a pure time payment and the time period involved is normally monthly or yearly. Non-manual workers are usually salaried.

Payment by results is related to the actual work done. The work done can be measured in terms of *(a)* piece-work; and *(b)* time allowances. In the case of piece work the worker is remunerated according to the number of units of output he has produced *i.e.,* the unit of output is priced as the criterion for payment. In time allowances the output is fixed than priced. Each work requires certain period of time for its completion or performance. There is a normal or standard time required for each work. The payment is based on this time allowed. The individual may take more or less time than this to finish the work. But he will be paid based on the standard time to be taken rather than the actual time taken.

A distinction is to be drawn between income, wages and earnings. Income is the flow of returns from the property, estate or wealth. Wages are the reward or payment for the work or employment. Earnings refers to total of all types of receipts from any profession. Earning will be more than wages. Wage is the minimum that one gets from a profession or job where as earnings are the maximum that one can receive from the profession or job and income is independent of profession.

The general trend is that there is a positive association between education and earnings. Therefore, education is considered to be an influential variable in explaining earning differentials between individuals. Human capital model is the most commonly used model for explaining earning differential among individuals.

8. Labour Mobility

Labour mobility refers to the movement of labour force. Mobility can be spatial which denotes movement of labour from region to the other region or from one country to the other. This is sometimes referred to as labour migration. Migration within the confines of a country is called internal migration and between nations is called international migration.

Mobility can be from one employment status to another. This is more common where internal labour markets exist and promotion possibilities are wide-spread. This is referred to as vertical mobility.

Mobility can also be from one occupation to another occupation. The occupation may be of similar status. This is referred to as lateral or horizontal mobility. Persons with narrow fields of specialization have less chances of lateral mobility though their chances of vertical mobility are better.

9. Education

Very often distinctions are drawn between education and training. Education implies general instruction and learning relevant to performance in an array of occupational roles where as training is specific instruction concerned with good performance of a particular task or a set of tasks making up a job or occupation (Staley: 1970). The level of training refers to the degree of socialization one has achieved in a particular occupational group whereas education refers to the professional knowledge or aptitude acquired and applied in a total system.

Educational level acquired by an individual is important factor in determining his job and earnings. Educational levels vary from literate in any language to doctorate in any subject. A person who can read and write with understanding in any one language is treated as literature.

The highest qualification acquired by an individual is recorded as his educational level. This is difficult to assess in certain cases especially if a person possesses more than one equivalent qualification. In Indian census when a person holds both general and technical qualification of equivalent level the technical qualification is recorded. When general educational level is higher than the technical education level or when it is not possible to decide which of them is relatively the higher qualification, the level of education as entered by the person is taken into account and he is classified accordingly.

In the case of a person who is still studying in a particular class, the highest qualification attained by him will be the one which he has actually passed and not the one he is studying. So his highest acquired qualification is recorded.

NOTES

1. It may be noted that working age population refers to population between the age-groups of 15 and 64 (World Bank: 1987).
2. In Indian census workers are some times divided into two—main workers and marginal workers (census: 1981). Main workers are those who have worked for major part of year preceding the enumeration. Marginal workers are those who have worked any time at all in the year preceding enumeration but have not worked for the major part of the year. Non-workers are those who have not worked anytime at all in the year preceding enumeration. Non-workers include *(i)* full time students who do no other work; *(ii)* persons engaged in unpaid household duties; *(iii)* dependents like children not attending schools and

permanently disabled; *(iv)* retired persons, rentiers etc. who do no other work; *(v)* beggars vagrants etc.; *(vi)* prisoners and inmates of charitable institutions; *(vii)* persons seeking employment for the first time; and *(viii)* persons employed before but are out of employment and are seeking jobs at present.

3. See Varghese (1986) for details on the empirical picture in India.
4. However ILO provides conversion tables to make the figures comparable.
5. There are two concepts used in measuring unemployment *(i)* persons rates; and *(ii)* time rate (Krishna: 1984). Time rate is the number of person days of unemployment as a proportion of person days of labour supply per week. Person rate is the number of persons counted as unemployed on the basis of their status during the reference period divided by the number of persons in the labour force in the same period. It can be seen that time rate is a flow rate and person rate the stock rate of unemployment.

REFERENCES

Arrow, K.J. (1973) "Higher Education as Filter", *Journal of Public Economic,* Vol. 2, pp. 192-216.

Bhagawati, J.N. and T.N. Srinivasan (1977) "Education in a Jobladder-Model and Fairness in Hiring Principle", *Journal of Public Economics,* Vol. 7, pp. 1-22.

Census of India (1981) *Provisional Population Totals: Workers and Non-Workers,* Seres-1, India Paper 3.

Fields, G.S. (1974): "Private Demand for Education in Relation to Labour Market Conditions in Less Developed Countries", *The Economic Journal,* Vol. 84, pp. 906.19.

ILO: International Labour Organisation (1969) *International Standard Classification of Occupations,* (Revised), Geneva, ILO. ILO: International Labour Organisation (1984) *Unemployment and Economic Growth,* Geneva, ILO.

Krishna, Raj (1984) *Growth of Aggregate Unemployment in India,* World Bank Staff Working Papers No. 638; Washington D.C.

Monly, J. and E. Costa (1981) *Employment Policies in Developing Countries,* Geneva, ILO.

Nurkse, R. (1953) *Problems of Capital Formation in Under Developed Countries,* Oxford, Blackwell.

Reich, M; D.M. Gordon and R.C. Edwards (1973): "A Theory of Labour Market Segmentation", *American Economic Review*, Vol. 63, pp. 359-65.

Robertson, D.J. (1961) *The Economics of Wages and Distribution of Income*, London, Macmillan.

Sanyal, B.C. (1985) "Graduate Unemployment and Education" in *International Encyclopedia for Education*, Oxford, Pergamon Press.

Schultz, T.W. (1961) "Investment in Human Capital" *American Economic Review*, Vol. 51, pp. 1-17.

Sen, A.K. (1975) *Employment Technology and Development*, Delhi, Oxford University Press.

Spence, M. (1973) "Job Market Signalling", *Quarterly Journals of Economics*, Vol. 87, pp. 355-75.

Staley, E.C. (1970) *Planning Occupational Education and Training for Development*, New Delhi Orient Longman.

Thurow, L. (1972) "Education and Economic Inequality" *Public Interest*, Summer.

Uthoff, A. and E.M. Pernia, (1986) *An Introduction to Human Resources Planning in Developing Countries*, Geneva, ILO, 1986.

Varghese, N.V. (1986) *Education and Labour Market: A Survey of Indian Evidence*, (A Study Sponsored by IIEP), NIEPA, New Delhi (Memeo).

Varghese, N.V. (1988) *Education and Employment Relations: A Case Study of Organised Sector in India*, Occasional Paper, Paris, IIEP (Forthcoming).

Watts, A.G. (1983) *Education, Unemployment and Future of Work*, Milton Keynes, Open University Press.

World Bank (1987) *World Development Report*, Washington, D.C. World Bank.

3

Education and Employment: A Global Development Scenario

S. Lourié

1. Introduction: Limits on a Discourse

Setting the stage for the International Course which is about to begin, calls for an explanation of the extent to which education and employment are related and how other factors overlap this relationship.

This implies however two self-imposed limits. The first is that we do not start off with considerations on education as a 'fundamental right' which in no way can be justified by economic considerations alone. Likewise, we shall not begin this presentation with an explanation of the dimensions of education which relate to cultural attainment levels, to individual satisfactions and to the pursuit of societal well-being through the production, acquisition and development of knowledge for its own sake. We shall therefore purposely begin this discourse on education by relating it essentially to one of its economic dimensions which is its impact on, and enhancement of, the productive labour force seen as a key instrument in promoting economic and social development.

The second limit we shall set is that while we do not suggest that economic and social development depend exclusively on the availability of a relevant productive work force, we will not discuss those considerably important historical, cultural, ethical and social factors which condition the political definition of the scope and magnitude of any type of economic development. Socio-cultural trends, value systems, behaviour and attitude are more likely to explain the shape of economic development programmes and their successes or failures than sheer quantitative analysis of manpower requirements.

That, however, having been clearly spelt out at the start, it is just as essential to recall that there can be no national 'development' if there is no self-sustaining economic growth. We shall therefore attempt to understand the symptoms and some causes of economic growth. This calls for an insight on individual sector growth and on the relationship between changes and increases in production and in added value on the one hand, and the availability of a capable and competent work force which, in turn, is largely conditioned by the education and training received either before or during its economically active life, on the other.

We shall then identify forces which affect what ideally would be a simple relationship between economic growth, patterns of distribution of occupations by sectors of economic activity and expected outputs of school and of training programmes whose presence in given numbers and qualifications will ensure future growth.

We shall therefore indicate that manpower planning while it cannot ignore assumptions about the economy must take into consideration delicate choices emerging from national conditions and—more imperatively still—from international economic factors which make nations more interdependent than ever before.

Thus, shall we hang the backdrop on the scenery of this course.

2. Economic Growth Objectives and Education: Three Asian Cases

Before analyzing somewhat more abstractedly the proposed issues, let us briefly look at economic development as a concrete reality in three Asian countries. Out of these experiences, future references to concepts may become more tangible:

2.1 Japan

It was its First Economic Plan, designed in 1955 for a six-year period, which put Japan's exceptional economic performance on orbit. It seems interesting therefore to check on what the objective were. That particular Plan, the first of its kind, identified four central policy goals which had to be met in order to achieve economic self-reliance.[1]

(a) the first was that the most important economic policy objective should be a major expansion of exports through industrialization, enhancement of productivity and restriction of imports to conserve foreign exchange;

(b) the second goal was expansion of employment calling for a maximum possible growth of the Japanese economy. This was promoted through the encouragement of industrial sectors at all levels, especially medium and small-scale businesses in order to absorb the expansion in the labour force;

(c) the Plan set stable economic growth as the third goal. It held that economic growth rate targets should be established within the limit set by the balance of payments 'ceiling';

(d) finally, the Plan sought to harmonize overall economic expansion and structural changes by re-orienting industry towards development of the domestic and international markets, centering on the heavy and chemical industries. The Plan thus called for structural changes to encourage the adoption of new technology, industrial rationalization, productivity growth as well as improvements in management methods, business finance and industrial relations.

This led to Japan achieving between 1966 and 1970 an average 10 per cent growth rate per annum which was followed in spite of the oil crisis by an average of almost 5 per cent between 1971 and 1981 and preserving almost a 4 per cent average between 1982 and 1985.[2]

2.2 Korea

The first step towards growth was to transform tenural conditions through land redistribution. This was followed by technological and institutional innovations that raised productivity. Then a massive investment was made in primary education to achieve universal education in rural areas, later to be followed by an expansion of secondary and university education.

Korea thus found itself with an abundance of highly educated human resources though it had no natural resources to speak of. An acceleration of growth could therefore be based only on labour-intensive industrialization. At first, this was oriented towards import substitution; because of the earlier rural development, internal markets were gradually being established. By the late 60s however, import substitution possibilities were exhausted and economic objectives shifted towards export-oriented, labour-intensive development. That effort which also depended on large foreign capital in-flows was successful in terms of growth as well as of distribution.[3]

2.3 China

This third case points to a framework for action in matters of employment and education. China's development strategy was shaped by two major constraints: an extreme shortage of arable land in relation to population and isolation from the main streams of world technological development. The Chinese response to these constraints has been two-fold. First, following an initial phase of property redistribution, poverty reduction was based, on the one hand, on local resources and initiatives and, on the other, on economy and technical improvisations. Poverty reduction was further achieved through rural development and the provision of basic social services and food security by means of large-scale transfers. Second, communes established some industries in rural areas but industrialization was based primarily on centrally mobilized resources using mainly technologies developed in the 1950s. Though the initial distribution of assets and by controlling to some extent the distribution of the gains from productivity, China achieved a per capita growth rate which is above the average of other low income countries.[4]

Thus, we note that Japan's new technology, industrial rationalization and productivity growth depended on the introduction of professional skills in areas of science and technology to be sure, but also in management, finance and industrial relations. The high premium given to its own unique brand of highly competitive school achievements, the close involvement of each graduate in the socio-cultural web of the employing institution and a modern programme ensuring the constant updating an re-training of professionals show the linkages between economic growth and skill building.

Likewise Korea's successful shift to exports of quality controlled manufactured goods is to a very large extent due to its exceptional reserve of qualified school graduates.

Finally, China's gradual industrialization and technical progress was due to the importance given to adapting emerging local know-how to modern criteria. The establishment after the Cultural Revolution of workers colleges enabling young workers to rapidly and intensively acquire broad-based vocational techniques and industrial leadership is another striking example of the relationship between growth and skill development.

Those three illustrations taken from Asia are meant to suggest that both employment and education and training and intimately woven into a general fabric, some strands of which may turn out to be of a sociological and cultural nature. Essentially they are based on universally accepted objectives of self-sustained growth as a pre-condition for redistribution and general human welfare.

3. Growth, Labour Force and Unemployment: National Resources

When then are the assets a country needs to possess in order to attain growth, development and welfare? These naturally are found in the accumulation of goods and services which a country can produce and which it can reinvest for further production.

Generally, this is obtained by responding to growing needs of the domestic market and by promoting exports, at competitive prices, of commodities, manufactured goods and capital goods.

A brief look therefore at the 'Gross Domestic Product' (GDP) which reflects this production capability and at its distribution by sectors, on the one hand, and at the distribution of its labour force through the sectors, yields indications for a given year or suggests trends if such analyses are conducted over time (see Table—3.1).

Table—3.1: Structure of GDP: Developing Regions, 1960—80 (in percentage)

	Agriculture		*Industry*		*Services*	
	1960	1980	1960	1980	1960	1980
All developing countries	31.0	17.3	29.9	38.5	39.1	44.2
Latin America and Caribbean (low-income countries)	26.2	17.2	27.7	32.0	46.1	
Latin America and Caribbean (middle-income countries)	16.2	10.0	36.7	39.0	47.1	51.0
China	n.a	n.a	n.a	n.a	n.a	n.a
India	51.0	37.0	19.4	25.0	29.5	38.0
Asia (other low-income countries)	48.1	33.0	17.5	27.0	34.4	40.0
Asia (middle-income countries)	34.8	18.0	21.0	36.0	44.2	46.0
Africa and Middle East (low-income countries)	54.4	41.0	13.3	17.0	32.4	42.0
Africa and Middle East (middle-income countries)	33.0	20.0	28.3	35.0	38.8	45.0
Africa and Middle East (capital surplus oil producers)	25.8	8.0	51.1	63.0	23.2	29.0

Note: n.a = not available

Source: ILO, World Labour Report, 1984, Ch. 1.

The structure of GDP in developing countries reveals that between 1960 and 1980, there were considerable shifts as to the relative role of each of the three main sectors (agriculture, industry and services (see Table—3.1). Thus, while in 1960, agriculture represented 31 per cent of GDP for all developing countries, it only represented 17.3 per cent twenty years later. Likewise, industry which barely reached 30 per cent in 1960 grew to 38.5 per cent of GDP by 1980 and finally, services which were of the order of 39 per cent in 1960 reached 44 per cent in 1980. Looking at the case of Asia and separating within Asia, the case of India, that of the low income countries and the situation of middle income countries, we find the following shifts in the 20-year period: the share of agriculture dropped by almost 30 per cent in India and in other low income countries, while for middle income countries, the shift was of the order of 50 per cent.

As this drop in the agriculture content of GDP took place, a parallel rise in the relative magnitude of industry also took place. Thus, in India, it grew by almost 30 per cent, by more than 50 per cent for other low income countries, and by over 70 per cent for middle income countries of Asia.

In the meantime, services also grew. In India by 29 per cent in the other low income countries by 16 per cent, and in the middle income countries by 4 per cent only.

If we compare now the distribution of the labour force within the three sectors for Asia, we shall see that whilst there were shifts comparable to the ones we have just noticed within the GDP, they are of considerably less magnitude (see Table—3.2). Thus India, whose labour force was essentially concentrated in agriculture in 1960, saw its share fall by 16 per cent by 1980, while in the other low income countries, it fell by 14 per cent and in the middle income countries, by 23 per cent.

These figures should now be compared to the gradual growth of the labour force in industry. Taking again the case of India, we note that the labour force in industry grew by 52 per cent, whilst at the same time, in the other low income countries, the industrial labour force share increased by 46 per cent. What is most remarkable is the case of the middle income countries where it increased by 60 per cent.

Table—3.2: Labour Force Structure: Developing Regions, 1960—80 (in percentage)

	Agriculture		*Industry*		*Services*	
All developing countries	72.6	59.1	12.8	19.9	14.5	21.0
Latin America and Caribbean (low-income countries)	63.5	49.3	14.8	19.8	21.7	30.9
Latin America and Caribbean (middle-income countries)	45.6	31.8	20.7	25.8	33.6	42.4
China	74.8	60.0	15.4	25.8	9.8	14.2
India	74.0	62.2	11.3	17.2	14.7	20.6
Asia (other low-income countries)	76.4	65.5	8.1	11.8	15.5	22.7
Asia (middle-income countries)	68.0	52.5	12.2	19.4	19.8	28.1
Africa and Middle East (low-income countries)	87.6	80.0	5.1	8.6	7.3	11.4
Africa and Middle East (middle-income countries)	69.8	55.6	12.2	19.0	18.0	25.4
Africa and Middle East (capital surplus oil producers)	68.8	51.8	11.2	18.3	20.0	29.9

Source: ILO, World Labour Report, 1984, Ch. 1.

Finally, a quick look at the sector of services indicate a parallel growth, in the distribution of the labour force showing that as the agriculture labour force went down, part of the migration towards the cities was absorbed by the services.

What is noteworthy (see Table—3.3), however, for the three sectors, is that the relationship between the GDP distribution and the labour force (LF) distribution indicates that the improvements in productivity (the quotient of GDP/LF) of industry, because of more rapid transformations and introduction of technology, were obviously greater than in agriculture.

The above considerations might have been considered both sufficient and necessary to determine proper 'fit' between education and employment. For a given development policy, there could follow a corresponding economic growth rate and the ensuring employment structure. From the latter, including the occupational distribution pattern, would emerge an indication of manpower and/or skills required at different periods for each sector and within the latter, for each branch. Thus, one could project the expected output of education and training programmes for differing years.

Table—3.3: Sectoral Rates of Growth 1960—1980; GDP and Labour Force (in percentage)

	GDP	India LF	LIC GDP	(Asia) LF	MIC GDP	(Asia) LF
Agriculture	–30%	–16%	–31%	–14%	–50%	–23%
Industry	+30%	+52%	+50%	+46%	+70%	+60%
Services	+29%	+40%	+16%	+46%	+4%	+42%

Source: Based on ILO World Labour Report, 1984, Ch. 1.
Note: GDP = Gross Domestic Product; LIC = Low Income Countries; LF = Labour Force; MIC = Middle Income Countries

Yet an appreciation of the labour force is not a determining indication of the employment situation. Indeed, despite high rates of growth in industrial production and continued general economic growth, too much of the labour force remained in low productivity and low income employment. The benefits of growth were not being widely spread to the lower income groups.

The extent of the problem can be partially shown by limited indicators of open unemployment (see Table—3.4). Thus, for all developing countries, open unemployment in 1980 represented some 6 per cent of the total labour force. The corresponding figure for India was 4.6 per cent, for the low income countries of Asia, it was 4.5 per cent; and for the middle income countries of Asia, 3.4 per cent.

Some unemployment rates, particularly in countries with a great deal of wage employment, had reached high levels as early as in the 60s, as in Sri Lanka. Where rates were high in the 60s, they generally remained so. In a particular country, unemployment rate varies between urban and rural areas, between the young and the old and among the graduates of different types and levels of education.

Table—3.4: Open Unemployment (a): Developing Regions, Percentage of Labour Force

Unemploment percentage

	1960	*1970*	*1980*
All developing countries(b)	6.0	5.2	7.8
Latin America and Caribbean (low-income countries)	8.1	7.4	10.3
Latin America and Caribbean (middle-income countries)	5.6	7.8	8.4
China	n.a	n.a	n.a
India	4.6	3.3	7.3
Asia (other low-income countries)	4.5	2.3	10.2
Asia (middle-income countries)	3.4	3.4	3.4
Africa and Middle East (low-income countries)	14.8	15.9	12.6
Africa and Middle East (middle-income countries)	7.7	4.7	8.7
Africa and Middle East (Capital surplus oil producers)	5.4	6.1	4.0

Note: (a) Those who are not at work but have officially declared their intention to be employed.
(b) Excluding China.
n.a = not available

Source: ILO, World Labour Report, 1984.

As we can note from the above open unemployment situation, which says little of under-employment, especially in agriculture, but also amongst the educated, forecasts of human organisation are not easily predictable. Since our purpose is to understand the nature of the linkages between training and education, on the one hand, and employment on the other, let us ask ourselves how fluctuations in job offers are affected by the overall context in which development takes place. To do so, we propose to look at two key dynamic factors which affect any national development situation and which, in turn, have an impact on employment prospects as well as on the role that education and training may be expected to play. The first relates to one of the causes in industrial productivity: technological development, and its impact on economic growth and, in particular, on industry. The second, touches on the implace of the world economic conditions on individual nations' growth employment and training. These two factors will be discussed in the following two sections.

4. Industrial and Technological Development

Industrial growth does not just happen. Emerging national economies may purchase ready-made industrial potential and import full-fledged plants equipped to the last detail and ready to operate at the turn of a key to start off the first motor which will ignite the production growth. These are known as 'turn-key operations'. Or national economies may purchase industrial licenses or 'know-how' together—or without—the foreign personnel. But, most determinant is the ability of an economy to launch *its own* industrial processes through the discovery of new techniques.

In other words, modern nations as their economies progress tend to own or at least control the means of transforming matter into the awaited finished product. These innovations in new techniques and improvements of old ones are part of the overall technological development of a country. Technological change may be formally defined as 'the application of theoretical and practical knowledge to production through a sequential succession of techniques'. Such an application will alter the make-up of the labour force since technological change is basically a labour-saving process leading to output rise or, in other words, to productivity increase.

But such technological changes initiated nationally can only exist if prior research and testing have taken place. Research, which can start modestly in the form of a laboratory experiment or an equation written on a blackboard, can evantually lead to a vast and varied number of applications. This has been the case with fundamental research carried out on the structure of atomic nuclei, which led to the discovery of nuclear energy. Research on solid state physics has redically transformed or created an immense range of products and systems such as digital watches, television receivers, video-recorders, health care equipment and many other familiar products. Space research programmes have yielded many valuable benefits in fields such as telecommunications, remote sensing, new materials, and transport systems. The theoretical understanding of the part played by nuclei acids in the transfer of genetic information arose from the discovery of DNA but also promises a vast range of applications in the field of biotechnology, from health to food.

Incorporations of microprocessors into existing technologies can produce a generation of new products of improved performance. Advances in information technology combined with progress in computers, video-recorders, and telecommunications can transform education, increase the efficiency of organisations, and permit better use of human and material resources.

Robotics can free workers from hazardous and repetitive labour and can improve the productivity of industry. The same technology can be applied to the problems of the physically handicapped to produce artificial limbs and other devices that may help them.

Remote sensing can improve our capacity to protect our environment and to live in harmony with it, develop our natural resources, and predict our weather. Improvements in materials can create new technologies and enhance existing ones. The evolution of catalysis from an art to a science and improvements in membrane technology offer the possibility of new and more efficient chemical processes. Biotechnology has vast potential for the production of pharmaceutical products such as insulin, the synthesis of industrial chemicals, the development of new agricultural species and the more efficient recovery of mineral resources.

In the field of energy, fast breeder reactor technology will soon offer a major increase in the efficiency of electricity generation from uranium. In the longer term, thermonuclear fusion, one of the most challenging technologies ever conceived, may offer a virtually inexhaustible source of energy from ordinary sea water.

Technologies being applied today are founded upon the scientific research and development of yesterday. Hence, the well-being of society in the next century will rest on the application of scientific research which is being carried out now. The importance of fundamental scientific research in the birth of new industries cannot be over-emphasized. Vital to the aspect of development is the role of government support of science to inspire the future economic and social development of all countries.

The purchase of technology from abroad by developing countries has often put them in great difficulty as, in exchange, they could offer nationally grown or extracted basic commodities, the relative price of which has decreased when compared to the rising cost of imported technology.

From the point of view of developing countries, this means that a situation of 'dependency', is maintained as their economies have to import machines and industrial inputs and consequently have to stimulate exports (especially of primary goods) to generate the necessary foreign exchange. Many developing countries still do not have a well organised sector of capital goods (machine-producing industries). Thus, they have not had the opportunity of making capital-saving innovations simply because they have not had the capital goods industry necessary from them. Under these circumstances, import of capital goods from abroad, has meant that they have not developed the technological base of skills, knowledge, facilities and organisation upon which further technical progress so largely depends.

Repeated imports of knowledge and equipment do not provide an adequate response to local conditions in terms of demography or of available natural resources. It is therefore of prime necessity to base national sovereignty of developing countries on their ability to master locally the flow of needed knowledge and equipment. An effort in this direction has indeed been taking place as the number of science graduates and engineers from many developing countries has increased several-fold in the last 20 years: Investments in developing countries, R & D, although still limited when compared to developed countries are beginning to grow.

It seems therefore capital to clarify the impact of the unquestionable and felt need for technological development, and of the measures taken to respond to it, on the employment situation.

Characteristically, technological change proceeds more rapidly than social change. The institutions and attitudes which were once favourable to earlier forms of technical and social development may become an impediment to the spread of new technologies. Thus, while 'optimists' see automation, information technology and robots as freeing workers from the drudgery of work, creating leisure, earlier retirement and a return to traditional values, 'pessimists' see new machines and organisations as accelerating de-skilling, reducing work creativity, creating mass unemployment and further, standardizing consumption.[5]

The optimists stress the positive aspects of technological advances. From their point of view, even if there is an initial decline of employment opportunities because of the introduction of new technologies, in the long run jobs are created in newly emerging industries because of the expansion in total demand. In this way, technology is expected to create more jobs than it displaces.

The pessimists, on the other hand, emphasize the labour-saving effects of a new technology. They argue that these effects tend to be most pronounced in stagnant economies. A low rate of economic growth will make it difficult to increase demands for products and consequently the creation of new job opportunities through derived demand will become exceedingly difficult. Thus, 'technological unemployment' will add to the number of jobs already lost as a result of recession and in the long run, the introduction of new technologies will tend to result in reduced employment opportunities.

A realistic assessment (between the optimists 'and pessimists' views) of the impact of technology must take account of the different nature of the jobs that are eliminated and those that are created. While the jobs lost are merely semi-skilled or unskilled tasks, these created require considerable technical knowledge. This trend will translate in the longer term into a fast pace of growth of professional and technical employment opportunities, which in turn, will alter radically the pattern of demand for occupational qualifications. Inevitably, by increasing the need for educated technicians, professionals and highly specialized skilled operators and decreasing the demand for workers in the lower skilled ranges and blue-collar occupations, the diffusion of new technologies poses a real danger for the disadvantaged individuals and groups in society.

In general, it may be said that if the most important skill, in an automated process becomes personal reliability, then the general level of education will acquire a particular significance, not just to allow the worker to understand the working of the limited operation for which he is responsible, but also to enable him to absorb the successive training and re-training which technical change is sure to entail at the level of the factory, of the occupation and of the industry.

The overall picture which emerges and should concern students of the relations between employment and education is that the unquestionable imperative technological requirements for economic growth call for skills which in numbers have no relationship to massive individual aspirations. Technological development must be nurtured by specialists having received high-or specialized-level training and education for a relatively limited number of them so they may occupy intermediate and high rungs of the occupational ladder. This state of affairs is obviously not compatible with the social and ethical aspirations of a policy offering 'education for all' which cannot be met on the strength of economically-founded technological development objectives.

5. International Economic Conditions

We have seen that technology is an indispensable asset for growth with its consequent challenges to the occupational distribution pattern and to individual perceptions of education and training as instruments of employment achievement. We need now to understand better another set of obstacles most developing countries will have to overcome to attain self-sustaining growth in a dramatically worsening international economic climate.

World economic growth is undergoing a marked slow down. International competition has brought about a disparity of development between industrialized countries and a polarization in the development of the less industrialized and developing countries. It may be said that the present slow down is built on the cyclical recession of Western countries. As an example, we shall simply recall that the United States' national debt which has doubled in the last six years, amounts today to some Two thousand billion dollars, whilst, at the same time, its trade deficit is reaching some 150 billion per annum.[6] Some say this situation finds its root in the collapse of the Bretton Woods Agreement (the end of the gold and the dollar parity), which coincided with the oil crisis and subsequently in the unique impact of US domestic fiscal policy. Whatever may be the cause of the present situation, it is unquestionable that it is affecting 'broadside' most developing countries which face today a bleak outlook for their export earnings and drastic drops in their commodity prices. This gradually came to be through protectionist policies developed by industrialized countries, themselves confronted with internal structural dislocations and rising unemployment. Thus, industrialized nations from the 'West' increased agricultural subsidies to their own farmers. This, in turn, has led to severe export limitations from developing countries, reducing in some cases to a trickle the earnings which they so desperately need.

As a result of past investments, developing countries are presently in a situation of impressive external debts amounting to a total of one thousand billion dollars. This, to a large extent, may be explained in terms of the great volatility of exchange rates, on the other hand, and of high interest rates which have brought up the cost of capital, on the other. As a result, developing countries have not been able to reach high rates of domestic savings. We are also witnessing a growing excess capacity in their production process, whether it be commodities, light manufacturing or in the steel, chemical and mineral industries.

In human terms, this has led to persistent poverty, especially in the rural and poor urban sections of the country, a gradual erosion of living standards of the lower and upper middle class and to a marked rise in unemployment. Let us look specifically at the latter as it affects our global outlook for this course. Unemployment statistics for developing countries are in most cases unsatisfactory and difficult to interpret. By and large, however, it is recognized that between 1973 and 1980, a large number of countries have experienced a significant increase in such unemployment (see Table—3.5).

As the above Table shows, unemployment recorded from the labour force sample surveys increased spectacularly in some countries (3.5-fold in Egypt). Unemployment recorded in employment offices (predominantly urban) in India showed an increase of 140 per cent. For Indonesia and Thailand, open unemployment increased by 312 per cent and 165 per cent, respectively over these years. There are however a number of countries where open unemployment remains constant or actually declines. They include countries of exceptionally rapid rates of economic growth. Thus total unemployment in the Republic of Korea and Singapore remained practically constant and low over the 70s, whilst in Malaysia, total unemployment actually declined in the 70s, although it increased in the 80s. In Pakistan, total unemployment recorded by employment offices also declined, probably due to a combination of high economic growth and a large outflow of labour to the Middle East.[7]

It is accepted that a transition from the traditional rural society to the more urban does not mean a direct transformation to modern large scale production of goods and services using modern technologies. What has been called an 'urban informal'

Table—3.5: Growth on the Number Unemployed in Developing Countries (thousands).

	1973	*1975*	*1978*	*1980*	*1982*
Egypt (LFSS)	145	233	355	536	–
Madagascar (EOS)	18	13	36	41	26
Mauritius (EOS)	27	21	16	31	74
Tunisia (EOS)	37	29	59	66	78
Argentina (LFSS)[1]	173	97	102	82	220
Brazil (LFSS)	968	–	1003	2023[2]	–
Colombia (LFSS)[3]	–	253	261	349	–
Costa Rica (LFSS)	–	41[4]	33	46	78
Chile (LFSS)	48	158	169	152	272
Jamaica (LFSS)	176	175	230	270	–
Peru (LFSS)	192	237	342	394	417
Burma (EOS)	194	197	415	486	656
India (EOS)	7714	8918	11837	15317	18646
Indonesia (EOS)	89	115	157	233	367
Korea (LFSS)	461	510	442	749	656
Malaysia (EOS)	155	125	107	73	69
Pakistan (EOS)	168	20	146	144	144
Philippines (LFSS)	690	581	694	878	975
Singapore (LFSS)	38	39	35	34	30
Syrian Arab Rep. (LFSS)	77	89	90	82[5]	–
Thailand (LFSS)	72	67	173	204	–

Source: International Labour Office, Yearbook of Labour Statistics, 1983.

Note: Source of national statistics indicated in parenthesis: LFSS, labour force sample survey; EOS, employment office statistics.

[1]Buenos Aires; [2]1981; [3]seven main cities; [4]1976; [5]1979.

sector, occupying a position between the traditional rural and the modern and in close connection with, or overlapping both, has almost always been an integral part of the urban society. In many developing countries, this sector accounts for a large proportion of the urban population and urban economic activity. In some cities of Asia (Bombay, Djakarta), informal sectors account for in between 50 and 70 per cent of total employment[8] Parallel to the 'urban informal sector' there is also a 'rural informal sector' with similar characteristics. Job-seekers unable to find jobs in the modern sector, either because of lack of skill and previous training and education or inadequate overall demand for labour, are often forced into the informal sector, which thus absorbs at least partly those who would have otherwise been openly unemployed. It is also often viewed as a sector to which many of the emigrants from the rural areas are primarily attracted at the beginning of their job search.

In conclusion, we note the deleterious effect of economic recession on the lives of millions. This is particularly striking in South Asia where, even if there were a 5.6 per cent average growth rate per annum until the year 2000, the range of per capita income would not exceed $200 to $400 at the end of the century.[9]

Under such circumstances where growth is inhibited and employment curtailed, what connection can be made with education and training as an *economic* necessity? Obviously, the answer lies not in a simplistic relationship between levels of education or achievements in training skills and production or export targets but rather in the complex web of societal change, which depends on education as an inevitable catalyst, and which is likely to bring about new forms of domestic and international dialogues.

6. Polarization of Development and its Challenges

From the two preceding sections, we may note that, on the other hand, to ensure self-sustained growth through the development of high levels of technology, there prevail sophisticated demands for skills while, on the other, as urban and rural unemployment grow together with the informal sector, there are apparently weaker economic justifications for massive educational and training prerequisites.

Put bluntly, there is beginning to emerge with greater focus the existence of a situation characterized by the presence of two 'poles' in the development of many of the 'poorer' countries.

On the other hand, there is a vital need for the development of a technological capability and the skill development processes it entails whilst at the other end, there prevails a level of extreme poverty which is not likely to be profoundly affected in the short term by growth trends and, consequently, by an influx of school graduates. In other words:

(a) where technology is a must for survival, education and training policies become key areas of action in order to prepare people and society for the new technological culture, to provide a more flexible labour force and to prepare young people and shift workers to newly emerging occupations and skills;

(b) at the same time, for the category of the unemployed and underemployed, the immediate demands are for lower mortality rate, eradication of the worst forms of poverty, raising of the level of literacy, and a framework for food security, nutrition and well-being.

For governments, the challenge of technology mainly requires changes in basic curricula in order to give students at all levels an understanding of the newly emerging technological culture, provision of a broad-based work-related education for young people, in order to overhaul apprenticeship and training arrangements in the light of emerging technologies and support for these measures by promoting geographic and occupational mobility. In addition to such measures, vocational training, pre-professional and professional education at the secondary and higher levels as well as in-service training must be founded on the principle of chartering the shortest route between the learning sites and the production place. No government, whether from industrialized or developing states, can afford to subsidize or finance the entire range of institutions which are specialized at these levels. Many government-financed vocational schools and professional universities, removed from the production scene, are equipped today with antiquated material, laboratories and workshops which in no way prepare their graduates for entrance into a labour market which is therefore neither interested nor willing to absorb them. This imposes a necessary linkage between production and education and training justified by the need to ensure relevance of the latter. This is further buttressed by quite autonomous consideration based on the dwindling of government financial resources for education. Governments will increasingly need to seek involvement, both professional and financial, of production sectors, whether public or private, in the training of the nation's future scientific, technological and industrial cadres.[10]

Such a strategy, in addition to its intrinsic merit in offering a response to demands of scientific, technological and industrial development corresponds to the unquestionable responsibility of the State to attend to the social, cultural, ethical and the long-term economic demands of society in favour of illiterates, school dropouts, unemployed and underemployed school, college and university graduates.

Governments, central or local, will gradually concentrate their limited resources on attending to the educational needs of the majority of populations whose short-term direct involvement in technological development is most unlikely. There is therefore a case to be made, together with an attempt at establishing a 'fitness' between technological development and the concomitant skills requirement, for a broad-based education and training, including an understanding of the new technological dimensions in order to make it possible for all, notwithstanding their likelihood to find employment in the short term, to reach the minimum 'cultural' waterline from which future social mobility may become credible.

In conclusion, governments faced with the duality inherent in growth objectives (compatible with self-sustainment and international competition) and in the unfettered advancement of their economically inactive population, must learn both to share the resource load for skills training at all levels with other productive 'actors' and to 'go it alone' in search for equity as it offers basic education 'to all' notwithstanding linear and short term economic justifications.

It is precisely strategies responding to such paradoxical and simultaneous forces that we shall wish to examine during this course, concerned essentially with the 'fitness' issue between employment and education. It was therefore with an intent that this opening lecture singled out the extremes of the present situation. It is the purpose of our programme to review with deliberate attention the intermediate stages and variety of choices open to decision-makers in the light of the unique conditions they face and at such time at they become manifest.

7. Conclusion in the Way of an Introduction

Given the above, it behooves me to introduce you to the approach we followed in designing this regional training course. It was felt that from the beginning of this workshop each one of the participants should be given an opportunity of individualizing the situation which I have presented in very global terms and which, by definition, cannot apply specifically to any of the countries from which have come participants to this course. It was felt therefore that national cases should be presented by each participant and discussed by at least one other if not by more.

In diagnosing the education and employment situation of the countries of each participant, we shall try and clarify some basic concepts which I may have used rather rapidly in my overall presentation (GDP, labour force, sectors, employment, productivity, etc.).

Subsequently, we shall then confront the first technical 'module' of the course which is to deal with the manpower approach to educational planning. In other words, we shall have to appreciate the extent to which it is possible to forecast or at least anticipate emerging strategies for education on the strength of assumptions about manpower requirements in the various sectors of the economy and for some years to come. This is where exercises will take place on the projection of such manpower demand.

Discussions will then ensue around these exercises as well as on estimates of manpower supply. With the latter, we shall attempt to assess the extent to which educational and training systems, within formal institutions or within industry, are capable of responding to the demand from the labour or employment market at levels and in numbers corresponding to what the economy can effectively absorb. Given the limitations of this approach, we shall want to discuss it critically.

We shall then go on to examine other approaches relating education with employment, basing ourselves on different theories of the labour market, on statistical techniques which can be used to understand better the actual 'signals' from the labour market and their receptivity by educational and training authorities.

We shall move on to a discussion of an economic dimension of educational planning based on the application of 'earning functions' which enable us on the one hand, to compare the costs of education both to society and to individuals with the benefits derived by both through additional earnings gained throughout one's active life, and on the other, to analyze the role of different factors and variables on income distribution, career promotion, etc.

We will then examine empirical studies which follow school and university leavers of various institutions into the labour market. This technique of checking on the career of former graduates is known as 'Tracer' studies which will be presented, analyzed and discussed.

The next module will be devoted to understanding empirically and very concretely how forces operate in the employment and labour market. In order to achieve this, we shall produce questionnaires meant to gather information reflecting the nature and magnitude of the relationship between education and employment.

As an overall conclusion to our training course, we shall attempt to look at various strategies for a better match between education and employment and to identify these intermediary stages between the two poles I described earlier. We shall thus look at specific solutions that have been tried out in various countries and draw some lessons for all of us.

I should like to conclude by trying to make you aware of the need to live in a state of uncertainty as you learn to rely less on linear, causal, simplistic extrapolations. No matter how well figures are collected and understood, no matter how well certain phenomena are identified and described—and all these are essential pre-requisites—there still remains the potent force of political, cultural and social externalities which are those that generally shape an economic situation as I tried to show at the outset with my illustrations of Japan, Korea and China. Together we have just seen how some such externalities like technological development objectives and the consequences of international structural adjustments (some call it the International Division of Labour) affect national purposes.

Planning today cannot consist in deciding a priori not only 'where' to go but 'how' to get there. Means and resources in today's economic crisis are evanescent and unreliable. Their future availability cannot be predicted reasonably. Planning today means therefore choosing between situations over which one has relatively little control. The sole important consideration is the objective to be reached. How and when this will take place will depend on the ability to make 'good' choices based on partially unpredictable circumstances. That is the meaning we give today to 'strategic planning' as we learn to navigate between difficulties and to apply gentle pressures, within the very limited margin of movement actually given to decision-makers, to pursue our route in the general direction given by the agreed objectives.

NOTES

1. U.N.U. "Work in Progress, Vol. 10, No. 2, Tokyo, May 1987.
2. OECD, "Main Economic Indicators", Paris, May 1987.
3. ILO. "World Labour Report", Vol. I, Chapter 1, Geneva 1984.
4. Ibid. ILO, Ch. 1.
5. Material for this section was culled from the United Nations "1985 Report on the World Social Situation" Ch. VII, U.N., N.Y. 1985.
6. In 'Foreign Affairs', Vol. 65, No. 3, see Leonard Silk "The United States and the World Economy".
7. Ibid, U.N. Chapter VII.
8. Ibid.

9. G. Gunatillake, Director, Marga Institute, Sri Lanka in APDC Newsletter, Vol. 6, No. 2, Feb. 1987, Kuala Lumpur.
10. For a More Detailed Treatment of Financing Strategies for the Diversified Forms of Education, see IIEP Publication Series: "IIEP Contributions", No. 1, 1987; Sylvain Lourié "New Strategies for Financing Diversified Forms of Education and Training".

4

Strategies for a Better Match Between Education and Employment

Brahm Prakash & N.V. Varghese

1. Education and Productive Work

Work was never degraded in any society. But the status of being a worker was considered to be infra dig. This was partly due to the dichotomy that existed between intellectual and manual work. This dichotomy could exist in the early periods because of various reasons. First, the technology of production was of very low order and work done was mainly manual in nature. Second, education had not well developed into a system whereby it is treated as a major source of production of skilled manpower. Education in the traditional sense meant involving in intellectually curious but socially less useful activities.

Industrial revolution brought out changes in this mode of thinking essentially emanating from the developments in the economic structure. Post-industrial revolution period required a large number of skilled manpower to maintain, if not to further advance, the technological developments achieved during the industrial revolution. This necessitated a change in the educational and the production system. Production came to be centered around factories employing large number of workers with varying skills. And system of training for these skills became necessary. Increasingly this role was assumed by the educational institutions. In other words, educational system became a major source of developing skilled manpower.

The need to link education with work is emphasized by philosophers from very early periods. However, this assumed significant in the recent periods because of economic reasons. Over the years, the changes in the production sectors, primarily due to technological advances, were very fast and very often the educational system could not respond favourably and instantaneously to these changes in the production field. In the colonial countries the deteriorating linkage between education and work has another dimension. The colonies borrowed, to a greater extent, the educational system from the imperial nations which did not have any link with the work situations in these countries. Different countries follow different strategies to link education with work.

In the present context the need to link education and productive work is felt mainly on the grounds of teaching the students the dignity of human labour; to appreciate traditional link between man and nature so as to make development more indigenous and self-sustaining; and to prepare children to participate increasingly in productive work while they are in the school and after they leave the school.

The method through which education can be integrated with work can be either through *(a)* integrating work experience in the educational process or *(b)* by taking education to work situations. The suggested stages in this process are:

(a) Introduction of work oriented vocational courses separately.

(b) Introduction of work experience as an optional course as well as vocational subjects in all general secondary schools.

(c) Introduction of work experience as a compulsory subject for all general secondary schools.

(d) Extension of work experience to senior secondary schools.

(e) Introduction of work experience in the perspective of life long education.

Programmes to link school education with work exist in almost all countries. The SUPW (Socially Useful Productive Work) programme of India and Community School programme of Bangladesh are live examples of attempts to link school education with work. However, in all countries, implementation of such programmes are subjected to difficulties of varies nature and success of such programmes is only to a limited extent.

2. Vocationalization

Schooling system attempts to equip students with adequate skills to enable them to enter into the world of work. Imparting of such skills makes the transition from schools to places of work smoother. Programmes of work experience in schools help the students to familiarize with work where as vocationalization helps in picking up and practicing skills which are useful on the job.

Irrespective of the nature of the programme, the progression of events from orientation of work to employment can be noted in stages. The first stage is learning about work. This stage may be descriptive and theoretical. The next stage is 'work observation' in which students are given a chance to see and observe actual work and work situations. Work observation is followed by providing students with some work experience. Work experience can be of two types—one intended to 'taste' the work and the other 'exploratory' in nature. Then comes the stage for vocationalization of education. Vocationalization facilitates learning and practicing skills. Learning and practicing of skills enhances one's own work experience which eventually equips one to regular employment.

Vocationalization is introduced with the objectives of:

(a) Providing knowledge about the world of work.

(b) Inculcating practical skills.

(c) Improving motivation of students.

(d) Inculcating positive attitudes which help in improving the employability as well as productivity of individuals.

(e) Improve the links between school and work.

(f) Improve career choices.

(g) Imparting knowledge and skills needed for employment.

Arguments for vocationalization centre around increased employability of vocationally educated; improving the quality of education by providing relevant education; improving economic efficiency in terms of returns to education and equity objectives. Critics of vocationalization point out that vocational schools do not enhance employment opportunities and many a time students from vocational stream are treated to be inferior in the employment market. It also creates inequities in society by providing vocational educational to the poor and academic education to the elite. Moreover, cost of vocational education, very often, are very high and returns from it are not very high.

The empirical evidence on the employment and earning potentials of the graduates are not very encouraging. Review of world bank projects concluded that:

(a) Vocationalization was successful in meeting quantitative targets of manpower.

(b) Vocationalization did not change pupils' attitudes towards practical and manual work.

(c) Vocationalization did not result in improving the quality of education.

(d) There were serious doubts about the cost effectiveness of diversification projects.

(e) Vocational education in diversified schools did not increase either the chances of employment or the earnings of school leavers.

(f) The rate of return to vocational streams is often lower than to academic streams.

(g) Vocational education did not reduce the private demand for higher education.

Despite all these negative points vocationalization is emphasized in all developing countries as an effective strategy to link education and employment. This may partly be due to the fact that vocationalization has not yet become wide-spread to take advantage of the economies of scale. Vocationalization in the initial stages involve a high investment. With wide-spreading of vocationalization the per student cost may perhaps be coming down. More significantly, the scheme has not been in operation for a long enough period to make an assessment regarding its cost-effectiveness. Therefore, emphasis on vocationalization as a strategy to link education and employment finds a place in the policy formulation of many of the countries.

3. Diversification of Post-Secondary Education

In response to the changes in the production sector and thereby changing skill needs, education especially at the post-secondary level needs to be diversified. Diversification becomes all the more essential when technological changes are very fast. In the present context there are many compulsions to diversify post-secondary education:

(a) Education objectives have become more diversified.

(b) Demand for education by new client groups like adult learners, disadvantaged and handicapped youth etc. has necessitated diversification.

(c) Widening of the process or resource mobilization, allocation and utilization has resulted in the diversification of higher education.

(d) New modes of programme delivery and management contributed to diversification.

Linking education with work through diversification of higher education involves *(a)* development of relevant courses; *(b)* modularization of courses; *(c)* combination of courses to cut across the disciplines; *(d)* flexibility in course options; *(e)* orientation of teachers; *(f)* proper mechanisms of resource allocation and utilization; and *(g)* introduction of proper planning and management practices.

Diversification in the traditional formal system takes place either by restructuring of the existing courses or by introducing new courses. Diversification all over the world has resorted to one or the other form though the specific reasons for introduction of diversification may vary between countries. In Germany, for example, diversification was introduced with the twin objectives of increasing participation of workers in management and meeting the needs of specific skills by upgrading the work force within the firm. Similarly experiments in industrial democracy for increasing workers participation in decision making necessitated introduction of diversification of education in Sweden.

In India, establishment of industrial training institutes, polytechnics, engineering colleges, institutes of technology, institute of management are examples of attempts to diversity post-secondary level of education. In the field of agriculture education opening of agricultural universities paved the way for wider scope of diversification. The University Grants Commission initiated a scheme of restructuring under graduate courses in India. The response from the universities was not very encouraging. However, of late attempts are made by many universities to restructure courses.

In the present day context diversification takes place through new modes of delivery system. Correspondence courses and Open University system are very significant from this point of view. Open university system was initiated in England in 1969 with the objective of increasing accessibility to higher education for those who could not otherwise have access to it. Ever-since Open University was established in England many other countries are trying to follow the same path. Thailand and Pakistan have their Open Universities. In India two Open University at the National level is already established in 1986 and attempts are under way to start Open Universities at State levels. The American programme of co-operative education and workers colleges in China are examples of attempts to integrate on-campus classroom study with off-campus work experience. In Pakistan open universities have taken employability as the sole criterion for its operation. The university does not offer courses in the traditional system. It can be seen that diversification can be through the introduction of new courses or by restructuring of the existing courses or through correspondence courses or through open learning systems.

Positive consequences of diversification are many: *(i)* it provides job specific skills; *(ii)* in incorporates latest developments in science and technology; *(iii)* it permits the traditional formal education to compete with new types of delivery systems; and *(iv)* it continuously updates educational programmes to cope with changing skill needs in the production sectors.

Diversification has posed problems of management. With diversification the network of delivery system becomes really difficult to co-ordinate, monitor and manage. In other words the traditional management system has to undergo changes to respond to the management challenges created by diversification. Financial and other difficulties stand in the way of diversification. Despite the difficulties, diversification is considered to be a concerted effort by our higher education system to respond to the changing societal needs.

4. Informal Sector

The session on information sector focussed on the role of this sector in the process of development. It was pointed out that during the last two decades this sector had emerged as a significant area of research. Several policy analysts have evinced their interest in its functioning and its possible uses for broadening the scope of development. It was pointed out that during the 70s several studies were undertaken under World Employment Programme of ILO in most of the leading cities of the developing countries.

It was observed that informal sector tended to be chimerical in character and took different forms under different socio-economic conditions. Consequently comparisons in the observed pattern of informal sectors in one city could not be straightway made with the formal sector elsewhere. However, this is not to say that there are no common underlying theoretical postulate which can help one to have a more comprehensive and cohesive view of this proliferated reality.

Some of these postulate were then articulated in the presentation. Several instances of the informal sector from the city of Bombay based on ILO standard study were provided. Data relating to work force participation, their pattern of employment and related occupational characteristics were discussed. Keeping in view the focus of the seminar the evidence on the informal sector was also presented by stratifying it according to educational levels.

5

Diagnosis of Employment Situation: Some Basic Concepts

Bikas C. Sanyal

1. Introduction

The attempt in this article is to introduce the readers to some of the basic and elementary concepts useful in diagnosing the education and employment situation in a country. The concepts discussed in this note are classified under different headings. *Section 2* introduces the concepts of GNP and GDP. *Section 3* introduces the concept of labour force and work force. *Section 4* deals with the concepts of employment and work. It also deals with industrial and occupational classification of employment. *Section 5* elaborates on the concepts of unemployment. *Section 6* deals with the labour market. *Section 7* introduces the concept of wage. *Section 8* deals with labour mobility.

2. Gross National Product (GNP) and Gross Domestic Product (GDP)

GNP measures the total domestic and foreign output of residents and is calculated without making deductions of depreciation. It comprises gross domestic product adjusted by net factor income from abroad, *i.e.*, the income residents receive from abroad for factor services (labour and capital) less similar payments made to non-residents who contributed to the domestic economy (World Bank: 1989).

GNP per capita is arrived at by dividing gross national product by population of the country. For purposes of international comparisons, the World Bank converts GNP to US dollars. This procedure of conversion generally uses a three-year average of the official exchange rate, after adjusting the rates for differences in relative inflation between the country and the United States.

GDP measures the total final output of goods and services produced by an economy—that is, by residents and non-residents—regardless of the allocation to domestic and foreign residents. It is calculated without making deductions for depreciation (World Bank: 1989).

GDP by industrial origin is measured at producer prices or at purchaser values. GDP at producer prices is equal to GDP at purchaser values less import duties. GDP at producer prices is referred to as GDP at factor cost and GDP at purchaser values is referred to as GDP at market prices.

The economy is broadly divided into three sectors—agriculture, industry and services. These three sectors are sometimes referred to as Primary, Secondary and Tertiary Sectors. The agricultural sector comprises agriculture, forestry, hunting and fishing. Industry comprises mining, manufacturing, construction, electricity, gas and water. All other branches of economic activity are categorized as services. The share in GDP of each of these three sectors is taken as an index of level of development of the economy. With advances in economic development, the share of agriculture in GDP comes down and correspondingly the shares of other sectors increases.

3. Labour Force

The total population of a country can be divided into those who are economically active and those who are not. Economically active means all persons who furnish the potential supply of labour for production of economic goods and services. The labour force comprises all economically active persons aged ten and above (ILO: 1989). It includes the number of persons employed and unemployed but excludes the economically inactive population. Two measures of economically active population are: *(i)* usually active population measured in relation to a long reference period such as a year; *(ii)* currently active population measured in relation to a short reference period such as one day or one week (ILO: 1988).

International classification by status categorizes the economically active population under the following headings (ILO: 1988):

(a) ***Employer:*** a person who operates his or her own economic enterprise or engages independently in a profession or trade and hires one or more employees.

(b) ***Own account worker:*** a person who operates his or her own economic enterprise or engages independently in a profession or trade and hires no employees.

(c) ***Employee:*** a person who works for a public or private employer and receives remuneration in wages, salary, commission, tips, piece-rates or pay in kind.

(d) ***Unpaid family worker:*** a person who works a specified minimum amount of time (at least one-third of normal working hours) without pay, in economic enterprises operated by a related person living in the same household.

(e) ***Member of a producers' co-operative:*** a person who is an active member of a producers' co-operative regardless of the industry in which it is established.

(f) ***Persons not classifiable by status:*** experienced workers with status unknown or inadequately described and unemployed persons not previously employed.

The data on the economically active population do not include students, women occupied solely in domestic duties, retired persons, persons living entirely on their own means and persons wholly dependent upon others.

Labour Force Participation Rate (LFPR) is the percentage of total labour force to the total population aged ten and above, *i.e.* total numbef of persons employed plus unemployed divided by total population aged ten and above multiplied by a hundred.

The labour force is to be distinguished from workers and work force. Workers denote those who are participating in any economically productive activity. This participation can be physical or mental, direct or indirect involvement (supervision etc.) in work. The total sum of the workers constitutes the work force. Work force participation rate is the percentage of workers to the relevant age group population (ten years and above).

Sometimes a distinction is drawn between labour force, work force and supply of labour. As mentioned earlier, the labour force includes employed and unemployed persons; work force includes only employed, *i.e.* labour force minus unemployed gives the work force. Supply of labour on the other hand includes hours worked and intensity of working effort (Uthoff; Pernia: 1986).

Historical behaviour of labour force participation rates exhibits certain discernible patterns (Uthoff; Pernia: 1986).

(i) LFPR of men and women below the age of 25 tend to decline over a period of time as a result of access to higher education.

(ii) LFPR of men and women above sixty decline because of old-age benefits and the social security system.

(iii) Male LFPR between the ages of 25 and 55 show only a marginal declining trend.

(iv) Female LFPR vary between geographical areas depending upon cultural traditions and agricultural structure. Women are mainly engaged in primary sector activities. Female LFPR is sensitive to total income of the family.

4. Employment

The employed comprise all persons above a specified age who are in paid employment and self-employment. Paid employment means working for a wage or salary.

Employment and work are sometimes used interchangeably. However, a distinction needs to be drawn between the two. Perhaps a wage is the criterion by which these two can be distinguished.

Productive activities which directly take place in the realm of market forces are treated as employment. Market denotes exchange and in this sense work which has a direct exchange value is employment. In other words, when work is directly exchanged for a wage, it becomes employment. Work, on the other hand; does not necessarily mean earning a wage.

For example, those who are engaged in household economic activities may not be receiving a wage as a direct for the work they perform; but they may be receiving or sharing the profit borne out of the output that they produce and market.

Sen (1975) notes that the concept of employment is vague in any economy in which the wage system is weak and self-employment and unpaid family labour are common because the criterion of 'being paid a wage' cannot be reliably applied. Accordingly, this vagueness is a problem confined to less developed economies where the market system is less developed.

Employment has three aspects (Sen: 1975):

(a) it gives an income to the employed;

(b) it yields an output;

(c) it gives a person the recognition of being engaged in something worthwhile.

Recently the concept of work and employment and distinctions between the two assumed a different dimension even in the well developed market economics primarily resulting from the changing technological conditions of production. During the industrial stage, employment was organised in a central place, say in a factory, all people had uniform working hours and uniform frequency in the payment of wages. In the post-industrial phase, 'contractual systems of employment' emerged (Watts: 1983). Now work need not necessarily be organised in a central place. At present, with the revolution in the communication and information network, work can be very easily organised in the household itself. Therefore, people undertake contractual work and locate themselves away from the bureaucratic setup and industrial concerns. They finish the job and receive the payment. And this payment is not the same as wages. This is different from the conventional type of employment.

Self-employment means working for oneself. The self-employed are those who during the reference period performed some work for profit or family gain. This is different from wage employment, when one works for others for a fixed wage. Self-employment is increasing rather fast in many of the less developed economies. Often it is suggested that the educational systems should be re-oriented to equip individuals to be self-employed.

Another term which is very often used in literature on employment is under-employment. Under-employment exists when persons in employment who are not working full-time would be able and willing to do more work than they are actually performing at present (ILO: 1984). Under-employment is of two types—visible and invisible. Visible under-employment means working less than a certain number of hours per year. This number of hours may be either the number of hours desired or the number of hours considered normal or appropriate. People are invisibly under-employed if more of them are engaged in a certain activity than would be needed to produce the output which they produce (Monly; Costa: 1981). Their earnings are abnormally low, and their jobs do not permit full use of their capacities or skills. Under-employment of the educated is a serious problem in many of the developing economies.

Classification of the Employed

Employment is very often discussed in terms of industrial classification and occupational classification. Industrial classification denotes the distribution of the employed by sectors of activity. According to the International Standard Industrial Classification of Economic Activities, the major divisions of industries are:

- Agriculture, hunting, forestry and fishing.
- Mining and quarrying.
- Manufacturing.
- Electricity, gas and water.
- Construction.

- Wholesale and retail trade, restaurants and hotels.
- Transport, storage and communication.
- Financing, insurance, real estate and business services.
- Community, social and personal services.
- Activities not adequately defined.

It is generally believed that the relative distribution of workers between sectors is an indicator of the level of economic development achieved by any economy. The process of economic development is associated with a gradual shift of the work force from primary to secondary and further to the tertiary sector. Thus the least developed economy will have the highest proportion of its work force engaged in primary sector activities and the most developed economy will have the highest proportion of its work force engaged in the tertiary sector activities. It is to be noted here that of late this shift is not from primary to secondary to tertiary; in many of the less developed countries the tertiary sector is growing faster than the secondary sector. This is primarily due to the growth of service sectors in the tertiary sector due to the increased welfare measures adopted by the public authorities.

Occupational classification denotes distribution of employment between different occupational divisions. Till the seventies data on employment were collected according to the International Standard Classification of Occupations (ISCO) adopted by ILO in 1958. In 1968 ILO revised the occupational classification. In the revised classification there are eight major occupational groups, 83 minor occupational groups, 284 unit groups and 1,506 occupational categories. Because of this change in the occupational classification data are not strictly comparable over a period of time.

The International Standard Classification of Occupations gives the following major groups of occupations:

- 1. Professional, technical and related workers.
- 2. Administrative and managerial workers.
- 3. Clerical and related workers.

- 4. Sales workers.
- 5. Services workers.
- 6. Agriculture, animal husbandry and forestry workers, fisherman and hunters.
- 7/8/9. Production and related workers, transport equipment operators and labourers.
- 10. Workers not classifiable occupation and members of the armed forces.

5. Unemployment

Unemployment is the state of not working. Unemployment can be voluntary and involuntary. Those who are not working and not seeking an employment are treated as voluntarily unemployed. They do not come under the category of the economically active population. Involuntarily unemployed are those who are not at work but are seeking work or available for work at the on-going wage rate. This category is important from the economic point of view. In discussions, unemployment unless otherwise qualified, refers to those who are involuntarily unemployed. Unemployment rate refers to the percentage of total unemployed population to the total labour force.

The general definition used by the ILO for unemployment includes all persons above a specified age who, on the specified day or for a specified week, came into one of the following categories:

(a) workers available for employment whose contract of employment had been terminated or temporarily suspended and who were without a job and seeking work for pay or profit;

(b) persons who were available for work (except for minor illness) during the specified period and were seeking work for pay or profit, who were never previously employed or whose most recent status was other than that of employee (*i.e.* former employers, etc.) or who had been in retirement;

(c) persons without a job and currently available for work who had made arrangements to start a new job at a date subsequent to the specified period;

(d) persons on temporary or indefinite lay-off without pay.

The following categories of persons are not considered by the ILO to be unemployed:

(a) persons intending to establish their own business or farm, but who had not yet arranged to do so, who were not seeking work or pay for profit;

(b) former unpaid family workers not at work and not seeking work for pay or profit.

Unemployment is, very often categorized into various types. Frictional unemployment denotes unemployment caused by industrial friction such as immobility of labour, ignorance of job opportunities; shortage of raw materials, breakdown of machinery or plant etc. Seasonal unemployment refers to unemployment which is due to seasonal variations. Those employed in agricultural activities are subjected to seasonal unemployment if they do not plan for their employment in the off seasons in agriculture.

Structural unemployment refers to unemployment arising from structural changes in the economy. Technological changes will result in structural changes in the production process. It may displace labour and result in structural unemployment.

Cyclical unemployment refers to unemployment resulting from the business cycles in the economy. During periods of depression many people are thrown out of employment and they are referred to as cyclically unemployed.

Perhaps the most important and most commonly discussed type of unemployment is disguised unemployment. Disguised unemployment means that withdrawal of a part of the labour force from the traditional field of production would leave the total output unchanged (Sen: 1975). "In technical terms this will mean that the marginal productivity of labour, over a wide range, is zero" (Nurkse: 1953). Disguised unemployment is very common in all agriculture-based labour surplus economies. A distinction is to be made between incidence and duration of unemployment. Incidence of unemployment is the percentage of unemployed in a given population group. It is the unemployment rate. Duration of unemployment denotes mean years or months unemployed since leaving education (Sanyal: 1985).

6. Labour Market

The labour market is the institution which mediates between demand and supply of labour. It used to be believed that the price of labour—wage—was determined in the labour market depending upon the relative supply and demand for labour.

The classical economists assumed full employment and hence the primary function of the labour market was considered to be to ascertain the price of labour services at a given point in time. Given the assumptions of homogeneity of labour units and flexibility of wages, equilibrium in the labour market was a general case and dis-equilibrium was only a temporary aberration. The neo-classicists though, did not subscribe to the classical assumption of homogeneity of labour units and considered that the primary function of the labour market was to allocate and rationally adjust labour skills and labour demands so as to establish equilibrating wage rates.

From the educational point of view, different economists have emphasized different aspects of education which are given a premium in the labour market. In the human capital version, it is cognitive skills (Shultz: 1981), for Arrow (1973) it is the filtering or screening role, for Spence (1973) it is the signalling role of education which employers consider for recruitment. To Thurow (1972), Fields (1974) and Bhagawati; Srinivisan (1977) it is the hiring practice which is very important. However the radicals have shown that the labour market is segmented (Reich, *et al.* 1973). According to the theory, labour markets are divided into two: *(i)* primary, and *(ii)* secondary labour markets. The primary labour market is characterized by employment stability, high wages, better working conditions and internal labour markets. Secondary labour markets are characterized by low skill requirements, low wages, poor working conditions, high labour turnover and no promotion avenues.

Some versions of the segmentation theory further divide the primary segment into two—upper and lower tiers. Jobs in the upper tier required decision-making abilities whereas those in the lower tier involve routinized activities. Educational qualifications become a requisite for entry into the primary sector whereas they are not so essential in the secondary sector of the labour market.

A mention of internal and external labour markets is in order. Internal labour markets refers to the labour market internal to an organisation primarily for promotion into higher posts. The external labour market is the usual recruitment place for any job. In an internal labour market, only employees of the same organisation are candidates whereas the external labour market is primarily for the unemployed though the employed may also be part of it to improve their job prospects.

7. Wages

Wages, in the wider sense, are the reward for the factor of production, namely labour, and hence include any payment for work whether it is work done for an employer or that of a self-employed person. In a narrow and more commonly-used sense wages refer to payment to employed persons. Wage rate is the stated amount at which a person is hired.

Sometimes a distinction is drawn between wages and salaries. Wages are associated with lower-level manual workers paid on an hourly, daily or weekly basis whereas salaries refer to monthly or annual payments usually for white-collar employees.

Two important bases for wage payment or wage determination are: *(i)* payment by time; *(ii)* payment by results (Robertson 1961). Payment by time means deciding and paying a fixed amount of money to an individual with given and known characteristics for a certain specified period of time. Salary is the most common payment based on time. Salary is the pure time payment and the time period involved is normally monthly or yearly. Non-manual workers are usually salaried.

Payment by results is related to the actual work done. The work done can be measured in terms of (a) piecework; and (b) time allowances. In the case of piecework the worker is remunerated according to the number of units of output he has produced, *i.e.* the unit of output is priced as the criterion for payment. In time allowances the output is fixed rather than priced. Each work requires a certain period of time for its completion or performance. There is a normal or standard time required for each work. The payment is based on this time allowed. The individual may take more or less time than this to finish the work. But he will be paid based on the standard time to be taken rather than the actual time taken.

A distinction is to be drawn between income, wages and earnings. Income is the flow of returns from property, estate or wealth. Wages are the reward or payment for work or employment. Earnings refer to the total of all types of receipts from any profession. Earnings may be more than wages. Wage is the minimum that one gets from a profession or job whereas earnings are the maximum that one can receive from the profession or job and income is independent of profession.

The general trend is that there is a positive association between education and earnings. Therefore, education is considered to be an influential variable in explaining earning differentials between individuals. The human capital model is the most commonly used model for explaining earning differentials among individuals.

8. Labour Mobility

Labour mobility refers to the movement of the labour force. Mobility can be spatial which denotes movement of labour from one region to another or from one country to another. This is sometimes referred to as labour migration. Migration within the confines of a country is called internal migration and between nations is called international migration.

Mobility can be from one employment status to another. This is more common where internal labour markets exist and promotion possibilities are widespread. This is referred to as vertical mobility.

Mobility can also be from one occupation to another occupation. The occupation may be of similar status. This is referred to as lateral or horizontal mobility. Persons with narrow fields of specialization have less chances of lateral mobility though their chances of vertical mobility are better.

REFERENCES

Arrow, K.J. (1973). "Higher Education as Filter", *Journal of Public Economics*, Vol. 2, pp. 192-216.

Bhagawati, J.N.; Srinivasan, T.N. (1977). "Education in a Job Ladder-Model and Fairness in Hiring Principle", *Journal of Public Economics*, Vol. 7, pp. 1-22.

Fields, G.S. (1974). "Private Demand for Education in Relation to Labour Market Conditions in Less Developed Countries", *The Economic Journal*, Vol. 84, pp. 906-19.

ILO: International Labour Organisation (1969). *International Standard Classification of Occupations*, (Revised), Geneva, ILO.

ILO: International Labour Organisation (1984). *Unemployment and Economic Growth*, Geneva.

ILO: International Labour Organisation (1989). *Yearbook of Labour Statistics*, Geneva.

Monly, J.; Costa, E. (1981). *Employment Policies in Developing Countries*, Geneva.

Nurkse, R. (1953). *Problems of Capital Formation in Under-Developed Countries*, Oxford. Blackwell.

Reich, M; Gordon, D.M.; Edwards, R.C. (1973). "A Theory of Labour Market Segmentation", *American Economic Review*, Vol. 63, pp. 359-65.

Robertson, D.J. (1961). *The Economics of Wages and Distribution of Income*, London, Macmillan.

Sanyal, B.C. (1985). "Graduate Unemployment and Education", *International Encyclopedia for Education*, Oxford, Pergamon Press.

Schultz, T.W. (1961). "Investment in Human Capital", *American Economic Review*, Vol. 51, pp. 1-17.

Sen, A.K. (1975). *Employment Technology and Development*, Delhi, Oxford University Press.

Spence, M. (1973). "Job Market Signalling", *Quarterly Journal of Economics*, Vol. 87, pp. 355-75.

Thurow, L. (1972). "Education and Economic Inequality", *Public Interest*, Summer.

Uthoff, A.G.; Pernia, E.M. (1986). *An Introduction to Human Resources Planning in Developing Countries*, Geneva, ILO, 1986.

Watts, A.G. (1983). *Education, Unemployment and Future of Work*, Milton Keynes, Open University Press.

World Bank. (1989). *World Development Report*, Washington, D.C., World Bank.

6

Diagnosis of Employment Structures: Basic Concepts

F. Caillods and T. El Hachem

Very useful information concerning the employment situation and the education employment relationship can be obtained from the analysis of census data and other survey data (household surveys, manpower surveys) which are regularly collected in the different countries. Censuses for example are now available in (almost) all countries from two to three years. Most countries have indeed conducted censuses in the 1960s, 1970s and 1980s.

The object of this lecture and of the following exercise is to show how one can prepare a diagnosis of the employment situation and of the education employment relationship using data which is normally available and to illustrate the sort of conclusions that can be drawn in terms of medium-and long-term prospects. The information to be analysed will concern:

- the population structure by age sex urban and rural areas;
- the level of the economically active population and its structure by age, sex, urban and rural areas (labour supply);
- the level of employment (labour demand).

At all stages we will analyze the structure by educational level and the education-employment relationship.

It is useful to recall first a number of definitions. The discussion will then be illustrated with examples from different countries.

1. Evolution and Structure of the Population

Three major indicators will be analysed:

- the population growth rate,
- the urban population growth rate,
- the percentage of the population living in urban and rural areas, as they have an incidence on the number of pupils to be enrolled and on the size of the population seeking employment.

2. Level and Structure of the Economically Active Population

2.1 *Definitions*

— *The economically active population* comprises all persons who furnish the potential supply of labour for the production of economic goods and services. It is measured in relation to a given period of reference (as much as a year, or as little as one day or one week) (ILO 1988).

The economically active population, which is also called the labour force, includes the employed and the unemployed persons.

— *The working age population* depends on the school leaving age and on the age of retirement. In developed countries the working age population includes all persons aged between 15 and 59 or 64 years. In developing countries, the working age population is not so easily defined. Education is not necessarily compulsory, and child labour is a reality even if it is not well measured. There is no official age of retirement for large portions of the population (the self-employed in particular).

— *The labour force participation rate (LFPR)* is the percentage of the labour force over the working age population.

2.2 Discussion

Although it seems easy to define the economically active population, there are great variations in the way countries include, or do not include, unpaid family work, self employment, domestic activities and women's activities in general. In practice the EAP or the labour force often refer to those engaged directly in paid employment.

The labour force participation rate varies according to the age, the gender, the educational level of the persons, the country, its level of economic development, the proportion of the population living in urban areas, the salary level and the country's dominant culture.

The male participation rate varies very little except that there is a certain tendency of the LFPR for the 10-24 age group to decrease, as a result of schooling. The female LFPR on the other hand varies a great deal according to the above mentioned criteria, and the definition of the labour force (this definition can vary from one census to another). The increase in female labour force participation is in many countries one of the main source of increase in the labour force. The increase in the female educational level tends to increase their LFPR.

3. Employment and Unemployment Level

3.1 Definitions

- *The employed* comprise all persons who on a specified day or for a specified week were in paid employment or self employment, including the unpaid family worker.
- *The unemployed* comprise all persons who during a specified period were not employed and had no job but actively seeking work for pay or profit. It includes persons actively seeking work for the first time.
- *The unemployment rate* for a specific group refers to the number of unemployed in this group over the group's labour force.

3.2 Analysis

The unemployment rate should be analysed by age, gender, and educational level. The factor influencing the unemployment rate will be discussed in a specific lecture on this subject.

As important as unemployment is the problem of under employment.

Underemployment exists when persons in employment who are not working full time would be able and willing to do more work than they are actually performing at present (ILO 1984).

Underemployment is of two types: visible and invisible.

Visible underemployment means working less than a certain number of hours per year (desired or considered normal or appropriate).

Invisible underemployment exists when more people are engaged in a certain activity than would be needed to produce the output which they produce (Monly and Costa: 1981). Their earnings are abnormally low and their jobs do not permit full use of their capacities or skilis. Underemployment of the educated is a serious problem in many of the developing economies.

4. Employment Structure and Structure of the Labour Force

4.1 Classification

Employment and the labour force are often analysed in terms of:

— Sector of activity

The employed are classified according to whether they work in the primary sector (agriculture and mining), the secondary sector (manufacturing, electricity, gas and water) or the tertiary sector (commerce and service).

— Industry

According to the International Standard Industrial Classification of All Economic Activities (ISIC), the major divisions of industries are:

- Agriculture, hunting, forestry and fishing
- Mining and quarrying
- Manufacturing
- Electricity, gas and water
- Construction
- Wholesale and retail trade, restaurants and hotels
- Transport, storage and communication
- Financing, insurance, real estate and business services
- Community, social and personal services
- Activities not adequately defined

— Status

ILO distinguishes six categories (ILO 88)

- ***Employer:*** a person who operates his or her own economic enterprise or engages independently in a profession or trade, and hires one or more employees.
- ***Own account worker:*** a person who operates his or her own economic enterprise or engages independently in a profession or trade and hires no employee.
- ***Employee:*** a person who works for a public or private employer and receives remuneration in wages, salary, commission, tips, piece-rates or pay in kind.
- ***Unpaid family worker:*** a person who works a specified minimum amount of time (at least one-third of normal working hours), without pay, in an economic enterprise operated by a related person living in the same household.
- ***Member of producers' co-operative:*** a person who is an active member of a producers' co-operative, regardless of the industry in which it is established.
- ***Persons not classifiable by status:*** experienced workers with status unknown or inadequately described and unemployed persons not previously employed.

— Occupation.

The International Standard Classification of Occupations has been adopted by ILO in 1958 are revised in 1968. Given all the criticisms raised by the classification which was generally considered as not adapted to developing countries, it has been further revised in 1987. The new ISCO classifies the persons according to the tasks he/she performs. The main criterion used to define groups and sub-groups has been the skill requirements *i.e.* the skill level and the skill specialization. The former 1968 ISCO which inspired most censuses identified ten groups as follows:

1. Professional, technical and related workers.
2. Administrative and managerial workers.
3. Clerical and related workers.
4. Sales workers.
5. Service workers.
6. Agriculture, animal husbandry and forestry workers, fishermen and hunters.

7/8/9. Production and related workers, transport equipment operators and labourers.

10. Workers not classifiable by occupation and members of the armed forces.

4.2 *Analyses which can be carried out*

The structure of the labour force can be analysed in the following way:

- by sector of activity;
- by status;
- by industry;
- by occupation;
- by industry and occupation;
- by industry and status.

To highlight the relationship between education and employment, it is useful to analyse the labour force:

- by sector and educational level;
- by industry and educational level;
- by occupation and educational level.

It is useful to compare the structure of the labour force for different years (how it evolved over time) and between countries at different levels of economic development.

- It is generally believed that a country's structure of employment is a function of its level of economic development. One does notice that the process of economic development is associated with a gradual shift of the work force from the primary sector to the secondary and tertiary sectors, from self-employment to wage employment and that the proportion of scientific and technical personnel in the overall employment increases with the GDP per capita. In spite of such 'heavy trends' however, variation in the employment structure of countries at similar level of development can be observed which reflects their specific economic structure, the role of the public sector in their economy and their history in terms of educational development.
- The educational structure of the labour force is as much a function of the country's past education policy than of its level of economic development. The fact that the labour force is educated can in turn influence the structure of employment (supply effect).
- There is no fixed correspondence between education and employment and the educational level of people employed in one occupation vary in time and between countries. The education profile of an occupation depends on the demand and supply on the labour market.

Any further analysis introducing age, sex and income level as additional variables would help refine the analysis of the relationship between education and employment.

EXERCISE

Diagnosis of the 'Education Employment' Relationship the Case of Country X

I. Working-age population, labour force and labour force participation rate.

The economically active population or labour force comprises all persons of either sex who furnish—or would like to furnish—the supply of labour for the production of economic goods and services. It includes employed and unemployed persons and excludes students, women purely occupied in domestic duties, retired persons, etc.

1. Complete Table—6.1.
2. Analyzing Tables—6.1 and 6.2, state a number of factors which influence the labour force participation rate of men and women (and therefore the size of the labour force).
3. To what extent can education influence the labour force participation rate.
4. How do you explain the evolution of the labour force participation rate between 1981 and 1991.

Table—6.1: Working-age Population, Labour Force and Labour Force Participation Rate by Sex, 1981.

		Total	*Male*	*Female*
1.	Working-age population (10 years old and over)	9354	4839	4515
2.	Employed population ('000)	3649	2838	811
	Unemployed Population			
3.	Unemployed actively seeking work	504	306	198
4.	Unemployed not actively seeking work	335	168	167
5.	Sub-total unemployed (3 + 4)	839	474	365
6.	Labour force (2 + 5)	4488	3312	1176
7.	Labour force participation rate (6/1)	47.9%	...	...

Table—6.2: Labour Force Participation Rate by Age and Sex, country X 1991 (in per cent)

Sex/Age	10-14	15-19	20-24	25-34	35-44	45-64	65 & over	Total
Total	4.0	29.9	57.8	63.6	62.6	50.4	20.9	44.4
Male	5.5	40.4	78.7	91.5	93.5	79.9	37.8	64.8
Female	2.4	19.0	36.8	35.2	30.5	18.1	4.0	23.1

II. Level of unemployment (1981)

1. Complete Table—6.3.
2. Comment on Tables—6.3 and 6.4.

   How would you define the situation of unemployment in Country X in 1981?

   Who is primarily hit by unemployment (by sex and educational level)?

   How does education affect: the chances of somebody being unemployed?

Table—6.3: Unemployment Rate by Sex, Country X, 1981

	Total	*Male*	*Female*
1. Total labour force (000')	4488	3312	1176
2. Total unemployed population (000') Rate of unemployment (2/1 x 100)	839	474	365
3. Unemployed actively job-hunting (000') (3/1 x 100)	504	306	198

III. Structure of the employed population

1. Structure of employment by status. Comment on Table—6.5.
2. Employment structure by industry. Complete Table—6.6 and comment. How would you describe the growth of employment between 1973 and 1981 and between 1981

Table—6.4: Unemployment Rate by Educational Level, 1981

Educational level	*Total labour force 000'*	*Unemployed (000')*	*Unemploment rate*
No schooling	941.6	100.9	10.7%
Passed grades 1-10	3154.4	614.7	19.5%
GCE 'O' Level in 6 or more subjects	287.1	112.7	39.2%
'A' Level in 3 or more subjects	74.5	6.8	9.1%
Degree equivalent or higher	30.4	3.9	12.8%
Total	**4488.0**	**839.2**	**18.7%**

Table—6.5: Composition of the Employed Population by Employment Status and Occupation (in per cent).

	Paid employee	*Employer*	*Self-employed*	*Unpaid family worker*	*Total*
Professional and technical workers	93.2	2.2	4.4	0.2	100.0
Administrative and managerial workers	89.5	7.2	2.8	0.5	100.0
Clerical workers	99.2	0.3	0.4	0.1	100.0
Sales workers	45.2	18.7	33.2	2.9	100.0
Service workers	88.5	2.8	6.6	2.0	100.0
Agriculture workers	49.8	1.4	39.7	9.1	100.0
Production workers	87.7	2.7	8.8	0.8	100.0
Total	**66.6**	**3.1**	**25.0**	**5.2**	**100.0**

Table—6.6: Employment Structure by Industry: Evolution from 1973, 1981, to 1991

	1973		1981		1991	
	(000)	%	*(000)*	%	*(000)*	%
Agriculture	1693	53.27	1829	50.11	1876	45.53
Mining and qua.	10	0.31	13	0.36	34	0.83
Manufacturing	313	9.85	349	...	425	10.32
Construction	86	2.71	104	2.85	134	3.25
Commerce	268	8.43	344	9.42	437	10.61
Transport	133	4.19	179	...	200	8.45
Finance	20	0.63	25	...	57	1.38
Services	655	20.61	807	22.11	957	23.23
Total	**3178**	**100.00**	**3650**	**100.00**	**4120**	**100.00**

and 1991? Which economic sector employs the most people? How did the situation evolve in this respect between 1973, 1981 and 1991?

3. Employment by occupations and the occupation/industry matrix. Analyse Table—6.7 and complete Table—6.8. Comment on these tables: Which industry employs most qualified manpower (here: Professional/technical and administrative/managerial personnel) and how did the situation evolve between 1981 and 1991? Which factors can explain this evolution?

Table—6.7: Employment Structure by Industry and Occupation in 1981

	Professional/ technical	*Admin. and managerial*	*Total*
Agriculture	1904	475	1828977
Per cent	0.1	0.0	100.0
Mining	127	51	13079
Per cent	1.0	0.4	100.0
Manufacturing	4986	2130	348972
Per cent	1.4	0.6	100.0
Construction	2485	255	103561
Per cent	2.4	0.2	100.0
Transport	2738	979	178876
Per cent	1.5	0.5	100.0
Commerce	2132	2526	343768
Per cent	0.6	0.7	100.0
Banks and Finance	3292	1157	24945
Per cent	13.2	4.6	100.0
Services	160824	6344	806693
Per cent	19.9	0.8	100.0
Total	**178508**	**13924**	**3649571**
Per cent	**4.9**	**0.4**	**100.0**

Table—6.8: Employment Structure by Industry and Occupation in 1991

	Professional/ technical	*Admin. and managerial*	*Total*
Agriculture	1283	1476	1875828
per cent	0.1	0.1	100.0
Mining	193	151	33814
Per cent	0.6	0.4	100.0
Manufacturing	8639	8522	424715
Per cent	...	2.0	100.0
Construction	5670	2322	133968
Per cent	...	1.7	100.0
Transport	3853	2201	199574
Per cent	1.9	1.1	100.0
Commerce	3117	5400	437318
Per cent	...	1.2	100.0
Banks and Finance	6613	4939	56927
Per cent	11.6	8.7	100.0
Services	217016	8675	957211
Per cent	...	0.9	100.0
Total	**246384**	**33686**	**4119355**
Per cent	**...**	**0.8**	**100.0**

4. Employed population by educational level and occupation. Complete Table—6.9 and make general comments. How does the educational profile evolve with the occupation? Is there one typical educational level for each occupation? If not, could you make some suggestions on how to break this big occupational categories into more homogeneous ones as far as education is concerned. Do you think it feasible to define occupations perfectly homogeneous as far as their educational profile is concerned? Why not? Given what you have seen regarding the level of unemployment of school leavers, how is the educational profile of each occupation likely to change in the future?

5. Which information would be available in your own country?

Table—6.9: Distribution of Employees by Occupation and Educational Level, 1981

Occupations	*Education attainment*					Total
	University degree	A level in 3 or more subjects	O level in 6 or more subjects	Grade 1-10	No schooling	
1. Prof./tech.	22296	57004	44039	47665	7484	178488
Per cent	12.5	...	24.7	26.7	...	100.0
2. Adm./manager	2207	838	3070	6770	1032	13917
Per cent	15.9	...	22.1	48.6	...	100.0
3. Clerical worker	2539	4624	55632	113220	10129	186114
Per cent	1.4	2.5	29.9	60.8	5.4	100.0
4. Sales and service	624	1295	23542	371282	73502	470245
Per cent	0.1	0.3	5.0	79.0	15.6	100.0
5. Agricultural worker	607	1293	15779	1182151	582304	1782134
Per cent	0.0	0.1	0.9	66.3	32.7	100.0
6. Production worker	1250	1655	26377	755631	141578	926491
Per cent	0.1	0.2	2.8	81.6	15.3	100.0
7. Others	952	1003	5975	58797	24729	91456
Per cent	1.0	1.1	6.5	64.3	27.0	100.0
Total	**30475**	**67712**	**174414**	**2535516**	**840758**	**3648875**
Per cent	**0.8**	**1.9**	**4.8**	**69.5**	**23.0**	**100.0**

7

Tracer Studies to Relate Education with Employment for the Development of Human Resources

Bikas C. Sanyal

1. Introduction

Research on the relationship between education and employment has received significant attention in recent years among educational decision-makers, planners and administrators. It is now well recognized that simple quantitative forecasts of manpower needs cannot provide precise enough direction for the development of the education system. The relationship between education and employment can no longer be based on such forecasting models alone. The fact that there are aspects of this relationship which remain unknown makes it more complex. Researchers have to look into this unknown area, particularly at a time when the problem of unemployment among youth is becoming more and more critical. Overall open unemployment has been increasing at a very fast rate in almost all countries, except those where the economic recession has not been serious. However, the number of such countries are very few.

The problem in magnitude started increasing in the seventies. Although economic stagnation was believed to be the main cause behind this problem, it was also felt that many other factors were contributing to such a situation. These were sociological, psychological, administrative and organisational factors, which researchers had to identify in order to provide new tools for decision-makers to remedy this problem. However, such research has not always followed the same conceptual framework; different points of view about the relationship between education and employment have been the basis for different types of research. At one extreme, there is the point of view that the relationship between education and employment is artificially imposed by the society and vested interests plays a dominant role to keep a 'status quo' in such a relationship, thus perpetuating social hierarchy, discrimination and segmentation in the society. At the other extreme, it is held that educational systems could be reformed to provide skills to meet the social and economic development needs, as well as to meet individual expectations for upward social mobility, without going into the socio-psychological complexity of the relationship, reducing the analysis to the traditional quantitative forecasting exercises.

In what follows, we attempt to take into account the influence of the social structure on the development of education in relation to employment, based on the belief that reform measures if properly planned and implemented can reduce the problem of unemployment. A combination of two approaches has been utilized, as described in the following sections.

2. The Conceptual Framework of the Relationship

It is argued that interdependence between educational development and the overall socio-economic development of a country in general, and development of employment in particular, calls for an analysis of the resource potential in natural, physical and human categories. To develop each region in a balanced way, the development strategy of a country should take account of whatever natural resource potential is available in that region. The process of exploitation and the choice of technology will be determined *inter alia* by natural resource potential. The exploitation of these resources needs skills, which must be provided by the education system. The way in which natural resources are exploited, therefore, influences the educational development strategy in structure and content. It is also dependent on the available and potential physical resources such as building equipment, transportation and communication facilities. Development of these physical resources depends in turn on the development of education and vice versa. An analysis of physical resources potential therefore becomes an important task in ascertaining the role of education in the overall development strategy of a country.

In the analysis of the development of human resources, traditions, customs and beliefs cherished by the people cannot be ignored. Demographic changes influence the human resource potential as well. Education, for that matter higher education, has to be planned in such a way as to develop this human resource potential in order to respond to the needs of the social and economic development of the country, while considering the expectations and attitudes of the people. An analysis of human resource development therefore becomes imperative in the overall analysis of the relationship between education and employment.

The conditions of work, recruitment and promotion policy of the employment market influence the type of qualification that an employee would have. A full employment policy, on the one hand, has to guarantee a job for every individual but, in countries where this policy does not prevail, individual initiative is necessary for obtaining employment. Therefore, the development of human resources becomes dependent on the operation of the labour market and the prevailing employment policy. The policy of human resource development for economic and social needs calls for an analysis of the skills needed for the various activities of the economy. The output of the education system, by type of skills taught, has to be known for proper utilization of the human resources in generates. Before the education system can be planned with respect to intake, content and structure, it is only logical that demands for such skills in quantitative terms should be estimated beforehand to whatever extent possible. These estimates of demand, which traditionally have been called manpower demand, but in our conception are broader than that because of the consideration of the qualitative aspects, are susceptible to inaccuracy due to economic uncertainties and the changing nature of the perceptions, attitudes and expectations of the different segments of the society. However, some guidance is needed as to the direction that the development of education in general, and higher education in particular, should take in quantitative terms to cater for the future needs for skills as to avoid unemployment, underemployment, or shortage of skilled human resources.

It is considered that these segments, if properly prepared, can provide such guidance. These quantitative estimates of needs for skills can be checked with the actual values to identify the degree of inaccuracy and to form a checklist of missing parameters and variables. They are also useful for setting the foundation of the strategy for the development of the structure and organisation of the education system.

It is assumed that where higher and vocational education is concerned the estimates are easier to make, because of the increased degree of correspondence between the skills imparted in the education system and the skills needed on the job, than for other types of education. Having regard to the problems of estimating future needs for highly qualified manpower, an analysis of the matching between the quantity of trained people and the quality of the training content demanded by the economy and responsiveness of the institutions of higher education becomes particularly useful. This analysis of matching brings out the shortcomings of the education system, not only quantitatively but also qualitatively. A careful diagnosis of the education system forms the basis of any future strategy for the higher education system and also provides a yardstick for achievements in restructuring the social system through change in the educational system, and illuminates the problems encountered in achieving the targets of socialization and equality of opportunities in the world of work. These problems may be seen in the various education 'paths' of different population groups,

Figure 1: Macro Aspects

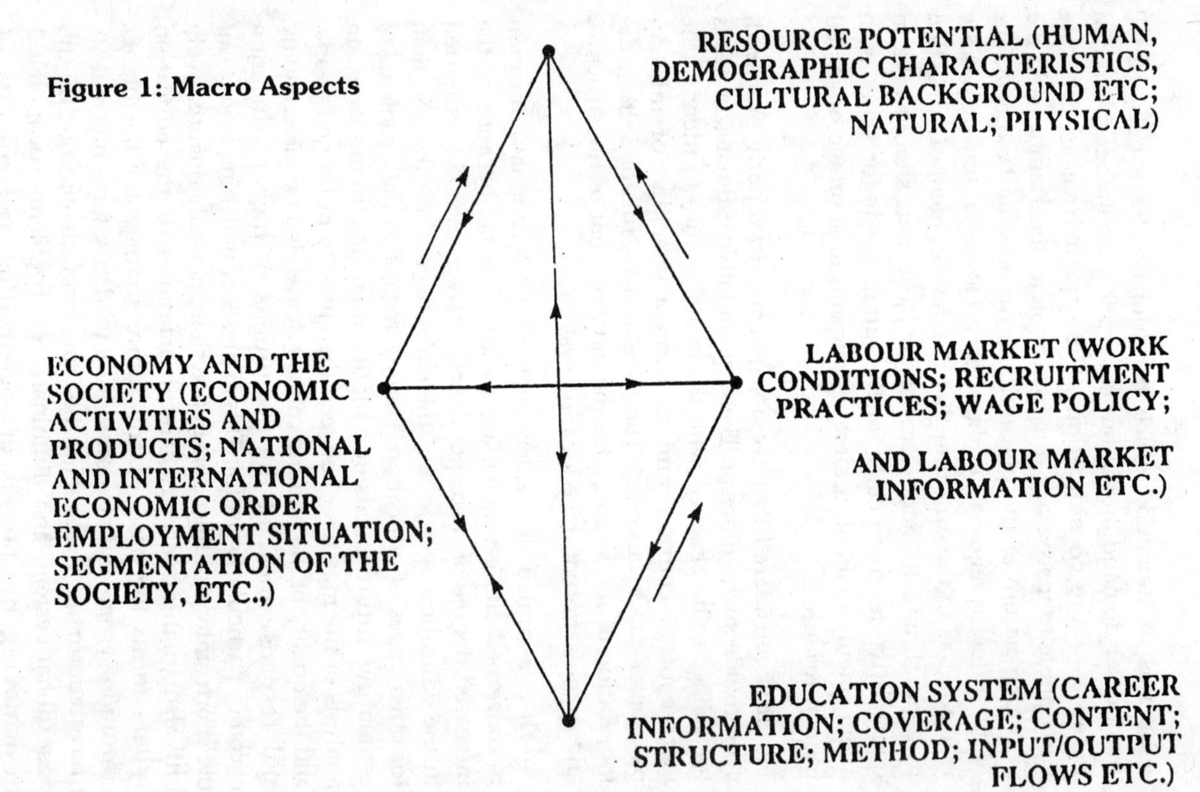

which result in the different working opportunities in the labour market. This relationship is demonstrated in *Figure 1*.

What is more important however are the micro aspects of the relationship. In the analysis of the relationship between education and employment, we are concerned with individual human beings and individual enterprises. Their background, attitudes and expectations play an important role in this relationship. What goes on in the labour market is a reflection of the social set-up including the educational system. We believe that the economy and the society, the human resource potential of the country and the education system as it is, influence the behaviour, attitudes and expectations of the individuals, their families, their community, and their educational history (see *Figure* 2). These factors again influence directly the expectations of each individual in respect of his or her social role, as does the operation of the labour market through its selection criteria, recruitment practices, labour market information system, etc. But the occupational expectations are also indirectly influenced by resource potential, economy and the society and the educational system through the individual characteristics (sibling position, family size, parents/guardians' occupation, education and income), the community characteristics (home region, religion, ethnicity, tribe) and the early educational history (type of school, type of education, academic performance etc.) (see *Figure* 3).

Similarly, motivation in respect of education is generated directly by the motivation in respect of occupation, functioning of the education system, the individual, family, community and early educational characteristics, and indirectly by the resource potential, economy and the society, and the education system through the individual, family, community and early educational characteristics. It is considered that if a society is to be democratized, the education system, the economy and the society have to give emphasis to changing the micro characteristics so as to generate egalitarian occupational and educational expectations which would then lead to egalitarian educational and occupational careers of individuals.

Figure 2: Macro-Micro Interrelation

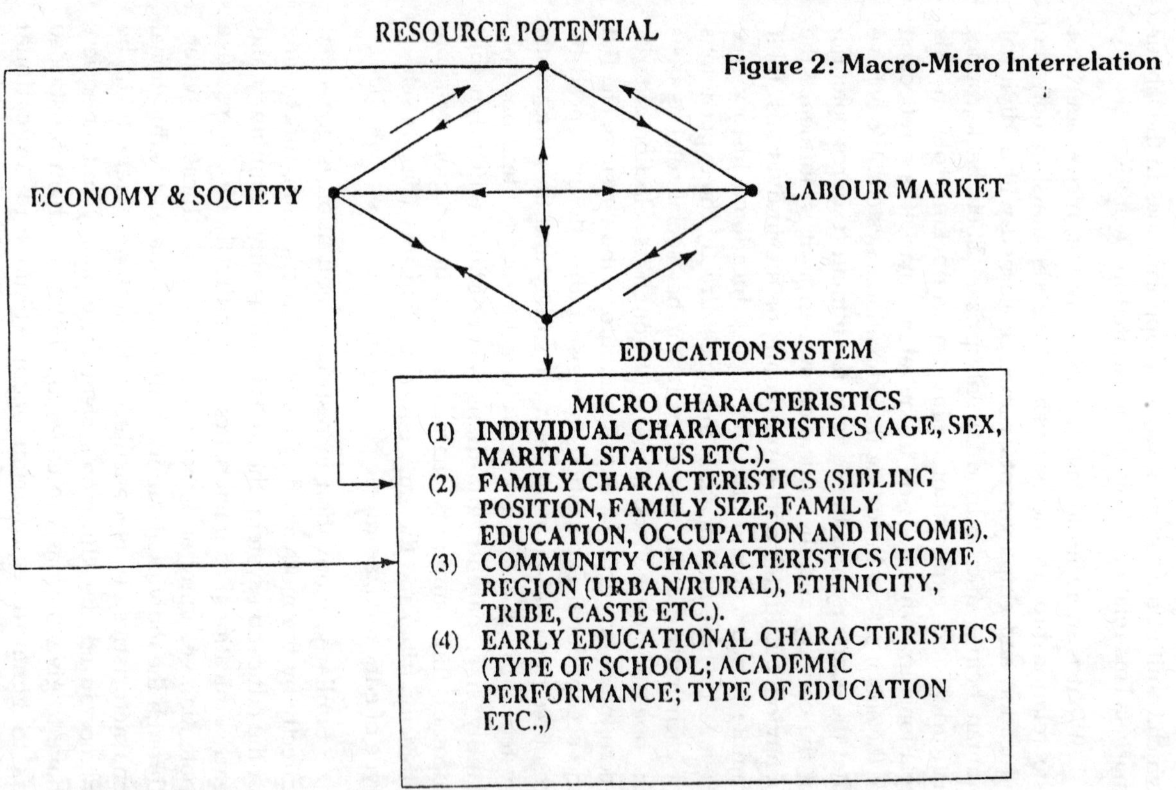

Figure 3: Occupational Expectations Derived from the Macro-Micro Interface

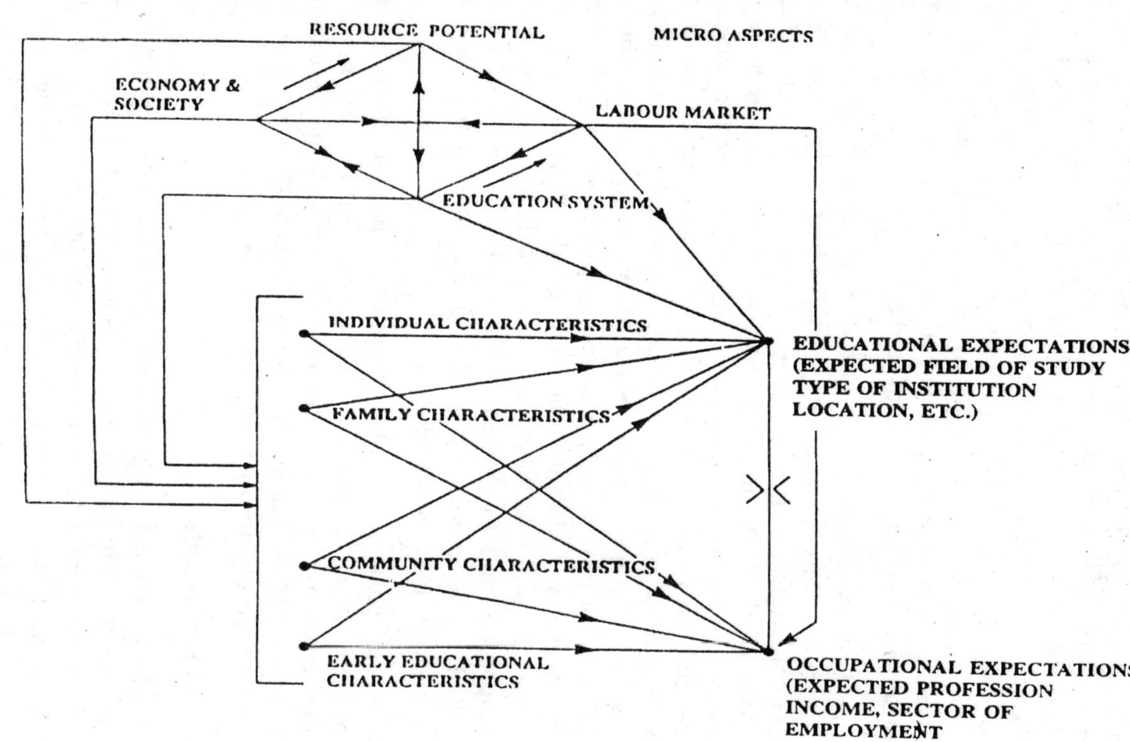

The educational career of the individual is directly influenced by the educational expectations, the education system, the individual, family, community and early educational characteristics, and indirectly by the occupational expectations, the economy and the society, and the resources potential through the micro characteristics (see *Figure 4*). The important factors in educational career are type of institution attended and its location, field of study pursued, academic performance, change of subject during the course of studies, etc.

The occupational career is dependent directly upon the educational career, the labour market situation, the occupational expectations, and individual, family, community, early educational and occupational characteristics, and indirectly upon the economy and the society, resource potential and the education system. The factors to be noted in occupational career are career information received, placement services used, recruitment methods and selection criteria used, waiting period to obtain a job, type of post held, type of firm, location, salary, satisfaction on the job, and utilization of training/education on the job (see *Figure 4*). Some of these items are also in the domain of the employers and thus need to be checked with them to find whether the experience of the graduates matches with the employers' perceptions.

The basic thrust of our approach is that the education system as an important instrument for human resource development can change the characteristics of the individuals, families and the community, so as to make the transition from institutions of education to work smoother.

3. Data Needs

A conceptual framework as described above requires a lot of data and information on the resource potential, economy and social structure, education system, and on the labour market. A list of such data needs is given in Table—7.1 along with the possible sources. The analysis of the individual, family, community, early educational and occupational characteristics,

Figure 4: Occupational Career Derived from the Macro-Micro Interface

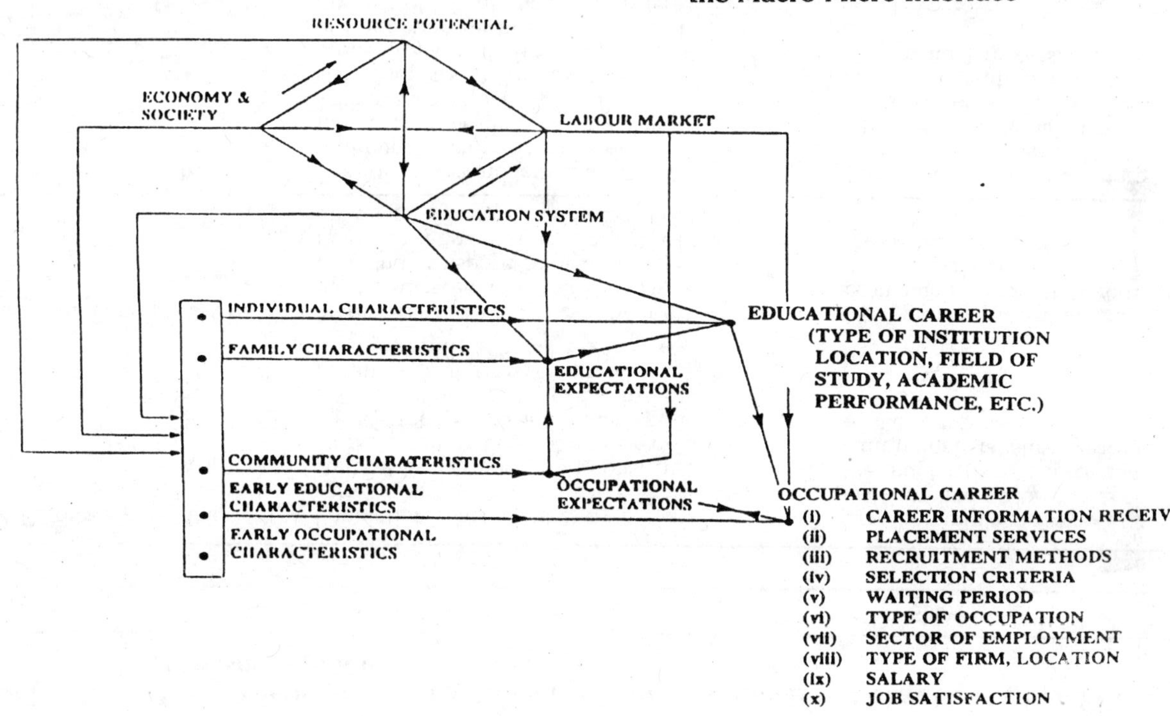

Table—7.1: Data Needs for Macro Aspects of the Relationship between Higher Education and Employment

Items	*Required information/statistics*	*Sources*
1	2	3
1. Resource potential: (*a*) Human:	Population characteristics by region, social groups, age group and sex; cultural background: traditions; customs; working population, labour force participation by social groups, age and sex; educational participation by social groups, age and sex; emigration and immigration.	Census, sample surveys, historical and social studies on the country; labour force and educational statistical yearbooks of the country.
(*b*) Natural and physical:	Nature resource reserves: underground, on the surface and underwater; water and land transport; climatic conditions, flora and fauna; physical infrastructure: buildings, equipment and other facilities.	Geological, agricultural and economic surveys of government non-government and international agencies.
2. Economy and the society:	The role of the modern and the traditional sector, the industrial origin of the gross domestic product; level of saving, income per capita; the characteristics of the new international economic order (NIEP), namely terms of trade, transfer of technology and division of labour, the role of external operators in the national economy; social stratification; employment situation.	Economic surveys are reports of the country prepared by national and international agencies, sociological studies, studies on political economy, employment reports, etc.

(*Contd...*)

Table—7.1 (Contd...)

1	2	3
3. Labour market:	Selection criteria, recruitment and promotion practices, wage policy, labour market information. etc.; the traditional labour market; the rural labour force.	Statistics on employment and earnings; reports of recruitment committees, salary commissions; statistics on labour force; census and sample surveys.
4. Education system:	Statistics on enrolment by type and level of education (past and present), by sex, region and social groups; statistics on physical facilities, teachers and budget, flow rates by year of study, level and type of education; availability of career information; information on content and structure of the education systems in school and out of school; coverage of education; internal and external efficiency of the system.	Ministry of Education, Ministry of Finance, at Ministry of Planning; other reports and nation and international level.

occupational and educational expectations, educational and occupational career actually held by the individual also need considerable data, which are not usually available in published documents. Instruments have to be designed to collect such data. Three instruments are designed in the form of questionnaires: one for the students, one for the graduates (separately for employed and unemployed if it is feasible to cover them) and one for the employees. The data needs for the micro aspects of the relationship between education and employment are given in Table—7.2 (for students and graduates) and Table—7.3 (for employers). The data on the employers are needed for comparing the perceptions of the employers with the experiences of the graduates, as well as for identifying the relationship between education and employment as perceived by the employers.[1] The drawing up of the necessary questionnaires to collect the data will be discussed later in the course.

4. Collection of Data

Representative samples are drawn from the student, graduate and employer population based on the random sampling technique; where such a technique fails, purposive sampling to cater for the special needs and scope of the study is adopted.

5. Analysis of the Data

A list of hypotheses is prepared to verify the conceptual framework described above and to derive policy measures. These are tested by standard statistical analysis, as described in the session on statistical techniques.

6. Results

As stated before, results of such research are to be related to the specific socio-economic context of the country. The implications for planning of education related to employment are derived separately for each country studied. The results from a study in Solomon Islands are giving in Tables—7.4 to 7.11 for discussion.

Table—7.2: Data Needs for Micro Aspects of the Relationship between Higher Education and Employment: the Students and the Graduates

	Items	*Statistics/Information*	*Source*
	1	**2**	**3**
1.	Individual characteristics:	Age, sex, marital status	
2.	Family characteristics:	Sibling position, family size; education, occupation and income of parents/guardians.	
3.	Community characteristics:	Home region (urban/rural), ethnicity, religion, tribe, educational opportunity in the community, etc.	
4.	Early educational characteristics:	Type of school, location, type and level of education, academic performance, financing; other training activities.	Sample surveys conducted with specially designed questionnaire.
5.	Early occupational history:	Whether worked as a student: if yes, nature and earnings; whether worked breaking studies: if yes, nature and earnings.	

(Contd...)

Table—7.2 (Contd...)

1	2	3
6. Occupational expectations:	Type of occupation expected, type of post, sector of employment, type of firm; expected waiting period; expected salary motivational factors for working in rural area, expected selection criteria, placement services and recruitment methods.	
7. Educational expectations:	Type of specialization desire; type of institution, location, type of performance expected; type of educational career information received.	
8. Educational career:	Career guidance, admission criteria, reasons for the type of specialization pursued, type of institution attended, location, academic performance, changes if any in field of study during educational career; role of career information; relevance of education received.	Sample surveys conducted with specially designed questionnaires.
9. Occupational career. (1)	Career information, placement services, selection criteria, recruitment methods, waiting period, type of occupation, education/occupation match, sector of employment, type of firm, location, job satisfaction, motivational factors for work in rural area; reasons for delay in obtaining a job.	

(1) For graduates only. The statistics relate to the employed graduates; information on unemployed graduates is very useful if a survey can be conducted; only the first and last elements, namely career information and causes for remaining unemployed have to be included.

Table—7.3: Data needs for Micro Aspects of the Relations between Higher Education and Employment: the Employer's Perceptions

	Item	*Information/statistics*	*Sources*
1.	Characteristics of employers:	Data of establishment, type of control, size, industrial group, nature of products and services.	
2.	Employment characteristics:	Criteria for selection, method of recruitment, availability of job description mechanics, number of type of graduates employed, estimates of needs for graduates in the future, salary structure.	Sample survey of employers conducted with specially designed questionnaire.
3.	Relationship with higher education institutions:	Relevance of higher education programmes for job performance; organisational mechanics for in-service and on-the-job training; methods of co-operation with the institutions of higher education; best methods of organising educational programmes related to the needs of the world of work.	

Tracer Study Results for Solomon Islands

Table—7.4: Factors Important in Choice of Course (percentage of graduates)

	Males	*Females*	*Total*
Lead to desired jobs	95	81	92
Help in work	90	81	91
Help in promotion	75	67	73
Lead to higher way	75	52	70
Work in new field	41	37	40
Obtain scholarship	72	59	69
Interest in subject	51	74	56
No place on desired course	11	11	11
No scholarships as desired	7	4	6
Only course accepted into	18	22	19

Table—7.5: Factors held Important in Choice of Occupation (percentage holding factor as important)

	Total
Good income	75
Knew something about it	82
Expected high demand	87
Community respect for it	62
Followed teachers' advice	17
Followed parents' advice	15
No particular reason	8

Table—7.6: Methods of Obtaining First Job after Graduation (in percentage)

	All graduates
Job guaranteed by sponsor	59
Careers officer at institution	6
Employment/Labour Office	8
Gazette/Newspaper/Magazines	8
Visited firms directly	4
Family/friends	3
Became self-employed	0

Note: The percentage may be greater than 100 since respondents may have indicated the importance of more than one factor, or add to less than 100 because of an 'other' category not shown in Table.

Table—7.7: Category of First Graduate Employment

	Number	*Percentage*
Govt./Stat./Parastatal	116	89
Private Sector	4	3
Religious Non-profit	6	5
Not stated	4	3
Total	**130**	**100**

Table—7.8: Category of Graduate Employment by Programme

	Govt./ Para	*Private[1]/ Sector*	*Relig./ Non-profit*	*Not Stated*
Agriculture/Vet Science	12	–	1	–
Arts/Humanities	1	–	1	–
Business/Ec/Mgmt/Admin	44	1	–	–
Computing	1	–	–	–
Education/Teaching/TESL	13	–	2	–
Engineering	4	–	–	–
Law/Legal Studies	1	–	–	–
Medicine	6	–	–	1
Marine	–	–	–	1
Nursing	2	–	–	1
Science/Forestry/Nat. Res.	20	–	1	–
Secretarial	4	2	–	1
Social Science	8	–	1	–
Telecommunications	–	1	–	–
Total	116	4	6	4
Percentage	89	3	5	3

(1) The numbers in the sample employed in the private sector are very small. While this may be partly explained by a small bias in the sample (because graduates in the private sector may have been more difficult to trace) the general conclusion that the private sector has not been a major employer of post-secondary institution graduate remains valid.

Table—7.9: Expectation of Job before and after Working

	Before working		*After working*	
	Very good	*Poor*	*Very good*	*Poor*
Salary level	42	5	31	8
Promotion prospects	64	7	40	20
Relevance of qualification	80	2	79	5
Providing relevant experience	78	1	80	2
Appropriateness of job level	71	2	61	6
Job security	79	1	83	1

Table—7.10: Percentage finding Course useful in Work Requirements

	All graduates
Theoretical and conceptual	95
Practical and technical	88
Computer/technology	58
Professional relations with colleagues	95
Client relations	92

Table—7.11: Reasons for not attempting Self-employment

	All graduates
Expected job shortly	69
More money as employee	10
Lack of finance	57
Could not risk savings	22
Lack of appropriate training	8
Lack of demand	37

Notes: 1. In some cases, data have been collected from academic staff to better the relationship.

8

Human Resources Development Perspectives in Educational Planning

Tun Lwin

1. Introduction

Educational planning, unlike planning of other economic sectors, has goals and objectives which cannot be confined to the education sector alone. Most often, these extend beyond the boundary of the education, into complex human dimensions of multi-sectoral developmental processes; indeed some of these goals and objectives encompass the whole spectrum of human development issues so that they may be regarded as societal goals as such. Today educational planners cannot afford to confine their work to the quantitative input-output relationships among variables within the education sector alone; they have to be sensitive and responsive to society's call for a much broader human resource development strategy in the planning of educational development. The purpose of this chapter is to examine the imperatives of educational planning within the context of integrated human resource development strategies, with particular reference to the needs and priorities of countries in the Asia-Pacific Region.

One of the basic issues which the planners have to cope with is the conceptualization of human resource development itself. Chinapah, Löfstedt and Weiler argued that, for educational planning to become a more effective tool in the development of human resources, it will have to re-establish its linkages with a broader range of human competence beyond what is needed in the world of work, and become part of a wider array of social and educational interventions both within and beyond the formal education system. They stress that the conceptual key to this argument lies in a re-interpretation of the notion of human resources and their development. The re-interpretation recognizes the need for thinking of human resource development as encompassing a much wider range of human competence, that is, not only the kinds of competence that are relevant to productive work in the economic sector, but also those that human beings need to protect and improve people's health, to keep population growth within reasonable limits, to sustain and develop cultural traditions and identities, to enjoy recreational activities, to put nutritional resources to the best possible use, to preserve a less hazardous and endangered environment, and—last but not least—to assume and play an active role as a citizen. All of these kinds of competence constitute, in the aggregate, society's 'human resources'.

In its deliberations on the issue of human resource development, the Economic and Social Commission for Asia and the Pacific has observed that, while the human factor plays a decisive role in economic and social progress, it is also the people who are the intended beneficiaries of development. Human resource development is, in this perspective, much more than an instrument for development: it is the ultimate objective of the development process.

2. Dimensions of Human Resource Development

The Jakarta Plan document stated:

> "From a broad conceptual point of view, the full range of economic and social development processes may be characterized as human resource development. It has sometimes been argued that concepts which seek to be all-inclusive tend to have little explanatory or operational value. Nevertheless, approached from the perspective of human resource development, the main concerns and priorities of the development process take on a clear focus and direction. This clarity is enhanced when the key

problems of human resource development are classified in accordance with three major themes of employment and manpower development, science and technology and the quality of life".

Within an integrated analytical framework, the three dimensions mentioned above comprise a set of complementary and interrelated issues. None of them can be fully examined without reference to the others, yet each provides unique insights into the nature of the overall problem and the means whereby it can be resolved effectively and efficiently.

3. Demand-focused Versus Supply-focused Approach to HRD

The Jakarta Plan postulates that human resource development may be approached from the supply side or from the demand side. The supply-side approach deals with the generation of the means for human resource development, on the assumption that the demand already exists. The demand-side approach is concerned with the utilization of these means. The numerous policies and programmes for human resource development that have been implemented by governments of developing countries of the Asia-Pacific region have concentrated largely on supply-side issues. Yet the level of human resource development in many countries, particularly among their rural populations, remains obstinately low, while the need for effective human resource development continues to be an urgent priority. This suggests that a supply-focused may not be sufficient.

The limitations of existing programmes for human resource development suggest that more demand-oriented strategies are required. The absolute poor, rural landless, urban slum dwellers, women, members of minority groups and other disadvantaged groups, especially those is isolated and backward areas, confront a wide range of economic, social, psychological and physical obstacles to the development of their human resources. The disadvantaged sections of society form the obvious target for human resource development, not only because of the egalitarian and humanitarian ideals that would be served thereby, but, equally important, because of the high long-term social rate of return on investment that would be achieved.

4. Priority Issues and Strategies for Human Resource Development

Within the context of the Asia-Pacific region, the Jakarta Plan has identified three priority issues, namely: employment and manpower development; science and technology; and the quality of life.

(a) Employment and Manpower Development

Forecasts to the year 2000 indicate that many countries in the region will continue to have rapid population growth. Labour supply will also grow rapidly. In the face of a relatively slow-growing demand for labour, this will lead to a substantial rise in unemployment. Especially serious situations are likely to arise in the agrarian sector and the market for unskilled labour. For many developing countries, additional problems in matching labour demand and supply will be associated with unstable and possibly deteriorating domestic and international demand conditions, strengthening of protectionist tendencies and obsolescence of many skills in the presence of changing technological circumstances and other factors.

(b) Science and Technology

Rapid accretions to the international fund of scientific knowledge and technology are fast revising the region's agenda of development opportunities. The implications of recent scientific and technological progress in such fields as information, biotechnology, micro-electronics, material sciences and energy technologies indicate that, unless vigorous steps are taken immediately to adapt the region's human resources to the new realities, the development potential inherent in modern science and technology will be lost. At the same time, efforts must be made to adapt the new technologies to the region's labour-dominant factor proportions and to its pressing human resource development needs. The interface of the region's science and technology capabilities and its human resource profile thus requires that attention to devoted to both the generation of manpower for the promotion of science and technology and the utilization of science and technology to upgrade the full range of human resources.

(c) Quality of Life

The evident failure of the development process to generate substantial improvements in national and international equity and eradicate poverty in many developing countries has little likelihood of being overcome in the foreseeable future unless carefully co-ordinated remedial strategies, policies and programmes are introduced in a number of key sectors, including education, health, population, urbanization and the environment. In many developing countries of the region, seriously disadvantaged population groups continue to comprise the great majority of the people. Tapping the potential of these under-utilized human resources would generate significant socio-economic progress, while simultaneously enhancing the quality of life of these groups. Consequently, improvements in the quality of life of these groups would raise their productive capabilities. Practical measures for improving the living conditions of disadvantaged groups and increasing their level of participation in society will need to be identified and rigorously implemented if these benefits are to be realized. The disadvantaged target groups to be accorded priority attention can be identified as, among others, the rural and urban poor, the landless, the unemployed, women, youth, disabled persons, the ageing and minority groups.

5. Educational Planning and Integrated Human Resource Development

The International Congress on Planning and Management of Educational Development, Mexico City, 26-30 March 1990, examined, *inter alia*, the theme relating to educational planning and the human dimension of development. In this Congress, general agreement was reached regarding the concept of human resource development as comprising not only education but also culture, health, employment, science and technology, basic human rights, etc. The Congress highlighted that planning for human resource development was a complex and wide-embracing task, going far beyond the education area, involving government agencies a charge of science and technology, health and employment sectors, among others, as well as actors in the private sector and non-governmental organisations.

Particular priorities were discussed by participants in the Congress. Among them, special attention was given to the issues of illiteracy and basic education for all. It was suggested that the provision of education should be particularly concerned with access to literacy teaching and schooling for the most disadvantaged social groups.

With regard to secondary vocational education, emphasis was laid on quality with a view to allowing students to choose between continuing their studies and entering the labour market.

In a different connection, the question of training opportunities for women at all levels of schooling and in different types of education was highlighted. This priority stemmed from a number of considerations regarding inequality of opportunity and associated economic and social problems.

The perceptions of the Mexico Congress on integrated human resource development and educational planning have shown significant areas of convergence with the Jakarta Plan of action on this issue. The Jakarta Plan recommends, *inter alia*, the following:

(a) Basic Education for All

Education is an essential foundation for human resource development. In addition to literacy and numeric skills, basic education for human resource development, involves the inculcation of attitudes and abilities that will promote both a demand for, and the capacity to undertake, further human resource development. Literacy and numeracy and at least a rudimentary understanding of scientific principles and methods are essential pre-conditions for a productive and adaptive population that can utilize and adjust rapidly to new technologies and other exogenous changes. Efforts should therefore be intensified to provide universal basic education. In particular, governments should ensure that basic education is extended to disadvantaged population groups. Proposals for specific action include:

(i) Appropriate measures being introduced to provide for universal basic education in those countries where this has not yet been achieved, and to enhance its quality in all developing countries of the region.

(ii) The qualifications of teachers, especially those responsible for primary and basic adult education programmes, should be upgraded to enable them to provide students with a sound education foundation for a lifelong process of human resource development.

(iii) Curriculum development should be undertaken to enhance the quality of primary school education, including the acquisition of learning skills, rather than rote knowledge alone, as a basis for lifelong human resource development.

(iv) The potential of modern educational technologies including the use of the electronic media, should be developed to improve access to basic education for all. In this regard, special attention should be given to the opportunities afforded by advanced communications technologies as educational infrastructure for the least developed, land-locked and island-developing countries and for isolated communities and disadvantaged population groups in other countries.

(b) Upgrading Secondary and Higher Education

Access to secondary and higher education should be ensured to all qualified candidates and its quality should be improved. In view of the need for the region's secondary and higher education system to attain international standards of excellence, action should be taken to improve curricula, strengthen teachers' capabilities and upgrade support facilities. Steps should also be taken to provide opportunities for all qualified students to continue their education to the higher levels in order to realize the full potential of each individual member of society. Proposals for specific action include the following:

(i) Curricula in all educational fields, particularly at the secondary level; should be revised to emphasize the understanding of humanistic values, scientific and analytical methods of thinking in order to develop in

the population a capacity to adapt to change and participation in lifelong education for human resource development.

(ii) Action should be taken to counteract the current reliance on formal paper credentials, rather than actual capabilities, in identifying human resources qualifications.

(iii) The adequacy of teacher training methods for secondary education should be reviewed and improved methods should be devised and instituted to upgrade the qualifications of teachers at this level. Special emphasis should be given to the training and upgrading of science, mathematics and technical teachers at the secondary level.

(iv) Steps should be taken to facilitate the inter-country exchange of educational personnel in the region, especially at the post-secondary level and among teacher training personnel, as a means of sharing country experience and human resource development perspectives in educational systems.

(c) *Vocational and Technical Training*

Vocational and technical training should be made relevant to current and prospective employment conditions. Its capacity to prepare graduates to adapt to technological and other changes in the workplace should be enhanced. To meet these needs, access to vocational and technical training should be increased and the quality of such training as a basis for productive employment should be improved. Proposals for specific action include the following:

(i) Recent advances in science and technology appropriate to the conditions in individual developing countries should be incorporated into the vocational and technical training curricula of their educational systems.

(ii) Vocational and technical training programmes should be encouraged to emphasize a broad approach to human resource development and promote the capacity of skilled manpower to adjust to changes in the labour demand. Narrow specialization in technical training should be avoided where possible. Similarly, vocational and professional training should be designed to expose students to a wide range of skills.

(iii) Work-study programmes and apprenticeship schemes should be incorporated into vocational and technical programmes to increase the relevance of training to actual employment conditions.

(iv) Short-term vocational and technical training and retaining programmes should be designed to retain workers whose skills have become redundant as a result of changing production requirements. Training models directed towards specific skill groups within the labour force should be developed to meet this need in the context of rapidly changing employment conditions.

(v) Vocational and technical education curricula should be broadened to inculcate entrepreneurial values and positive work ethics. Curricula should be designed to include exposure to the full range of skills required for the operation of small-scale enterprises.

(d) Non-formal Education and Training

Formal education, even if available to all school-age children and youth, cannot alone sustain human resource development because such development is a lifelong process. Furthermore, many young people are excluded from formal education owing to various circumstances. Non-formal educational channels, including adult education, should therefore be developed and strengthened. Within the non-formal education system innovative programmes should be devised to develop skills, attitudes and capabilities not covered by formal education curricula. Priority in the development of such programmes should be directed towards the needs of disadvantaged population groups not adequately served by the formal educational system. Specific proposals for action include:

(i) Adult education programmes should be developed to teach basic literacy and numeric skills and elementary science to those with little or no formal education, especially women, as a critical means of improving their prospects of employment and enhancing their quality of life.

(ii) Continuing education programmes should be developed as non-formal adjuncts to the formal education system to support lifelong education. They should be designed to facilitate the upgrading of under-utilized human resources and enhance the capacity of all individuals to adapt to changing social and economic circumstances.

(iii) Women's educational self-help networks should be supported to provide women, especially those wishing to enter the labour force, with basic education and vocational training. Vocational training programmes should be related to existing and emerging employment opportunities to increase women's active economic participation.

(iv) Innovative programmes should be developed to increase the awareness of local-level government officials and service delivery personnel regarding the special needs of disadvantaged groups and to enhance their capabilities for implementing human resource development programmes for disadvantaged groups.

(v) Out-reach training programmes should be developed for workers and the self-employed in the informal sector. Such programmes should be structured as field exercises, focusing on training for income and employment generation for those population groups that would not ordinarily seek out formal training opportunities.

6. Recapitulation and Conclusion

The human factor plays a decisive role as a productive agent in development; at the same time, it is the people who are the intended beneficiaries of development. Human resource development thus serves as both as essential means and the ultimate end of development.

Human resource development contributes to the attainment of such fundamental development objectives or ideals as the eradication of absolute poverty, full employment, universal basic education, universal access to secondary education and vocational training, national self-reliance in science and technology, satisfaction of basic needs and full participation of all population groups in the development process.

In view of the pervasive interaction between human resource development and all facets of economic and social progress, an integrated approach to the planning and execution of human resource development is required, involving the active participation of all sectors.

Education is an essential foundation of human resource development. Literacy and numeracy and at least a rudimentary understanding of scientific principles and methods are an essential pre-condition for a productive and adaptive population that can utilize and adjust rapidly to new technologies and other exogenous changes. Efforts should therefore be intensified to provide universal basic education. Access to secondary and higher education should be ensured to all qualified candidates and its quality should be improved. Access to vocational and technical training should be increased and the quality of such training as a basis for productive employment should be improved. Formal education, even if available to all school-age children and youth, cannot alone sustain human resource development, because such development is a lifelong process. Furthermore, many young people are excluded from formal education owing to various circumstances. Non-formal educational channels, including adult education, should therefore be developed and strengthened.

Recognizing that human resources can be effectively developed only with the active participation of all economic and social sectors, as well as the public and private sectors, an integrated approach to human resource development planning is called for. Educational planners are required to take into full account the human resource development perspectives in the conceptualization and elaboration of educational development plan and programmes. Appropriate methods and mechanisms should be developed to ensure that an integrated approach is adopted to human resource development planning and implementation strategies.

Some of these aspects are the subjects of study in the subsequent sessions of Module 4: "Strategies for a better match between learning and work".

REFERENCES

V. Chinapah; J.-I Löfstedt; H. Weiler. *Integrated Development of Human Resources and Educational Planning*.

ESCAP. *Jakarta Plan of Action on Human Resource Development in the ESCAP Region*. Final Report.

C.K. Ming. *Review and Prospects of Educational Planning and Management in Asia and the Pacific*.

K. Nishida. *Strategies of Educational Planning for the Development of Human Resources*.

UNESCO. *Planning and Management of Educational Development*. Mexico City, 26-30 March 1990.

9

Manpower Approach to Educational Planning

N.V. Varghese

Manpower approach is one of the most commonly used approaches to plan education. This approach argues that provision of supply of adequate manpower with varied skills is the main function of the educational system and therefore education should be planned as per the manpower requirements. The projection of demand for different categories of manpower forms the basis of determining enrolments and provision of educational facilities in the schools and colleges.

1. Methods of Manpower Estimate

There are various methods to estimate manpower demand. Perhaps the simplest method is to ask each employer regarding his future requirements of manpower. In micro situations this is applicable. However, for planning at the macro level it is difficult to rely upon this method. Alternatively, sometimes international comparison method is used to plan education. This method involves in observing the occupational and educational structure of a country at a more advanced level of development and hypothesize that this is the desired structure for the country for which the forecast is made. Similarly sometimes model firm comparison methods are used to derive the occupational structure. In this approach the occupational structure of the most modern and efficient firms within a country considered as the ideal one is examined and the occupational structure of that firm is used to plan education. Incremental Labour Output Ratio (ILOR) and density ratio methods are also used to project manpower. ILOR method extrapolates particular type of manpower in an occupational category and its corresponding output or national income. Density ratio method consists of estimating stable fractions of qualified manpower in an economic sector and applying these to the total labour force forecasts in various sectors.

2. The MRP Method

The method that was adopted as the method for forecasting manpower in this training programme was the methodology used in the OECD's Mediterranean Regional Project (MRP). This methodology was adopted for two reasons: *(i)* this is the most commonly used method for manpower forecasts in many countries; and *(ii)* it provides detailed and systematic steps for manpower planning. MRP methodology involves five main steps in assessing the required number of workers by educational levels in the target year of the plan.

The first step is to estimate the future level of output (GDP) for the target year. This estimate GDP is very often divided by the total population and expressed in terms of GDP per capita. The next step is to estimate the structural transformation of the economy or the distribution of GDP by economic sectors. In general in all the developing countries the share of primary sectors will be very high. But during the process of development the share of agricultural sector comes down and that of manufacturing and service sectors goes up. Therefore, this change envisaged in each sector is to be estimated and incorporated because such structural changes will have direct implications so far as the nature of labour skills demanded in concerned. Very often the structural changes depend upon the growth rates in each industry which are often predetermined by policy.

The third step is the estimation of labour productivity by economic sector for the targeted year. Measurement of labour productivity itself is subject to controversies. However, for the purpose at hand labour productivity is defined in a very crude form as the sectoral GDP divided by the number of workers in that sector. Estimation of labour productivity for the targeted year will help us in deriving the number of workers required in the target year. The figures for sectoral GDP (step II) have already been estimated. Sectoral GDP divided by the labour productivity in that sector gives the required number of workers in that sector. And their summation across the sectors gives us the total number of workers.

The fourth step involves estimating the occupational structure of the labour force in each of the economic sectors. Mostly international standard classification of occupations is used to categorize the workers into different occupations. The relative position of each occupation may change. Some occupations may attract more qualified workers, while others may remain the same or reduce the deployment of labour force.

The fifth step is to estimate the educational structure of the labour force in the given occupations in different economic sectors. This involves estimating educational levels of the workers in each occupational category.

Each occupation will have persons with different levels of education. The proportion of different levels of educated within each occupation is computed. This proportion forms the basis for future projections. Based on the projections of the proportion for the target year, the educational levels of workers in each occupation are estimated. It may be noted that since the total number of workers is already estimated (in step III), this gives the workers by educational levels in all occupation. An aggregation of workers by levels of education across occupations gives the total number of workers required by occupational levels. To work out the total number of workers by levels of education in each occupational category in each economic activity is the main task of this exercise.

3. Estimation of Manpower Supply

Next, an attempt is made to project the number of persons with the required levels of education over time. The projection of manpower supply takes this into account. The expansion of educational system can either be strictly planned on the basis of required manpower or be a result of the spontaneous expansion based on social demand. Very often expansion of the educational system in the developing countries is based on the social demand approach. In this context demographic factors influence and determine enrolments in the primary levels of education, and the pattern of students flow between classes and stages determines the number of graduates produced by the system. The participation rates of graduates of each level give the number of persons actually available for work.

Methods of projection of manpower supply in its simplest form is based on the students' flow rates. Any student entering the educational system can have only three possibilities—either he or she is promoted to the next grade or is a dropout from the school or is a repeater in the same grade. Based on all these three possibilities the flow rate method estimates the number of graduates for any given number of enrolled students with the help of promotion, repetition and dropout rates. Depending upon these three factors one can decide the excess number of students to be enrolled in each level of education to get the projected number of graduates as workers. This also has to be adjusted for the labour force participation rates of each level of educated. Once the enrolments are estimated provisions of other educational facilities can be planned.

4. Balancing Demand and Supply

Once the demand for and supply of manpower are estimated, the next step involved is to balance between the two. This step is more important if supply estimates are based on the social demand rather than on estimations of manpower demand. This adjustment or balancing is an iterative process whereby both demand and supply aspects may be adjusted. It may be noted that it is not the total number of graduates but the number adjusted for the participation rate that is used for balancing supply to manpower estimations with the use of computers this process has become easier.

5. An Overview

Manpower approach to plan education is in general criticized at two levels. First, at the philosophical level where treating educational system as a factory to produce the manpower to be used in the production sectors as the only function of education is questioned. It is considered to be a narrow and partial view. In fact education is emphasized for good many non-economic and non-employment reasons. Therefore, considering this model as the basis for educational planning is not desirable. Second, this approach is criticized on the ground that even when this approach may be desirable, it is not feasible because of the difficulties in making reliable manpower estimates. Discussions in the group tended to focus around the difficulties of applying this approach rather than the desirability of this approach.

Manpower estimates are based on the assumptions of fixed co-efficients of production and non-substitutability of different categories of manpower. There are different problems associated with these two assumptions. Firstly, it is very difficult to estimate the relevant parameters accurately. The issue of estimating labour productivity was taken as an instance. Measurement of productivity of itself is controversial and hence its accuracy and reliability are not beyond doubt. Second, to assume these parameters to be constant in their value over a period of time is far from the real world situation. In fact, the present day world is characterized by changes, marginal or substantial, in these parameters depending upon various factors which directly influence economic development. This phase of development is characterized by fast changing technology. And these technological changes are not easily amenable to reliable forecast which indirectly invalidates the assumption on the constancy of co-efficient of production. Another factor which further complicates the situation, is that technological changes are not always endogenous especially in the case of developing countries. Technological changes and decisions on them depend upon the international context in which the particular country is placed. In the case of most of the developing countries they depend to a great extent on the developed countries for technological advancement. But how far a country actually is amenable to changes from outside depends on the national policy. If the economy is more open then the role of influence of exogenous factors on development will be more. The specific cases of Sri Lanka and China came in for detailed discussion in this context.

Related to this is the pattern of development of economy. Manpower approach assumes that there exists a reliable economic planning in the economy. Therefore this approach is not applicable if economic planning is non-existent. Manpower planning is based on the envisaged path and rate of growth of the economy as assumed by the economic planning. However, it is to be noted that this approach does not presume a socialist or centrally planned economy. In fact MRP project was for non-socialist and market based economies. What is more crucial is that there should be economic planning to provide the manpower planners with GDP and its sectoral distribution for the target year. This approach is dependent upon these factors. Many a time, rates of economic growth fall short of the targets. Under such circumstances, it is natural that the manpower projections could be wrong. Perhaps, the manpower planner should not be blamed for this. On the other hand, if economic growth takes place as planned and still manpower projections go wrong, then the responsibility will be with the manpower planners.

Many a time manpower forecasts take into account the formal system of education. In all economies, skill formation through the non-institutional means or outside the educational system is quite common. This is more so in the informal sectors of the economy. In the manpower planning many a time this aspect is not given due consideration. Same is the case with on-the-job training which is common with many employers. This job-specific and firm-specific information is not easily available and hence does not get taken into account while estimating manpower supply.

If one allows market forces to be taken into account, then manpower planning becomes more difficult. One may notice that costs of education and relative earnings of individuals are not taken into account while forecasting manpower. In fact, it needs to be emphasized at this point that the term used in manpower 'requirement' than manpower 'demand'. This approach again does not take into account the costs of producing the projected manpower. In the labour market one finds that wages and hiring practises are sensitive to the demand and supply conditions of educated manpower. In many an instance wages are fixed to jobs than to the qualifications of individuals. However, recruitment pattern undergoes a change when there is unemployment. This change will be in favour of more qualified personnel. Employers, in their recruitment policy prefer persons with higher levels of qualifications. This policy leads to various types of distortions in the labour market and the assumption of non-substitutability of different categories of manpower gets violated under such circumstances. Eventually the education occupation relation also gets distorted. In most of the countries, this problem is more pronounced in the general education based occupations than in the professional and technical education based occupations.

Many other difficulties in this approach were also focussed upon the discussions. But it was pointed out that at least some of these problems stem from non-availability of detailed data. In this context the need for developing a systematic data base as a basic input into the manpower planning was highlighted. Because of the difficulties confronted, some of the participants expressed the view that manpower analysis may be preferred to manpower forecasting. It was also emphasized that some of the difficulties expressed are common to any type of forecast and is not strictly confined to manpower forecasts. In general it was agreed upon that manpower forecasting provides broad directions and guidelines for development of educational system. Therefore, exclusive reliance on the exactness of the projected figures is not always desirable. It was felt that manpower planning should be seen as a method to provide guidelines rather than as a method to given precise numbers. A caution was added that even when this approach is resorted to, this by itself should not be seen as the only approach to plan education. Instead, this along with other approaches should be adopted, depending upon specificities of the country.

10

The Use of Simulation Models in Educational Planning

Anita Nazareth

1. Introduction

Why is educational planning necessary? What is mission of educational planning? Whom does educational planning serve and benefit? How does the educational planning process operate? What types of tasks are suitable for the educational planning process? What relationships exist between educational, urban, transportation, economic planning and other types of planning?

Banghart, F.W; Trull, A. Jr. 1973, p. 5.

These questions have to be addressed in order to elucidate the components of educational planning. The initial need for planning arose with the evolving complexity of modern society. Problems such as growing population, manpower needs, the ecology, decreasing natural resources and widespread application of scientific developments all place demands on educational institutions. If the educational organisations are to be able to meet these demands, then competent planning becomes mandatory.

Planners in various fields, especially educational planners, are recognizing the need for inclusive planning that considers the social and physical, as well as economic aspects of any given problem. Solving problems in this three-pronged manner is becoming an important task in educational planning.

Banghart, F.W; Trull, A. Jr. 1973, p. 5.

2. What is Educational Planning?

Educational planning is a process of preparing a set of decisions for future action, directed at achieving goals by optimal means. Overall educational planning is a continuous systematic process involving the application and co-ordination of social research methods, and of principles and techniques of education, administration, economies and finance. It requires the participation of the general public, in private as well as public activities, with a view to securing adequate education for all the people with definite goals, and in well-defined stages. The ultimate aim is to provide everyone with an opportunity for developing his/her potential and making the most effective contribution to the social, cultural, and economic development of the country.

3. Approaches Used in Educational Planning

The essence of planning and learning is its concern for the educational environment of the human community. Thus, the planner must be aware of and supportive of the values, the goals, and the social structure of the community in order to serve it.

Traditionally, educational planning is said to have four basic approaches at the national level: *(i)* estimation of social demand; *(ii)* manpower planning; *(iii)* rate-of-return analysis; and *(iv)* cost-effectiveness analysis. In practice, planners combine all these different approaches to supplement each other.

Educational planning, or for that matter any kind of planning, is intimately involved with politics and policies resulting from the political process. This relationship has been characterized by Chapin, F.S. (a teacher and researcher of urban planning), who wrote, "Thus, in a very fundamental sense, the planning process must play an important role in supplying policy alternatives and pressing for decisions from the earliest and broadest level of policy formulation on down to the more detailed levels of policy determination".

Learning is the principal output of an educational system and estimating future school enrolments is one of the most important factors in quantitative educational planning. Using these enrolments as a base we can start to calculate all other future needs of the educational system including the number of teachers, of classrooms, as well as equipment and supplies and ultimately the cost of financing the system. Forecasting enrolment is therefore a starting point in costing all the needed resources for carrying out an educational development plan.

There are numerous mathematical models available and used in educational planning to make projections. The most commonly used are *Flow Models* which describe in numbers, the entry of students into an educational system, their transition through various classes, up to the time they eventually leave the system.

As a start it would be useful to make a distinction between the three terms: *projecting, forecasting* and *setting objectives/targets* that are often used when speaking of future evolution of enrolments.

Projecting

A conditional proposition of the future obtained by extrapolation of past tendencies in the system. The proposition is conditional as it is only valid if the past rends continue unchanged during the period covered by the projections.

Forecasting

Shows a more probable evolution of future school enrolments.

The difference between projecting and forecasting, is that the former only gives an idea of the future educational needs if past trends continue, while the later, more ambitious tries to show the evolution which has the greatest chance of occurring, taking into account future plans and the most probable changes in past trends.

Setting Objectives/Targets

Often National Development Plans announce decisions such as:

"By the year 2000 all children between the ages of 6 and 12 will have access to schooling."

or

"By the year 2005 there will be a primary school within one mile walking distance of any child."

It is then on the basis of those types of targets that an educational planner can calculate what the capacity of the educational system should be in order to achieve the target.

An educational planner may use all these methods in a number of different models to prepare alternative scenarios for consideration. The *projection* method, which presupposes that trends exhibited by salient parameters continue into the future, may lead to interventions when the planners realises that the outcomes are not generally desirable. The *forecasting* method allows government policies and changes to be taken into consideration in preparing likely scenarios. And the *target* method gives strong indications of what needs to be done and what inputs are necessary for the target to be achieved.

4. Types of Educational Planning

Long-term or Perspective Plan

10 to 20 or 25 years. Type of society desired, level of literacy, number and types of graduates, labour force desired.

Medium-term Plan

3 to 7 years as a backdrop to long-term planning, prepared on a rolling basis extending one year at a time and usually linked to the National Five Year Development Plan.

Short-term Plan

Usually a work plan on an annual basis. The annual plan is also the controlling plan of a particular sector which matches the resources available to the results desired. While the medium- or long-term plan sets directions, the short-term plan assists in its ultimate achievement.

Single-purpose Plan

It is an administrative operation plan with a particular objective to implement a reform/measure, build an institution or to test a pilot legislation.

5. Why Use Computers in Educational Planning?

Much of the work done on educational systems has been mainly the forecasting of the number of students in the system at some future point in time. This methods is adequate when the system operates in a stable environment. Conventional approaches to planning fail to yield satisfactory results during periods of rapid social or educational changes. Developing countries often also experience rapid political changes which can lead to fundamental shifts in policy direction over a relatively short period of time.

It is for these reasons that we make use of *computer modelling* as an aid in the decision-making process of educational planning. In usual circumstances, all the parameters which influence the educational sector cannot always be determined ahead of time. Those parameters which are known also change over time and hence a dynamic representation of the system in necessary. This dynamic aspect is taken care of in the form of equations relating one variable to another. The level of detail incorporated in a model is contingent upon the extent to which all the variables affecting the system are taken into consideration.

Details of the steps will be clear in the following scenarios.

11

Theories of the Labour Market

Maureen Woodhall

1. Introduction

The previous module of the course has been concerned with the "manpower approach to educational planning", which rests on a number of crucial assumptions:

- In order to achieve a desired level of output, or economic growth, the economy of a country 'requires' or 'needs' certain minimum inputs of labour, physical capital and raw materials.
- There is a fixed, or constant, relationship between the input of skilled manpower in different occupational categories in an industry, sector or the economy as a whole, and the level of output. This means that it is possible to identify, and to project or forecast, the manpower structure 'required' to achieve desired output targets.
- There is a fixed, or constant, relationship between the educational qualifications of workers and the occupational structure.
- The main purpose of educational and manpower planning is to ensure that the educational system produces the right combination of skilled manpower, in

order to achieve the desired level of output and to avoid shortages or surpluses of skilled manpower.

These assumptions, which you have examined in more detail in previous session, have been challenged by critics of the 'manpower forecasting approach' to educational planning. An alternative approach has been advocated, based on the concept of 'human capital'. This approach is based on the idea that education is a form of investment in human capital, which provides workers with knowledge and skills which raise their productivity in employment, and therefore increase future levels of output and national income.

The idea that education is a form of investment in human capital, which in analogous to investment in physical capital and which can be analyzed using the same techniques of cost-benefit analysis, or rates of return, was developed in the 1960s by American economists such as Schultz (1963) and Becker (1964) and has a number of important implications for educational planning.

But just as the advocates of the human capital approach reject the assumptions of the manpower forecasting approach to planning, so there have been many attacks and criticisms of the underlying assumptions of human capital theories and the cost-benefit approach to educational planning. Mark Blaug (1970) has summarized the conflicting theories and assumptions underlying the two approaches in terms of "two views of the state of the world", which represent "nothing less than totally different views of how economic systems work" (Blaug 1970, p. 214).

The simple dichotomy that he describes in terms of two views about the labour market for educated manpower has been made more complicated in recent years by the development of new theories of the labour market. The concept of human capital has been attacked by those who argue that education does not directly increase the productivity of workers by imparting knowledge or skills, but simply acts as a 'screening device' or 'filter', which enables employers to identify workers with particular characteristics. In order to evaluate these alternative theories we need empirical evidence about how the labour market works.

But some economists argue that there is not one labour market but a series of 'segmented markets' with different characteristics for different groups of workers. We are thus faced not simply with two views of the world but with a series of alternative theories of the labour market for educated manpower which rest on conflicting assumptions and give rise to different policy implications.

We will examine each of these theories in turn, and finally, in the discussion and practical exercises that follow this lecture, we will test some of the hypotheses generated by the theories and explore the policy implications.

2. The Theory of Human Capital

The idea that education is a form of investment in human capital, and that the profitability of different types of investment can be measured using cost-benefit, or rate or return analysis, rests on the following crucial assumptions:

- education makes workers more productive, by giving them knowledge and skills that improve their work performance and enable them to achieve higher levels of output than uneducated workers;
- markets for goods and services are competitive, so that the prices of both labour and capital reflect their marginal productivity. This means that employers will employ more labour only if the value of the extra output produced exceeds the additional cost (measured by wages or salaries). If wages or salaries are higher than the marginal productivity of labour, then employers will substitute capital for labour, in order to maximize their profits;
- the relative wages of salaries of different workers also reflect their marginal productivity, so that educated workers will have higher earnings than uneducated because of their higher productivity. Employers will employ skilled or educated workers only if the value of their extra output exceeds the additional cost; if not, then employers will substitute unskilled labour for educated workers;

- the extra lifetime earnings of educated workers can therefore be used to measure the direct economic benefits of education both for the individual (private benefits) and for society as a whole (social benefits) (see Figure 1). In order to measure the total social benefits, some allowance must also be made for indirect, or 'spill-over' benefits (externalities);

- private and social benefits can be compared with the opportunity cost of education to give a measure of profitability (the benefit-cost ratio, net present value or rate of return) of different types of education, to help explain the private demand for education and provide a guide for resource allocation and educational planning (see Figure 2 and Table—11.1).

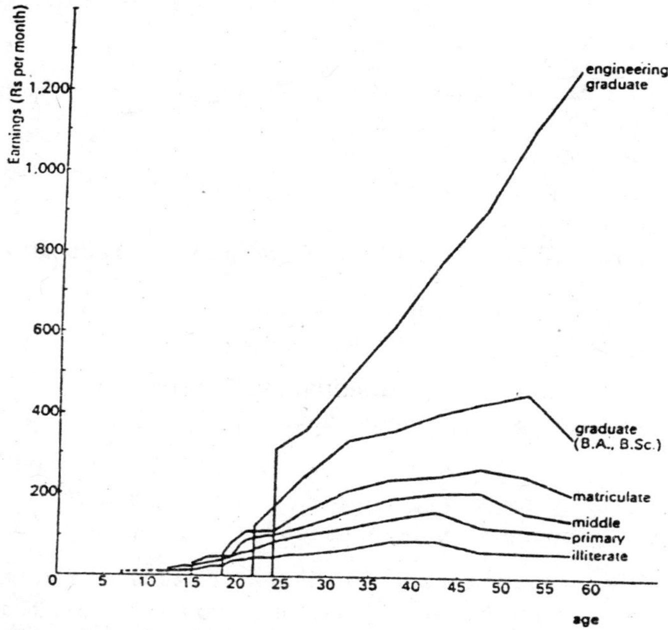

Source: Blaug, Layard and Woodhall (1969).

Figure 1: Are earnings profiles for Indian workers by level of education, 1960

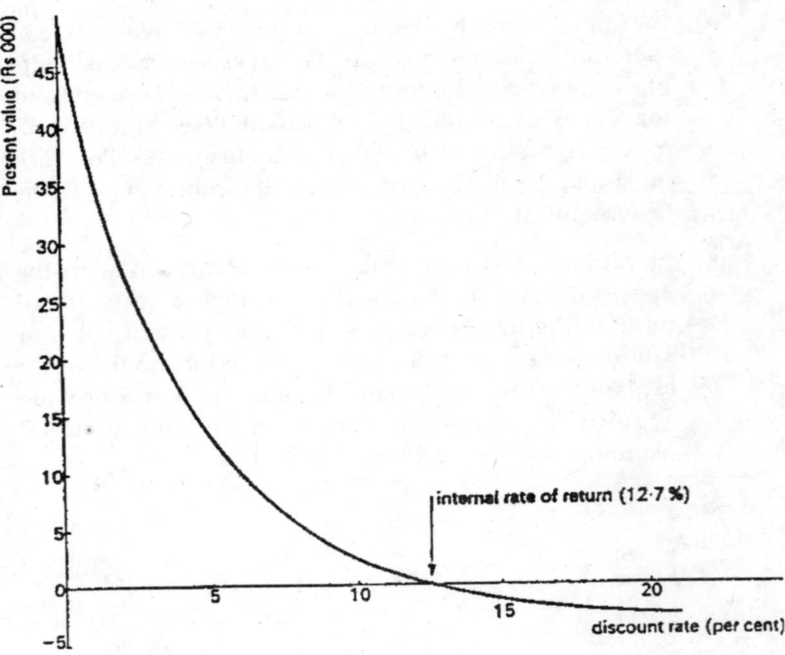

Source: Blaug, Layard and Woodhall (1969).

Figure 2: The rate of return to Indian higher education 1960.

The human capital model of the labour market therefore relies heavily on three basic assumptions:

- markets are competitive, so that prices can be used as a measure of relative demand;
- prices of goods and salaries will move up and down in response to changes in demand or supply, in order to maintain an equilibrium between demand and supply;
- techniques of production are flexible, so that employers can substitute capital for labour or unskilled labour for skilled or qualified workers.

All these assumptions are challenged in alternative theories of the labour market. The manpower forecasting model challenges

Table—11.1: Returns to Investment in Education, by Country, Type and Level

Region		*Social*			*Private*			*Number of countries reporting*
		Primary	*Secondary*	*Higher*	*Primary*	*Secondary*	*Higher*	
Africa		28	17	13	45	26	32	16
Asia		27	15	13	31	15	18	10
Latin America		26	18	16	32	23	23	10
Europe, Middle East, and North Africa		13	10	8	17	13	13	9
Developing countries		24	15	13	31	19	22	45
Developed countries		–	11	9	–	12	12	15
Asia								
Hong Kong	1976		15.0	12.4		18.5	25.2	
India	1965	13.4	15.5	10.3	17.3	18.8	16.2	
	1978	29.3	13.7	10.8	33.4	19.8	13.2	
Indonesia	1977				25.5	15.6		
	1978	21.9	16.2	14.8				
Malaysia	1978					32.6	34.5	
Pakistan	1975	13.0	9.0	8.0	20.0	11.0	27.0	
	1979				14.6	6.7	9.4	
Philippines	1971	7.0	6.5	8.5	9.0	6.5	9.5	
	1977			8.5			16.0	
Singapore	1966	6.6	17.6	14.1		20.0	25.4	
South Korea	1967		9.0	5.0				
	1969		11.0	9.5				
	1971		14.6	9.3		16.1	16.2	
	1973		12.2	8.8				
	1980		8.1	11.7				
Taiwan	1970		26.5	15.0		17.6	18.4	
	1972	27.0	12.3	17.7	50.0	12.7	15.8	
Thailand	1970	30.5	13.0	11.0	56.0	14.5	14.0	
	1972	63.2	30.9	18.4				

— Data were not available because no control group of illiterates was available.

Note: Private returns take into account only the cost of education to the individual. In contrast, social returns are based on the full costs of education to society, so they are comparatively lower.

Source: Psacharopoulos 1985.

the assumption that labour markets are competitive and flexible. Blaug summarizes the different assumptions of the human capital and manpower forecasting model in terms of the 'two views of the world' shown in Figure 3. He admits that "Needless to say the real world lies somewhere in between", but the question is "does it lie nearer to the right or to the left of the continuum?" Blaug's "two views of the world" suggest that the basic question is whether the labour market is competitive and flexible. But other models of the labour market raise other fundamental questions.

The Man-power forecasting view of the world	*The Rate-of-return view of the world*
1. Students acquire more education for consumption reasons.	1. Students acquire more education for investment reasons.
2. Students choose major subjects in ignorance of, or with no regard to, career prospects.	2. Students are well informed and attentive to career prospects.
3. All education is specialized and specialization starts early.	3. All education is general and there is no specialization at any age.
4. All input-coefficients in schools are fixed: complete indivisibility are specificity of teachers, plant and equipment.	4. All input-coefficients in schools are variable: complete divisibility and non-specificity of teachers, plant and equipment.
5. The demand curves for different skills shift discretely.	5. The demand curves for different skills shift smoothly.
6. Near-zero elasticities of sub-stitution between skilled men.	6. Almost infinite elasticities of sub-situation between skilled men.
7. Near-zero elasticities of demand for different skills.	7. Almost infinite elasticities of demand for different skills.

Figure 3: Two views of the world.

3. The "Screening" or "Filter" Theory

The human capital theory predicts that educated workers will have higher lifetime earnings than less educated or illiterate workers, and data for more than sixty countries confirm that education does, indeed, lead to higher average lifetime earnings. The question is what does this prove? Human capital theories suggest that it is the knowledge and skills imparted by education that make qualified manpower more productive, and that employers pay higher wages and salaries, in order to benefit from the higher levels of output of educated workers.

An alternative theory, known generally as the 'screening' or 'filter' hypothesis, suggests that educated workers are paid more, not because of their superior knowledge or skills, but because employers recognize that they have higher innate ability and certain characteristics and attitudes that make them more useful as workers than those who lack the experience of formal education. In the 1970s American economists such as Arrow (1973), argued that education did not directly improve workers' productivity, but simply acted as a convenient 'filter', 'signal' or 'screening device' which enabled employers to identify those with superior ability and personal attributes, such as motivation, self discipline and positive attitudes to work, authority or modernization, which would make them more productive.

If this is true then education would still be a profitable *private* investment, since it would enable individuals to enjoy higher earnings, but if education has no direct effect on productivity, it would represent a vast waste of *public* resources. This argument was taken up by Dore (1976) who warned of the dangers of 'credentialism', leading to the 'diploma disease'. If the number of highly qualified workers is relatively small, then a university degree may be regarded by employers as an effective 'filter' or 'screening device'. But rapid expansion of university education would mean that employers would require a more effective 'filter' and so would begin to demand higher and higher qualifications, in order to identify those with the required ability and attributes.

One way to test the screening hypothesis is to use earnings functions to measures the independent effect of different factors, such as age, educational level ability (as measured by IQ tests) on earnings. But even though earnings functions demonstrate that education *does* have an effect on earnings, after other factors such as innate ability are taken into account, it does not show *why* employers pay educated workers more. If it is because long experience has convinced them that only graduates have the knowledge and mental skills required for particular jobs, then this supports the human capital model. But if in fact they care nothing for these cognitive skills, but pay graduates more simply because they believe graduates will be more determined or more disciplined, than less educated workers then education would indeed be no more than a 'filter'.

Once again, we have two views of the world, or at least two views of employer behaviour, and once again the real world lies somewhere between. In fact there are two versions of the screening hypothesis:

- the 'strong' version, which, suggests that education does nothing to improve workers' productivity. In this case we might predict that the earnings differentials of educated workers would narrow over time, as employers begin to use direct evidence of workers' performance on the job to determine wages or salaries, rather than educational qualifications that enabled them to be appointed to the job in the first place. But in fact earnings differentials tend to widen, rather than narrow, over time.
- the 'weak' version, which suggests that education does act as a screening device, but that this is socially useful, since it enables employers to identify those with motivation, positive attitudes towards work and the ability to learn new skills quickly, on the job.

If we accept the 'weak' version, then this model does not destroy the human capital model, but simply adds another dimension. By emphasizing the importance of motivation and attitudes, it suggests that education improves productivity not simply by imparting knowledge and cognitive skills, but by inculcating or changing attitudes and by developing social and communication skills. According to this argument, the early version of the human capital theory were not wrong, so much as incomplete. They ignored, or underestimated some of the indirect benefits of education.

One of these indirect benefits is that education performs the socially valuable function of improving selection for jobs, by giving employers better information or 'signals' about workers' attributes. In fact it can be argued that it is both more efficient and more equitable for employers to use educational qualifications as a 'filter' than to use other personal characteristics, such as sex, race, religion, caste or social class.

However, this brings us to another objection to the human capital model, which is that there is not a single labour market but a series of segmented labour markets' for different groups of workers, and that characteristics such as sex or race determine access to these.

4. Segmented Labour Market Theories

The first version of this model emphasized the difference between the 'modern' and the 'traditional' sectors of the economy, and suggested that the characteristics of jobs in these two sectors were so different that the two sectors represented dual labour markets:

- the 'primary' labour market, with modern techniques of production and capital, and large-scale employers offering skilled jobs with job security;
- the 'secondary' labour market, with traditional techniques, limited capital and small-scale employers offering 'dead-end' or temporary jobs, with the high rate of labour turnover.

According to this model, high productivity is a characteristic of jobs, rather than people (Carnoy 1977) and this leads to the 'job competition model', which suggests that education provides access to high productivity jobs, in the modern sector, but it does not directly affect the productivity of the workers themselves.

Labour economists such as Doeringer and Piore (1971) developed the idea of a 'dual' labour market and emphasized the importance of 'internal labour markets' which operate in large-scale organisations, where employers offer on-the-job training and promotion only to their own employees. Educated workers are more likely to have access to such 'internal labour markets', and therefore the higher earnings of the educated may simply reflect this access to a restricted 'segment' of the labour market, rather than higher productivity.

More radical labour market theories go further, and economists such as Carnoy (1980) have developed the theory of labour market segmentation and argue that access to certain 'segments' of the labour market is restricted to particular groups of workers. According to this model, the segmentation of labour markets reflects the basic conflicts of a capitalist system, with its class struggle and the desire of capitalists to weaken the working class by dividing and fragmenting the labour force.

There is plenty of evidence that different groups of workers have access to different types of jobs. In many countries women and ethnic minorities are more likely to be concentrated in temporary, low-paid and low status jobs, with no job security and no prospects for on-the-job training. But this does not prove that the arguments of the extreme segmented labour market theories are valid; nor does that fact that workers in urban areas have access to better paid jobs than rural workers. There are several studies that show that rates of return to education are higher in urban areas than rural areas. This is entirely consistent with the human capital theory.

What is important is the degree of mobility between different types of jobs. If education and on-the-job training increase the mobility of workers, then this is simply another example of the economic benefits of investment in human capital. If on the other hand, mobility is very restricted, then this would support the segmented labour market model.

5. Conclusion

We are left not with two views of the world, but with several views, which provide different explanations for:

- the associations between education and earnings;

- the hiring practices of employers;
- the distribution of income.

Some of these models of the labour market lead to mutually inconsistent predictions, and therefore to different conclusions about how to improve the links between education and employment, and in particular to different conclusions about the value of 'vocationalizing' education. In other cases, alternative theories can be regarded as providing new insights, rather than conflicting models of how labour markets actually work. As Blaug emphasized in 1970, the real world lies somewhere between the extreme theories summarized in this lecture. More recently, he has argued (1985) that if we add together certain concepts emphasized in these theories, for example the notions of 'screening' and 'internal labour markets', then "we arrive at a picture of the economic value of schooling that is simply miles removed from the old-fashioned belief that education makes workers more productive and that employers pay them more because they are more productive."

Nevertheless, even if the original formulation of the concept of human capital can be criticized for over-emphasizing this 'old-fashioned belief', the concept of investment in human capital remains a powerful theoretical tool. Rather than destroying the validity of this tool, the alternative theories have demonstrated that the relationship between education and employment is far more complex than was first supposed.

REFERENCES

Arrow, K.J. (1973) "Higher Education as a Filter", *Journal of Public Economics* July, pp. 193-216.

Becker, G. (1964) *Human Capital*. New York: Columbia University Press.

Blaug, M. (1970) *An Introduction to the Economics of Education*. London: Penguin Books.

—(1985) "Where are we now in the Economics of Education?", *Economics of Education Review*, Vol. 4 (1), pp. 17-28.

Blaug, M., Layard, R., Woodhall, M. (1969) *The Causes of Graduate Unemployment in India*. Allen Lane, Penguin Books.

Carnoy, M. (1977) *Education and Employment: A Critical Appraisal*. Paris: IIEP (Fundamentals of Educational Planning Series).

—(1980) "Segmented Labour Markets", in M. Carnoy, H. Levin and K. King, *Education, Work and Employment*, Vol. II. Paris: IIEP.

Dore, R. (1976) *The Diploma Disease: Education, Qualification and Development*. London: George Allen and Unwin.

Doeringer, P.B. and Piore, M.J. (1971) *Internal Labour Markets and Manpower Analysis*. Lexington, Mass.

Psacharopoulos, G. (1985) "Returns to Education: A Further International Update and Implications", *Journal of Human Resources*, Fall, pp. 583-604.

Schultz, T. (1963) *The Economic Value of Education*. New York: Columbia University Press.

12

Theories of Labour Market

N.V. Varghese

Introduction

Individuals differ in the incomes they receive: this is an indisputably observed phenomenon in different economic systems (Taubman: 1975). In traditional society, higher individual incomes were closely associated with the material wealth one possessed. Consequently, an analysis into the origin of differential incomes will in fact be an analysis of the rise and extent of differential property ownership. On the other hand, in modern or non-traditional forms of society, the relative significance of property incomes has diminished and correspondingly the share of earned incomes has gone up (Denison: 1962; Kuznets: 1966). This was mainly because of diversification and expansion of white-collar occupations. Moreover, it was also shown that only a quarter of the variance of income can be attributed to inequalities of property holdings and the remaining three-fourths to inequalities of earnings from jobs (Pen: 1971). Subsequently the focus of analysis was shifted from income to earnings. Again, it was found that there existed differentials in earnings among individuals. Further enquiries brought to light the dominant role played by education in the earnings of a person (Schultz: 1961; Hansen: 1963; Becker: 1964; Psacharapolous: 1973; Taubman: 1975 etc.)

Better educated people earn more than the less educated and this positive association between education and earnings has 'near-universal character' (Bhaduri: 1978) and is often characterized as the "most striking finding of modern social science" (Blaug: 1974). However, the mechanisms by which education influences earnings is a less agreed area of enquiry. Spurred on the different view points, various economists have put forward differing postulations. The attempt of this paper is to critically scrutinize the main trends in the postulations on the relationship between education, employment and earnings.

The plan of the paper is as follows. Section 2 analyses the relationship based on the human capital theory. Section 3 discusses the affective skill development model. Section 4 deals with screening and signalling. The job-competition model is explained in Section 5. Bumping and pooling hypotheses are discussed in Section 6. Section 7 highlights the salient features of the job-ladder model. Labour market segmentation forms the focus of analysis in Section 8. The last Section compares the various explanations and attempts to draw some policy implications for planning education.

2. The Cognitive Skill Development Hypothesis

The first theoretical explanation of the education-earnings relationship was provided by the advocates of the human capital theory (Schultz: 1961; Becker: 1964; Mincer: 1974 etc.). According to this theory, education develops cognitive skills which enhance the productivity of and contribution by an individual to total output. Since individuals are paid according to their relative contribution to total output, the more productive will be paid more. And the more productive, in this frame of analysis, will be those who are more educated. Consequently, people are competing to invest more in education. Logically enough, differences in earnings arise because of the differences in the amounts invested in individuals.

According to this postulation, money spent on education is like any investment expenditure and therefore, the demand for education is an investment demand. In fact, it is a derived demand and is a function of the rate of return. The investment in education will continue to the point where the marginal rate of return is equal to the cost of schooling. As in the capital market, this rate is subjected to diminishing returns while cost of education is an increasing function of levels of education.

In general, the human capital model describes output as a function of capital and labour. Since labour is not homogenous because of various levels of education and because the human capital theory assumes that the more educated will contribute more to the total output and wages are paid according to marginal productivity the wage of the more educated will be higher than those with less education.

This particular argument shows that in the human capital framework the distribution of income is mainly affecting only one section of society, *i.e.* employees. From the employer's point of view there is no significant change: the only difference being what was previously distributed among many would now be distributed among a few. However, such an explanation provides an insight in theory into how earning differentials can arise through investment in education even when the total product does not necessarily increase. Education, in fact, contributes to output both in qualitative and quantitative terms. And, therefore, it will be less realistic to assume that employers are not affected by it. Very often, a change in the composition of the labour force from less educated to the more educated favourably affects the employer because he need not always distribute the due share of the increased returns to the workers.

Models using the human capital framework are invariable based on the marginal productivity theory of distribution which assumes perfect competition. If this assumption is true, then economists need not directly have to analyze productivity as a variable intervening between education and earnings. Provided labour markets function competitively, earnings are a satisfactory measure of productivity and if markets are perfectly competitive then earnings are exact measures of the same (Blaug: 1972). But the more important question is: Are the markets really competitive? If not, what we characterize as earnings from education involves more factors.

Education creates barriers to entry in the labour market. By insisting on educational qualifications for job entry, the job market creates barriers to entry for those who do not possess the required qualifications. Under such circumstances the earnings of the educated as revealed in the market reflect an element of monopoly rent.

"Much of higher earnings is not a return on education but a monopoly rent on *(i)* the scarcity of the parents who can afford to educate their children well; and *(ii)* the restrictions on members permitted into a profession in which existing members have a financial interest in maintaining scarcity" (Balugh and Streeten: 1963).

In a strictly human capital framework this monopoly element cannot continue in the long run because competition in the labour market will eventually eliminate it in the process of market clearance. Moreover, employers are also equally or more interested to eliminate it. Very often they adopt a policy of lowering the hiring standards and provide the new recruits with on-the-job training. This will result in a competition between the new entrants and the previously recruited highly educated in similar jobs. And, eventually, this competition will reduce the excess wage which used to accrue to the more educated; and in the long run the wages will be brought down to the initial position where they equal the marginal productivity of the individual.

To sum up according to the human capital theory, the relationship between education and earnings is established through the productivity-increasing role of education; productivity is positively associated with the levels of education. Hence the more educated earn more than their less educated counterparts.

3. The Affective Skill Development Argument

According to this postulation, education is an instrument used as a mechanism of social reproduction. Therefore, any analysis of the educational system would remain incomplete if its inter-relationships to other institutions and social relations are ignored. In a typical capitalist economy education performs dual functions:

(a) it plays a role in production; and

(b) it plays a role in social reproduction *i.e.* perpetuates the existing social order (Bowles and Gintis: 1975). Every individual knowingly or unknowingly performs these functions through his/her schooling.

Educational system develop many traits which are valued highly by the employers. Therefore, the market value of a worker depends on an array of personal characteristics such as cognitive, affective and ascriptive. The schooling system, through its structural correspondence with the production systems, helps in developing these characteristics. For example, the nature of social relations in education requires the student to function routinely and over long periods which is similar to the role performance in bureaucratically structured enterprises. Even the grading system in classrooms reflects the reward to the development of traits necessary for job performance (Gintis: 1971).

Employers in their hiring practices embark upon certain worker traits and wages are fixed accordingly. Education produces these worker traits not through its curriculum content in the cognitive sense but through the socialization process in the affective sense. However, this does not mean that all the affective traits exhibited by an individual are the result of his/her schooling. The persons graduated from the same school may have different traits. To some extent these traits depend on the social class origins of the individual concerned. In other words, the social class origins are also important elements in determining the personal characteristics that are valued highly by the employers (Bowles: 1972).

To sum up, this postulate, too, supports the basic premise that education enhances earnings. But the mechanisms by which this is facilitated differs from that of the human capital model. According to this postulation, schooling affects earnings through a process of socialization that takes place in the schooling process. Schooling develops certain characteristics or traits which are affective in nature. But these affective skills, too, enhance the productivity of the individual.

4. Screening and Signalling

Screening (Arrow: 1973) and Signalling (Spence: 1973) theories hypothesize that education does not develop productive capabilities in any individual. A degree or diploma acts as a credential or signal for the employer. It serves more as a measure of performance ability rather than as evidence of acquired skills. A diploma serves as a screening device in the sense that it sorts out individuals of differing abilities and conveys this information to the employers.

Employers have very poor information about the productivity of the employees at the time of hiring. But from past experience, they have very good statistical information of the distribution of productivities of individuals with varying attributes. And education provides this information. Employers depend upon this information to filter out the more productive from the less productive.

According to the filtering hypothesis, those who go for higher education are more talented and relatively more able than those who do not. The role of education is simply to find out or search out who is more talented. In the absence of a screening device like education, there is a possibility of misplacement of the talented with the less talented. Employers will continue to use educational credentials for job selection because it is the easiest and for them the cheapest way of knowing a person's potentials. Individuals are also eager to provide this information because this will enhance their chances of being selected and better rewarded. If the individuals know their ability and the market does not, then all the individuals will be treated alike. In this case those who are with higher ability will be the losers. Therefore, individuals with higher ability are interested in being identified and therefore they are willing to spend money on a device which labels their potentials and which will enable them to 'capture their ability rents" (Stiglitz: 1975).

According to the signalling theory, hiring is an investment under conditions of uncertainty. The employer is uncertain about the productive abilities of employees at the time of hiring. So hiring is like purchasing a lottery ticket. At the time of hiring, employers get information regarding two types of attributes—*(a)* attributes like sex, race etc. which are fixed; and attributes like education which are manipulative. Given the combination of 'signals and indices' (Spence: 1973), the employers may be able to distinguish individuals, based on their past experience regarding the productive capacities of employees with certain attributes.

Signalling theory differs from the screening hypothesis as regards feedback from the responses of employers. According to Arrow, allocative efficiency need not be achieved through screening because it needs information regarding marginal productivities of individuals and in a complex production process the employer may not obtain it. The signalling theory, on the other hand, considers that there is always information feedback to employers and the employer's beliefs are readjusted accordingly; so are wages. The 'upward filtration' model (Taubman and Wales: 1974) indirectly supports this claim. Since firms do not know the productivities at the time of hiring, those who are in comparable positions are paid equally and later they introduce performance-based promotions and income on accomplishment.

Empirical testing of the screening hypothesis is, perhaps, more difficult than its theoretical differentiation with the human capital theory. Studies (Taubman and Wales: 1974; Layard and Psacharapoulos: 1974; Haspel: 1978 etc.) show that screening exists; but the results cannot tell us whether productivity increments are due to education or to the inherent talents an individual possesses.

To sum up, these two hypotheses support the basic postulation that there exists a positive correlation between education and earnings. But they do not subscribe to the view that higher earnings are caused by any skills developed by the educational system. Higher education does not develop any skills. It only identifies or screens out the better talented and gives this information to the employers. Since the higher educated, according to these hypotheses, are intrinsically more talented, employers prefer to hire them and higher wages are paid accordingly. Therefore, the higher educated earn more because they are intrinsically more talented and thereby believed to be more productive.

5. The Job-Competition Model

The job-competition model is an attempt to formalize the empirically observed phenomenon that despite education being more equally distributed income is unequally distributed (Thurow: 1974). In this model "instead of competing against each other based on wages, individuals compete for jobs based on their relative costs of being trained" (Thurow: 1975).

The function of education is not to confer skills but to certify trainability and to confer a certain status by virtue of certification. Jobs and higher incomes are then distributed on the basis of this certified status. According to this model skills are picked up on the job. The function of labour markets is to match the trainable individuals with training ladders. Employers are looking for the best matches so as to reduce the training costs. Therefore, trainability and training costs become important determinants of recruitment policy.

Individual jobs are the related incomes are determined by two sets of factors:

(a) one set of factors that determine their position in the queue; and

(b) another set of factors that determine their job opportunities in the economy.

One's position in the queue depends on the structure of the national labour queue. This national labour queue depends on three factors:

(i) the background characteristics like education, sex, race etc.;

(ii) employer's ranking of different background characteristics; and

(iii) distribution within each background characteristic.

Since education is an important background characteristic used for screening individuals in the labour market, one's position in the labour queue to a great extent depends on it. But this does not necessarily mean that education determines the actual distribution of income, because it is also a function of job opportunities. But if the differences among individuals are minimal they may be grouped together and therefore their expected values will always be around the group's expected value. In other words, groups have expected values in the labour market and not the individuals.

In the labour market employers rank their workers on a continuum from the best to the least potential trainees on the basis of the estimated potential training costs. If there is perfect correlation between the background characteristics and employer's ranking, then each group's position in the labour queue will be the same as that of their background characteristics. Under such circumstances background characteristics themselves can be seen as a proxy to determine the group's position in the labour queue.

The distribution of job opportunities in the economy is governed by:

(a) character of technical progress;

(b) sociology of wage determination; and

(c) the distribution of training costs.

Education can enhance the chances of getting a job because it reduces the training costs. After the initial job entry one gets skills through on-the-job training. After receiving this training, perhaps, the initially equal workers would have unequal skills and productivities and thereby unequal incomes.

A close look at the model will reveal that education is important in determining earnings of an individual or groups at least for two reasons: *(a)* employers are interested in education because it provides them with information regarding the probable training costs they have to incur; and *(b)* prospective employees are interested in education because their position in the labour queue is determined to a great extent on the basis of background characteristics among which education is an important one. These two factors will influence the demand for education and it will continue to grow.

To sum up, the emphasis in this model is on job, rather than on wage, competition. Labour markets do not mediate between the skill requirement and the skilled. Skills are picked up on-the-job. What employers are interested in is to reduce the training costs. So they are looking for the trainability of the individual. Education is an important background characteristic which is indirectly used as measure of trainability. Therefore, education helps in job entry. However, the actual earnings depend on the skills that one picks up on the job.

6. Earnings under Conditions of Bumping and Pooling

This model focuses on the hiring practices as an intervening variable in determining the education-earnings relationships, especially in the case of developing countries. In less developed countries wage rates are rigid and wages are fixed to jobs rather than to the educational levels of the employees.

According to the simplified version of the model there are two groups of workers—educated and uneducated. Similarly there are two types of jobs—skilled and unskilled. The unskilled jobs are divided into two—urban unskilled and agricultural unskilled in the rural areas. In the wage system urban skilled workers get the highest followed by urban unskilled and agricultural workers in the rural areas (Fields: 1974).

Education is productive and therefore employers hire persons with higher levels of education in a preferential order. The job seekers, on the other hand, try to maximize their incomes. When the number of jobs is higher than or equal to the number of educated persons, the functioning of the labour market is smooth and everybody gets a wage equal to his/her relative contribution to the national product. If the educated persons outnumber the vacancies in the skilled market, then this surplus educated labour can have two options before them:

(*i*) to go to the next best employment, *i.e.* urban unskilled jobs; and

(*ii*) to remain unemployed but look for a skilled job, since wages are less in the unskilled sector.

According to the bumping model, the employers follow a policy of preferential hiring practice and therefore the educated moves to the next lower level market *i.e.* the urban unskilled jobs. If unemployment of the educated continues to increase and employers continue to follow the same policy of preferential hiring practice then eventually the jobs in the urban unskilled job market will be filled by the educated. This will force the uneducated urban workers to seek jobs elsewhere. This process of driving out of the uneducated workers from urban unskilled jobs is called "Bumping out process". The options of those who are bumped out of the urban unskilled jobs are very limited. When they fail to find a job in the urban sector, they have to seek employment in the rural areas. This, again, will eventually displace the rural unskilled workers from their job. Thus one can see that the better skilled drive out or bump out the less educated from better paid jobs.

The pooling model is similar to the bumping model in many respects. It does not assume a preferential hiring practice based on education. Education is considered neither a hindrance nor a help to get jobs. In unskilled markets educated and uneducated job seekers have equal chances of being selected or rejected. Since wage differentials exist among the labour markets, educated people will be less interested to obtain unskilled jobs because such a shift will not increase their probabilities of employment. Therefore, educated job seekers would like to stick to the urban skilled jobs. Only under extreme differences in the levels of unemployment between the two labour markets will they be willing to come to the unskilled jobs markets.

According to the two versions of the theory, there is a difference between educated persons employed in skilled and unskilled job markets. In the bumping model those who choose to enter unskilled labour markets and get the on-going wages consider themselves to be fully employed whereas in the pooling model the same group considers themselves to be partially employed. So the present value of income that one expects in unskilled job market is lower. This implies that in the pooling model the opportunity cost of educated unemployed in the skilled market is lower than that in the bumping model, *i.e.* the educated in the pooling model may be able to tolerate prolonged unemployment better than they can do on the bumping model.

The private present value of earnings from a particular level of education is the motivating factor to obtain more education, and if demand for education is to be reduced then the government has to bring down the present value of the future earnings of the educated. This can be done in different ways:

(a) bring down the wage differentials between the skilled and unskilled in the labour market or change the tax structure by making it more progressive;

(b) change the hiring practice whereby a preferential hiring practice on the basis of education is not followed; and

(c) charge the full cost of education to students by providing them with loans.

To sum up, according to this model hiring practices followed by the employers play a dominant role in the determination of earnings of an individual. If preferential hiring practices are followed there may be absolute differences in earnings but the relative differences in earnings of the groups with different levels of education may not change substantially. In the practice in hiring is not preferential then both the relative and absolute differences between persons with the same and differential levels of education will continue.

7. Earnings in a Job-ladder Model

This model is very similar to the bumping model and emphasizes the primary function of education as a mechanism to improve one's own competitiveness in the labour market. According to the model, the economy is divided into three sectors. Sector I employs only educated labour, sector II employs educated labour as teachers and sector III employs both educated and uneducated workers at identical wage rates. Wages are rigid in sectors I and II. The excess supply of labour from the two sectors spills over to the other sector *i.e.* sector III (Bhagawati and Srinivasan: 1977).

In its pure form, this model assumes that sector I employs only educated labour. Sector III, on the other hand, needs only uneducated labour. Because of unemployment, there will be a spillover of the educated labour from other sectors to sector III. Since wages of the educated and uneducated are the same in this sector, the employers are happy to have the educated. But when fairness in hiring practice is introduced, those who have more education benefit more because, as in the case of preferential hiring practices, higher levels of education enhance competitiveness and thereby employment chances of the educated. So individual demand for education will continue to grow.

To sum up, the 'fairness in hiring' principle forms the basis of the theory. Fairness in hiring exists because of the existence of job ladders. If there are no job ladders then the fairness in hiring principle becomes redundant. Therefore, the best solution is to eliminate job ladders and to restore fully flexibility of wages. The second best solution will be to eliminate the use of educational attainment as a criterion in hiring practices and introduce a lottery system for all qualified and over-qualified applicants.

8. Earnings in a Segmented Labour Market

The labour market segmentation hypothesis focuses on the socio-institutional factors influencing jobs and wages. Based on the historical perspective on the evolution of the employment process and the reactions of the employers towards it, the theory argues that segmentation of labour markets is the result of the deliberate attempt by the employers to fight against the progressive homogenization and thereby the collective bargaining power of the workers. However, there are different versions to this theory based on the identification of factors chiefly responsible for the process of segmentation. Some of them emphasize social control ıctors (Reich *et. al*: 1973 and Edwards *et. al.*: 1975), other technological factors (Piore: 1975) and the basic contradiction in social structures (Carnoy: 1980). Though there are differences in the emphasis added, all of these different versions have a common framework.

According to the segmentation theory, the labour market is divided into two (primary and secondary) sectors. The primary sector is characterized by high technology, high wages and stable employment conditions, whereas the secondary sector is constituted of low technology, low wages and instability of employment. Some versions of the theory further divide the primary sector into two: upper and lower tires (Piore: 1975). Jobs in the upper tier involve decision-making abilities and those in the lower tier are constituted of routine tasks involving less decision making. Internal labour markets (Doringer and Piore: 1971) and promotion possibilities exist in the primary sector and are relatively absent in the secondary sector. Because of the low wages, instability of employment and absence of mobility, labour turnover is high in the secondary sector.

In the primary labour market, education becomes more important at the 'ports of entry' and workers not having the required qualification for particular entry level jobs are excluded from the primary sector jobs and promotion ladders therein (Reich *et. al*: 1973). In the upper tier of the primary sector employers are looking for workers with 'ability to do what one would have been told without being told' (Carnoy and Rumberger: 1976); and in the lower tier traits like dependability, rules orientation and responsiveness to authority are sought for. The jobs in the secondary sector require minimum or no skills. Some studies (Mazumdar and Ahmed: 1978) have shown that education counts more in the primary labour markets and experience in the secondary segments.

The primary concern of the hypothesis is that earnings in any of the segments of the market are based neither on education nor on experience. The wages are related to and based on exogenous factors like race, sex, etc. In fact the segmentation theory talks about the institutional structure of wages (Piore: 1973) rather than wages per se. In this frame of analysis, education is not a direct determinant variable influencing earnings. However, the theory does not repudiate the correlation between education, experience and earnings though it does not venture any causative arguments in this respect.

According to the theory, the correlation between education, experience and earnings does not establish that more education and experience contribute to higher productivity. So the link between education and earnings is not through productivity but through socio-institutional factors. Since incomes are attached to jobs rather than to individuals, job entry becomes crucial in determining one's wages. For job entry education is unimportant in the secondary sector. However, education is a relatively significant factor in the primary markets. This is because the educated can better meet 'the hierarchical needs and customs' (Carnoy and Rumberger: 1976). This again is due to the fact that the better educated come from well-to-do families which are in line with the organisational design of the enterprises. Therefore, the theory argues that whether educated or not it is the socio-economic background which influences earnings. Since there is a correlation between socio-economic background and educational levels of the employees (Bowles: 1972) there can be a correlation between education and earnings. But to derive any causative relation between education and earnings based on such evidence will not be justified.

To sum up, this theory also agrees that there can be positive correlation between education and earnings. But it does not agree that higher earnings are due to higher education. On the other hand, it argues that in the present social order those who get higher education and thereby higher earnings are people from a higher socio-economic background. So the educational factor in determining earnings is more of an incidental nature and the real correlation or relationship is between earnings and the socio-institutional factors.

9. Conflicting Implications of the Diverging View Points

In the earlier sections we have discussed conflicting explanations for the observed positive association between education and earnings. Based on the differences in the identification of intervening variables that facilitates such a positive correlation, the postulations can be grouped into four:

(*a*) productivity as the intervening variable;

(*b*) trainability as the intervening variable;

(*c*) hiring practices as the intervening variable; and

(*d*) socio-institutional factors as the intervening variable.

Human capital, screening and signalling hypotheses, in one form or the other, identify productivity as the variable intervening between education and earnings. All these three hypotheses agree with the fact that the higher educated are more productive. But they do disagree in explaining why the educated are more productive. To the human capitalists education develops cognitive skills which enhance productivity. Screening and signalling hypotheses, on the other hand, argue that higher educated are inherently more talented and hence more productive. To them, education screens out these talented individuals and signals this information to the employers, *i.e.* the role of education is productivity identification rather than productivity addition. Perhaps, the difference is that in human capital the concept of productivity enters through the front door whereas in the other two hypotheses it enters through the back door (Varghese: 1982). However, these two roles of education need not be contradictory to each other. In fact, Arrow argues that the filtering role of education, from the private point of view, is synonymous with the productivity adding role.

Implications of these hypotheses for educational policy formulations vary. To the human capitalists, education contributes to national output and individual earnings. Therefore, they encourage public and private expenditure on education. On the other hand, screening and signalling hypotheses argue that the total national product will not be enhanced because of more educated people. Accordingly the contribution of education to national product will be zero if educational costs are borne by individuals and negative if educational subsidies exist (Blaug: 1972). Therefore, these hypotheses discourage public spending on education. However, they do not discourage private expenditure on education because through education the more talented are identified and are paid accordingly.

The job-competition model identifies trainability as the important factor influencing job selection and thereby earnings. According to this model, productivity is an attribute of jobs and not of individuals. Skills do not exist in the labour market; they are picked up on the job. What the employer is interested in at the time of hiring is to reduce the probable training costs. Since the employer does not have information regarding specific training costs of specific individuals he/she uses education as one of the important background characteristics or proxy variable under the assumption that the more educated one is the less the training costs to be incurred on him/her. This gives the educated an opportunity to get better jobs and higher earnings.

This model encourages private and public spending on education for different reasons. Employers are interested in education because it provides them with the information regarding the probable training costs. Society is interested in education because it helps in altering the distribution of income. Individuals are interested in education because their position in the labour queue to a great extent is based on the level of education. But the individuals spend on education not as an investment but treat it as a defensive expenditure 'necessary to protect one's market share' (Thurow: 1974).

Bumping and job-ladder models emphasize hiring practices as an important factor in determining individual earnings. Both models agree that the educated are more productive and in this sense they are in line with the human capital theory. But unlike the human capital theory, they argue that the jobs the educated generally hold in less developed countries are such that their potential productivities can not be realized. This is because of the existence of unemployment and the hiring practice followed by the employers. During periods of unemployment the employer follows a policy of preferential hiring practice based on the educational qualifications. This practice is considered to be fair because the educated have spent more to acquire higher levels of education to increase their competitiveness in the job market. Under this hiring practice the more educated receive better jobs and higher earnings. The higher educated earn more not because of their productivity but because they were given preference in hiring. Since the educated are forced to jobs requiring less education, their contribution to the total product is not different from what the less educated would have contributed.

According to this theory public spending on education is a waste and therefore argues against public expenditure or higher education by the less developed countries. On the other hand, private spending becomes essential because of the preferential hiring practice. People spend on education not because they like it but because if X does not obtain higher education Y will and eventually it will reduce the market value of X. Hence X is forced to obtain higher levels of education.

The affective (Bowles and Gintis: 1975) and segmentation models emphasize the socio-economic factors influencing education and earnings. To the proponents of the affective skill development model education is an instrument of social reproduction and the role of education is to inculcate certain affective traits through the structural correspondence between education and production sectors. And these traits are valued highly by employers. So the educated are hired and paid higher wages. In a typical capitalist society the institutional factors are strong enough to restrict the entry of less privileged from the educational and employment sectors and therefore, the poor are deprived of better education and higher paid jobs. According to the segmentation theory the institutional barriers are a necessary condition for the smooth functioning of the capitalist system. So the capitalists are interested to maintain and increase the role of institutional barriers. Segmentation in the labour market is a reflection of this phenomenon. The capitalists try to reinforce the existing segmentation in the labour market because it is a very useful instrument in fighting against the organised labour force. And they use education as one of the important instruments of dividing the labour force. Those in the primary sector are paid higher salaries and education is made an essential requisite to enter to these segments. Since educational opportunities are unequally distributed, the better educated will invariably be from better socio-economic backgrounds. Therefore, by insisting on educational qualifications they, in fact, recruit people from better socio-economic backgrounds. The employers prefer this group because, by virtue of their social position, they will be more in agreement with and hence more useful to the employers in carrying out their designs. Here one can notice that the educated are recruited not because of their education but because of socio-economic characteristics. Education is one factor or perhaps an incidental factor influencing earnings.

According to these hypotheses, a marginal or substantial increase in educational expenditures by the public authorities or by the private individuals is not going to have any effect on the existing situation. What is needed is to change the very socio-institutional factors which reinforce the segmented nature of the labour market. Therefore, these hypotheses argue for the restructuring of the institutions which result in bringing about inequities in society. This calls for radical changes in the philosophy of the system in general and of the educational system in particular.

From the discussions in this paper, one can notice that each of the postulations provides a partial explanation for the observed positive association between education and earnings. However, the direction of the change in emphasis is worth noting. From human capital to the segmentation theory, there is a gradual shift in emphasis from individuals to groups to society at large. To the human capitalists, education is a powerful instrument to bring about equity in the distribution of income; to the segmentationists education can only reproduce inequities when social inequities exist. So the shift in emphasis is from an isolated analysis of education as an active agent of change to the marginal role of education in a given society. Education is treated only as one of the supporting instruments in an economy. This shift in emphasis brings to light the inter-dependent role of education and thereby the necessity of planning for education at its interface with a given social context.

REFERENCES

Arrow, K.J. (1973): "Higher Education as Filter", *Journal of Public Economics*, Vol. 2, pp. 193-216.

Balogh, T. and Streeten, P.P., (1963): "The Coefficient of Ignorance", *Bulletin of Oxford, University of Institute of Statistics*, Vol. 25, pp. 99-107.

Becker, G.S. (1964): *Human Capital: A Theoretical and Empirical Analysis, New York," NBER.*

Bhaduri, A. (1978): "Education and Distribution of Personal Income: Analysis of Issues and Policies", *Industry and Development*, Vol. 2, pp. 1-14.

Bhagawati, J.N. and Srinivasan, T. (1977) "Education in a Job-Ladder Model and Fairness in Hiring Rule", *Journal of Public Economics*, Vol. 7, pp. 1-22.

Blaug, M. (1972): "The Correlation between Education and Earning: What does it Signify", *Higher Education*, Vol. 1, pp. 53-70.

Blaug, M. (1974) *Education and Employment Problem in Developing Countries*, Geneva, ILO.

Bowles, S. (1972): "Schooling and Inequality from Generation to Generation", *Journal of Political Economy*, Vol. 80, pp. 219-52.

Bowles, S. and Gintis, H. (1975): "The Problem with Human Capital Theory: A Marxian Critique", *American Economic Review*, Vol. 65, pp. 74-81.

Carnoy, M. (1980) "Segmented Labour Markets", in *Education, Employment and Work* Vol. II, Paris, UNESCO.

Carnoy, M. and Rumberger, R.W. (1976): "Segmented Labour Markets: Some Empirical Forays", Paris OECD.

Denison, E.F. (1962): *Sources of Economic Growth in United States and the Alternatives Before Us*, New York, New York Committee for Economic Development.

Doringer, P. and Piore, M. (1971): *Internal Labour Markets and Manpower Planning*, Lexington, Mass, D.C. Heath.

Fields, G.S. (1974): "The Private Demand for Education in Relation to Labour Market Conditions in Less Developed Countries" *The Economic Journal*, Vol. 84, pp. 906-19.

Gintis, H. (1971): "Education, Productivity and Characteristics of Worker Productivity", *American Economic Review*, Vol. 61, pp. 266-80.

Hansen, W.L. (1963): "Total and Private Rates of Return to Investment in Schooling", *Journal of Political Economy*, Vol. 71, pp. 128-40.

Haspel, A.E. (1978): "The Questionable Role of Higher Education as an Occupational Screening Device", *Higher Education*, Vol. 7 pp. 879-95.

Kuznets, S. (1966): *Modern Economic Growth: Rate, Structure and Speed*, New Haven, Yale University Press.

Layard, R. and Psacharopoulos, G. (1974): "The Screening Hypothesis and Returns to Education", *Journal of Political Economy*, Vol. 82, pp. 985-98.

Mazumdar, D. and Ahmed, M. (1978): "Labour Market Segmentation and the Determination of Earnings: A Case Study", *Working Paper No. 278*, World Bank.

Mincer, J. (1974): *Schooling, Experience and Earnings*, New York, NBER.

Pen, J. (1971): *Income Distribution*, Oxford University Press, Oxford.

Piore, M. (1973): "Fragments of a Sociological Theory of Wages", *American Economic Review*, Vol. 63, pp. 377-84.

Psacharopoulos, G. (1973): *Returns to Education*, Elsevier Publishers, London.

Reich, M., Gordon, D.M. and Edwards, R.C. (1973): "A Theory of Labour Market Segmentation", *American Economic Review*, Vol. 63, pp. 359-65.

Schultz, T.W. (1961): "Investment in Human Capital", *American Economic Review*, Vol. 51. pp. 1-17.

Spence, M. (1973): "Job Market Signalling", Education and Distribution of Income," *American Economic Review*, Vol. 65.

Stiglitz, J.E. (1975): "The Theory of Screening, Education and Distribution of Income", *American Economic Review*, Vol. 65.

Taubman, P. (1975): *Sources of Inequality in Earnings*, Amsterdam, North Holland Publishing Co.

Taubman, P. and Wales, T. (1974): *Higher Education and Earnings*, New York, McGraw Hill Book Co.

Thurow, L. (1972): "Education and Economic Inequality", *The Public Interest*, Summer, pp. 66-81.

Thurow, L. (1974) "Measuring the Economic Benefits of Education", in Gordon, M.S. (ed.) *Higher Education and Labour Market*, New York, McGraw Hill Book Co.

Thurow, L. (1975): *Generating Inequality*, London, Macmillan Press Ltd.

Varghese, N.V. (1982): "Manpower Planning in a Developing Economy: A Study in Education-Employment Linkages", Ph.D. Thesis, Jawaharlal Nehru University, New Delhi.

13

Other Approaches to Relate Education and Employment: Theories of Labour Market

N.V. Varghese

Manpower planning is based on the assumptions of fixed relationship between input of skilled manpower and the level of output in the economy, and a reliable correspondence between level and types of education and job categories. These assumptions do not hold good especially in the present day context of many economies. Therefore, alternative theories of labour market, in contrast to manpower approach came into existence. Perhaps, the most prominent among them is the human capital version.

1. Human Capital Theory

Human capital theory postulates that expenditure on education is a form of investment—an investment in human beings. Like investment in any form, investment in human beings gives return. This return is reflected in the earnings of the educated. The theory postulates that schooling enhances skill and dexterity of individuals which in turn enhances the productivity of the workers. Workers are paid as per their contribution to the total national product. In other words, wages are paid according to the marginal productivity theory of distribution. Hence educated earn more than their less educated counterparts.

Human capital model is based on three basic assumptions:

(a) Markets are competitive which enable prices to be used as a measure of relative demand.

(b) Prices of goods and services change in response to changes in demand and supply; and

(c) Techniques of production are flexible enough to substitute capital for labour and between different levels of educated people.

In fact human capital theory forms the basis for rate of return analysis. Rate of return analysis compares the net present value of costs of and benefits from education. Costs of education includes both direct and opportunity costs. Benefits of education generally take into account those which are directly measurable. The stream of life time earnings adjusted by a discount rate is taken into account. There are various problems associated with the measurement of earnings and hence on the estimations of rate of returns.

Earnings depend on various factors. Therefore specification of earnings function is very important. The variables taken into account may vary from situation to situation. However, it is believed that education plays an important role in determining the earnings of an individual. Very often multivariate analysis is resorted to identify and isolate the extent of influence exerted by various factors influencing earnings. Some of the important variables influencing earnings and which are quite often taken into account in the multi-variate analysis are education, father's income, father's occupation etc. Rates of return studies, in general show that:

(a) investment in education is profitable;

(b) private rates of return are higher then social rates of return for any given level of education;

(c) rates of returns tend to be highest in primary education;

(*d*) rates of returns tend to be higher in less developed countries.

2. Screening Hypothesis

Another approach which questioned some of the postulations of human capital theory is known as screening hypothesis. Screening hypothesis in general agree with the fact that higher educated are more productive. However, they disagree with the fact that this higher productivity is due to education. On the other hand screening hypothesis considers that higher educated are more talented and what schooling does is to screen out or identify the more talented from the less talented. In this sense education acts as a convenient filter which enables employers to identify those with superior ability. Extreme version of screening hypothesis implies that education has no direct effect on skill inculcation. Thus if one could find some alternative way of screening, the expenditure on education could be deemed to be waste of public resources. However, the empirical evidence to prove whether higher earnings is due to higher productivity, or due to innate abilities is difficult to obtain.

There are two versions of the screening hypothesis. In its strong version, it suggests that education does nothing to improve workers' productivity. In this case one might predict that the earning differentials of educated workers would narrow over time, as employers begin to use direct evidence of workers' performance on the job to determine wages or salaries rather than educational qualifications. In its weak version the hypothesis shows that education acts as a screening device, but that this is socially useful since it enable employers to identify those with positive attitudes towards work and the ability to pick up skills quickly.

3. Education Escalation and Competition for Jobs

There are other explanations of the labour market process which lay emphasis on the changing hiring practices of the employers when there is unemployment. Employer's in general follow a policy of preferential hiring practice whereby more qualified persons are given a preference in the recruitment. This eventually leds to bumping out of lower level educated persons from the labour market. This will have a direct influence on the demand for education. Every prospective employee finds that since employers have enhanced the hiring standards, one has to seek higher levels of education to maintain one's relative position in the labour market. This will encourage higher demand for education. In can be seen that in this type of explanation persistence of unemployment distorts education employment relations.

Another version of the labour market theory commonly known as job competition model considers that trainability as the trait which is valued high by the employer in the labour market. Persons with higher levels of education are easily trainable and therefore, their training costs will be less. Therefore, employers hire more educated people to reduce the training costs. In this sense education becomes significant for job entry. However, actual wages will be determined on the basis of productivity which is directly related to the skills picked up during on-the-job training.

4. Segmented Labour Markets

Another explanation based on the Marxian framework view labour market as segmented. In its initial version labour markets were divided into modern and traditional sectors or into primary and secondary labour markets. Primary labour markets are characterized by modern techniques of production, high wages, and stability of employment. Secondary labour markets are characterized by traditional techniques of production, low wages, no employment stability and jobs are mostly dead end ones. Later versions of segmented labour markets, sub-divides the primary segment into two—upper tier and lower tier. Jobs in the upper tier of the primary segment require decision making capacities while jobs in the lower tier are characterized by routine activities.

More advanced and more radical versions of the segmented labour market divides the labour markets into four segments:

(a) The monopoly sector;

(b) competitive sector with high wages;

(c) competitive sector with low wages; and

(d) crafts' segment.

Educational qualifications and the class origins of the recruitees to each of these segments vary. The class origins become an important factor for job entry. And in a typical capitalist society education itself is unequally distributed and accessibility is related to the class origins. Therefore, while using education for job entry it indirectly tells us about the class origins.

5. Tracer Studies

The inter-dependence between educational development and the over-all socio-economic development of a country calls for an analysis of the resource potential in natural, physical and human categories. The exploitation of natural resources depends on the development of human resources and vice-versa. Human resource potential is influenced by demographic changes. Education plays a significant role in developing human resources. Therefore, there is a need to plan education to develop human resources. Educational achievement of individuals is influenced by the conditions of employment or unemployment, the recruitment and promotion policy. That is to say the development of human resource is dependent on the operation of labour market and the prevailing employment policy.

At the micro-level an analysis of the relationship between education and employment has to take into account the background characteristics, attitudes and expectations of individual human beings. The economy and society and to some extent education influence the behaviour, attitudes, preferences and expectations of the individual. The important micro characteristics on which one needs information are:

(a) Individual characteristics like age, sex, martial status etc.

(b) Family characteristics like family size, education, occupation etc.

(c) Community characteristics like caste, religion, urban, rural etc.

(*d*) Early educational characteristics like type of school, academic performance, type of education etc.

The educational career of an individual is directly influenced by educational expectations. The family background and future expectations decide the institutions in which one is to study, field of study pursued, academic performance etc. The occupational career of an individual, on the other hand depends on educational career, labour market situation, occupational expectations etc. The career information received, placement services used, recruitment method adopted, type of post held etc. are important factors in occupational career.

The basic thrust of this approach, is that the education system can change the characteristics of the individuals, families and the community so as to make the transition from institutions of education to work smooth. This method involves tracing back the history of each individual from his present position with respect to all micro-characteristics which are detailed above. In some cases tracer studies are also undertaken by following a cohort of students by eliciting information on their positions at fixed intervals say at five years over a period of time. In both cases one is tracing—whether forward or backward—the important socio-economic characteristics of an individual.

As can be seen this method involves a lot of data collection on various aspects. So far as macro information are concerned data can be collected from the secondary sources. For micro characteristics data are to be collected from the primary sources. Generally in tracer studies samples are drawn from the students, graduates, employees, unemployed, employers etc. And detailed questionnaire method is used to collect data on micro characteristics.

14

Estimation of Manpower Demand and Supply

Bikas C. Sanyal

1. Objective of the Session

The need for information on future requirements for qualified manpower has been emphasised to provide one of the bases for the planning of education. Some guidance is needed as to the direction that the development of education should take in quantitative terms to cater for future needs for skills. It is believed that forecasting of qualified manpower can provide this guidance. Although methods of forecasting have a lot of limitations, an increasing number of countries, especially from the developing world, are preparing manpower forecasts according to occupational and educational requirements within the framework of their development plans. The present session has therefore, as its objectives:

(a) to appraise participants of the different methods of projection of qualified manpower; and

(b) to sensitize them about the shortcomings of these methods as regards their adaptation to specific contexts.

2. Different Methods of Projection of Qualified Manpower Needs

A variety of methods have been used to derive manpower forecasts in different countries. The dominant model is known in the literature as the 'manpower requirements' method. The different steps of this particular model will be outlined and then discussed.

We shall adopt the methodology used in the OECD's Mediterranean Regional Project (MRP). This is for two reasons: first, this project provides the most extended number of 'steps' in generating the manpower forecasts and, second, the MRP model (or some slight variant of it) is the one still used today by a great number of countries.[1]

The three major steps in qualified manpower forecasting are: (a) projecting the demand for educated manpower, (b) projecting the supply of educated manpower, and (c) balancing supply and demand. In what follows, we mainly consider the first step and its main stages, since we are dealing here with the manpower forecasts. Let us introduce the following symbols:

P = Population
L = Labour force
X = Output
i = Economic sector
j = Occupation
k = Educational level (or type)
T = Target year of the plan
0 = Base year of the plan

3. The Demand Side

The MRP methodology uses five main steps is assessing the required number of workers by educational level in the target year of the plan. These are as follows:

3.1 Step 1: Estimating the Future Level of Output (X_T) for the Target Year

We know $\frac{X_{0-}}{P_0}$ = GDP per capita in the base year.

Let r_1 represent the desired average annual grov th rate in GDP per capita and r_2 the estimated growth rate of population.

Then GDP per capita in the target year T will be

$$\frac{X_{0-}}{P_0} (1 + r_1)^T$$

and output in the target year will be

$$\frac{X_0}{P_0} (1 + r_1)^T \times P_0 (1 + r_2)^T = X_0 (1 + r_1 + r_2 + r_1 r_2)^T = X_T$$

3.2 *Step 2: Estimating the Structural Transformation of the Economy or the Distribution of GDP by Economic Sector*

$$\frac{X_{i-}}{X}$$

According to the International Standard Industrial Classification of Economic Activities, the major divisions of industries are:

i = 1. Agriculture, hunting, forestry and fishing
i = 2. Mining and quarrying
i = 3. Manufacturing
i = 4. Electricity, gas and water
i = 5. Construction
i = 6. Wholesale and retail trade, restaurants and hotels
i = 7. Transport, storage and communication
i = 8. Financing, insurance, real estate and business services
i = 9. Community, social and personal services
i = 10. Activities not adequately defined

In tabular form the structural distribution can be demonstrated as shown in Table—14.1 for the base year 0.

Economic development, in particular, industrial development will change the share of different industries in the total GDP resulting in structural transformation of the economy.

Table—14.1: Distribution of GDP by Economic Sector (base year)

Industry	*GDP*	*GDP share of total*
Agriculture	$X_{1.0}$	$p_{1.0}$
Mining	$X_{2.0}$	$p_{2.0}$
Manufacturing	$X_{3.0}$	$p_{3.0}$
	.	.
	.	.
	.	.
Services	$X_{9.0}$	
Others	$X_{10.0}$	$p_{10.0}$
Total	X_0	1.0

The structural transformation will change the value of p_i (i = 1, 2, ... 10) depending upon the growth rates of each industry, which are often predetermined by policy.

$$P_{i.T} = \frac{X_i(1+s_i)^T}{X_T} = X_{i.T} = \frac{X_{i.T}}{X_T}$$

Where s_i is the average annual growth rate of the industry i.

Let us remember that $\sum_i p_{i.T} = 1$

and $\sum X_i\,(1+s_i)^T = X_T$

X_{iT} is target year contribution to GDP of the industry i, i = 1, 2, ...10

This will result in Table—14.2 for the economic structure of the country in the target year T.

Table—14.2: Economic Structure of the Country in Target Year T

Industry	*GDP at year T*	*Share of GDP*
Agriculture	$X_{1.T}$	$p_{1.T}$
Mining	$X_{2.T}$	$p_{2.T}$
Manufacturing	$X_{3.T}$	$p_{3.T}$
	.	.
	.	.
	.	.
Services		
Others	$X_{10.T}$	$p_{10.T}$
Total	X_T	1.0

3.3 *Step 3: Estimating Labour Productivity by Economic Sector for Target Year and its Change between base and Target Year*

$$\left(\frac{X_i}{L_i} -\right)$$

The productivity of labour for each sector is estimated from the GDP of each sector divided by the number of workers in that sector. For the base year, this can be represented in Table—14.3.

Due to changes in the technology, means of production and organisation of work, labour productivity will change in varying degrees for the different sectors. These changes are estimated from (1) past trends or (2) model country productivities or (3) international comparison or (4) experts' judgement or (5) a combination of several of (1) to (4).

Let the productivity growth rate estimated as above for the sector i = u_i, then

$$q_{iT.} = q_{i.0}\,(1 + ui)^T$$

Where q_{iT} = productivity of the sector i in the target year T. This gives us Table—14.4 for the target year.

The overall labour productivity can then be estimated as: $q_T = X_T/L_T$

Table—14.3: Labour Productivity of GDP by Economic Sector (Base tear)

Industry	*GDP*	*No. of workers*	*Labour productivity*
i	X_i	L_i	X_i/L_i
Agriculture	X_1	L_1	$X_1/L_1 = q_{1.0}$
Mining	X_2	L_2	$X_2/L_2 = q_{2.0}$
Manufacturing	X_3	L_3	$X_3/L_3 = q_{3.0}$
	–	–	–
	–	–	–
Services	X_9	–	–
Others	x_{10}	L_{10}	$X_{10}/L_{10} = q_{10.0}$
Total	X_0	L_0	$X_0/L_0 = q_0$

Table—14.4: Labour Productivity by Economic Sector (Target year)

Industry	*GDP in year T*	*Productivity in year T*	*No. of workers in year T*
Agriculture	$X_{1.T}$	$q_{1.T}$	$X_{1.T}/q_{1.T} = L_{1.T}$
Mining	$X_{2.T}$	$q_{2.T}$	$X_{2.T}/q_{2.T} = L_{2.T}$
Manufacturing	$X_{3.T}$	$q_{3.T}$	$X_{3.T}/q_{3.T} = L_{3.T}$
	–	–	
	–	–	
Services	$X_{9.T}$	$q_{9.T}$	$X_{9.T}/q_{9.T} = L_{9.T}$
Others	$X_{10.T}$	$q_{10.T}$	$X_{10.T}/q_{10.T} = L_{10.T}$
Total	X_T		L_T

3.4 Step 4: Estimating the Occupational Structure of the Labour Force within each of the Economic Sectors in the Target Year

$$\frac{(L_{ij})}{(L_i)}$$

The International Standard Classification of Occupations gives the following *major groups of Occupations*

j = 0/1. Professional, technical and related workers, for convenience let j = 1 in our case

j = 2. Administrative and managerial workers

j = 3. Clerical and related workers

j = 4. Sales workers

j = 5. Service workers

j = 6. Agriculture, animal husbandry and forestry workers, fishermen and hunters

j = 7/8/9. Production and related workers, transport equipment operators and labourers, for convenience let j = 7 in our case

j = 10. Workers not classifiable by occupation and members of the armed forces, for convenience let j = 8 in our case.

First let us examine the occupational structure of the labour force within each economic sector for the base year. Within each sector we shall compute the proportion of each occupation listed above. (See Table—14.5).

Table—14.5: Labour Force by Occupation and Economic Sector (Base Year)

Industry/ occupation	*Profess-ional*	*Adminis-trative*	*Produc-tion*	*Others*	*Total*
Agriculture	1_1	$1_{1.2}$	...	$1_{\cdot 1.8}$	1.0
Mining	$1_{2.1}$	$1_{2.2}$	...	$1_{2.8}$	1.0
Services					
Others	$1_{10.1}$	$1_{10.2}$	...	$1_{10.8}$	1.0

Note that $l_{ij} = L_{ij}/L_i$ = proportion of labour force in sector i with occupation j.

$i = 1, 2 \ldots 10; j = 1, 2 \ldots 8.$

For the target year, the proportions will change because of changes in the economy, technological changes, changes in the means of production and in the organisation of work, changes in the qualification level in the labour force, etc.

The method of incorporating these changes will be discussed later. For the time being, let us assume that: $1_{ijT} = a_{ij}$ 1_{ij0} where 1_{ij0} is the proportion of labour force with occupation j in the economic sector i for the base year and 1_{ijT} is the same for the target year.

a_{ij} is the proportional change in 1_{ij0}

$a_{ij} \geq 0$

For example, a_{ij} could be equal to $(1 + r_{ij})^T$, where r_{ij} is the growth rate in the proportion on average per year.

So we can have the target year labour force for each occupation within each economic sector once 1_{ijT} values have been calculated because from Table—14.4, we already know the total labour force for each sector in the target year and $L_{ijT} = 1_{ijT}$ x L_{iT} where L_{ijT} is target year labour force in occupation j and sector i and L_{iT} total labour force in sector i in target year (see Table—14.6).

Table—14.6: Labour Force by Occupation and Sector (Target year)

Industry/ Occupation	*Professional*	*Administrative*	*Others*	*Total*
Agriculture	$L_{11.T}$	$L_{1.2T}$	$L_{1.8T}$	$L_{1.T}$
Mining	$L_{2.1T}$	$L_{2.2T}$	$L_{2.8T}$	$L_{2.T}$
	–	–		
	–	–		
Services	–			
Others	$L_{10.1T}$	$L_{10.2T}$	$L_{10.8T}$	$L_{10.T}$
Total	$R_{1.T}$	$R_{2.T}$	R_{8T}	L_T

R_{jT} = Total no. of workers with occupation j.

This leads us to the final step:

3.5 Step 5: Estimating the Educational Structure of the Labour Force in given Occupations within Economic Sectors in Target Year

$$\frac{L_{ijk}}{-L_{ij}}$$

As before, this is also done on the basis of the base year observations. First the educational levels and types (k) are determined and the number of workers with different levels and types of education within each occupation are noted. The proportion of each level and type of education within each occupation is computed. This proportion is the basis for future projection. The base year values of proportions (e_{jk}) can be demonstrated in Table—14.7.

Table—14.7: Proportion of Educated in Different Occupations by Level and Type of Education (Base Year).

Occupation/ Education	*Level and type*						
	Post graduate	*Graduate*	*Senior secondary*	*Junior secondary*	*Primary*	*Others*	*Total'*
Professional	e_{11}	e_{12}	e_{13}	e_{14}	e_{15}	e_{16}	1.0
Administrative	e_{21}	e_{22}	e_{23}	...	...	e_{26}	1.0
Agricultural workers	.						
Production and related	.						
Services	.						
Others	e_{81}	e_{82}	e_{83}	...	...	e_{86}	1.0

The changes in these proportions are also determined for the target year in the same way as the changes in the occupational structure.

Let us assume that $e_{jkT} = a_{jk}\ e_{jk0}$

In a particular case we may have $a_{jk} = (1 + r_{jk})^T$, where r_{jk} is the average annual growth rate in the proportion of labour force with education k within occupation j.

e_{jkT} = proportion of labour force for the same in target year (T) and e_{jk0} is the same for the base year, a_{jk} is the change in the proportion e_{jk0} for education j and occupation k. Since we know the total number of workers for each occupation in the target year, we can easily obtain the total number or workers for each type of education in that occupation by multiplying the total number of workers by e_{jkT}

For example, to get the number of professionals needed with post-graduate degree (E_{11T}) we have to simply multiply R_{1T} by e_{11T} (see Table—14.7) or in general $E_{jkT} = R_{jT}\, e_{jkT}$, j = 1, 2, ... 8; k = 1, 2, ... 6. This gives us Table—14.8.

In the Table, F_{kT} = Total no. of workers required for the year T with education k to achieve the economic growth rate envisaged in our forecasts, based on the assumptions given above.

Table—14.8: No. of Educated Needed for the Different Occupations by Level and Type of Education (Target year)

Occupation/ Education	*Post-graduate*	*Graduate*	*Senior secondary*	*Junior secondary*	*Primary*	*Others*	*Total*
Professional	$E_{1.1.T}$	$E_{1.2.T}$	$E_{1.3.T}$	$E_{1.4.T}$	$E_{1.5.T}$	$E_{1.6.T}$	$E_{1.T} = R_{1.T}$
Administrative	$E_{2.1.T}$				$E_{2.6.T}$		$E_{2.T} = R_{2.T}$
Agriculturists							
Production							
Others	$E_{8.1.T}$					$E_{8.6T}$	$E_{8.T} = R_{8.T}$
Total	$F_{1.T}$	$F_{2.T}$	$F_{3.T}$	$F_{4.T}$	$F_{5.T}$	$F_{6.T}$	L_T

It should be noted that steps (1) to (3) pertain to general economic planning. Our concern as educational planners will be the last two steps which deal with occupational and educational forecasting. As indicated above, we shall give the different methods of forecasting the occupational structure below.

Several alternative ways have been used in different countries in their attempts to forecast the occupational structure:

(1) *International models, i.e.,* to observe the occupational structure of a country at a more advanced level of development and hypothesize that this is the desired structure in the country where the forecast is being made.

This may consist in the use of Model country comparisons, for example, Puerto-Rico utilized the coefficients of the United States, and Italy those of France.

It may also be Group country comparisons such as the use of parameters estimated from many OECD countries.

(2) *Model firm comparisons, i.e.,* to observe the occupational structure of the most modern or efficient firms and stipulate that their occupational structure can be adopted for the plan.

In the socialist countries, for instance, the 'model firm' is taken to be the one using the latest technology.

(3) *Staffing norms, i.e.,* to follow the advice of experts or simply initiative insight of the planner and specify certain desired ratios of engineers-to technicians, doctors-to-nurses, and so on.

This technique is often used in the agricultural sector in general and in the socialist countries.

(4) *Time series extrapolation,* to predict the occupational structure simply as a function of time following past trends:

This method has been used extensively in French planning.

$$L_{ij}/L_i = f(t)$$

In most cases, more than one of these methods is used depending on the economic activity being analyzed, as mentioned earlier.

It should be noted that changes in the occupational structure due to changes in the economy, especially technological changes, are to be taken into consideration at this stage.

3.6 Forecasting the Educational Structure

There exist, in general, two distinct classes of methods for expressing the forecast in educational terms: those working from occupation to education, and those which by-pass the occupational dimension and produce directly the forecast in terms of education. We have considered above the first class of methods.

The educational content of given occupations is found according to a typical, idealized structure (methods followed by French planners). It could also follow the international model, group country comparison or model country comparison method described above.

It should be noted here that possible substitution between education and occupation can be taken into account at this stage.

3.7 By-Passing the Occupational Forecast

In this case, the educational structure is derived as a direct function of labour productivity, *i.e.*

$F_k = f(X/L)$ or from a more general production function where a labour utilization coefficient (b) links output to educated labour, *i.e.*

$$F_k = b.X$$

4. The Supply Side

4.1 Based on Manpower Demand

From the total number of workers required for the year T with education k obtained in Table—14.8, one can estimate the intake to the relevant education/training. However, it should be remembered that output of a particular level and type of training depends upon the duration of the training. For example, let us estimate the intake necessary for the supply of Fkt number of workers required for the year T with education k. Let us assume that it take n years to graduate from this level and type of education. We can construct the following Table—14.9 remembering that in the base year o there are already students in the course for n years of studies, who will graduate during the next n years batch by batch. Those who were admitted in year -n (I-n) will graduate in year o (Go) and will be added to the workforce in year 1 (w1). Those who are admitted in year o (Io) will graduate in year n (Gn) and will be added to the workforce in year n + 1 (wn + 1).

Table—14.9: Intake forecasts for Manpower Supply with Education Type and Level k for Target Year T

Year 1	*Intake* 2	*Graduates* 3	*New workers* 4	*Adjusted stock from previous years* 5	*Total No. of workers* 6 = 4 + 5
–n	I–n				
–(n–1)	I(–n–1)				
o	Io	Go	wo	Wo	Fo
1	I1	G1	w1	W1	F1
n–1	In-1	Gn–1	wn–1	Wn–1	Fn–1
n	In	Gn	wn	Wn	Fn
n + 1	In + 1	Gn + 1	Wn + 1	Wn + 1	Fn + 1
	In + 2	Gn + 2	wn + 2	Wn + 2	Fn 2l
T–n–1	I T–n–1	G T–n–1	w T–n–1	W T–n–1	F T–n–1
T–n	I T–n	G T–n	w T–n	W T–n	F T–n
T–1	I T–1	G T–1	w T–1	W T–1	F T–1d
T			wT	WT	FT

Now let us look at Table—14.9. Column 1 gives the years starting from –n going through o, T–n ending at T, the target year of our forecasts. The year –n is included in the table because the students admitted in year –n will graduate in year o and are included in our stock of manpower. Column 2 gives the students admitted in a year corresponding to column 1 and are denoted by In for the year n. Column 3 gives the number of graduates corresponding to the intakes of Column 2. Note that it takes n years to graduate. So Go is the number of graduates in year o from an intake I –n n years earlier. The values in the column of graduates are obtained by multiplying the intake values by the corresponding transition rates from intake to graduation. These rates take account of dropout, repetition and failure. For simplicity it is expressed by one compact indicator say g.

For practical purposes this may remain constant. Then

$$G_O = I_{-n} \cdot g$$

and $G_n = I_O \cdot g$

$$G_{T-1} = I_{T-n-1} \cdot g$$

Not all graduates will join the work force the following year. Some will drop out because of emigration, home conditions, personal and other reasons. Let the participation rate be h.

Let us denote the additional workers in year n by wn. Then

$w^1 = Go \, . \, h$

$w^n = Gn\text{-}1 \, . \, h$

$w^{n+1} = Gn \, . \, h$

$w^T = {}^{G}t\text{-}1 \, . \, h$

These values are given in column 4. Note that wn + 1 is predetermined because Gn is predetermined because Io is the intake in year o which should be known. Column 5 is the stock in a year adjusted from the previous year for loss due to death, resignation, emigration, retirement etc. Let us call this rate f.

The stock in previous years is given in column 6 as the total number of workers in a particular year. We know Fo the stock of manpower with education k in year o. We know also

$$F1 = Fo\ (1\text{-}f)\ (=W1) + w1\ (=Go.h)$$

Similarly we know all the values of F up to Fn + 1 but no more. And we know FT the target year requirement of total number of workers with education k from Table—14.8. How are intermediate values obtained? Let us assume a linear increase Δ in the number of workers for the years from n + 1 to T as follows:

Years	Total No. of workers
n + 1	Fn + 1 (known)
n + 2	Fn + 1 + Δ
n + 3	Fn + 1 + 2Δ
.	
.	
.	
T - 1	$Fn + 1 + (T-n-2)\Delta = F_{T-1}$
T	$Fn + 1 + (T-n-1)\Delta = F_T$

$$\text{Therefore } \Delta = \frac{FT - Fn + 1}{(T-n-1)}$$

Replacing Δ by the calculated amount, we get total number of workers for each year from n + 1 to T

Now WT = FT–1 (1–f)

and wT = FT – WT

Since we know the participation rate among the graduates

$$\text{we know} \quad G_{T-1} = \frac{WT}{h}$$

$$\text{and} \quad I_{T-n-1} = \frac{G_{T-1}}{g}$$

Similarly we can compute all the values from I T–n–1 to I 1. So the intakes I1 to I T–n–1 will provide us with the necessary manpower FT with level of education k in the target year T based on the rates of transition, participation and loss due to resignation, retirement, death, emigration etc. as assumed in the model.

Applying the same method, we can compute the intakes for all other types and levels of education.

The supply projections based on social demand involve three basic steps:

1. Making population projections by school age groups. These projections take place according to any standard demographical model or, in certain cases, they are simple time extrapolations;

2. Assessing the number of graduates by educational level and type. This follows the social demand model, namely school level transition probabilities are applied to the base population cohorts. These are followed through time until they exit the educational system, formal or non-formal.

3. Determining the labour force participants. This is achieved by applying the sex-age-educational level specific labour force participation rates to the graduates generated in the previous step.

5. Balancing Supply to Demand

It is very unlikely that the demand for qualified manpower matches exactly the spontaneous supply. It is for this reason that a final exercise has to be undertaken, that is the adjustment to equate both sides, supply and demand.[2]

5.1 Revising the Demand and/or Supply Projections

This is usually done in two simultaneous ways that are not mutually exclusive.

If (Ejk) as estimated from the demand side is very difficult from the (Ejk) assessed from the supply side, the manpower planner will most likely go back to his computations and revise some of the assumptions used in demand and supply projections.

It might be realized, for example, that, the productivity coefficients used for future labour on the demand side were too *optimistic*. Or else, for instance, the participation ratio adopted regarding the labour force on the supply side was too pessimistic. Several other assumptions could be re-examined in light of certain factors. By selecting other parameters than those assumed originally the planner can reconcile a great deal of the discrepancy between future supply of and demand for qualified manpower.

5.2 Formulating the Final Plan

This step is the only genuine policy action for identifying manpower surpluses or deficits not likely to be covered automatically by spontaneous supply and then arranging for the output of educational programmes to equal supply and demand at the target year of the plan. The output has also to be phases year by year up to the target year. The policy of intake is to be based on these output figures, taking into account failure, drop-out and repetition parameters and other losses and additions.

The supply of educated manpower may also be balanced with demand by computing the required output for each level and type of education adjusting for losses and additions. The intake to each level and type is to be computed from the required output, taking account of failures, drop-outs and repetitions. The total intake for each level and type is then to be distributed for each year among the institutions.

5.3 Other Methods of Projecting Qualified Manpower Needs

(a) Tinbergen model: this is one variation of the MRP model. It bypasses occupational forecasts, neglects primary education enrolments and goes straight to estimating educational, requirements, giving special attention to the required number of teachers, delineating the path of enrolments from the base year to the target year. It also pays special attention to the replacement of expatriates by national qualified manpower.[3]

(b) Saturation norms method: saturation norms are ratios of qualified manpower to the total labour force or total production. These norms are established for different groups of enterprises and for different types of qualified manpower. When the total labour force or total output of production in the future is estimated, the number of qualified manpower needed can be determined.

(c) Personnel nomenclature method: the nomenclature is a list of posts to be filled by qualified manpower. It is drawn up by means of expert analysis of each sector of the economy, group of enterprises or even a single enterprise, for the target year based on an analysis of the existing situation and future means of production of goods and services. The coefficients of qualifications structure for each sector, group of enterprises or single enterprise (ratio of specialists with higher education to those with specialized secondary education, for example) are used to determine the number and type of qualified manpower which will be necessary.[4]

In addition there are several other methods of projecting qualified manpower needs, namely, the input-output model, linear programming model, social demand model, labour absorption model, etc. These, however, do not have much practical application. (For details one may read the works referred to in the article by G. Psacharopoulos and M. Debeauvais cited earlier).

6. Problems Encountered in Projecting Qualified Manpower Needs

The problems arise principally from the assumptions incorporated in the methods when they are put into practice. These are:

(a) The occupation distribution in an economic sector is not as rigid in practice as is assumed in the MRP method. Inter-occupational substitution occurs, generally due to economic changes, but especially due to technological changes, making the projection inaccurate.

(b) The educational distribution of the labour force for an occupation is also not as rigid in practice as is assumed in the MRP method. Substitution of a level and type of education within an occupation by another level and type does take place, further contributing to inaccuracy of the projection.

(c) In countries where the educational system is extremely diverse, it becomes difficult to relate the level and type of education to an occupation.

(d) Depending on wages, prices and availability, enterprises produce given amounts of output with widely varying

mixes of labour and machinery, making any forecasting of manpower extremely difficult.

(e) Uncertainties about the economic growth of each sector, productivity changes, variation in the participation rates of the labour force and in the educational system, mobility of manpower, etc., especially when forecasts made relate to a long time period (as in the case of qualified manpower needs), make the task of projection extremely difficult.

(f) In the saturation and personnel nomenclature methods, the total labour force or the total output are often over-estimated in practice because of extensive and intensive involvement of the enterprises and the influence they exert on the estimations which is often subjective. The norms applied for determining the different types of qualified manpower are also subject to bias of the experts. Objective analysis is often impossible.

Finally, the available projection methods have not been able to take into account the rural-urban imbalance in manpower distribution and the costs of executing a manpower plan.

In spite of the above defects, these methods do provide some indication as to the direction education should take, especially when a country is committed to modernization, and an attempt is made to relate education with employment. With an improved information base, some of the defects can be rectified, although economic uncertainties will always exist. New methods of projection are expected to be developed using an information base which will provide signals for steering the development of education, with a continuous monitoring, feedback and control system.

NOTES

1. Psacharopoulos G. and Debeauvais M. "Forecasting the needs for Qualified Manpower: Towards an Evaluation" in *Forecasting Skilled Manpower Needs: The Experience of Eleven Countries* Edited by R.V. Youdi and K. Hinchliffe, UNESCO, Paris 1985.

2. The supply of manpower as projected in 4.1 will automatically match with the demand projections.

3. Tinbergen J. and Bos H.C. "A Planning Model for the Educational Requirements of Economic Development" in Econometric Models of Education, Paris, OECD, 1965.

4. Ivanov I.V. "Skilled Manpower Planning, Forecasting and Training in the USSR" in R.V. Youdi and K. Hinchliffe, op. cit.

15

The Earnings Function

Bikas C. Sanyal

1. Objective

The education is not the determining factor for employment, nor is employment the only objective of education. Employment of an individual depends on several factors. The employment career is subject to similar phenomena. Earnings and employment reflect in a certain way the performance of individuals in their employment career. The objective of this session is:

1. To demonstrate the association of different factors, including education, with earnings of workers.
2. To identify the relative importance of different factors.
3. To acquaint participants with earnings functions and demonstrate how they can be constructed with the use of computers.
4. To show the use of earnings functions in explaining different views of relating education to employment.
5. To sensitize the participants to the limitations of earnings functions in explaining the relationship between education and employment.

2. Age-Earnings Profile by Level of Education

Figure 1 shows that the Philippines earnings of individuals vary (1) with age and (2) with level of education. For each level of education, earnings vary with age, and for each age, earnings vary for different levels of education.

3. Earnings Profile by Age, Education and Sector of Employment

Earnings also vary for each age group and for each gender by sector of employment of the individual as shown in Tables—

Figure 1. Annual family income by age and education in the Philippines

Sharing in development

Pesos (in thousands)

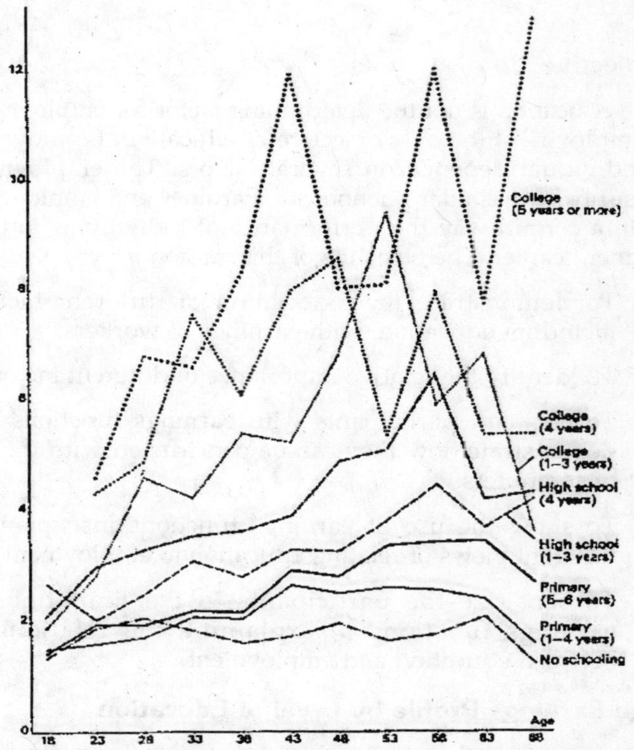

Source: Bureau of the Census and Statistics: *Family income and expenditures survey,, 1971.*

15.1 and 15.2. Of course, earnings vary by level of education as shown in Table—15.3.

Table—15.1: Actual Pay by Economic Sector and Age (graduates file)

Age group	*Private sector*	*Public sector*
30-	611	623
30-40	902	785
40+	1254	1153

Table—15.2: The Sex Earnings Differential by Economic Sector (graduates file)

Sector of employment	*Male earnings (pesos)*	*Female earnings (pesos)*	*Male earnings advantage per cent*
Private	956	575	39.9
Public	1042	726	30.3

Table—15.3: Means Earnings by Educational Level of Two Generations (Pesos)

Educational level	*Father*	*Mean monthly earnings respondent*
No education	884	a
Primary school	953	a
Secondary school	964	a
Vocational school	1017	566
B.A.	1446	782
M.A.	1396	1054
Ph.D.	2150	2451

(a) The graduates sample does not include persons with secondary educational qualifications or less.

Source: Psacharopoulos, G, and Sanyal, B., Student expectations and labour market performance: the case of the Philippines Higher Education 10 (1981) Elsevier Scientific Publishing Col, Amsterdam.

4. Earnings Profile by Sex Gender, Ethnic Groups, Field of Study, Socio-Economic Status and Type of Institution Attended

Table—15.4 shows the percentage distribution of graduates of Malaysia by their actual salary levels. This demonstrates the extent of variation in the earnings by gender, ethnic groups, field of study, socio-economic status of the graduates (defined by their parents' education, occupation and income), and type of institutional attended. (Comment on the details)

5. Earnings Function

The relationship between earnings and the influencing variables can be expressed in mathematical form: Earnings = f (age; education; sex; sector of work, occupation..)

The simplest form of this functional representation is given by a linear relationship between earnings and the other variables as follows:

Earnings = a + b_1 (age) + b_2 (education) + b_3 (sex) + b_4 (sector of work) + b_5 (occupation + ...)

This can be further simplified by limiting the influencing variables (explanatory variables) to those which are quantitative. For example:

y (earnings) = a + b_1 (age) + b_2 (number of years of education completed) + b_3 (parents income)

In this case, a, b_1, b_2... can be given some precise interpretation, b_1 = change in earnings for unit change in age when other variables remain the same. b_2 = change in earnings for unit change in years of education when other variables remain the same. b_3 change in earnings for unit change in parents income when other variables remain the same and a is a constant term giving the theoretical earning when all other variables become zero.

Such a mathematical function explaining the earnings is called an earnings function. (Qualitative variables such as sex, ethnic origins... can also be considered an explanatory variables and their relative effects measured).

Table—15.4: Actual Salary of Graduates in the Private Sector by Sex, Ethnic Group, Field of Study, SES and Institution

Variable	*M$500*	*M$501- M$800*	*M$801- M$1,000*	*M$1,101- M$1,400*	*M$1,401- M$1,700*	*M$-1,701- M$2,000*	*M$2,001- M$2,500*	*M$2,500*
1	2	3	4	5	6	7	8	9
Sex								
Male	1.1	1.5	7.7	10.4	19.0	9.1	24.8	26.3
Female	6.5	6.5	15.1	15.1	22.6	7.5	18.3	8.6
Ethnic Group								
Biunputera	4.0	0.5	6.5	8.5	25.1	9.0	27.6	18.6
Chinese	0.9	2.2	8.8	11.9	17.3	9.7	23.6	25.5
Indian	–	6.8	9.6	16.4	12.3	8.2	21.9	24.7
Field of Study[b]								
Arts-based	3.0	3.9	10.8	10.3	17.2	4.7	25.9	24.1
Science-based	0.8	1.2	6.2	13.2	22.9	12.4	22.9	20.5
Professional	–	–	1.5	9.1	18.2	15.2	27.3	28.8

(Contd...)

Table—15.4 (Contd.)

1	2	3	4	5	6	7	8	9
SES								
High	1.0	1.0	7.2	11.3	20.6	7.2	24.7	26.8
Middle	2.0	2.8	9.4	13.0	19.7	9.4	23.2	20.5
Low	0.2	0.2	8.5	11.1	17.1	9.4	29.9	18.8
Institution								
Universiti Malaya	2.7	1.6	4.9	8.6	13.0	6.5	32.4	30.3
Universiti Kebangsaan Malaysia	–	–	25.0	25.0	16.7	–	25.0	8.3
Universiti Sains Malaysia	11.5	3.8	–	11.5	19.2	7.7	38.5	7.7
Universiti Teknologi Malaysia	–	–	–	25.0	25.0	–	25.0	25.0
Universiti Pertanian Malaysia	3.8	–	3.8	7.7	65.4	7.7	7.7	3.8
Institut Teknologi MARA	6.3	–	31.3	12.5	12.5	6.3	12.5	18.8
Overseas Universities	0.3	1.7	8.5	12.6	20.5	11.6	22.2	22.2

Notes: *(a)* Includes Sri Lankans and Pakistanis.

(b) See note to Table—6.2 in Chapter 6.

Source: Aziz, U. *et. al*.: *University Education and Employment in Malaysia*, IIEP, Paris, 1987, p. 169.

The values of a, b_1, b_2, b_3 etc. can be calculated from data on earnings of individuals and the corresponding values of other variables for these individuals, by computer with the use of a suitable computing programme (the most popular is called SPSS). The method of analysis is called multiple regression analysis. a, b_1, b_2... are called 'regression coefficients'.

The computer also gives (1) indications if a particular coefficient is significantly different from zero, and (2) the coefficient of determination R^2 showing the extent (in per cent) that the function (model) has been able to explain the variation in earnings (the prediction capacity of the model).

6. Example

A recent survey of a representative group of workers in a country gave data on earnings (y), age of individuals (x_1, number of years of education (x_2) and number of years of training (x_3). The following equation was obtained as the earnings function. Earnings in the relevant monetary unit, (y) = $-731.6 + 24.9x_1 + 52.4x_2 + 46.2x_3$ and $R^2 = .46$.

This shows that for unit change in age *i.e.* one year increase or decrease in age, earnings will increase or decrease by 24.9 units. One year additional year of education will increase earnings by 52.4 units and one additional year of training will increase earnings by 46.2 units. The model has been able to explain 46 per cent of earnings *i.e.* 46 per cent of the difference in workers' earnings are associated with differences in their age, education and training. The remaining 54 per cent of the earnings variation is due to factors which were not considered in the model.

7. Exercise

The following earnings function was derived from a survey of workers in a country. Earnings (Annual) = 2000 + 1.5 (parents income in Baht) + 12 (work experience in years) + 20 (number of years education) + 5 (number of months of in-service training) $R^2 = 0.52$.

1. If all other variables remain the same, what should be the additional earnings for an additional year of education for it to be worth undertaking?
2. Which is the more attractive proposition? To have one additional year of experience on the job or an additional year of education?
3. Which variable has the strongest influence on earnings—an additional year of formal education or an additional year of in-service training?
4. What percentage of the variation in earnings has been explained by parents income, work experience, education and training?

REFERENCES

Aziz, Ungku, Chew Singh Buan, Lee Kiong Hoek, B.C. Sanyal: *University Education and Employment*, Malaysia, IIEP, Paris, 1987.

Norusis M./SPSS Inc. *SPSS/PC Base Manual* SPSS Inc. Chicago 1988.

Psacharopoulos, G. and Sanyal, B.: *Student Expectations and Labour Market Performance: the Case of the Philippines. Higher Education 10 (1981)*, Elsivier Scientific Publishing Company, Amstardam.

16

Earnings Functions: Theory

B. Camara

Wage and income policies are a matter of great concern in developing countries especially in Africa where various countries are undergoing adjustment programmes in order to overcome the acute economic and social crisis When studying the present situation of wage and income distribution, one has to consider different factors that determine to a great extent the dynamics of the of the phenomenon.

The historical approach shows the colonial heritage in terms of salary and income distribution. Many African countries have maintained the structural imbalances left by the previous political period. Moreover, the inequalities have worsened, creating a dramatic situation in rural areas as well as in urban ones. Therefore, the inter-relations between growth, employment, education and earnings must be given due attention in the search for long-lasting solutions to the development of African economies and societies.

As far as study of the inter-relations is concerned, there are useful methods of statistical and econometric analysis which can provide a better understanding of the underlying relationships. Particularly in the area of earning functions, tools are available for relevant identification and analysis of relations linking salary levels and other quantitative and qualitative variables.

I. Identification of Underlying Relationships

Data collected from specific surveys on salary distribution constitute a basis for sound analysis of relations. Obviously the quality of the analysis depends very much on the quality of data used. Necessary statistics do not relate only to salary variables but include also information on factors and variables that may have a significant influence on the level of earnings, such as economic growth, productivity, inflation, educational level, type of occupation etc.

According to the wage theory adopted, a specific set of explanatory variable is used. However, the testing of assumptions is a crucial step in the study of earnings functions. Before choosing the variables, it is important to analyze the economic and social links within the context referred to. The choice must not be made at random. The mechanisms which determine the level and evolution of earnings need to be highlighted. This analysis can help in reducing the number of preliminary explanatory variables. That is the case when two or more variables are strongly inter-related. As an example, one can find a close relationship between age and number of years of experience. Thus in order to consider both variables as explanatory variables, we may retain only one, say experience instead of age to explain earnings level.

The following figure shows some basic links between certain economic and social variables and salary.

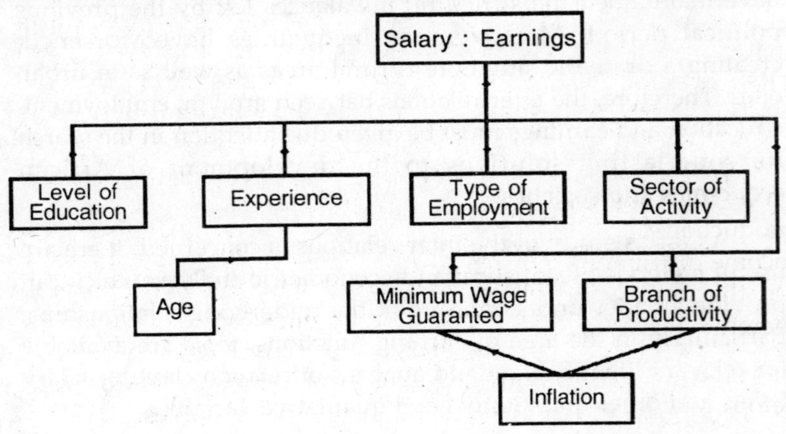

As one can see, salary is explained by both social and economic variables and by quantitative and qualitative variables as well. The qualitative variables chosen are: the Level of Education (LE), the Type of Employment (TE) and the Sector of Activity (SA), these variables are expected to play a significant role in the determination of the salary. In fact the wage policy is generally based on the type of employment linked with the level of education particularly in the modern sector. Cadres with engineering or business administration occupations very often have the highest salaries in the economy and they belong to the sub-population of graduates. If we look at the situation of school teacher having secondary level education, their salaries are lower than those of graduates and post-graduates. Moreover, as to workers with primary education level or illiterates, the salaries are usually very low compared to other groups. As a matter of fact, they constitute the majority of the available labour force or manpower, with the lowest earnings and standard of living.

In African developing countries, inequalities also exist according to the sector of activity. Distribution of salaries in the agricultural sector may differ from the distribution in the industrial sector or in the sector of trade and services. These differences can be explained by various factors such as the importance given to a sector, almost at the expense of the other sectors, the basic structure of the economy, the balance of power between actors in the economic field, sector productivity, category of workers paid at that level. In addition to this, the other sectors may also adjust according to increases of the minimum wage. There is a sort of cascade effect generated by the variation of this explanatory variable.

As regards productivity, sectors with high productivity often have high salaries, due to capacity and achievements in production. Improvement in productivity may have an impact on income distribution, especially for workers with limited earnings. On the other hand, inflation increases production costs, and therefore, undermines the potential of productivity.

A preliminary economic analysis has to be undertaken before carrying out any statistical or econometric methods. The main difficulties to be dealt with relate to the combination of both academic theories and empirical studies on wages and earnings.

II. Description of Retained Variables

Several statistical methods can help in the confirmation of certain assumptions or relationship. Nowadays, with graphic editors on micro-computers, various scenarios are easily and quickly performed, thus enhancing the accuracy of empirical studies. Simple graph editing contributes to showing the trend of evaluation of explanatory variables compared to the evolution of the explained or dependent variable, here the salary. When analysing the trends the number of retained variables may be modified if the result of the data plotting is not satisfactory.

Apart from graphic editing, the dummy variables are commonly used in building earning functions based on both quantitative and qualitative independent variables. For qualitative variables, once their modalities are defined, the use of dummy variables containing only two figures: 1 & 0, provides a means to characterize each modality. As an example, one of the qualitative variables noted previously, say the level of education, may be classified into three modalities: Primary, Secondary, and Higher Education levels. If the observation relates to the Secondary level, the corresponding dummy variables gives 0 for Primary, 1 for Secondary, 0 for Higher education. The procedure is the same if the observation refers to any of the other modalities.

Econometrics has developed the technique of dummy variables, mainly for processing of qualitative variables, an example is as follows:

A set of six observations:

Primary	Secondary	Higher	Total
1	0	0	1
0	1	0	1
0	1	0	1
0	0	1	1
0	0	1	1
1	0	0	1

If we add the values of the three modalities per observation, we obtain the unit-vector composed of the figure 1. This has an important consequence on the form of the earnings function which can be derived from the first analysis. In fact, one cannot use all modalities in an earnings function if there is an intercept *i.e.* a constant term already in the equation set.

Say SALi = a0 + al*PRi + a2*SCi + a3*HIi

a0 is the constant term

a1, a2 and a3 are respectively the coefficients of Primary (PR),

Secondary (SC) and Higher education (HI) dummy variables. The index i denotes the observation being processed.

Let us write the equation in a vector form; the following relation is obtained:

SAL = X*A; with

SAL 1 1 1 0 0

SAL 2 1 0 1 0

SAL = : 1 : : :

SALi X = 1 : : : A = (a0, a1, a2, a3)

: 1 : : :

SALn 1 : : :

Considering the X matrix, we notice as indicated earlier, that the first column is equal to the sum of the three other variables; therefore, its column is a linear combination of the remaining three columns. So, the X matrix is a singular one: its determinant is zero.

In regression calculus, this is a key point for the validity of the method. Thus to avoid the constraint, we have to drop one of the dummy variables, which will be considered as a reference basis for the other complementary dummy variables.

Hence, the resulting equation will be:

SALi = a1 + a2*SCi + a3*HIi + Ui

Instead of having three explanatory variables, only two are included in the equation. The coefficient of the dropped variable has become the intercept (a1) of the earnings function. The last term Ui is the random error in the regression analysis.

Now, if we consider the two other qualitative variables mentioned in the figure, we may determine several modalities for each, according to data availability and analysis purposes. We shall identify four modalities for type of employment, and three modalities for sector of activity.

Type of employment (TE)	Sector of activity (SA)
—Cadres and managers (TE1)	—Primary sector (SA1)
—Technicians and employees (TE2)	—Secondary sector (SA2)
—Skilled workers (TE3)	—Tertiary sector (SA3)
—Unskilled workers (TE4)	

Finally we get the following set of variables in the econometric analysis of the earnings function:

SA = f (LE, EX, TE, SA, MW, BP)

As previously stated, one must drop one of the dummy variables for each qualitative variable. For the type of employment, we chose unskilled workers as a reference basis; and also the primary sector for the same purpose. Thus, the earnings function comprises seven (7) dummy variables (LE2, LE3, TE1, TE2, TE3, SA2, SA3) and three quantitative variables (EX, MW, BP).

III. Estimates and Validity of Earnings Functions

Econometric methods such as regression analysis, give estimates of the coefficients of the earnings function and also test the validity of the equation. When carrying out regression analysis attention must be paid to the following two problems.

Multicollinearity: this means that two or several explanatory variables are highly correlated. One way of identifying multicollinearity is, after the preliminary economic and social analysis, to compute the correlation matrix which contains all correlation coefficients for each combination of two variables among the entire set of variables. If a correlation coefficient is almost equal to 1, there is no need to retain both variables in the function; one will be sufficient.

Autocorrelation: For various events which occur regularly at short intervals such as salary payments the preceding values of both explanatory variables and dependent variables may have a relative impact on the current value of the explained variable. Whenever that is the case, it is necessary to use the autocorrelation test known as Durbin-Watson test. If autocorrelation exists, one way to correct it, to a certain extent, is to introduce lagged variables. For example, with first order autocorrelation of dependent variables we can have:

SALt = a0 + al*SALt-1 + a2*MWt + a3*BPt

In this function the salary at period t is explained by the salary at period t-1, and by the minimum wage and branch productivity at period t.

Autocorrelation analysis may lead to the study of sophisticated econometrics methods such as ARIMA models (Autogregressive integrated moving average models), which is not the purpose of the present paper.

Presentation and Analysis of Results

'Student' or t-Test

The standard way of displaying econometric results is to give, in addition to the equation, the corresponding values under each coefficient; for the coefficient of determination R2 (R squared); the value of the Durbin Watson test DW; the standard error of estimate (SEE); and the number of observations or time period.

SALi = al + a2*SCi + a3*HIiR2: No:

(ta1) (ta2) (ta3) DW: SEE:

The values in parentheses represent the null hypothesis test for each coefficient. Given the number of observations, one computes the degrees of freedom which are equal to (n-k); n is the number of observations, and k, the number of coefficients:

Example: SALi = 3.4 + 5.2*SCi + 13.2* HIi R2: 0.92 n:30

(5.2) (1.7) (2.8) DW: 1.97 SEE: 18

Analysis

Having chosen a critical point, say 1 per cent, which means 99 per cent probability, the statistical table in this test gives us the critical value corresponding to the degrees of freedom computed.

For the above example, the function has 27 degrees of freedom :n-k = 30 – 3 = 27.

At 1 per cent of critical point, the t distribution gives the critical value: 2.743. Therefore, if a figure in parenthesis is greater than the critical value, the null hypothesis for the relevant coefficient can be rejected. In other words, the corresponding variable has a significant impact on the dependent variable, which is the salary.

Examining the computed student values in the equation given, one may notice that only the coefficient of the variable SC is not significant. Thus secondary education level does not have a significant impact on the level of salary, according to the set of data processed, whereas for primary and higher education levels, the impacts are notable.

R2 expressed the proportion of explained variance according to the explanatory variables. The more R2 approaches 1, the greater the significance. For the function analyzed, 92 per cent of the total variance is explained by the retained variables.

As seen earlier, the Durbin-Watson test is a test of autocorrelation. If the value of DW computed is around 2, then one can conclude there is no autocorrelation of random errors. Otherwise the Durban Watson statistical table gives the values of DL and DU corresponding to Durbin lower and Durbin upper.

If DW < DL there is autocorrelation

DW > DU there is no autocorrelation

DL > DW DU no conclusion can be reached.

The results presented above give 1.97 for the value of the Durbin-Watson, which is almost 2. More precisely, the Durbin-Watson statistical table indicates (for 30 observations at 1 per cent critical point): DL = 1.07 and DU = 1.34. So in our case, DW being greater than DU, we can conclude there is no autocorrelation.

As concerns the Standard error of estimate, which is the last element of the results, it helps in approximately defining an interval for the dependent variable.

If the estimate of SA is 150, the corresponding interval is: SA-SEE = 150 – 18 = 132; and SA + SEE = 150 + 18 = 168.

Thus the acceptable values of the salary estimate should be found within the range 132; 168.

Fisher Test

Apart from the student test or t test, the Fisher test which applies the null hypothesis to all coefficients at the same time, can also be used. This test deals with two parameters: k – 1 and n – k.

k – 1 is the number of explanatory variables; and n – k equals the degrees of freedom.

F (k – 1, n – k) at 1 per cent critical point, gives for k = 3 and n = 30, the derived value 7.63. In n were equal to 28 the value read on the table would be 7.77.

Similar to the student test, if the Fisher value computed is greater than 7.63 we can reject the null hypothesis. Otherwise the set of coefficients is not significantly different from the zero-vector; consequently the earnings function is not appropriate.

One should note that the overall test of coefficients by the Fisher method, does not provide much information on the accuracy of a coefficient for a given explanatory variable. It is the t test which gives a more relevant appreciation for a precise variable. Thus the tests are complementary. Furthermore the Fisher value has a defined link with R2, the coefficient of determination:

$$F = \frac{R2/k-1}{(1-R2)/n-k}$$ F and R2 are used in the analysis of variance

Due to this fixed relation between F and R2, once we have the student values and R2, an appreciation of the validity of the earnings function can be obtained.

IV. Application: Average Earnings in Swaziland

Study of the earnings function is facilitated by available tools such as computer packages using econometric methods. Among these programmes the most well known are SPSS (Statistical Package for Social Sciences); TSP (Time Series Processing); Lotus 123 which is a spreadsheet package. For econometric analysis, the first two packages are more efficient.

However, with Lotus, we do have regression results like: the estimates of coefficients, their standard deviation and the R squared. The use of Lotus is easier than the preceding packages. Moreover graphic editing and modelling can also be efficiently done with this package.

Application to the case of Swaziland gave the following results:

Comparing earnings functions in private and public sectors, we find that for the public sector the field or sector of activity and the type of occupation have a significant impact on average earnings, whereas for the private, only the type of occupation and gender have a significant impact. In the private sector particularly the regression results are not acceptable when we use absolute values of earnings, but when we run regression using the logarithm values of average earnings, then R2 jumps from 0.47 to 0.70. This means that the variations in earnings between categories are large.

For the public sector, using logarithm values of average earnings, R2 improves: .84 as against .72 previously. Therefore one can conclude that earnings inequalities are greater in the private sector than in the public sector.

As far as gender is concerned, this variable has notable impact on earnings in the private sector, but not in the public sector since the coefficient in statistically equal to 0. Thus gender equality is more effective in the public sector than in the private sector.

The following Tables are based on the statistics provided by the Central Statistics Office of Swaziland for the year 1987. The example analyzed shows in importance of appropriate methods for a better understanding of economic and social reality.

Public Sector

Earnings Explained by Sector of Activity and Type of Occupation

(absolute values of earnings)

Regression output:

Constant	–38.5009
Standard error of estim. Y	238.8077
R square	0,716283
Number of Observations	79
Degrees of freedom	70

Coefficient(s) X 338.4078 274.7249 –70.2025 746.7309 980.0541 258.1428 392.9771 184.2080

Stand. devi. coef. 87.46634 77.27050 54.28505 92.27219 92.07238 90.26083 94.09889 92.07238

Students values 3.869 3.555 –1.293 8.093 10.644 2.860 4.176 2.001

Public Sector

Earnings Explained by Sector of Activity, Sex and Type of Occupation

(logarithm values of earnings)

Regression output:

Constant	2.054220
Standard error of estim. Y	0.131568
R square	0.838636
Number of observations	79
Degrees of freedom	70

Coefficient(s) X 0.249385 0.238124 –0.05309 0.703639 0.803653 0.384638 0.470354 0.305817

Stand. devi. coef. 0.048188 0.042571 0.29907 0.050836 0.050726 0.049728 0.051842 0.050726

Student values 5.175 5.594 –1.775 13.841 15.843 7.735 9.073 6.029

Public Sector

Earnings Explained by Sector of Activity and Type of Occupation

(Logarithm value of earnings)

Regression output:

Constant	2.025086
Standard error of estim. Y	0.133548
R square	0.831370
Number of observations	79
Degrees of freedom	71

Coefficient(s)X 0.254953 0.239861 0.709995 0.805925 0.384638 0.474957 0.308089

Stand. devi. coef. 0.048809 0.043200 0.051473 0.051473 0.050476 0.052556 0.051473

Student values 5.223 5.552 13.794 15.657 7.620 9.037 5.985

Private Sector

Earnings Explained by Sector of Activity, Sex and Type of Occupation

(Absolute values of earnings)

Regression output:

Constant	523.0668
Standard error of estim. Y	558.3506
R square	0.471543
Number of observations	104
Degree of freedom	95

Coefficient(s) X −141.567 −166.391 −329.407 1089.222 1155.722 248.0555 530.7221 58.94444

Stand. devi. coef. 150.7619 142.1224 110.1317 186.1169 186.1169 186.1168 199.7046 186.1168

Student values −0.939 −1.171 −2.991 5.852 6.210 1.333 2.658 0.317

Private Sector

Earnings Explained by Sector of Activity, Sex and Type of Occupation

(Logarithm values of earnings)

Regression output:

Constant	2.368733
Standard error of estim. Y	0.207679
R square	0.705187
Number of observations	104
Degree of freedom	95

Coefficient(s) X 0.022407 0.033082 –0.18177 0.766753 0.753617 0.373502 0.502067 0.142033

Stand. devi. coef. 0.056076 0.052862 0.040963 0.069226 0.069226 0.069226 0.074280 0.069226

Student values 0.400 0.626 –4.437 11.076 10.886 5.395 6.759 2.052

Private Sector

Earnings Explained by Sex and Type of Occupation

(Logarithm values of earnings)

Regression output:

Constant	2.390770
Standard error of estim. Y	0.205951
R square	0.703972
Number of observations	104
Degrees of freedom	97

Coefficient(s) X –0.18150 0.766753 0.753617 0.373502 0.502876 0.142033

Stand. devi. coef. 0.040614 0.068650 0.068650 0.068650 0.073619 0.068650

Student values –4.469 11.169 10.978 5.441 6.831 2.069

17

Science, Technology and Large Scale Enterprise Development

John W. Forje

Introduction

There is a virtually no country in the world which has not boarded the technological train which started in the West. It speeds along towards an unknown destination. The carriages are the different countries and peoples. Besides its negative impact on the environment, this situation also threatens the earth's cultural diversity. No one can slow the train down since the engine has no driver.[1]

Cameroon is part of this process; its society is being revolutionized by advances in science and technology. The development of the oil industry in Cameroon opens new avenues for inter-linkages between higher education and industry, but the absence of such linkage between the two bodies has and continues to be an impediment to socioeconomic transformation of the country. The great divide between poverty and affluence lies not in the quantity and quality of natural resources found within the frontiers of a country but in its human resources capability, *i.e.* the know-how and capacity to convert these resources into usable products for the common good.

Today, three major groups of technologies are revolutionizing industry around the world. These are the enabling or frontier technologies—information and communication technologies, biotechnology, and advanced industrial materials—and they are responsible for creating a multitude of new products and services and transforming production methods in almost every sector of the economy.

The structure of the educational curriculum for human resources development in Cameroon has implications for the development of the oil industry and the overall industrial transformation of society.

This paper will examine the inter-relatedness between human resources development and industrialization. The pattern of higher education—industry co-operation and collaboration determines the structure and pattern needed for the economic and industrial development of an emerging industrial country like Cameroon.

Certain recommendations are advanced for a mechanism to create an alliance between higher education and industry and establish a cordial relationship to help forge and enhance the industrialization of the country. These recommendations are based on the premises of certain deficiencies inherent in the country's colonial and post-colonial development. Some of these can be listed as follows:

- national policy for education and human resources training has been articulated and aggregated without due consideration of the policy for exploitation and development of the oil industry and the industrial sector in general;
- the non-existence of a coherent national science and technology policy;
- technological development in the oil industry is constrained due to the lack of highly trained manpower capacity/capability;
- the non-existence of a university-research-industry accord;

- development of the oil industry has not significantly affected or influenced the country's pool for manpower or the quality of its manpower.[2]

Seen within this framework, there is an urgent need for a concerted educational curriculum that inter-marries university education, research and industry; to formulate and implement a concerted science and technology and research and development (R & D) policy; the need for a formal education system to intervene in the training of manpower for the industrial sector, to allocate adequate financial resources for R & D and to promote and encourage technical subjects at an early stage in the educational system.

These postulations as Sanyal *et al* (1990)[3] point out, need to be verified if future educational planning and policy-making is to respond positively to the scientific and technological development needs of the country.

As we know, the scientific and technological needs of the country are many and varied; inadequate human resources development; poor institutional infrastructure and lack of inter-sectoral linkages impair technological advances. These factors mitigate against the economy benefiting immensely from the establishment of the oil industry and in taking advantage of advances in the scientific and technological domain. The patrol chemistry industry is one that opens many possibilities for development since it has multifarious linkages with agricultural and other industrial sectors.

Misconceptions

Since independence many African States have continued with the economic structures developed during the colonial period. This policy approach has had great consequences for the development of the region and Cameroon in particular.

Africa's independence at the early stage was dominated by two misconceptions about technological development in the region. The first myth was that the existence of scientific research institutions was the factor that contributed to economic change. The second focused on the belief that technology was readily available and could be easily obtained through technology transfer arrangements.

The 1962 United Nations Conference on science and technology for the underdeveloped countries asserted that developing countries could 'leap frog across the centuries' by applying or harvesting the technologies already available in the market. These good intentions have failed to materialise due to vested western interests that continue to hinder the transfer of technology to developing countries. The failure of the high hopes of the 1962 UN Conference and other emerging issues led to the 1979 United Nations Conference on Science and Technology for Development (UNCSTD) in Vienna, Austria.

The first misconception contributed to the proliferation of science and technology institutes and research councils in many African countries. Most of these institutions lacked both the legal and financial support necessary to effect the generation of endogenous technologies in the development process. Some of them tried to deal with local problems and come up with technical innovations, but most of these have remained at design or prototype levels. The second assumption, that the technology transfer to Africa continues to be afflicted with numerous problems. In short, the assumption of technology transfer has been and continues to be misleading. In some cases, it led to the massive accumulation of enormous foreign debts due to importation of inappropriate technology and wrong investment strategies—which have often ended as 'white elephant'.

Calestons Juma concludes that the high rate of technological failure has fostered an 'anti-technological' climate in some sections of African society. Technology is seen as the main cause of social problems.

Furthermore, we should also note that the wind of political independence came at the time of the publication of the earliest quantitative studies in the industrialized nations on the role and impact of technological change in economic development and socio-economic transformation. Sad to say, the implications of the studies were not grasped by African nations, hence, science and technology policy continued to be ignored until recently through the Lagos Plan of Action (LPA) and the recommendations of the Conference of African Ministers Responsible for the Application of Science and Technology to Development [CASTAFRICA] I and II.

What is noticeable throughout the continent is the persistent lack of endogenous technological advancement and greater dependency on exogenous technologies. Technological advancement constitute a vital component of economic development and growth.

Africa's economic underdevelopment can be explained through its inheritance of a raw material export policy approach. In addition, there has been few incentives to establish a strong scientific and technological base as a tool for self-reliant development and as a mechanism to enhance participation in international competition. These biases were inherited at independence, and the application of technology still remains peripheral in many African countries.

As stated earlier, only recently have attempts been made in the continent to recognize the role of research, technology and economic transformation as an essential ingredient in human resources development. The creation of Ministries of Scientific Research, Technology and Higher Education, academies of sciences and scientific organisations gives new impetus to the importance attached to the need and generation of an endogenous development attitude.

In some countries, the wind of change is strongly focused on the restructuring of the educational system to reflect the long-term and urgent technological requirements and needs of the country. But much has yet to be done to create the appropriate climate for the integration of infusion of endogenous technological innovations in the mainstream of economic development and growth.

We have also to appreciate the realities that certain development undertakings can hardly rely on endogenous technology alone—in such cases—for example the oil industry—we have no choice but to depend on foreign high-tech currently not available within the country; and in which we lack both skilled manpower capacity and capability, not to mention the necessary infrastructures.

The plethora of problems facing the region calls for a complementary approach and application of technologies—endogenous and exogenous—to remedy the situation and not least, to avoid the development approach of reducing socio-economic complexity to merely technical problems. Socio-economic development and growth and technological advancement and interwoven complexities that must complement not alienate each other in order to attain a better life for all people.

In other words, various factors interact to produce the ultimate results. It is imperative at this juncture to appraise the existing realities that 'recent developments in the industrial and agricultural sectors indicate that the main agent of long-term socio-economic development and growth is not necessarily the relative endowment of land, labour and capital (or factors of production in neo-classical parlance) but the capacity to undertake technological innovation. It can be argued that African development and growth has lagged behind not necessarily because it has been exploited, but because the exploitation has gone hand-in-hand with limited scientific and technological advancement. To provide a more realistic picture of Africa in relation to the changes in the global technological map, it is important to conceive of social systems as non-linear. They change through the introduction of new information and technologies as well as institutional reorganisation. For this reason, the introduction of technological systems into the economy reorganizes it and allows it to change its method of production and patterns of resource utilization'. [Calestous Juma (1989), The Gene Hunters, Zed books, pp. 31-32, London].

The resources exist in Cameroon but the various patterns of resource utilization are still marginalized and not fully exploited because of the prevailing policies on science and technology. To fall back on the views of Calestous Juma, 'African countries' capacity to undertake the required adjustments, depends on the ability of political leadership to grasp the significance of technological change and institutional reorganization.'

A shift in attitude is required. The entire problematique of the oil industry, the generation and utilization of science and technology in the socio-economic transformation of Cameroonian society requires an urgent shift in mentality and attitude towards human resources development, without which the benefits of development can hardly trickle down to the marginalized rural and urban poor. The trickle down approach in this context necessitates linkages between education—research—and the industrial sector to produce an appropriate delivery system to narrow the rural-urban imbalance; the meshing of modern and traditional technologies; openness towards change without destroying the cultural setting of the society in question.

Jacques Hallak states that 'a developing country's capability of participating in the benefits of technological progress, and of contributing actively to technological innovation, depends on a number of educational prerequisites. High-level researchers, engineers, and technicians must be trained and used effectively. It is not because developing countries must look to others to provide technology that they need not produce their own professionals, managers, technicians and skilled workers. Without them, they cannot assess the possible choices, select appropriately, or apply what they choose to their own contexts. Without them, there is no choice but to fall behind forever. A country's engagement in the development and use of new technologies has serious implications in terms of employment and skill requirements'. [Jacques Hallak (1990), Investing in the Future: Setting Educational Priorities in the Developing World, Pergamon Press, IIEP,. pp. 47-48, London.]

In a nutshell, this statement outlines the main problems underscoring Cameroon's technological backwardness and why fundamental changes not only in basic education but also the development of education at all levels is a necessary prerequisite in overcoming the underdevelopment which continues to plague Cameroon. A plea is made in this direction to begin to shift current emphasis on law, the humanities and the social sciences towards more emphasis on science-related disciplines.

Jacques Hallak notes that the experience on the newly industrialized countries also shows that basic scientific education with strong emphasis on technology and engineering must be attained before a country can expect to diffuse or adapt new technologies to local conditions on the shopfloor (1990: 53).

It goes without saying that current day interest in science and technology must be fostered and encouraged in the proper perspective with greater interaction between education, research and the productive or industrial sector. The introduction of science parks could be a way of promoting such a linkage. What is required at this stage is for the country to set out its priorities, establish an efficient management and organisation system and to draw heavily on the successes and failures of other nations in meetings its human resources development requirements.

Socio-Economic and Political Setting

Cameroon has a chequered political history; first as a German colony; later as a United Nations Trust-territory under British and French administration; and finally independence following the reunification of the two dependencies in 1961.

The different stages of the country's political evolution and transition have in different ways contributed to the non-emergence of a coherent and consistent policy strategy for national development. Unity in diversity only touches the tip of the iceberg of the realities of the problems facing the two communities that make up the Republic of Cameroon. Economically, the country is still an agricultural society since more than 80 per cent of the population depends on the primary sector for its livelihood.

The exploration and exportation of oil since 1977 could be visualized as a turning point and blessing given the falling world prices for the country's cash crops—cocoa, coffee, cotton, tea etc. The exploitation of petroleum as a dominant factor in the Cameroonian economy eased the pressure on the cash crop sector to earn much needed foreign exchange and provide govenmental revenue for various activities. For example, between 1977/78 and 1983/84 oil production rose from one-half of one per cent of GDP 14 per cent, while agricultural production fell from 32 per cent to less than 25 per cent of GDP. Such changes require indigenous creation, adaptation and application of modern technology not only in the oil industry, but also in other sectors of industry.[4]

Cultural diversity persisted since more than 200 ethnic groups make up the nation. Administrative diversity is prevalent due to the legacy of British and French structures of administration introduced and practiced in the region. This diversity is also evident in the educational system. As a result, attitudes towards the labour market, public duty and accountability are different between the Anglophone and Francophone communities. Thus the great Anglophone/ Francophone divide remains a major obstacle to overcome. So far, genuine efforts towards total integration, particularly in the field of education have not been made to redress these significance differences. Disparity also exists in the natural resources of the two Cameroons. In addition, in terms of climate and vegetation, Cameroon can be grouped under three ecological zones; forest, semi-arid and savany zones making it a true replica of the African continent in miniature.

Benard Nantang Jue notes that whatever natural endowments the country possesses, it is evident that its economic success, *i.e.* development, reposes on the economic policies of the Government as well as on the vicissitudes of the international market. The importance of the latter factor cannot be overemphasized, as the country which is heavily dependent on trade is vulnerable to fluctuations in the terms of trade in the world market. On the other hand, the former cannot be ignored as they provide the framework for the regime, *i.e.* the political environment within which economic processes are carried out. (Jue, 1990: 4).

Furthermore, the divergences in colonial policy coupled with the disparity in natural resources has had consequences for the pattern of national integration and development in the different parts of the country. Cameroon stands at the cross-roads of the inter-linkages of different factors which if not adequately addressed could lead to maldevelopment in the midst of plenty.

The Evolution and Structure of the Petro-Chemical Industry

Oil exploration dates back to the 1950s through a French exploration company. Société National ELF-Aquitaine (SNEA) and its local subsidiary ELF-SEREPCA. These companies concentrated their activities on on-shore exploration. It was in the early 1960s that they switched their interest to off-shore but still with limited success: the exploration activities of ELF-SEREPCA reached a turning point in 1972 when oil was pumped out in Btika, in the South-West Province, close to the frontier with Nigeria. It took another four years before oil was found in large enough commercial quantities to attract industry. Actual oil production started in 1977 through a joint venture between the Cameroon public Co-operation—Société National des Hydrocarburas (SNH) and the French company ELF-Aquitaine. By 1984, Cameroon was ranked the thirteenth oil-producing nation in the world. The State Oil Refinery, Société Nationale de Raffinage (SONARA) is responsible for the processing of the country's crude oil.[5]

Over the years, the petroleum industry has emerged as one of the strategic enterprises for the country's development. There are plans for extensive expansion of the SONARA petroleum refinery; a complex for the transformation of natural gas into ammonia/urea and methanol; establishment of a complex for further exploitation of natural gas; and construction of facilities for production of plastic materials from petroleum products. (See Sanyal, 1990: 37).

Undoubtedly, the current and envisaged activities of Cameroon's petroleum industry involving exploration; development of infrastructure; production-processing of crude oil; storage facilities for crude oil; storage of petroleum products and distribution of such products, and of course, development of petro-chemicals require skilled manpower currently not available in the country. Shortage of manpower capacity perpetuates dependence on foreigners and other mechanisms for sustaining this vital sector in the process of socio-economic transformation.

A study on the development of the oil industry in Cameroon indicates that the national gas complex would require a staff of

400 by the year 2000; 60 per cent professional and 40 per cent other workers; the administrative sector would require an increase of 25 per cent; the plastic complex will require 117 national professional technicians and four expatriates; the natural gas sector will need 427 and the methanol complex 309 staff members. (Sanyal, 1990: 37).

Given the gross deficiencies in trained scientific and technological human resources and infrastructures in Cameroon coupled with the mismatch between education and employment, dependency on imported technology and manpower capacity will be sharpened. The educational curriculum and methods of manpower planning and training must be given attention to meet challenging current and future needs.

Oil exploration and production in Cameroon is dominated by three foreign transnational enterprises: Production Cameroon (TEPCAM), a subsidiary of TOTAL LFP of France; ELF-SEREPCA, a subsidiary of ELF AQUITANE of France and PECTEN Cameroon, a subsidiary of American Shell. Production output for these companies is as follows:

Cameroon Oil Production

ELF-SEREPCA	65-70 per cent
PECTEN	25-30 per cent
TEMPLAM	10 per cent

The construction of metallic off-shore oil platforms is done under the aegis of the Union Industrie Cameroon (UIC), dominated by private foreign enterprises. Quality control of petro-chemical products is by foreign firms, Baroid and Hydrac. Hydrac is controlled by SNH created by a Presidential decree on 12 March 1980. Petroleum by-product firms in the country are GETRAM and BOSCAM. SNH has over 50 per cent shares in GETRAM. BOSCAM is foreign dominated. The marketing and distribution of petroleum products in the country is undertaken by AGIP, BP, MOBIL, SHELL, TEXACO and TOTAL. A Canadian firm (SAFIMAR) is in the process of developing an integrated network for the distribution of petroleum products. The firms involved have consolidated their activities under an umbrella group, Groupement Professional des Petroliers (GPP) to guard against aggressive inter-firm market competition.

Educational Curriculum

Education contributes to a nation's well-being through its trained manpower who contribute to advances in technology, the development of new products, and manufacturing processes, enhanced skills of the workforce, and the improvement of management practices.

Cameroon is unable to compete effectively in the global market because of the alienation of its educational system from the mainstream of development. The structure and functioning of the country's educational system is not aligned to the urgent and fundamental realities of the society, incorporating the development of domestic technological capability and based on the natural resources endowment of the nation. Its system of education still bears the imprints of colonial legacy, hence the functional existence of two separate systems of education, with eight of Cameroon's ten provinces under the tutelage of French domination, while two anglophone province (North and South West) remain under the influence and practice of the English educational system.

Theoretically, the University of Yaounde and other institutions of higher learning are bilingual. Practically, this is not the case. Higher Education structures on the French system helps in alienating potential anglophone students in furthering their education in engineering and sciences-oriented disciplines.

The absence of a coherent national science and technology policy, and an integrated higher education-industry related approach coupled with the down-grading of the status of engineering and sciences oriented careers in the public service, makes the overall output of scientific and technical graduates low and incompatible with the pressing needs of the country. Too few students are trained in science and technology as compared to the number of graduates in letters, law and social sciences, which are held in high esteem by the administration.[6]

Furthermore, the lack of maths and science teachers in secondary schools contributes to the vicious circle of under-supply and training of manpower potential in engineering and science-related subjects. In their study, Sanyal *et al* (1990: 51) noticed a sharp decline in the output of graduates from the Advanced Technical Colleges (ENSP). The Faculty of Science, Yaounde University which constitutes 25 per cent of the total number of students also suffers from the lack of institutional infrastructures and facilities, making it impossible for the facility to carry out its academic properly and efficiently.

The unemployment rate amongst graduates in general is extremely high, partly due to the current economic crisis; partly to the non-linkage or orientation of manpower needs to the modern economic sector, and not least, due to an inconsistent development strategy adopted over the years. In addition, the rush for white collar jobs and the neglect by the authorities in promoting and encouraging technical subjects from primary to university levels all add to existing deficiencies in S & T and R & D activities in the country.

Unlike other oil producing countries in Africa (Algeria, Libya, Nigeria) neither the university of Yaounde nor any of the university centres and a Advanced Technical Schools operates a department of petroleum studies. The absence of such a department increases the country's dependence on foreign institutions for the training of Cameroonians in the petrochemical industry.

In-House Training

To overcome some of the deficiencies created by an unco-ordinated educational and industrial policy approach, the oil industry has set up its own training system. In 1997 LEF Cameroon opened a centre in Douala for the training of oil personnel. The course or training programme focused on general safety in process operations, first aid, fire fighting, instrumentation, compressor pumps; process control and maintenance etc. The establishment of a refinery training centre by SONARA in 1981 contributed to the decline of ELF training activities. Prior to this (1978-80) SONARA trained the nucleus of Cameroon engineers and technicians in foreign refineries, particularly in France.

SONARA training objectives are motivated and geared towards the needs of the corporation with a desire secure some degree of skilled manpower self-reliance and technology transfer, independence and profitability. It is with these goals in mind that a training department comprising three sectors, administration, logistics, teaching staff and printshop under the leadership of a manager and deputy has been created.

In-house training is a necessity for oil industries to up-date knowledge and skills; to reduce costs, increase output and profits and enhance the progress of the enterprise. So far, the system of training developed by the oil industry at their local refinery training centres is quite impressive and encouraging given the existing realities of the country in the field of education. The flexible approach adopted gives the firms scope to train people in different skills and levels either in Cameroon or in academic institutions abroad.

The seven year-course for an 'agent de maîtrise' training management staff through different departments helps in creating a cadre of skilled technical staff. About 16 types of training course including computer, law, boiler-making, management safety etc. are provided. So far 68 per cent of the employees of producers of crude oil had received in-service training; and 82 per cent of those in the refinery; a lesser proportion, 46 per cent of employees in distribution and stocking had been trained in company. Most of the in-service training is given to skilled workers (67 per cent), but even at higher levels more than half had also received some training either in the form of seminars or missions abroad. (Sanyal 1990: 133).

While such in-house training schemes are essential for the maintenance and progress of the oil industry, it is equally important for the public sector to step up activities particularly in the structures and functioning of the formal educational system to put at the disposal of the private sector the bulk of qualified manpower needed in the secondary sector.

The success of the measures described depends on the vigorous realization of a reform programme. In order to stimulate interest in scientific technical solutions among companies, the economic prerequisites and educational reforms have to be provided, not only with particular industrial sectors but for those dealing with high-tech and innovative enterprises. Some of the measures to be taken require a tripartite corporate approach with:

- strong emphasis on basic science and mathematics in secondary schools; at present these subjects are unsatisfactory;
- the performance of secondary technical schools has to be improved by (a) linking them more closely to industries; (b) making courses more work related; (c) recruiting qualified teaching staff, especially in mathematics and science, with a national incentive system; and (d) transferring, if possible, part of the training to the industries;
- the University of Yaounde should in co-operation with the industry and government, strengthen its scientific and technical branches; a post graduate course in science and technology policy and in technology should be established either at the university or in the Advanced Technical Schools;
- the unco-ordinated relationship between government, education and industry means that policy articulation for the oil and other industrial sectors and for education does not consider changes found desirable in the education system, as the industrial sector develops. It is evident that the general weakness in technical education can only be overcome in the long-term but that does not preclude certain short-term measures being taken now;
- to help develop local technological capability, the country should take advantage of the infrastructure of SONARA or those provided by other industries as well as its willingness to start work on research and development in the oil industry. (See Sanyal 1990: 134-135).

It is thus necessary to develop a tripartite co-operative or comprehensive programmes between the government, university and industry to stimulate and promote the scientific and technological building capacity of the country.

The western industrialized countries attach a pivotal role to technology in sustaining economic gowth or, to put it more succinctly, view technology as a strategic variable for economic progress. Cameroon's aims should not be different, *i.e.* grappling with the paradox of accelerating economic growth, technological change and enhancing competitiveness in a world increasingly characterized as 'globalized'. For a country like Cameroon, the urgent and immediate task assigned to education, S & T and R & D as the 'motors of economic growth', is to enhance economic development and the social welfare of the population; new modalities to ensure success must be developed.

Perhaps some lessons could be drawn from the long-term objectives of the Cameroon refinery training centre to provide a reservoir trained and experienced Cameroonians, to actively participate in the industrialization process of the society. However, the efforts of the oil industry should extend even further, for example, to assist the educational system in devising an option on basic petroleum studies in the formal educational structure of the country.

The absence of a coherent educational policy involving education and industry, coupled with the failure of many secondary schools, absence of more technical secondary colleges and the incapability of Yaounde University to provide students with specific occupational skills helps to explain why a relatively large proportion of workers at technical and professional levels have and continue to go abroad to acquire further training. Table—17.1 shows the type of training considered most useful to supplement formal education.

An opinion survey of workers shows how important it is for the country to link government-university-industry as a means of harnessing and enhancing the manpower potential of the country. According to the survey, 69 per cent of the employees thought that the challenge of technological self-reliance lay in developing university-government-industry relationships and research (56 per cent) while a lesser proportion were concerned with changing methods of instruction (38 per cent), and introducing new subjects (34 per cent).

Table—17.1: Type of Training Considered Useful to Workers

	Type of Training	*Percentage*
1.	Company inservice training	43.3
2.	Company training abroad	23.0
3.	Training in another country abroad	18.0
4.	Training in another company in Cameroon	15.5
5.	Correspondence courses	9.3
6.	Other	8.6
7.	Short term courses in R & D institute abroad	3.3
8.	Short term course in university abroad	3.3
9.	Short term courses in Yaounde University	3.3
10.	Short term courses in R & D institute in Yaounde	8.8

Source: Sanyal *et al* (1990), Development of the oil industry in Cameroon and its implications for education and training: IIEP Research Report No. 79, Table VI. 2, p. 79.

Looking at the type of problems faced with regard to formal education when adjusting to jobs, the same survey found out that opportunities for practical work are lacking in the education system. The survey shows that workers felt their formal education to have been too theoretical (51.0 per cent), gave no information on industry (40.0 per cent) and did not promote creativity (24.0 per cent).

The interviews further showed that the most useful forms of training needed to supplement their formal education were company in-service training either in Cameroon and abroad (43 per cent and 23 per cent respectively), that is the need for practical training was found wanting at secondary and higher education levels.

Resolving Inconsistencies

Regretfully, one observes increasing inconsistencies in Cameroon between thought and action. Findings at the theoretical level are never implemented widely enough among the population. Action must follow words. There is an urgent need to resolve existing contradictions in the higher education-research-industry relationship if the industrial sector is to contribute meaningfully in the development process. To do so, it is necessary to modify the structure of education; and harmonization is necessary even though the survey by Sanyal indicates that only 27 per cent of the workers thought a restructuring of the educational system was necessary. Budgetary allocations should be stepped up, a task which depends not only on the Ministries of National and Higher Education, but also on the government and private sector in general.

The technological and scientific manpower capacity of the country cannot be improved and increased if the present discriminatory relationship between the various disciplines continues to exist and if the poorer groups do not play a greater role in society, *i.e.* if the gaps separating the poor from the privileged group, the disciplines of letters/law from science subjects, and while collar and blue collar activities are not substantially reduced or totally eliminated.

It is not proper to emphasize the role of education as a forge for development while the education system—split up into sub-systems of Anglophone/Francophone patterns with conflicting aims—accentuates the social differences within society. It is thus necessary to strongly advocate as a priority educational harmonization enforcement for the country, so as to improve its potential to develop manpower resources.

There is a need to accelerate the reform of the education structure to ensure greater efficiency, qualitative and quantitative output of human resources and to take advantage of S & T advances in other parts of the world. Currently the educational policy is one that trains an army of dependence, that is, it is creating needs rather than responding to needs; technical education is neglected and there is no priority given to science education. Technical education is the bastion of the industrialization process; hence, the industrialization of an underdeveloped society requires in the first place the establishment of an engineering sector.

The transfer of technology is not enough and indeed not even the main issue, which is that of the development of an indigenous technology base. The establishment of the oil industry is a major breakthrough in the industrialization process. Industrialization is a process of economic development where an increasing proportion of home resources is mobilized to establish a technologically up-to-date and diversified economic structure. Such an economy is characterized by a dynamic industry producing both consumer goods and the means of production. This approach could be called the central development strategy which involves the government, education and the productive sectors. The gaps between these three can not be closed unless there is some way of requiring users of technology to employ the local manpower available.

With regard to training and related issues, a number of aspects should be taken into account:

- an objective and realistic debate as to the kind of society the people want to construct; the role of education in the society and its broad aims and guiding principles;
- reformation of the education system so as to bridge the gap that divorces it from reality, making it a component of the development process, recognition of the links between real life and education for socio-economic transformation;
- a review of the development strategy in practice and a rigorous planning of scientific development to reflect more the acute and urgent needs of society.

As a direct result of the technological gap, the inherent policy inconsistency and low productivity, the country is unable to derive much from its national resources. Cameroon remains a victim of the dictates of foreign investors since the development priorities of the country were wrong to begin with and have contributed to numerous socio-economic problems.

To begin with, the education and scientific systems continue to suffer because of the lack of sufficient investments in infrastructures and human resources development. Unstable forms and inconsistent policy approaches, organisation and financing have destroyed the establishment and continuation of long-term development perspectives. The pace of research as well as the acquisition of equipment is slow, and of course, dependent among other things on the development of external trade—the earnings of foreign exchange.

Because of this negative list one finds at the company level, a growing lack of trust in the scientific and technological potential within the country; hence, Cameroon technological know-how is under-rated. It involves less effort for some companies to find solutions for their technical problems with the use of foreign manpower and technological equipment than to search for development possibilities locally. This is because the educational structure and policy approaches does not establish a linear connection between education, research, innovation, technology and production; and in no way does it in fact encourage the improvement of endogenous technology or the manufacture of domestic products. The dependency of the country on the North means that Cameroon has little freedom of choice. That attitude and relationship has to be reversed. Education and awareness creation is an important instrument in this context. Only an enlightened public can bring out effective and meaningful development.

Changes in Curriculum Structure

Changes in the educational curriculum are necessary and should radically link education on training to the productive sector. Secondly, there is a need to establish a national committee for Education, Research, Technological Progress and Industrial Productivity to thoroughly examine the mechanisms for relating education to industrial activities and for the maximization of the natural resources of the country.

The national body responsible for education, scientific, technical and industrial activities (ESTIA) should establish a system responsible for the realization of activities by means of commissioning, financing and providing motivating stimuli for ESTIA.

A planning and selection system should be charged with the duties of selection and implementation of themes for research and development with intensified involvement of the industrial sector, to encourage eventual emergence of a self-managing self-financing and independent enterprise. This should act as an endogenic force on innovation and as a long-term plan for scientific and technical advancement. Some of these changes could include appropriate mechanisms to establish a government-education-industry relationship; the establishment of petroleum studies in higher education institutions as well as encouraging such studies in secondary/technical colleges, and creating infrastructures to organise and develop R & D activities in the country.

Table—17.2: The Linkage of Science/Technology and the Educational System

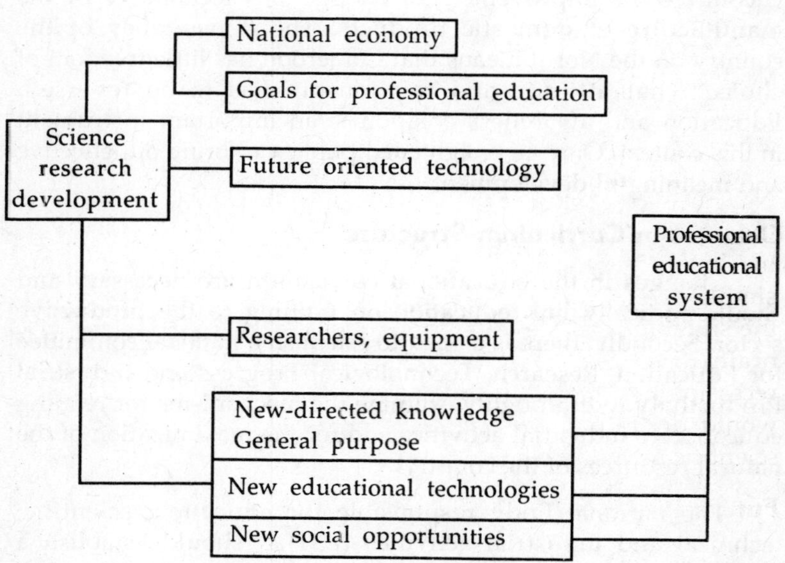

Stimuli

Apart from new educational developments needed to link education to industry, additional incentives are necessary to stimulate interest in the practical use of the results of research activities. One reason for the current undesirable separation between education and industry is Cameroon's failure to devise an effective way to transfer technology from the laboratory to industry. So far, the educational system does not permit/ encourage the growth of such enterprises so as to contribute significantly to the national economy; nor have the policy makers devised effective ways of transferring science and technology (S & T) results into large state enterprises. Consequently, Cameroon can only expect to see a widening of the technology gap with the industrialized nations and a growing lack of vitality in its high and medium technology industries.

The sharp dichotomy between pure and applied science imposed by the educational and development strategy of the country has to retrospect cost the society dearly. For example, most research establishments have had and continue to experience a long period of turmoil which has left its participants exhausted and with no incentives to innovate or link their research results to industrial productivity. The few researchers, scientists and engineers are made to conclude that society does not value their contribution to societal change and development. Not much has happened during the past decade or so to change the fundamental deficiencies in the country's science/technology machinery or education, research and industry relations for the simple reason that resources and a true willingness to change the situation are lacking. Fortunately for the country, a massive brain drain has been averted due to the current economic recession in surrounding countries, but given the opportunity, it would do so and present a serious dilemma for endogenous scientific activities.

Future Prospects

In view of what has been said above, and that the role of education and training in Cameroon has yet to be thoroughly and critically defined and studied, for the moment, the main conclusion is that the educational system of the country is not tailored to meet the needs of the industrial sector. The oil industry in particular has been forced to establish a training scheme to respond to its immediate needs. Conversely, the oil industry has no direct impact on the growth and development of the education system and cannot therefore influence a readjustment in the existing educational curriculum. If the present confusion persists in the country as a result of the growing inconsistency in the educational system, the organisation of research and development and eventual industrial take-off could be delayed. In other words, high-tech industry (like the oil industry) cannot be expected to flourish in Cameroon within the framework of its own manpower resources and capability with the consequence that the country is doomed to be a backwater in the high technology drived 'third industrial revolution'.[7]

Inconsistent educational policy approach and development strategy continue to cripple day-to-day scientific activities and this in turn contributes to the demoralization of engineers, researchers, technicians and scientists. It is true that a high-tech specialized sector like the oil industry cannot just depend on the educational system and output of manpower for its needs; an inhouse training policy is required to meet pressing and specific needs. However, the secondary and higher educational output provides the bastion of needed manpower as the first stage for further specialized training. That is why secondary technical schools, the polytechnics and university science faculties should be strengthened and expanded to provide manpower for the industrial sector.

The bulk of secondary schools, 70.8 per cent (technical stream) in the country are privately owned—the expansion of these institutions is greatly influenced by social demand and the immediate benefits to the owners. That is why the public sector must redouble its efforts to produce young citizens with technical qualifications. The City and Guilds Certificate; the Higher National Diplomas in addition to other technical qualifications should be encouraged. Currently, the higher education system produces few science and technology graduates since it also experiences enormous problems in giving enough practical training. The Advanced Technical Institute, currently an elite establishment as regards resources, comprises only 2 per cent of the total student body. Generally, this institution should provide the bulk of high level technical manpower needed in the oil industry and other high-tech industrial establishments.

The problem that plagues the oil industry in Cameroon is that of paucity of participation—that is, the industrial sector does not participate in the decisions which affect the educational curriculum of the country and that very frequently when they do participate they have no authority to do so, which is the prerequisite for making participation meaningful. The industrial sector remains marginalized and that is why the establishment of a government-education-industry advisory board is necessary to stimulate meaningful co-operation and participation from the private sector.

It is not necessary that new institutions should be established but existing ones restructured to meet challenging needs as well as redress existing problems and constraints.[8]

Perhaps the policy/strategy adopted by Korea in establishing the Korea Technical Qualification Testing Agency could be a good example for the Cameroon oil industry in particular and the industrial sector in general to implement within a Cameroonian environment. It would help establish a roster of people with specialized skills gained in industrial training for employment in certain posts of crucial importance or requiring specialized skills. To start, the infrastructure of SONARA could be used to promote training, research and development in the oil industry.

An integrated approach (industry-education-oriented-training) should constitute the basis of a new education curriculum with the industrial sector playing a fundamental role in the formulation and implementation stages of the policy.

Isolation of scientists, engineers, researchers and technicians from the mainstream and thrust of the development process, and difficulties in commercializing research results due to compartmentalization within and across industries and of the overall industrial strategy of the government, has to be radically addressed before S & T and R & D activities can become the engine of growth for an industrial take-off.

As a late-comer to the industrialization process, many advantages exist for Cameroon to avoid committing the same mistakes as earlier industrial nations. The knowledge and technology exist. How can Cameroon exploit and adapt existing knowledge to its own environmental setting? What is essential in the entire exercise is to initiate a radical domestic reform process. Any form of economic and educational reform must pay due consideration to the need for a domestic order, to a rapidly changing world environment and relationship in the modernization process and co-existence between nations.

In this context, the function of joint ventures—where greater emphasis is placed on learning by doing, *i.e.* linking education to industry, and establishing links between R & D and between S & T & E and the production sector, as opposed to direct technology transfer, as is the case now, should be explored. What is the likelihood for this new approach succeeding in Cameroon? What modalities could ensure success? Above all, why should a new approach not be tried? The challenge facing Cameroon in the next two decades is specific and requires a specific response particularly from the educational sector and physically marginalized areas.

Conclusion

A common thread in this discussion paper is that better S & T performance for better economic performance and socio-economic transformation is closely linked to reforming the education system in Cameroon per se. But a re-evaluation of the education system without radical changes in the development strategy would have little or no impact on the industrialization process. A common opinion is that importing technologies without a sound endogenous capacity and capability will have no impact on S & T and R & D activities in the country—Cameroon will only continue in the backwater of technological dependence and underdevelopment. Therefore, there is the need to revive the education system to guarantee rapid innovation in industry and increase productivity as well as provide basic human needs to the entire population. For this, more radical changes in the education and economic management systems are needed.

Of course, educational reform will produce organisational and managerial changes that cannot presently be anticipated. Human nature being what it is, it is sometimes slow to take up anything new. But these changes in the long run would be of maximum benefit to the country. This is a choice we have to make here and now. Knowledge is being lost.

The failure of much of our development strategy, however, points to several important lessons for the future. What is clear is that experiences elsewhere of education-research-industry co-operation show the need for the collective organisation of interest groups and these can only be successful where public and private as well as individual efforts favour and work towards change. An education system that is innovative is a healthy one. As with the bare foot doctors in China and the Japanese economic miracle, Cameroon can also generate its own economic and industrialization miracle. The potential and possibilities for such a transformation exist within the country. But the process of harmonizing the education system and of linking education to the productive sector requires political will and broad radical change of old attitudes. Above all, it requires an acceptance that this will all take time, that errors will be committed and adaptations will prove necessary.

REFERENCES

1. See Science Policy Vol. 12, No. 3. October 1990, Ministry of Higher Education and Scientific Research, Holland.

2. See Bikas C. Sanyal *et. al.* (1990), *Development of the Oil Industry in Cameroon and its Implications for Education and Training*. IIEP Research Report No. 79, p. 3, UNESCO, Paris.

3. Bikas C. Sanyal (1990) *Technological Development and its Implications for Educational Planning*: IIEP Research Report No. 85, UNESCO—Paris.

4. See Sanyal *et. al.* (1990) *op. cit.* and Benard N. Jua (1990), *Economic Management in Neo-Colonial States*. The Case Study of Cameroon, Leiden, p. 4.

5. For further information see Cameroon Sixth Five Year Economic, Social and Cultural Development Plan 1986-1991, Ministry of Plan and Regional Development, Yaounde, 1986.

6. See R. Sack and E. Stuman (1985), *University Level Manpower Supply and Demand in Cameroon. Status and Prospects,* 30 January 1985, UNESCO, Paris. See also John W. Forje (1988), Science, Technology and Development Policy in Cameroon, Lund-Sweden.

7. See John W. Forje (1989), *Science and Technology in Africa*. Longman London.

8. John W. Forje (1989), *Science, Technology and Development Policy in Cameroon,* Lund-Sweden.

18

Education and the Informal Sector

Boubacar Camara

Analysis of the interrelations between Education and the Informal sector is a crucial step in the overall study of socio-economic development in developing countries, especially in Africa. For more than three decades now, African societies have been experiencing tremendous difficulties related to the educational and economic policies being implemented. Since 1980, with the adjustment programmes progressively extended to most African countries, socio-economic imbalances have been aggravated by the negative effects of both policies and the international environment.

With respect to the present critical situation, there is an urgent need not only to understand the interrelations between Education and Development, but moreover to define innovative development strategy giving due consideration to the informal sector, and to the development of diversified human resources through education.

1. Education: New Contents and Role in Development

The crisis of the education systems in Africa constitutes a basis for the definition of new contents more relevant to development. Research in this area is not specific to the continent. At world-wide level, educational specialists and actors are trying to identify the key elements of a new education which can help in solving problems of human resources development, and global development.

The Jomtien Conference on Education for All held in March 1990, stands as an important event which resulted in the adoption of the World Declaration on Education for All, and the Framework of Action to meet basic learning needs. The concept of basic education including formal, non-formal and informal education activities has been clarified.

For human resources development, in particular in developing countries, basic education is a fundamental development factor. In countries where the illiteracy rate is high and the enrolment ratio low, such as Sahelian countries, basic education for the development of the society is a first priority.

This type of education must provide a minimum of knowledge, know-how better understanding of/and interaction with the environment, for improving education and training and for more efficiency in participating in the socio-economic and cultural development of the society.

Education is not only for modern formal sector of the economy; Education is the common base for all sectors of the economy and society. The interaction of the various types of education and the various sectors of activity appears as a key element in understanding the problematic of development, notably in developing countries. The systematic approach, which is a dynamic and integrated approach, will help in finding the major trends and factors leading to the development of all sectors and to social progress. The informal sector as a significant part of the socio-economic system in Africa will benefit from education and particularly from basic education for all.

2. The Nature and Role of the Informal Sector

In Africa, there is a long tradition of small scale of production activities. Before the colonial period, several activities such as metal work, weaving, leather work, jewellery, commerce of different kinds, have been undertaken in order to meet social demand.

With the event of the colonial era, modern activities were introduced; oil factories, mills, storehouses, manufacturing, public administration, new types of management, etc. These activities which form what is called the modern sector have evolved according to a great number of factors: political, cultural, social and international.

The post colonial period is characterized among other things by the existence of a modern sector which is limited in term of jobs and active population, and a widespread sector called the informal sector covering the majority of the active population, more than 70 per cent in most countries of the continent.

What are the characteristics of the so-called informal sector?

In fact, the informal sector is not so informal as it is called. This sector has its own dynamics, its own laws of evolution. The complexity of the sector due to the diversity of the activities, has led to the use of simplified name: informal sector. One can say, that the informal sector has always existed. It preceded the modern sector. Moreover, the informal sector contributes a great deal in meeting the needs of the population. More than 80 per cent of social demands in many developing countries are dealt with, within the informal sector.

This fact is mainly explained by the competitiveness of the informal sector in various activities: it provides cheap and appropriate goods especially in rural areas and sub-urban areas regrouping more than 80 per cent of the total population in African countries.

The structure of prices in the modern sector is often so rigid that the final price is unaffordable for many people. The informal sector is playing several kinds of roles within the socio-economic system.

A Sector which is Complementary to the Modern Sector

As the modern sector is not sufficiently developed to meet all the needs of society, the informal sector tends to fill the big gap in providing numerous products and services. Processing activities and commercial activities are an important component of the informal sector.

To develop these activities, the informal sector needs inputs from the formal sector, from abroad, but also from its own production. The following diagram shows some indications of the functioning of the informal sector. For example, the output of the mills factory can be used by the informal sector for bakery, poultry and cattle breeding, etc. In some cases the informal sector behaves like a retailer, in other cases, it behaves like a manufacturer—by processing crude material and semi products. The same situation appears with inputs from abroad. Nowadays, many goods from new industrial Asian countries are commercialized through the informal sector: clothes, toys, knives, lamps, etc.

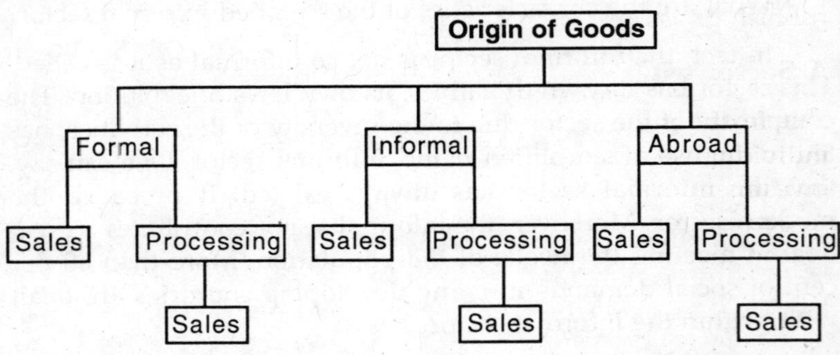

Even if the informal sector has a complementary function to play, it is also competing with the modern sector particularly in the area of clothing. The import of clothes has an impact on local industry. This competition must be taken into account in the search for a solution to the development of both the informal sector and local industry. The competition within the informal sector is another contradiction. The commercialization of ready-made clothes affects to a certain extent the activities of local tailors and dressmakers.

A Sector which is Supporting the Modern Sector

Building activities of the informal sector constitute an important contribution to the development of the modern sector. In West African countries, most houses are built by workers of the informal sector. The comparatively low cost of construction in the informal sector again explains the role played by this sector in meeting construction demand. Very often, for large building, bricklayers of the informal sector are given specific subcontracts. The construction sub-sector is a dynamic component of the informal sector.

The car repair sub-sector represents another crucial area which reflects the support of the informal sector to the modern one. Vehicles of the modern sector are generally maintained and repaired by garages of the informal sector in most West Africans countries. This activity has a great impact on the market for spare parts. There are other activities showing the support of the informal sector to the modern sector such as retail activities rubbish processing, etc.

A Sector with Great Saving Capacities

In the informal sector, according to the types of business, individuals, co-operate in order to save money for short term investment.

This informal banking system has great advantage since it is based on a spirit of solidarity among members of the group. Especially among businesswomen of the informal sector, this type of saving mechanism is used continuously. Even for women at home, a similar system is set up among friends and relatives, and periodically one of several members receive the total amount of money collected. The actual amounts depend on the financial power of members of the group, in some cases millions of francs are dealt with at each meeting.

Obviously, the modern banking system, is interested in recycling the considerable liquidity with the informal sector. Efforts are being made to link the informal saving mechanism and the modern banking system through the opening of accounts. But it is not an easy task. There is a great deal of confidence in this mechanism.

One can say that the informal sector often looked at as a backward sector has huge potential for the overall development of society. The modern sector must learn a lot from it. But to get dynamic and fruitful interaction, the informal sector must be supported in improving skills, managerial capacity and the cultural level of its actors.

3. Education and Training Requirements of the Informal Sector

Paradoxically, in the new informal sector, all levels of education are present. This is due to the negative effects of the socio-economic crisis on modern activities and modern employment. More and more graduates are unemployed and have no choice. Self employment becomes a matter of survival. The graduates or post graduates of the informal sector are undertaking activities which do not require such a high level of education. From a technical point of view, they are prepared to manage their business and to take advantage of several facilities of the modern sector such as credit.

However, for the majority of the informal sector in West African countries, workers are illiterate. The need for basic education is an urgent one. Non-formal education activities in the informal sector are strongly needed, which must be integrated, in productive activities and skills improvement. An example of this is the programme of the International Labour Office which is implementing small scale projects in several countries: Togo, Rwanda, Mali to help tinsmiths, and other manufacturing activities. Education is part of the support programme.

But efforts have to be intensified since there are increasing needs for basic education, in relation to the growing number of primary school and secondary school leavers and to the rural exodus. Education authorities should elaborate appropriate strategies to help the informal sector in the area of relevant non-formal education.

In the process of the follow-up of the World Conference on Education for All, Plans of action on a long term basis are being prepared. It is necessary to give due priority to a sector with such a development potential for society. Moreover, co-operation within the informal sector must be initiated and supported. Available human resources in the informal sector will play a significant role in contributing to the education of other actors of the sector. A new partnership in the informal sector and between the modern and the informal sector should be set up and developed in order to overcome the present crisis that has lasted too long.

19

Education and the Informal Sector: An Overview

S. Seegolam

1. Introduction

The type of education is functionally related to the model and level of development which a country has achieved or aspires to achieve. World experience clearly indicates that countries have been called upon to effect necessary reforms in their educational systems in the light of changing economic conditions. The role of education is today more exhaustive and planners at both the macro and micro levels cannot ignore the fact that any mismatch between the system of education/training and the requirements of the economy can no longer be perpetuated.

In most cases developments in education appear to be linked to the evolution of the formal sectors of the economy while the informal sector seems to have remained an outlet for the educationally unsuccessful. It is a common scene in our country to find these 'educational unfortunates' working either with the local mechanic, the small furniture manufacturer, the village cobbler, the local handicraft centre, the lory helper, the local mental workshop or the farmer. We have long believed that the informal sector can be left to itself and that we should prepare our human resources for the more formal sectors.

However, the complementarity between the informal-formal sectors of an economy and the supportive roles which the informal sector is called upon to play in the process of sustained economic development requires that the labour force employed in these informal sectors should be educated, *i.e.* they should possess the basic numeracy and literacy skills which would allow them to become a more efficient 'labour unit'. The human being becomes a resource when he is educated, trained, developed and allocated to productive work. It is being increasingly recognized that the manpower available to any organisation is the most important resource, albeit the most complicated one. The success or failure of an enterprise will, therefore, depend to a very large extent, on the quality, education and dedication of its labour force.

It is in this light that I propose to discuss the role of education in the development of the informal sector.

2. The Role of Education

In its broadest meaning, education is any process by which an individual gains knowledge or insight, or develops attitudes or skills. Such education can be

(a) *formal, i.e.* acquired through organised study or institution,

or

(b) *informal, i.e.* arise from day-to-day experiences or through relatively unplanned or undirected contacts with communications media.

The function of education is both social and individual. Its social function is to help each individual become a more effective member of society by passing along to him the collective experience of the past and the present. Its individual function is to enable him to lead a more satisfying and productive life by preparing him to handle new experiences successfully. The need to balance these functions, personal and social, poses the perennial issues of education.

The link between education and the level of economic development cannot be ignored. Studies indicate that education accounts for around 20-25 per cent of economic growth. It would also appear that one of the major reasons for the spectacular development of the Newly Industrialized Countries (NICs) has been the high educational level of their labour force.

So far, educational facilities and institutions seem to cater more for the formal sector requirements and there appears to exist very little effort by educational authorities to cater for the needs of the informal sector. Furthermore, it also appears that educational changes have not kept pace with the high rate of economic progress in many countries including Mauritius. This can be explained by the fact that educational systems are slow to change. In Mauritius and Rodrigues, we have nearly 400 schools with some 9,000 teachers. Each school has its own history, its own ethos and expectations, its own strengths and weaknesses. Each teacher has his or her own training, experience, habits and preconceptions.

What happens in a school in principally determined by what happened last year and the year before. Change tends to be gradual and incremental as established custom is not easily broken. Consequently, periods of rapid economic and social changes witness a growing mismatch between the educational system and the needs which it should serve.

The notion that formal schooling may affect what happens in the informal sector has become increasingly attractive to governments (including those in developed countries) faced with stagnant formal sector growth and a dramatic increase in unemployment. Many of the direct interventions in the informal sector—whether by non-governmental organisations (NGOs), government departments or external agencies—touch only a few hundred artisans here and there, and they may only last for a year or two. Basic schooling reaches hundreds of thousands or millions of young people for a longer period.

For this reason, a series of initiatives have been taken in recent years to link schools more directly to aspects of enterprise, to change attitudes and direct youth towards self-employment. Education can also provide the basic numeracy and literacy skills which help to accelerate the process of growth. These include:

(i) Educational policies to promote the informal sector.

(ii) Pre-vocationalization of intermediate and secondary education.

(iii) Diversification of secondary education cycles.

(iv) Introduction of productive work in school curriculum.

Schooling may, therefore, have a positive influence on work in the informal sector by introducing practical subjects into the curriculum or merely by ensuring that school leavers are literate and numerate. On a more negative note, the school system may prepare large numbers for the informal sector by not permitting them to continue their education beyond a certain level. In other words, what is commonly perceived as failure in schools operates as one of the first major orientations to informal sector jobs.

In this light, it would be right to have a brief look at the way of educational objectives have evolved in Mauritius. Historically, the country has placed a great premium on education which has resulted in high social mobility in the population.

More than two centuries ago, education was available to the French settlers but was not available to the slaves and the labour class. Gradually, government took over the responsibility for education and non-fee paying primary education was introduced for a small group of the population as far back as 1815. The emancipated slaves and the labouring class found out quickly that one of the basic pre-conditions for their complete liberalization was education. Thus the Labour Party, formed in 1936, had set itself the objective of free primary education for all.

Furthermore, the fact that in 1947 the right to vote was given to all those who could sign their names in any language increased the thirst for education amongst all workers. Consequently, educational facilities at different levels increased considerably.

The goals of education as stated in all the Development Plans since independence in 1968 lay stress on:

- Equality of opportunity.
- A diversified curriculum.
- Promotion of science, technical and vocational education.
- Improvement in the quality of education.

As from 1977, education was made non-free paying at all levels, including the tertiary level. A White Paper in 1984 gave a new orientation to the education system. Greater emphasis was placed on the review of the curriculum, examination and teaching methodology to adapt them to the changing needs of the country. In this connection, a Master Plan for the development of education was published in 1991. In the same year, education was made compulsory up to the age of 12.

The setting up of the IVTB in 1989 has given a new dimension especially in the fields of vocational and industrial training. IVTB's mission is to promote, co-ordinate and provide training to school leavers as well as to the existing workforce so that they may acquire the new skills needed by a fast-growing economy while at the same time ensuring better job prospects and a higher quality of life for one and all.

As the lead organisation in the training field, IVTB's commitment to the Mauritian nation is to:

- Train for excellence.
- Raise training awareness.
- Enhance quality through training of the workforce at all levels.
- Provide opportunities for flexible training to meet the demands of the economy.
- Optimize the use of human resources.

Such a role conferred on the IVTB augurs well for the evolution of the informal sector in Mauritius.

3. The Link between the Formal and Informal Sectors

Most of the developing countries have traditionally been subject to economic dualism whereby they had a modern sector which was highly productive, capital-intensive and offering high salaries and a traditional sector which covered all sorts of non-wage activities. It was assumed that as industrialization took place, employment in the modern sector would expand and gradually take over that in the traditional sector.

In practice, this has not occurred as the majority of developing countries have experienced a rural exodus and a slow rate of job creation in the modern sector. The fact that rural/urban migrations have continued to increase in most of the countries despite the lack of employment opportunities in the modern sector, has led to the development of further activities in the traditional sector in the urban areas, *e.g.*, handicrafts, small trades, small services, transport, etc., thus intensifying the activities in the traditional sector.

The growth of the informal sector is also explained by the 'linkages' between the formal and informal sectors. For example:

(*a*) Subcontracting of work between the large and small firms (this is common in the Mauritian textile sector).

(*b*) The multiplier impact associated with the growth of the modern sector (*i.e.* the development of the formal sector generates certain spill-overs in the form of small enterprises which are called upon to operate so as to provide support services), and

(*c*) The advantages of the small firms. They are formally more resistant and less affected during periods of declining economic activity. The small firms are more flexible and given the low capital investment, they can more easily adjust to economic changes.

4. Features of the Informal Sector

Although transactions in the informal sector have been taking place since the very early days, the concept of the informal sector has received public attention only lately (ILO mission to Kenya in

1972). In Mauritius, the sector presently comprises around 20,000 enterpreneurs compared to around 2,000 in the formal sector and it is estimated that total employment in this sector should amount to around 135,000 (one-third of the workforce).

The informal sector is not as invisible as it used to be. The sector has been growing and in many countries it is hard to miss it.

It is known that such sectors in most countries have:

- A heterogeneous phenomenon encompassing a wide range of income-generating activities for the poorest of the poor as well as for the relatively well-to-do small entrepreneurs who are only a few steps away from the formal sector.
- Low capital outlay (less than around $5,000) and the low capital labour ratios (less than around $1,000 for one labour unit).

Informal sector workers are mostly self-employed entrepreneurs or are helpers and apprentices. Once these helpers or apprentices attain the skills they either start their own business or they move to the formal sector for more lucrative employment. In this sense, the informal sector trains labour for the formal sector.

The average level of education of the workers in such sectors is improving despite its traditional conception as an outlet for the educationally unsuccessful. People in these sectors may not be literate but they have certain skills.

- Informal sector enterprises tend to have a high 'mortality' rate.
- Many of them are totally dependent on the formal sector, *e.g.* due to the subcontracting nature of works.
- Women play an important role as informal sector producers and traders.
- They have little access to credit, raw materials and new markets. These represent demand side factors pertaining

to the informal sector which should attract appropriate attention while planning and formulating policies.

- Most of their training is done on-the-job and through private training institutions as well as non-profit making training agencies such as religious organisations. Very few informal sector workers have ever attended courses in government institutions.

- The 'cyclical' and the 'structural' informal sector participants. This implies that from a macro perspective, the informal sector acts as a 'sponge' for all those who are temporarily out of work, for example during a period of economic recession. The sector at the same time includes workers who have integrated themselves more permanently following the outcome of an individual decision. A skilled craftsman, for example, may decide that, given his qualifications and his limited access to capital, employment in the informal sector will be more rewarding. In contrast, 'cyclical' participants would typically include employees of modern enterprises who have become redundant and are awaiting new opportunities in the modern sector.

The features of the informal sector and the issues discussed in the first part of the paper tend to have considerable significance especially for policy purposes both for education and training. Such policy should, however, ensure that both the demand and the supply side factors influencing development in the informal sector are considered simultaneously. Furthermore, the need for training and education should not be a foregone conclusion for the sector as training may or may not be an instrument in solving their problems. Education/training for this sector should emphasize self-employment as international trends indicate that we might not provide enough opportunities for wage employment in the modern sector.

Let us hope for the best.

20

Training Issues in the Informal Sector

Pradeep K. Joosery

I. Introduction

This paper attempts a synthesis of some of the key training issues related to the informal sector and analyses their implications for policy-making and planning. The paper is organised as follows: after a brief introduction of the coverage, scope and importance of the informal sector in LDCs, the training issues are addressed. It also provides an insight into the 'small and informal' sector in Mauritius and the importance of training in that sector.

1. Overview of the Informal Sector

The informal sector is present in all countries. Its size and importance, however, varies from country to country and from one phase of development to another. The informal sector started attracting the attention of planners, following ILO's report on the employment strategy mission to Kenya in 1972. The informal sector was viewed as mainly autonomous, providing employment as well as goods and services for low-income groups. The sector was also considered to be economically efficient and capable to generating a surplus to fuel economic growth.

Various attempts have been made to qualify the importance of the informal sector in the overall economy of different countries. Some of the findings have proved very useful to manpower planners and labour market analysts in the formulation of education and training policy. It must, however, be pointed out that such surveys are fraught with problems, both conceptual as well as practical. There is no consensus on the definition of the informal sector. This is partly due to its heterogeneous character. It encompasses a wide spectrum of activities which are not easily captured in statistical surveys. However, different approaches have been used to define and analyse the informal sector based on working arrangements, level of investment, establishment size, commercial features, etc. It covers all sorts of manufacturing activities, construction, trade and commerce, repair and other services. For example, informal sector enterprises are engaged in repairs of vehicles, watches, radios and TV sets; they sell food on the pavements, they transport goods and people, run small shops, and a whole host of their activities.

Some of the common characteristics of informal sector activities are:

- Small units of production, owned and operated by one or a few individuals with little capital.
- Dependence on unpaid family labour.
- Use of labour-intensive techniques of production.
- Ill-equipped and low level of technology.
- Low quality but relatively cheap goods and services.
- Inefficiency in production.

In spite of the above common elements, there are still some important differences in the informal sector from one region to another, or from one country to another.

The increased attention paid to the informal sector is mainly because of its growing capacity to absorb large numbers of workers and new entrants in the labour market who have been unable to find employment in the modern sector. According to some estimates, the informal sector accounts for 20 to 70 per cent of the urban labour force in different developing countries. The contribution of the informal sector to the GDP varies from country to country, but is estimated to be on average about 10 per cent.

In addition to the significant contribution of the informal sector to employment and GDP of developing countries, it is held to be an important generator of skills and human resource development in general. The sluggish growth of the modern sector in most of the African countries and its inability to generate adequate productive employment opportunities have led to increased reliance on the informal sector as an employer of last resort.

2. Training Issues in the Informal Sector

The transfer of knowledge, skills or attitudes, which is organised to prepare people for productive activities, or to change their working behaviour, is commonly referred to as training. Training is some cases also includes extension services and consultancy services. Whichever the form training may take, it is certainly not confined to what takes place in recognized institutions for one to three years to prepare school-leavers for entry in the labour market.

It needs to be brought out at the very outset that a trained workforce constitutes only a necessary and is definitely not a sufficient, condition for economic development. To be effective, training should be accompanied by an enabling business environment. This is borne out more clearly in the case of the informal sector. It is not evident whether training is the single most important intervention that needs to be attempted now in the informal sector.

The informal sector plays a very important role, much more important than the formal and non-formal education system, in skill formation in the developing countries. The most common method of acquiring and imparting skills in the informal sector is through the informal apprenticeship arrangement. This is one of the oldest systems of skill formation. Practically no initial skills or experience are required. Skill formation in this system takes place through exposure of the apprentices to working situations by the master craftsmen. The apprentice must be willing to undergo an extended period of training. Generally, there are no fees charged. In cases where fees are charged, they are usually very low, making the system one of the cheapest ways of acquiring skills, with virtually no expenditure on the part of the government.

In spite of the significant contribution of the informal sector apprenticeship system to skill formation, it must be pointed out that training is only incidental to production. The owner of the garage is interested in taking apprentices only so far as the volume of activities warrants it. This production-training nexus is an essential feature of the informal apprenticeship sector system which needs to be borne in mind, especially when any training policy is being formulated for the informal sector.

Practically all the evidence available points to the fact that the educational level of those working in the informal sector is generally lower than their counterparts in the formal or modern sector. This implies that most of the structured training courses designed for the formal sector, with specified initial educational requirements, are not accessible to the majority of workers in the informal sector. This argues in favour of special training programmes to be designed to meet the needs of the informal sector, keeping in view its specificities. Within the informal sector, there is evidence to the effect that those with basic literacy and numeracy fare better than those who lack these skills. This strengthens the need for basic education to be made universally accessible.

Training may also be inaccessible for informal sector workers because it cannot be afforded. The workers earn very low wages, in many cases just sufficient for their maintenance, and in any case less than those obtained in the formal sector for similar jobs. Even when the fee charged is only nominal the workers may still not be able to afford it as the transportation cost and expenses on instructional supplies may make the training too costly. Besides, informal enterprises may not provide for time off, as in the case of the modern sector.

In addition, as the workers in the informal sector are in many cases remunerated at piece rate, time lost through training involves forgone income, which they can ill-afford. A vicious circle exists: because of low wages trainees cannot afford to follow training courses, which in turn affects their productivity adversely and thus their wages, and so on.

In some cases it has been found that there is a fear on the part of employers that skills acquired through formal training of workers in the informal sector might result in demands for wage increases, a shift of the trained worker to the formal sector, or his loss to competitors. Hence, it is unlikely that such training will be promoted by the employers.

The difficulty which arises in formulating a training policy for the informal sector relates to its financing. With competing claims on the limited resources, it is unlikely a government will provide the necessary financial resources required to promote training for the informal sector. Even in those countries where training is financed through a payroll tax, the training system has been primarily geared to meeting the needs of the modern sector. In those countries where fiscal incentives, in the form of tax rebates, are provided to promote in-service training it has been found again to be biased in favour of large modern firms.

The informal sector has its own ethos which needs to be taken into consideration, especially when formal training methods are used to meet informal sector training needs. Thus, for instance, one of the strengths of informal training is its unstructured and improvised character from which it owes part of its *raison-d'être* and dynamism. This makes it flexible and adaptable to immediate employer needs. It is not certain whether this feature can be maintained through formal training involvement in the informal sector. This explains the scepticism often expressed about the formalization of informal training.

However, it may be argued that the prospects for the informal sector will depend on the degree to which it can be integrated into the whole economy. Through effective subcontracting this integration process has been made possible in some sectors such as clothing and footwear. This should extend to other sectors, through an upgrading of technology used in the informal sector. Training can be an essential element in the promotion of this technological change, although training alone cannot lead to such a goal.

The development of the informal sector and its integration into the overall economy will require more and more marketing and managerial skills (including elements of book-keeping and costing) from the small entrepreneurs. Such courses can be designed and organised by formal institutions. Marketing by word of mouth should give place to a more organised marketing strategy.

Many informal 'backstreet' training centres have sprouted in large cities of most countries. This is partly in response to the lack of training facilities in the formal sector, or the need to be more flexible on entry requirements and the time for conducting the courses. The quality of these courses vary widely. Some cater for national examinations, in academic as well as in a range of practical skills. Instead of having formal training institutions cater for the needs of the informal sector (with the risk that the training programmes may not be appropriate nor the timing suitable), it may be argued that steps should be taken to allow these 'backstreet' training centres to do a better job. This can be envisaged through the setting of standards and the formal training system developing customized training materials for them. In addition, fiscal and financial incentives may be provided by the government for the purchase of training equipment to enable them to improve the quality of training.

Other methods include the extension services, popularly used in the agricultural sector, whereby technical assistance, with a large training component, is provided to the informal sector. In some countries, the release approach to training is used, which involves regular on-the-job apprenticeship training and classroom instruction. This method enables the sector to benefit from formal sector training facilities.

3. Salient Features of the Small and Informal Sector in Mauritius

Apart from the population census which is held normally every ten years in Mauritius, there is no regular source of information on the small establishments and the informal sector.

First a word of caution: statistics available in Mauritius are not presented in the stylized form of formal and informal sectors, separately. In fact, the informal sector is not a well-defined term and has not been surveyed as such. The statistics have been commonly presented in the form of 'large' establishments and 'other than large' establishments and so have been the framework of most of the analyses. Certainly, not all those included under the latter category would qualify for the informal sector as used in the customary sense. This residual character of the implicit definition of the 'informal' sector makes comparison with other countries unfeasible.

Table 20.1 Provides the structure of employment classified into 'large' and 'other than large' establishments for the two census years 1983 and 1990. The statistics for 1990 should be used more as an approximation, pending the publication of official ones.

Employment in 'other than large' establishments in 1983, which was 103.1 thousand accounted for almost 35 per cent of total employment. The relative share remained more or less the same in 1990 with an employment of 150.5 thousand. The average annual growth rate of employment in 'large' establishments, which stood at 5.5 per cent, was matched by an equal growth rate in 'other than large' establishments, during the period 1983 to 1990.

Employment in 'other than large' establishments in agriculture increased significantly from 21.9 thousand, or 28.8 per cent of employment in the sector, in 1983 to 30.4 thousand or 44.5 per cent in 1990. The same increasing trend is observed in the share of Community, Social and Personal services. In contrast, employment in 'other than large' establishments in manufacturing declined from about 30 per cent of total employment in 1983 to 15.6 per cent in 1990.

Additional information on small establishments was obtained following a survey (defined as those establishments employing nine or less persons) undertaken in 1985 by the Central Statistical Office. It was estimated that there were 16,000 small establishments, excluding agricultural concerns as well as other industries without formal establishment like street hawkers,

Table—20.1: Structure of Employment, 1983 and 1990

Major industrial group	*1983*		
	Large establish-ment	*Other than large estab-lishments*	*Total*
1. Agriculture, hunting, forestry fishing and mining	54.1	21.9	76.0
2. Manufacturing	37.6	16.0	53.6
3. Electricity, gas and water	4.2	0.0	4.2
4. Construction	4.5	8.0	12.5
5. Wholesale and retail trade, restaurants and hotels	9.0	25.0	34.0
6. Transport, storage and communication	8.0	12.7	20.7
7. Financing, insurance, real estate and business services	4.7	1.6	6.3
8. Community, social and personal services	63.0	14.9	77.9
9. Activities not elsewhere classified	6.2	3.0	9.2
Total	**191.3**	**103.1**	**294.4**

Table (Contd.)

1	**2**	**3**	**4**
1. Agriculture, hunting, forestry fishing and mining	37.9	30.4	68.3
2. Manufacturing	117.0	21.7	138.7
3. Electricity, gas and water	3.4	0.0	3.4
4. Construction	11.0	19.3	30.3
5. Wholesale and retail trade, restaurants and hotels	16.9	31.5	48.4
6. Transport, storage and communication	12.7	15.5	28.2
7. Financing, insurance, real estate and business services	9.2	2.3	11.5
8. Community, social and personal services	65.8	29.8	95.6
9. Activities not elsewhere classified	4.6	0.0	4.6
Total	**278.5**	**150.5**	**429.0**

Note: Large establishments consist of:

(a) Agricultural establishments comprising:

(i) Sugar cane plantations where 10 hectares or more were harvested;
(ii) Tea plantations of 2 hectares or more;
(iii) All 'flue-cured' tobacco establishment, irrespective of acreage;
(iv) Other agricultural establishments employing at least 10 persons on the day of the survey.

(b) Non-agricultural establishments employing at least 10 persons on the day of the survey. It is to be noted that 'outworkers' are excluded; these are piece-workers who, although employed by an establishment, are working in their own homes on materials provided by the establishment.

(c) All central and local government departments.

---

vendors, etc. Large establishments with 10 or more persons numbered about 1,200. Some of the findings of the survey may be summarized as follows:

(i) Over half of the small establishments were engaged in the wholesale and retail trades. Community, social and personal services accounted for 23 per cent of the small establishments, while manufacturing industries made up another 18 per cent. Most of the rest consisted of restaurants, hotels and business services.

(ii) Nearly 60 per cent of these small establishments were situated in urban areas.

(iii) The number of persons engaged in these small establishments was 47,708—an average of three persons per establishment. More than half of this number were in the wholesale and retail trades, while personal services and the manufacturing industries each accounted for about 20 per cent of persons engaged.

(iv) The majority of persons engaged consisted of working proprietors (*i.e.* 42.3 per cent or 20,134) and unpaid family workers (15.7 per cent or 7,472). Employees numbered 16,090 or 33.8 per cent and apprentices 3,912 or 8.2 per cent.

(v) Of the total 47,708 persons engaged in small establishments 76.5 per cent were males.

(vi) The contribution of the small establishments was estimated at around 7.5 per cent of GDP. The small and informal sector was estimated to contribute about 10 to 11 per cent of GDP in 1985.

4. Training and the 'Small and informal' Sector in Mauritius

In the absence of any empirical analysis of the relationships between training and the 'small and informal' sector in Mauritius, the following broad observations can be made:

- There is only a small number of formal technical and vocational training institutions in the country and their enrolment capacities are very limited. Had it not been for the contribution of the informal apprenticeship arrangement the present shortage of skilled and semi-skilled workers (*e.g.* masons, plumbers, fitters, electricians, mechanics, etc.) would have been more acute. It is not uncommon to find workers trained in the small and informal sector joining formal establishments (in particular in such occupations as masons, welders, mechanics, painters, carpenters, etc.).
- The small and informal sector constitutes the main socio-economic outlet for a large majority of the drop-outs from primary schools, which presently number from 8-10,000 annually. The Industrial and Vocational Training Board (IVTB) has been setting up pre-vocational training centres to cater for the needs mainly of these drop-outs, through an initiation to the various trades in addition to basic literacy and numeracy programmes. The present capacity is, however, limited to about 800 pupils annually and with the entry requirements these centres are not accessible to many of the drop-outs.
- A large number of private training institutions have been set up in the recent years. They are all required, by law, to be registered with the IVTB, to be able to operate.

There are 41 of these centres registered with the IVTB which provide training in management, information technology, engineering, office skills, etc. Many of these institutions provide quality training. Although they do not cater specifically for the training needs of the small and informal sector, they are nevertheless more accessible to workers in that sector on account of their flexible timing and less strict entry requirements. These registered centres can benefit from duty-free facilities on their equipment and loans at concessionary rates from the Development Bank of Mauritius Ltd. The ultimate objective is to raise their standards and improve the quality of training.

- There are various organisations/institutions and training courses which cater specifically for the training of small entrepreneurs *e.g.* the Small Industries Development Organisation, Centre de Promotion de la Petite Entreprise, Mauritius Employers' Federation, the National Handicraft Centre and, at one time, even the University of Mauritius.
- The small and informal sector can also benefit from the facilities available in formal training institutions, especially in those fields in which the practical components is high. The training course in jewellery offered in one of its centres by the IVTB provides an example. In the selection of trainees, almost half the number of training places is provided to the children or close relatives of existing jewellers and the other half to school-leavers. Such a practice is possible especially for those occupations/trades which are transferable from parents to their children. It has been found that, in addition to the skills acquired by the trainees, the course has had an impact on the introduction of modern techniques and technology in the sector, which is characterized by the existence of a large number of small enterprises.
- The success of any training programme, and in particular, one designed for the informal sector depends

to a large extent on the availability of 'qualified' trainers with the right aptitudes who should preferably be of the same nationality as the trainees. The medium of instruction should be the one with which the trainees are most familiar. In Mauritius, however, there is a dearth of local trainers. In any meaningful action is to be taken to train workers in the informal sector, a pool of trainers needs to be trained from amongst the best apprentices or workers in the informal sector. This will have a multiplier effect and will ensure that subsequent training is conducted in a cost-effective way. The training of trainers courses should preferably be run on a part-time basis with a modular approach and using more visual and oral techniques.

5. Conclusion

The informal sector is playing an important role in most developing countries in providing employment to a large number of people, mostly the youth. Its contribution to GDP is not negligible. In addition, it contributes significantly to the generation of skills and human resource development in general. Its development will depend to a large extent on its integration in the overall economy. Training for the sector can be instrumental in this transformation process. However, the design of training courses and the methods to be used need to be adapted to deal with the specificities of the sector.

21

The Importance of Training in the Promotion of the Informal Sector Concept

Michael Axmann
Kanchada Poonpanich

In many developing countries, the urban population and urban labour force have been growing very rapidly in recent years. Much of this additional labour force is not absorbed by the organised medium-and large-scale industry or services sectors, but by means of very small-scale activities labelled as the 'informal sector'. Depending on the definition adopted, this urban informal sector accounts for 40 to 70 per cent of urban employment in several Asian countries (see Sethuraman, 1987).

Despite many attempts to define it, the concept of the informal sector, has remained very elusive (see Muqtada 1988). In a way it implies that there is a concept of a formal sector which is opposed to the informal sector. But how can a line be drawn between them? The informal sector is an extremely heterogeneous phenomenon. It brings together a wide variety of economic activities that tend to be overlooked in statistics, including all sorts of manufacturing activities, construction, trade and commerce, repair and other services. For example, informal sector actors make mattresses, cups and plates; their repair clocks, tuk-tuks and TVs; they write letters, lend money, run shops and restaurants; they transport goods and people on their motor-cycles and so on.

Informal sector activities are more often than not carried out in small units established, owned and operated by one or a few individuals with little capital; these are usually labour-intensive activities which result in low-quality but relatively cheap goods and services. Most informal sector units are not very well-equipped and have little infrastructure. Depending on the legislation, informal sector workers often find it difficult to abide by all the laws, but this does not mean that they are necessarily involved in illegal activities, as some observers say.

Nonetheless, there are probably as many definitions of the informal sector as there are researchers! The informal sector as it will be approached in this paper is a model for explaining economic activities, and specifically those informal sector economic activities that have growth and employment potential. To this end, the following definition is proposed that looks at that part of the informal sector that might eventually 'graduate' into somewhat bigger units, called small enterprises. This paper looks at economic activities, from which employment is derived.

A working definition for the informal sector that focuses on the scale of the operation as well as the manner in which the units function is suggested as follows:

> The "Informal Sector consists of units established, owned and operated by one or a few individuals who neither possess adequate capital, skills and know-how nor do they have free access to them as economic thinking would suggest" (see World Employment Programme, 1987, p. 8).

I. The Informal Sector as an Employment Promotion Concept

Currently there seem to be two different schools of thinking regarding the role of the informal sector in developing economies. The first argues that the informal sector is a symptom of parasitism, underemployment and falling efficiency in resource utilization. According to that paradigm, the only form of healthy employment promotion is to expand labour absorption in the formal sector, which will then gradually cause the informal sector to disappear. The other view is that it is the formal sector that is the parasite, and the informal sector is the market force that tries to correct the distortions, such as distorted prices, interest and wage levels. According to the latter school, efficiency of resources is much higher in the informal sector, and employment promotion should try to reduce and remove all legal and administrative constraints to its development.

Findings of studies undertaken by ARTEP in a number of cities in the region (Bombay, Manila, Bangkok, Karachi, Kuala Lumpur), seem to underline the second view and indicate that in many developing countries, the formation of the informal sector as one important source of employment is, in a way, a reflection of the failure of the development planning and policies pursued. The growth of employment in formal sectors of most Asian economies has not met either forecasts or expectations. In fact, little employment has been created in the formal sector despite its high investment levels and high potential for labour-turnover. Nonetheless, the small-scale sectors of Asian economies have long been neglected, since their employment effects were not visible at first glance.

In many of these countries, the urban drift and an ever-increasing demand for non-agricultural jobs have paved the way for the perception on the informal sector as an employment promotion concept.

Informal sector employment typically has several economic competitive advantages over formal sector employment:

First, it brings about employment with a lower capital investment per worker and this can be seen as making better and more effective use of human resources. This phenomenon can also be interpreted as one way of effecting an adjustment process in the absorption of labour that has not been steered properly by macro-economic policy interventions.

Secondly, employment in the informal sector provides a low cost means for people to earn income through self-employment. This is true for many, if not most of the sub-sectors of the informal sector. ARTEP research in many Asian countries indicates clearly that many parts of the informal sector have the capacity to create, at relatively low cost, subsistence for a self-employed and his or her family.

Thirdly, the small and micro-enterprise concept reflects individual entrepreneurial spirit, and may not only reach more potential small business people, but may also create more indirect employment effects (by creating employment for people who are working for small and micro-entrepreneurs) and even upstream and downstream employment effects (for example by involving other people who may become subcontractors or suppliers, etc.). Hence, the concept of entrepreneurship development for micro-enterprises is likely worth pursuing from an employment promotion aspect as well as from a human resource development point of view.

According to ILO statistics for Indonesia some 2.5 million new jobs must be created for all the new people entering the labour force in the next two years, just in order to keep the unemployment rate at its present level. More than 60 per cent of these new jobs will be in the informal sector. In the Philippines, the situation is similar: 600,000, or 60 per cent of the yet-to-be-created 1 million new jobs in the next two years, will be in the informal sector.

What then does the economic picture in Thailand look like?

Thailand is doing well in economic terms. The target for the annual rate of growth in gross domestic product (GDP) was set at 5 per cent in 1985. The performance surpassed this estimate: in 1987 GDP was 7 per cent, in 1988, nearly 12 per cent and in 1989, 9 per cent; 1990 could bring a solid 8 per cent again. Real per capita income is steadily growing and basic services, such as health come at a price. However, income distribution was worsened in recent years, with the richest 20 per cent of the population having close to 55 per cent of the total income. So far as unemployment is concerned it has turned out to be difficult to raise the productivity of the labour force and their incomes, with resulting problems of surplus labour not being adequately absorbed by the formal labour market. Seasonal unemployment remains high, and may affect up to a third of the labour force in the poorer regions. Open unemployment is at much higher levels since the 70s, now affecting 6 per cent of the labour force. In spite of growing employment opportunities, it has simply not been possible to absorb all the new entrants in the labour market (see Table—21.1 for data on Thailand's population and labour force).

There are again of course brighter spots in this picture. The recent high pace of economic growth in Thailand has increased the purchasing power of a growing middle class and has introduced new possibilities for adoption of new techniques of production. The widening of markets-basically externally-induced growth-has led to increased production, and start-up of new product lines, as well as improved quality of present products. If this is a trend with trickle down effects to the informal sector, will still have to be proven.

Another facet is the very fast multiplication of informal sector activities, especially where the capital requirements for newcomers are modest, such as in petty trading and certain forms of putting-out work. One recent ILO/ARTEP study suggests that expectations of higher incomes may motivate informal sector actors to move out of wage employment into self-employment. Probably the most important reasons lies in the substantial earnings differentials between the small and micro informal sector entrepreneurs and the workers they employ. The number of establishments in Thailand with employees by size and region shows that there is a considerable part of the labour force that finds employment in the micro-enterprises.

A recent study on "Employment and Growth in the Informal Sector of Thailand", undertaken for the ARTEP/ILO/Japan project "Strategic Approaches towards Employment Promotion", tried to gain some insight into the processes of change in the informal sector and the implications for the employment generation capability of this sector.

The study addressed three specific issues:

Table—21.1: Thailand's Population and Labour Force, 1989

Population	55,450,000	people
Labour force	30,423,000	people
Total employed persons	28,734,000	people

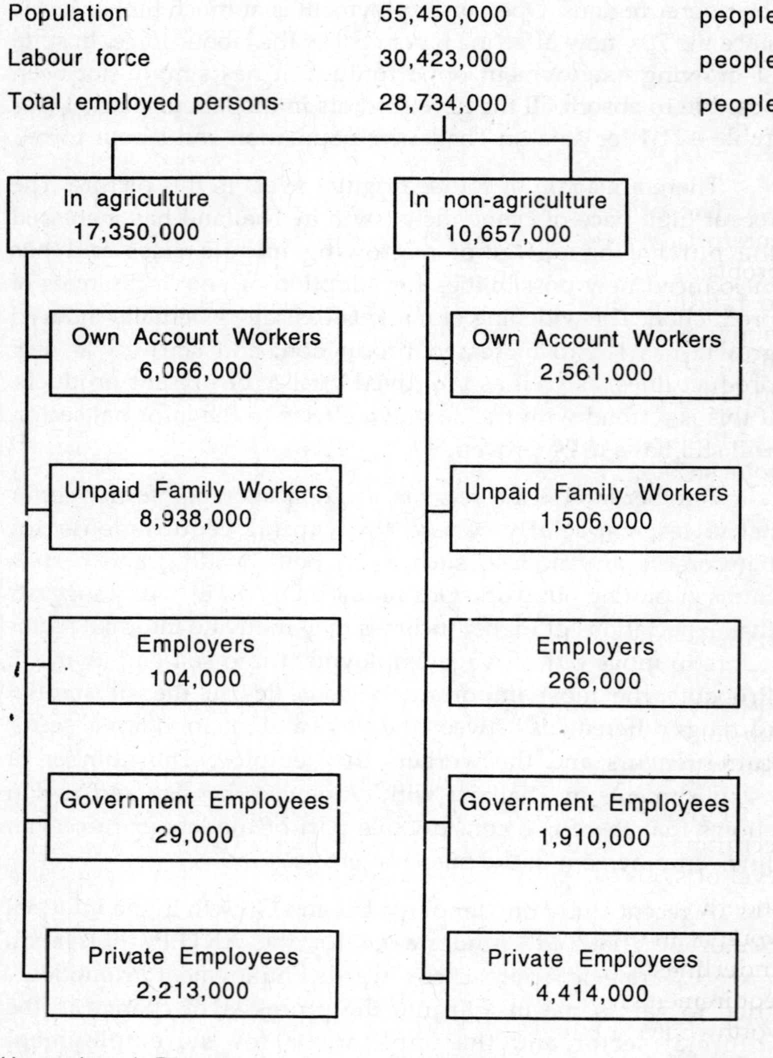

Unemployed Persons	1,689,000	people

Source: Labour Studies and Planning Division, Department of Labour.

(i) Evidence of growth of very small, micro-scale activities into somewhat larger, small-scale enterprises;

(ii) The major factors underlying growth and stagnation in informal sectors activities; and

(iii) The effects of growth in informal sector activities on labour demand, *e.g.* replacement of labour by capital and demand for scale.

The study started from the assumptions that micro-enterprises in the urban informal sector would face a number of problems in different fields, such as training, obtaining access to funding, developing viable marketing strategies, meeting labour and other regulations, recruiting skilled labour, facing high labour turnovers, being confronted with little or no government, and having little market information.

Preliminary findings and recommendations of this study point in the following directions: first, in order to be successful as an informal sector entrepreneur, considerable experience, knowledge and skills are required. The average age at the starting of businesses in the sample was around 35 years.

Secondly, the direction and nature of possible assistance and training probably has to be sector-specific. Skills training could contribute the lessening the vulnerability of the informal sector entrepreneurs and would enable them to do the activities without sub-contracting them to large enterprises. Skill training could also help them to expand their operations to other areas.

Furthermore, some enterprises reported difficulties in recruiting skilled workers (for a more detailed description of the level of skills of informal sector workers see Table—21.2). This underlines the very high proportion of semi-skilled and unskilled workers and the relatively low percentage of skilled workers and underlines the hypothesis that skills training is a definite requirement for the informal sector. Furthermore, it would be worthwhile exploring skills training for workers in formal as well as non-formal training institutions.

According to the study, a good labour market information system also needs to be established for the informal sector. Many entrepreneurs (57 per cent) in the study want the Government to assist in training entrepreneurs for and in the informal sector.

One crucial point given in many of the answers was the either inadequate or completely lacking access to funds for business start-ups. Business failure was almost always due to not being able to generate sufficient funds to take micro-enterprises through the first couple of years.

At the end of this first section it should be stressed again that employment promotion has to go together with human resource development. Thailand is on its way to acquiring the status of a Newly Industrialized Country (NIC) and in looking at the other NICs in the region, namely Korea, Singapore, Hong Kong and Taiwan, it is interesting to see that all those economies have shifted from labour-based lines of production to more skill—and entrepreneurship-intensive technologies.

In the human resource-driven strategy proposed for Thailand in the second part, the competitive edge of the Thai economy would not be low-wage labour as currently, but skill development and entrepreneurship development. These ideas should be kept in mind when thinking about training interventions in the informal sector. These are by no means complete, but are intended to give the policy maker some guidelines on how to design *Training for Work in the Informal Sector* (this phrase was first used by Fluitman, 1989).

II. 'Training for Work' in the Informal Sector

There are many possible interventions for promoting the informal sector. A list might include credit, training, organising people in the informal sector, providing advisory services, giving consultancy services, providing databases on small enterprises, etc.

Addressing possible interventions in the informal sector calls for a policy agenda and a package of policies tackling the above mentioned problems. The intention of this paper is not to set up a policy agenda for the informal sector nor to address all the possible interventions, but rather to focus on possible training interventions in and for the informal sector and derive some implications and recommendations.

Table—21.2: Number of Workers by Skill Level, Activity and Size Group

Activity of enterprises	Number of Enterprises	0-4 workers: Categories of labour — Skilled	Semiskilled	Unskilled	Apprentice
1. Garment	25	1	25	1	4
Per cent		3.2	80.6	3.2	12.9
2. Metal work	25	8	31	14	4
Per cent		14.0	54.4	24.6	7.0
3. Electrics, Electronics	25	0	21	9	0
Assembly and repair per cent			70.0	30.0	
4. Artificial flower making	25	0	6	5	5
Per cent			37.5	31.3	31.3
5. Motor vehicle and motorcycle	25	3	21	4	5
Repair per cent		9.1	63.6	12.1	15.2
6. Jewellery	25	2	47	9	0
Per cent		3.4	81.0	15.5	
Total	150	14	151	42	18
Per cent		6.2	67.1	18.7	8.0

(Contd.)

Table 21.2 (Contd.)

Activity of enterprises	*Number of Enterprises*	*5-20 workers*			
		Categories of labour			
		Skilled	*Semiskilled*	*Unskilled*	*Apprentice*
1. Garment	25	1	165	4	10
Per cent		0.6	91.7	2.2	5.6
2. Metal work	25	3	101	73	44
Per cent		1.4	45.7	33.0	19.9
3. Electric, Electronics	25	5	101	50	13
Assembly and repair per cent		3.0	59.8	29.6	7.7
4. Artificial flower making	25	0	43	70	42
Per cent			27.7	45.2	27.1
5. Motor vehicle and motorcycle	25	98	96	10	68
Repair per cent		36.0	35.5	3.7	25.0
6. Jewellery	25	1	175	111	2
Per cent		0.3	60.6	38.4	0.7
Total	150	108	681	318	179
Per cent		8.4	53.0	24.7	13.9

(Contd.)

Table 21.2 (Contd.)

Activity of enterprises	Number of Enterprises	5-20 workers: Categories of labour			
		Skilled	Semiskilled	Unskilled	Apprentice
1. Garment	50	2	190	5	14
Per cent		0.9	90.0	2.4	6.6
2. Metal work	50	11	132	87	48
Per cent		4.0	69.1	31.3	17.3
3. Electric, Electronics	50	5	122	59	13
Assembly and repair per cent		2.5	61.3	29.6	6.5
4. Artificial flower making	50	0	49	75	47
Per cent		0.0	28.7	43.9	27.5
5. Motor vehicle and motorcycle	50	101	117	14	73
Repair per cent		33.1	38.4	4.6	23.9
6. Jewellery	50	3	175	120	2
Per cent		1.0	58.3	40.0	0.7
Total	300	122	832	360	197
Per cent	100.0	8.1	55.1	23.8	13.0

Source: Labour studies and Planning Division, Department of Labour, Study on 'Employment and Growth in the Informal Sector of Thailand, 1989.

1. Definition of Training

Training comes to mind as a possible area of intervention in the informal sector, but what is meant by 'training for work' in the informal sector? Our definition should be the following:

8 "The term applies to any transfer of knowledge, skills and attitudes which is organised to prepare people for productive activities or to change their working behaviour. It may concern first time learners, and people who have worked all their lives; it covers in-and out-of-school efforts; it encompasses vocational, technical, managerial entrepreneurial, societal and other useful skills. It need not even be called training such as in the case of agricultural extension or business advisory services." (see Fluitman 1989, p. XV).

2. Taking a Sensible Approach

Governments and other development agencies should recall the *elephant in the porcelain shop before deciding to move in*. They should be aware that there is not a single right 'recipe' for all cases, but that there is a need for going about finding solutions in a systematic manner. Especially, it is essential to uncover the factors which explain success or failure in past interventions.

When it comes to government and development agency intervention, we will be looking at macro-level interventions that concern current policies, programmes and training systems as a whole. These interventions should help create an 'enabling environment' and should address the linkages between training and other areas. They should aim at building or strengthening a national framework which allows for transfers of competence to individuals (*i.e.* micro-level interventions) to be as coherent and effective as possible.

The informal sector is no longer as 'invisible' as it used to be. Not only is the informal sector very visible, but much more is known about the informal sector, *e.g.* that most people in the informal sector are self-employed, that they are increasingly well educated, that informal sector enterprises tend to have a high 'mortality rate', and that women play an important role as informal sector producers and traders. Furthermore, it is known that access to credit, raw materials and new markets are typical bottleneck.

If all this is know, what are the solutions and what should the role of government agencies and non-government organisations be in promoting the solutions?

3. Some Innovative Approaches to Informal Sector Training Programmes

This section outlines some of the most relevant new and innovative approaches that have arisen recently in designing education and training programmes for the informal sector. Although not an exhaustive list, these programmes and programme components are intended to give some idea of the many possible interventions that could be considered by policy makers and governments in Asia.

(a) Entrepreneurship Education and Work in the Informal Sector

Some policy makers complain that direct interventions in the informal sector are ineffective; they argue that these interventions touch only a few artisans here and there are only last for a year or so. One way to address this criticism is by introducing entrepreneurship into the educational curricula to help create a more entrepreneurial culture by incubating in students the values and attitudes which promote entrepreneurship. Basic schooling would reach hundreds of thousand of millions of young people for many years.

Formal 'education' and 'entrepreneurship' have so far not been related to one another. No studies or research have been done to determine whether one is essential for the other. Entrepreneurship Education is thus a new field and demands careful analysis and understanding. Perhaps the main reason why little examination has taken place in the area in an academic way is that most individuals in the field are practitioners rather than analysts, interested in the design and implementation of entrepreneurship development programmes rather than in the conceptual and theoretical issues. Some reasons for introducing entrepreneurship into education could be:

(i) to promote and develop values and a culture of entrepreneurship in students;

(ii) to expose students to the business world and allow them to explore entrepreneurial career opportunities thereby leading them to think in terms of self-employment and entrepreneurship as a career option rather than wage employment;

(iii) to develop entrepreneurial competencies, knowledge, skills and motivations of students to enable and motivate them to take up entrepreneurial activity and;

(iv) to establish linkages between small businesses and education, to give a more practical orientation to the educational system.

Entrepreneurial education could be introduced at different levels in the education system. In India, for example, the Entrepreneurship Development Institute of India in Ahmedabad (EDI-I) has introduced entrepreneurship education into the curriculum of vocational schools (11th and 12th level), consisting of courses such as (1) creativity, (2) entrepreneurship and economic development (country examples, entrepreneurial motivation, entrepreneurial competencies, self assessment (SWOT); (3) business opportunities; (4) linking business opportunities with oneself; (5) enterprise management (marketing, finance, production, managing people, working conditions) and (6) support to new entrepreneurs. For other institutes have really looked into entrepreneurship education to develop curricula along those lines. Among the few that have made an attempt at the university level are the Universities Merdeka Malang and the Institute for Technology in Surabaya, both Indonesian.

Introduction of entrepreneurship into the educational system seems to be an important issue in the present situation in Thailand, too, with a high rate of educated unemployed and a lack of clarity of goals among students. Its introduction has the potential to make a contribution to increasing the effectiveness of education itself, a 2nd could result in new ways of leading students to result-oriented learning.

However, Thailand has a serious handicap when it comes to mobilizing human resources for development. Only 29 per cent of the eligible age group is enrolled in secondary education, against 68 per cent in the Philippines, 41 per cent in Indonesia, 54 per cent in Malaysia and 95 per cent in the Republic of Korea. A major bottleneck is the shortage of skilled manpower. The basis for employing the labour force more productivity than in traditional agriculture, is therefore relatively weak right now and underlines how much skills training is needed, not only for the informal sector.

Slow, gradual, and careful introduction, allowing for experimentation and learning from experiences, can make entrepreneurship education successful. Such courses could develop self-confident youth who have a high potential to manage change and uncertainty and to become economically independent. This the contribution of entrepreneurship education to the development of countries like Thailand is limitless.

(b) Re-Orienting Formal Training Institutions

Literature on the planning of training provision in the past focused on an institution-centred framework. Training needs were defined, programmes developed and their relative accomplishments evaluated. Usually the whole process would take part in a training institution, to which trainees would come and receive classroom-based instructions.

Lately the emphasis has shifted: not only donor agencies but also governments and other actors in development have realized that going through informal networks and trying to get away from training in formal training institutions has not only been more effective, but also less expensive.

Especially in the more technical areas and production side, there is a need to combine theory and practical implications to a much higher extent than in formal training schemes. The assumption behind this close linkage is that unless they can see some immediate practical relevance, such as improved production or improved productivity, it will be difficult to persuade trainees to spend much time in a training course.

This makes a lot of sense from the trainees' point of view; it usually, however, requires a lot of rethinking of the training agency's role. If trainers act as management consultants or give technical assistance in improving production, they need to master both skills.

In a traditional mainstream courses of formal training agencies, trainers are usually teaching only a few or specialized courses; but, they are often several steps behind the technology actually used in the formal sector. Interventions in the formal sector require a broader perspective, and here the trainers are likely to be ahead of the technology being used.

In a recent article for the ADG/World Bank Seminar on Vocational and Technical Education and training', C. Dougherty (see Dougherty, 1990) argues that too much of the planning literature focuses on pre-employment training in formal training institutions or skill development centres. He continues by saying that in practice, for most occupations, in-service development of skills is far more important. And, this training is usually not given in formal training institutions, but on the job or in modules outside and without the help of formal training institutions.

This points in two directions. The first is definitely questioning the basis for manpower development planning and practised in may countries, which used to assume that supply and demand would develop independently from each other and that the objective of manpower planning would be to match these divergent components. Perhaps the development of 'trainability' rather than teaching specific skills should be emphasized by manpower development planning.

Secondly, what is true for the formal system of education is even more relevant for the informal sector. Most in-service skill development is demand-driven: skills are developed as needed and only when needed (and, whenever possible, training is done on-the-job).

One major obstacle for informal sector clientele, though, is getting access to non-formalized skill training. One solution could be for formal training institutions to come to the trainee and organize on-the-job, workplace-based 'hands on' instruction.

For example, trucks could be equipped as complete mobile workshops to be used as instructional centres. Through a schedule of regular visits, team members could assist small-scale owners to solve particular problems. Intervention would focus on the problem at hand. In other words, if the trainee does not come to the training institution, then the training institution must come to the trainee.

Universities may not only have a multiplier effect when it comes to education and training, but might provide educational extension services. In Thailand as well as in Indonesia, universities usually have a triple function in doing research, giving lectures as well as doing community development.

A third way of 'informalising' formal training institutions' problems would be to set up groups of informal sector entrepreneurs through local animators or village workers and organise distance training programmes by radio or TV to advise on solving problems.

'Distance training' describes a new way of learning and studying. Courses can be offered by non-traditional means, for example by watching videotapes, attending occasional tutorials and using self-instruction booklets. Distance training students can be supported by extension workers.

Distance training, using university students as extension workers in rural areas, and running mobile workshops are three of many ways how to re-orient formal training institutions and to make them more receptive to the needs of informal sector entrepreneurs. Formal training institutions can play a very active role in training for work in the informal sector, but these institutions have to realise that training for small and micro-entrepreneurs must become more flexible and adaptable to training needs and logistical requirements.

(c) The Group Development Model: A Bottom-up Approach

Training interventions in the informal sector often strongly emphasize the 'self': whether self-training, as in the support to urban informal sector enterprises in French speaking Africa, self-financing, as in the case of the Self-Employed Women's Association (SEWA) in Ahmedabad, India, or self-instruction and self-evaluation in the case of Business Improvement Groups (BIG) that support organisation of self-help support groups for small entrepreneurs. All of these programmes have a few things in common:

1. Learning is largely 'by-doing';
2. Learning is provided on the job in an appropriate work environment;
3. Learning establishes very close links with an effective demand for goods and services; and above all;
4. Education is looked upon as having a double function:
   (a) To become aware of the potential of a group to solve problems which it has analysed itself;
   (b) To acquire the skills which are needed to implement solutions preferably in a group situation.

(d) *Making Services Available: A Top Down Approach*

As contrasted to the group development model, another model of support for the informal sector looks at training as one of several elements in a package of complementary elements that need integration. This package could include elements such as training, finance, marketing, management, technology, improvement, attitudes development and consultancy.

To co-ordination mechanism then tries to make sure that training does not take place in a vacuum, but is integrated into a variety of strategies. It can looked upon as a small business development strategy to be handled by ministries or departments in a specific country.

The specific contribution of training as one of the elements in a package depends a good deal on which other institutions are involved. For example, training can help people to get credit when it is used as a screen for loan applicants after successfully completing a course in bookkeeping or costing.

Table—21.3: Selected Training Agencies for Small Entrepreneurship Development

Institute	*CDG*	*DIP*	*NISD*
Programme	SED	EDP	Entrepreneurship Training Course
Starting date	1987	1980	1984
Organisation	non-governmental	governmental	governmental
Objectives:	- to develop technical training center - to develop small entrepreneurship - to generate more employment	- to develop small and medium industries by creating new - entrepreneurs and strengthening the capability of existing entrepreneurs	- to promote small business - to reduce unemployment
Target group:	TOT - vocational instructors Local businessmen and entrepreneurs TPE - student and graduage UTC (rural potential entrepreneurs)	- potential entrepreneur - existing entrepreneur (*i.e.* owner of medium and small enterprise)	- educated unemployed - those completed NISD's training course
Location of training course:	Udon Thani Province	provinces	Bangkok
Training methods	PCW Lectures & Learning by doing	Lecture-oriented	Lecture-oriented

(Contd.)

Table—21.3 (Contd.)

Institute	*CDG*	*DIP*	*NISD*
Training content:	- pre-training (only for TPE) - marketing - how to set up own business - how to manage own workshop - how to train and guide apprentices - (TPE): plus project writing) - assessment (only for TPE) - post-training (only for TPE)	- entrepreneurial spirits and characteristics - marketing - production management - finance - feasibility study - firm registration, factory Laws, Labour laws, government services	- business administration - management - entrepreneurship - finance and bookkeeping - marketing - selling - location - advertisement - tax law and business law - field trip
Instructor	TOT - Thai experts on small entrepreneurship TPE - those completed TOT	university lecturers successful businessmen government officials	professionals experienced businessmen university lecturers
Training materials:	prepared by CDG in collaboration with STOU	prepared by each instructor	prepared by each instructor
Training fees:	free of charge	free of charge except 3-5,000 Baht for meals	free of charge except 200 Baht for refreshment
Training duration	TOT - 4 weeks TPE - 6 weeks	3 weeks	60 hours
Number of trainees	TOT - 30 - 35 persons TPE - 30 - 35 persons	30 - 35 persons	20 - 25 persons
Extended activity after training	non available	EDP club assessment run by DIP	annual evaluation run by NISD

Many studies have recommended that government agencies set up a support system for existing and potential micro enterprises. However, the role of the governments should always be indirect and basically concerned with providing an 'enabling environment' and providing material support as appropriate.

III. Sampling of Training Programmes for Small Entrepreneurship Development in Thailand

The development of small entrepreneurship in Thailand is in the 1980s recognised as the key to reducing the problems of unemployment and underemployment in Thailand. Many governmental and non-governmental institutions have organised training programmes for skills development: for instances, the Development of People's Organisation Project run by the Community Development Department the Vocational Rehabilitation Programme run by the Department of Public Welfare, the Occupational and Income Programme run by the Office of Accelerated Rural Development, the Pra Dabot Technical Training Programme and the Vocational Training Programme promoted by their Majesties the King and the Queen.

A common objective of these programmes is to promote income-generating activities among the rural poor and disadvantaged persons. The main component of these programmes is skills training. Some provide credit, material and equipment supply to the participants, but none offer entrepreneurship training.

There are, however, a few agencies which have launched package programmes to stimulate and encourage the establishment of small-scale industries: Among others, the training programmes run by the Department of Industrial Promotion (DIP), the National Institute for Skill Development (NISD) and the Carl Duisberg Gesellschaft (CDG).

These merit close attention because all share the same objective: to provide not only vocational skills but also technical and, partly, financial assistance to unemployed people for existing entrepreneurs for establishing or expanding small enterprises. In this section objectives, target groups, training approaches as well as constraints and problems of these programmes will be illustrated (see Table—21.3).

1. DIP and its Entrepreneurship Development Programme

In 1980, an Entrepreneurship Development Programme (EDP) was set up by the Department of Industrial Promotion as part of the Department's policy to develop small and medium industries in Thailand and to accelerate industrial decentralization to the provincial areas. The EDP was launched as a package programme to stimulate and encourage the establishment of small scale industry and provide assistance for the creation of new enterprises. This programme is divided into two categories: *(a)* creating new entrepreneurs; and *(b)* strengthening the capability of existing entrepreneurs.

The EDP promotes the development of entrepreneurs in rural areas and consists of the following phases: *(a)* selection of a potential investment area; *(b)* a techno-economic survey in the selected area in terms of existing enterprises; *(c)* an advertising campaign to attract potential local entrepreneurs to a symposium and where the concept and objectives of the EDP are presented and discussed; *(d)* the identification of potential and existing entrepreneurs who are interested; *(e)* design of a training programme appropriate to the needs of the target group; and *(f)* provision of follow-up and consultancy services in the areas of management, marketing, production, finance, technology and a project proposal for loan application.

The training approach is lecture-oriented together with a case study, group work and field trip. Each training course lasts about three weeks for 30-35 trainees who are required to pay for their meals themselves, while registration fees and instruction materials are provided free of charge. The training course comprises four packages: *(a)* entrepreneurial spirit and characteristics; *(b)* business administration (marketing analysis, policy and planning, production management, finance, and study tour; *(c)* feasibility study; and *(d)* how to set up your own business (firm registration, factory laws, labour laws, government services). Training materials and instruction medias are designed and prepared by trainers who are mostly university lecturers, successful business people and some government officials.

The EDP has conducted twenty courses, offering two courses per year. The trained people number about 599 from 11 provinces in all regions of Thailand. The early training courses were financed by Technonet Asia and UNDP. At present the Ministry of Industry takes responsibility for a major part of the total budget.

After training, entrepreneurs are grouped together to establish so-called 'EDP clubs' or entrepreneur forums for the purpose of exchanging business ideas, helping each other to solve business problems and to survey the market, and developing inter-trade relationship among group members. The forum meetings are held monthly in various provinces. Besides the above activities, the group also visits some modernized factories that have well organised systems or are capable of making use of other DIP services ranging from personal consultations, technical extension to financial support (through the Small Industries Finance Office--SIFO).

After the training, evaluation is done by looking into economic variables such as increased investment and increased employment; for example 800 million Baht have been generated and 2,000 people have become self-employed in the areas where the courses were conducted.

2. NISD and its Entrepreneurship Training Course

The National Institute for Skill Development (NISD) was established within the Department of Labour in 1969. The Objective was to improve the skill development by promoting standards of training and expanding training activities so that youths who enter the labour force would have more skills required by industries. The NISD has played a major role in skill promotion activities for industry, including the introduction and preparation of a National Trade Standard and Trade Test as required for upgrading and certification, the training of instructors and the development of curriculum and training aids. NISD has run various training courses which are relevant to employment needs, for example: pre-employment training, upgrading training, non-technical training, foreman training instructor training, training of officer courses and promotion of in-plant training.

Recognizing rising unemployment rates, especially for the educated unemployed, NISD initiated in 1984 a training project in small business promotion. The objective is: *(i)* to enable unemployed people to obtain knowledge and skills in order to become a small entrepreneur; *(ii)* to enable people with vocational skills in various fields to initiate or expand their small enterprises. An ultimate goal is to reduce the problem of unemployment and promote employment generation.

The entrepreneurship training course is offered to two target groups: those who have no job, but have completed medium and high levels of education and are willing to work in small business; and those who have completed NISD's training courses and started their business, but still lack business knowledge. Four training courses are offered for each fiscal year are each course has about 20-25 persons and is free of charge except for 200 Baht for refreshment. The course consists of 60 hours in class, offering lectures in the following subjects:

- basic knowledge of business administration;
- principle of management;
- entrepreneurship;
- finance and bookkeeping;
- marketing;
- selling;
- location;
- advertisement;
- tax law and business law;
- management; and
- study tour.

Moreover, trainees have a chance to practice project writing and to analyse the feasibility of their own projects.

The training methods comprise lectures, discussions, role playing, case studies, workshop, drills and project formulation.

The instructors are experienced businessmen from both the private and public sectors, and some are university lectures.

NISD joins with the Employment Service Division in screening, interviewing and selecting trainees. A major criteria is that trainees should be ready to run their own business.

NISD has so far arranged 24 training courses. There are 648 trainees and 533 passed the training. The age group addressed varied between 18 and 45 years. About 80 per cent of the participants were men, 20 per cent women. The venue of training is, however, in Bangkok. That means that so far only urban dwellers have the opportunity to participate in the courses. The training course is planned to be extended to the NISD's 7 regional centres situated in all regions with the objective of providing more training opportunities to potential rural entrepreneurs.

At the end of each training course, an evaluation is held through questionnaires concerning the kind of training, the topics and the time that they are dealt with, as well as the trainers and the approaches used. The results of evaluation indicate that a majority of the participants are satisfied with the topics covered in the courses. Still, about 40 per cent of the participants suggest that other subjects such as tax rates for various businesses, characteristics of leadership, public speaking, negotiating skills, procedures with bank and loan approval and sources of business information be included in the courses. Some participants suggest to extend the time spent on bookkeeping, budgeting, selling, business and tax laws. An extension of the period of the training course from two to six weeks has also been proposed. Other suggestions include an improvement in instruction methods and documents.

Furthermore, NISD usually runs a follow-up to get in touch with the participants after six months. About 200 people answered the NISD's letter explaining the reasons why they did not start a business. The problems are due to inadequate financial support, and the lack of the right location and the right production techniques and skills.

Through both evaluation and follow-up, NISD learns a number of constraints and problems of the programme. One constraint is that the instructors come from various firms and educational institutes and vary in experience of educational techniques and skills. At present, the NISD plans to organise a training of trainers course for NISD staff to prepare its own staff development. A second problem is that so far NISD has not set up other support services to the trained persons, such as facilitating access to credit, providing follow-up services for existing entrepreneurs, making information available or providing advisory services. Another constraint concerns a better technique for participants selection.

At present NISD is collaborating with the ILO/Japan project to overcome these difficulties and to improve the entrepreneurship development package. A more comprehensive curriculum will be developed and a training of trainer course will be organised. It is also planned to set up entrepreneurship development programmes in the different Regional Institutes for Skill Development.

3. CDG and the Small Entrepreneurship Development Project

Carl Duisberg Gesellschaft (CDG) is a German non-governmental organisation attached to the Asian Institute of Technology in Bangkok. In 1988 it set up a package programme for 'Small Entrepreneurship Development' (SED) in Udonthani Province through co-operation with the Department of Vocational Education. The overall goals of the project are to: *(i)* contribute to small industrial development in the provinces by generating and supporting on a self-help basis small entrepreneurs; *(ii)* create more employment in the provinces in order to slow down the migration and technical brain drain from provincial areas to the cities and especially the capital.

To achieve these goals, CDG selects the Udon Thani Technical College (UTC) as a focal point of small entrepreneurship development among potential students/apprentices, graduates and vocational teachers and trainers in collaboration with local businessmen and industrialists. It also forms a core group of local businessmen and entrepreneurs and vocational teachers to be trainers and develops curriculum and training material to spur entrepreneurship development.

At the end of each training course trained persons can apply for further expert advice and financial assistance on loan basis from CDG in setting up and manage workshops on a single and/or co-operative basis in their respective trades.

Apart from the training programme, CDG collaborates with the UTC in training apprentices/students of UTC in practical aspects after they have received basic training and guidance at the college first. Through an application of such a mixed dual vocational system CDG hopes to develop the UTC's capacity to increase its students' intake and related output of graduates who are not only technically fit—in theory and practice—but also commercially prepared to set up their own workshop and join the growing community of small entrepreneurs in the province.

The CDG Training programme comprises two training courses, the Training of trainers (TOT)—30-35 persons for each course, and the Training of Potential Entrepreneurs (TPE)—30-35 persons for each course. The training method used in the Project Casework-Based (PCW) which is a blend of mainly three types of active learning methods: *(i)* the prospective project method, its dominant attribute; *(ii)* the basically retrospective case method; and *(iii)* the interactive group work. This training approach is different from the conventional type of lecture-centred seminar or training in that PCW is action-oriented.

Its key principles are 'Learning by Doing' and the 'Role of the Intervenor', through realistic project thinking and acting. Its strong future and charge-orientation together with pre-structure tasks, like a case, for group work are to generate sufficient motivation and pressure to build together on viable solutions under pressure of time. Training curriculum and materials are designed in accordance with the training needs of the local people and are prepared by the CDG's officials with the assistance of educational technology specialists of the Sukhothai Thammathirat Open University.

The training courses for TOT (4 weeks) and PET (6 weeks) consist of 4 packages: marketing analysis, how to set up their own business, how to manage their own workshop, and how to train their workshop apprentices. Before and after each training course, for TPE pre-training, assessment, and post-training which concentrate mainly on follow-up of loan applications.

These are not the only programmes currently being run in Thailand. These case studies present a selection of the ones that are better known. Among other programmes in Thailand the ones of CARE, the Population Development Association (PDA), and the Department of Non-Formal Education should be mentioned. Nonetheless, many more training programmes need to be developed to address underemployment and unemployment effectively and that is true not only for Thailand.

In developing training for work programmes, policy makers might want to refer to an analytical tool to compare training design for the informal and formal sector. Table—21.3 gives profiles of training for work in both sectors and looks at aims and objectives, organisation and management and at characteristics of trainees and the training.

NOTES

The authors of this paper are staff members of the DOL/ ILO-ARTEP/Japan project "Strategic Approaches towards Employment Promotion" in Bangkok. ARTEP is the Asian Regional Team for Employment Promotion of the ILO. The basic goal of this project is the formulation of practical suggestions to the Government of Thailand, Department of Labour, through the design and planning of effective programme packages for employment creation, verified by means of pilot projects and based on investigative studies.

REFERENCES

1. Setheraman, S.V., *The Informal Sector: A Review of Evidence from Selected Asian Countries*, Geneva, ILO, 1988.
2. Muqtada, M. (ed.), *The Elusive Target: An Evaluation of Target-Group Approaches to Employment Creation in Rural Asia*, Geneva, ILO, 1989.

3. World Employment Programme (WEP), *Informal Sector and Urban Employment—A Progress Report on Research and Practical Activities.* Geneva, ILO/WEP, 1987.

4. Fluitman, F. (ed.), *Training for Work in the Formal Sector,* Geneva, ILO, 1987.

5. Dougherty, C. Education and Skill Development: Planning Issues, (working paper) presented at: Asian Development Bank/World Bank Seminar on Vocational and Technical Education and Training, Manila, January 22-27, 1990.

22

Human Resources Development for the Informal Sector

Henning Eriksen

Links between the educational world and the informal sector of the world of work are not too obvious. In order to be able to get a clearer picture of these links, it is first of all necessary to have a rough idea of what actually is the informal sector, and who are the workers in it.

Definitions and General Characteristics

At a conceptual level, it can be said that *economic activities* which are not officially regulated and which operate outside the intensive system offered by the state and its institutions belong to the informal sector.

At an empirical level, we are often referring to *enterprises* which employ less than 5 or 10 persons.

A typical pattern of the employment available is the following: low wages, inadequate job security, absence of official protection and trade union organisation, non-coverage by social security systems and minimal wage legislation. In short, no minimum labour standards.

Its enterprises can be characterized by their reliance on indigenous resources, family ownership, small-scale operation, labour-intensive and adapted technology, and skills acquired outside the small educational and training systems. The last point is vitally important. This means that the huge amounts of money and effort put into national education and training institutions, are basically not catering to the needs of what is often a majority of the working population. For example, in the early 80s, half of the total employment of Bangkok and Metro Manila belonged to the informal sector, 55 per cent in Calcutta, 60 per cent in Madras and 65 per cent or more in Dakar and Karachi. As most modern and formal sector enterprises are found in major cities, figures for total national economies will probably be even higher.

Talking about the informal sector in very general terms might of course be slightly misleading. It is a different thing in a rural and in an urban context, and it might very well vary in different national contexts. Even so, some general characteristics do exist.

Here in Bangkok for example, it has been found, comparising the formal and informal sector, that there is a tendency for informal sector *workers* to be mostly female, outside the primary working age and/or without completed primary education. And contrary to a common belief, it was found that the informal sector does *not* consist mainly of recent migrants to Bangkok. Almost 70 per cent of the workers had stayed more than 20 years in the city.

Generally, *earnings* are higher in the formal sector but, for instance, the self-employed had on average higher incomes than blue collar workers of the formal sector. And—most importantly—the potential for future increases in income is considerable, especially among the self-employed.

Despite the often poor *working conditions* are extremely long working hours which several groups in the informal sector suffer, quite a lot of them prefer their present employment. This of course can also be seen as a mere reflection of the fact that their informal livelihood is the only one available to them.

Adapted Training

What kind of training then suits the needs of informal sector workers? As these people are working already, it is preferable to place emphasis on retaining and upgrading. As the trainee cannot afford longer training periods spent away from the working place, it must be on-the-job, workplace-based and typically hands-on training. People will be highly motivated for short term practice-based training where they can see an immediate outcome, in contrast to longer theory-based training. The trainer will often be a practitioner himself and coming from the same community.

The Virtues of Informal Sector Training

In this connection it should be duly noted, that these features do not belong to some future hypothetical training system, but the features of the current training of a large number of people and, equally important of a relatively successful training system. In terms of cost-effectiveness, not very many formal training systems can compare with this apprentice-based form of training.

A recent World Bank Study of public pre-employment vocational education and training substantiates this. This study claims that training systems are often too large, poorly financed, inflexible and of low quality. Educational and training systems in developing countries were here found to be effective when they were allowed to do the job they do best—providing the *complementary* skills needed to raise productivity. Supporting the employability of specific weaker groups is another worthwhile task; for instance pre-employment vocational training in traditional (usually commercial and secretarial) skills has been found to increase women's access to wage employment.

Already at this stage then, we are able to draw a *conclusion* saying, that one training strategy—and definitely not the worst one—is *not* to interfere with the training provided through the informal sector. This means that, one, we should accept and even develop the huge potential of informal sector training, and two, in addition to that, strengthen our formal training systems via the adoption of some of the best features of informal sector training.

Recommended Action

As a general rule, try to link curriculum development of vocational training to the job functions actually performed, and avoid building large training institutions isolated from the enterprises and people who they are supposed to serve. It should be added that this is attempted in many developed countries with large and with what is considered well-functioning vocational training systems. But even in such circumstances it must be considered extremely ambitious, because planning future vocational training and implementing the plans usually takes a lot longer than changing existing jobs or introducing new technology in companies. Instead, certain specific measures can be taken, such as:

- bring in more teachers who are still active in existing manufacturing and service jobs,
- make advisory boards and even management of training institutions tripartite in nature.

This can be achieved by putting employers and workers on the boards of institutions.

- make courses short and practical in nature. A week or two providing skills through 'guided doing', perhaps from a mobile workshop, is a lot easier to plan and carry out than the management of big buildings with expensive equipment and long training periods,
- enrol employer nominees before everybody else and enrol untrained employees, *i.e.* wage earners and self-employed before unemployed. This might sound less acceptable to some because of its social implications, but remember that the overall purpose is to maximise returns of resources invested and raise productivity, which in turn will be of general value to everybody.
- place school drop-outs as trainees of master craftsmen by providing incentives such as equipment to the master craftsmen,
- make training systems performance-driven. Try to link the allocation of funds to the performance demonstrated.

This can be done through the establishment of criteria according to which funds are disbursed. Pay the institution in accordance with the number of trainees successfully placed in jobs or who set up successful enterprises after training.

- introduce separate schooling for working children. An example of this is UCEP (under-privileged children's education programme) in Bangladesh and Nepal.

Familiarization with Self-Employment

Before turning attention to the specific training needed for specific types of employment in the informal sector, there is an important function performed by the formal educational system to be noted. Not only in developing countries, but also in highly industrialized ones, it is being realised that stagnating economic trends can be reversed and job creation can be increased through among other things, familiarization at all levels in the educational system of working life as self-employed or as entrepreneur. You can only choose an option which is known to you.

Young people in primary school may be made familiar with employment prospects, working conditions, common technology and specific entrepreneurial skills needed in the informal sector. Development of feasible curricula in primary, secondary and higher levels of education, particularly in rural schools which contain skills of self-employment and entrepreneurship, is necessary.

There is a clear economic and social rationale behind this. As pointed out already, the earnings of some groups of the informal sector, and especially of entrepreneurs are higher than in some commonly available low income formal sector occupations. Usually, entry into entrepreneurship is by starting business at a fairly late stage in working life, when the necessary skills and capital requirements are acquired. But to pave the way for this development in the personal life of the individual, it is conditional that there is preparedness and knowledge about this common trend of progressing from formal or informal sector employment to small scale entrepreneurship in the informal sector.

This can be done in a variety of ways. Teachers must be taught about working life in the informal sector, students can spend one or more, shorter or longer periods of time in specific enterprises, and successful entrepreneurs can be asked to lecture in schools. Important subjects to be taught are attitudes information on sources of inputs, law and practices and common market outlets of the informal sector. Students at all levels may be given opportunities for achieving practical working experience while they are still in school. Certain Indian experiences give support to the view that an entrepreneurial culture can be taught in schools with considerable success.

Skills Needed

An entrepreneur is one who initiates, establishes and successfully manages an economic activity or an enterprise. Entrepreneurship can therefore be promoted through provision of the values and attitudes conductive to such behaviour. Students should be helped to identify and develop their personal entrepreneurial potential and competence. Their exploration during education, and acquisition of capability to identify appropriate opportunities in their environment, will enable them to take up a career in entrepreneurship at a later stage in life.

Specific entrepreneurship courses can be organised by labour administrations. Employment services should be in a position to access promising entrepreneurial options and organise courses based on this knowledge teaching the specific skills and techniques needed. In particular, a vocational guidance programme can be used for the purpose.

The more general skills and attitudes needed are initiative, problem-solving capability and preservance. Basic management principles, marketing, bank procedures, book-keeping and budgeting, and personnel management are all useful tools in addition to the specific craftsman-skills needed.

Teaching these things in class-rooms is one thing. To demonstrate them and especially to guide people in acute need of assistance is another. Instead of relying on class-room training only, extension services in specific trades can be set up. Mobile repair shops providing advice right on the spot can be extremely useful.

Another reason for this is that the introduction to working life will in itself stimulate avoidance of the common 'diploma disease'. A qualified guess is, that the large proportion of students enrolled at universities are there simply because they have never been presented with alternatives and because the social values of an academic career are never being challenged.

Importance of Primary Schooling

Many entry-level jobs—formal or informal—require little training. Individuals enter skilled employment via many training paths, of which pre-employment vocational educational is only one, and often the least important in terms of numbers. General education, combined with on-the-job training in enterprises, provides most of the skills needed in many countries. Completion of primary schooling, however, is the foundation for continued education and training and even more important in this respect, for succeeding as an entrepreneur.

Talking about skills needed in the formal sector, it can probably be said, that making people literate and numerate are the most important things in relation to human development. Illiteracy is the single most tenacious barrier to occupational progress. In many developing countries it is in all likelihood much more effective to embark on major literacy programmes than to invest in advanced and highly expensive higher level vocational training.

Here it should be remembered that there is a tremendous mobility between the formal and informal sector at the personal level. Workers in formal sector jobs are attracted by the greater earning potential of self-employment in the informal sector. Boosting primary schooling and basic vocational training in particular will therefore have a major impact on the informal sector also.

23

The Informal Sector from the Perspective of Training its Workers

A.T.M Nurul Amin

I. What have we Learned About the Informal Sector?

It is now about two decades that the academics and development policy makers have been using the term informal 'sector' to describe certain economic activities of the cities of developing countries. The usage of this term generated a lot of debate as to its definition (conceptually and empirically) and its role (functionally and potentially) in the process of econonic development. Despite the growth of a huge literature on this debate, no universal agreement exists either on its definition or its postulated role.

However, the promising sign is that the interest in the informal sector has now moved from debate to seeking actions. Let me first briefly state what all this debate has been about:

1. On concept (*e.g.* Informal Sector or Petty Commodity Production?)
2. On Entry Condition (*e.g.* Ease of Entry Vs. Barriers to Entry)
3. On Characteristics (*e.g.* Disadvantaged by Personal Characteristics or Disadvantaged by Socio-Economic Family Background?)

4. On Composition (*e.g.* Marginalized Labour or Dynamic Entrepreneurs?)
5. On Social/Political Dimension (*e.g.* Petty Bourgeois Aspirations Vs. Proletaranization)
6. On linkages/Relationships (*e.g.* Benign Relationship Vs. Subordinant/Dominant Explorative Relationship)
7. On future outlook (*e.g.* Continued Marginalization Vs. Growth Prospect of Dynamic Indigenous Entrepreneurs).

A considerable amount of research has been carried out on many of these aspects, which seems to have provided a number of consensus as presented below:

On Definition

At the conceptual level, the informal sector may be defined as comprising those enterprises which have in common one major and dominant attribute: official non-status. Thus enterprises and individuals within the informal sector operate outside the incentive or social security system offered by the state and its institutions. This status seems to emanate largely from the miniscule size of these enterprises and their unauthorized operations. At the empirical level, enterprises are distinguished by some easily identifiable physical features and legal characteristics. Thus rather than relying on the size of the enterprises as a sole criterion, the definition commonly adopted is comprised of those enterprises which employ less than 10 workers and satisfy at least one of the following additional criterion: the enterprise is not registered under the Factory or Commercial Enterprise Establishment Acts, it operates from an unauthorized location or for some other reasons it operates illegally, it operates from a temporary structure or from residence or backyard. Even in those instances where some enterprises may carry some permits to operate, the legal status is rather fluid for not meeting various employment and working conditions requirements.

On Entry Conditions

The evidence on entry conditions suggests that characterization of the sector by 'ease of entry' or 'barriers to entry' is not an accurate reflection of the actual situation faced by potential entrants to the sector. Accumulated evidence from different studies suggests prevalence of varying degrees of entry difficulties with different activities in the sector.

On Characteristics

It is now recognised that the sector's role is not limited to the absorption of secondary labour in the urban economy (*i.e.* as a second or supplementing income source). It is also not the young, and the old, the females or recent in-migrants who are in a majority in informal activities of many rapidly growing metropolises of the developing countries. The sector appears to absorb many prime candidates (*i.e.* of the age group, 25-44) in the urban labour market. Significant differences are found to exist between the labour force in the informal and formal sectors with respect to education an economic background. Thus any disadvantages in the personal characteristics of the workers of the informal sector are more likely to be socio-economic (*e.g.* in terms of their access to land or other means of production) in nature rather than purely demographic (*e.g.* young, old or female).

On Composition

The popular view of the informal sector has been as a provider of services. Some view these services as non-essential or unproductive. Studies carried out in many cities do show that trade and service activities are the major occupations in the informal sector. But it does not necessarily follow that these services do not constitute useful economic functions. The composition of the informal sector studies from many cities show that food and drink retailing, selling clothes, and businesses in wastes scraps, a variety of repair activities (*e.g.* shoe-repairing, lock and key repairing), tailoring mentalworks, furniture-making are some of the major informal sector activities which are operated from location-specific enterprises. Besides, the major activities in construction are earth digging or removing, work as helpers to masons, brick-breaking and brick-laying, carpentry, painting, masonry and plumbing, in the informal transport sector, an arch-type of informal activity is tricycle driving (*i.e.* samlors of Bangkok, rickshaws of Dhaka and becaks of Jakarta). The other notables in the informal transport system are the passenger shuttle services of the 'tempos' in Dhaka, or tuk in Bangkok and jeepneys of Manila, which complement the more organised services of buses are taxis, and goods-carrying services of land and bullock-carts, representing informal alternatives to modern truck services.

In view of the above composition of the sector, it seems unwise to dismiss the informal sector as a set of economically inconsequential activities simply because they appear so insignificant beside the glaring neon signs of modern business houses.

On Social/Political Dimension

Some viewed the informal sector as a growth of the urban proletariat who could create social unrest or could act as a strong ally to the revolutionary aspirations of the working class. Most studies indicate that the informal sector activities rather provide opportunities to fulfil (or the hope of fulfilling) the wide-spread petty bourgeois aspirations that are prevalent among participants in these activities, particularly the owners and the self-employed. The prevalence of petty bourgeois aspirations is noticeable from the evidence on entrepreneurs, planned expansion of enterprise. This becomes particularly evident from the specific intention in such plans: ownership of land and structures from which the enterprises are operated, ownership of vehicles in case of transport, intentions to improve, expand and modernize. All this points to the conclusion that, in place of a revolutionary proletariat or industrial reserve army hypothesis, a prevalence of petty bourgeois aspirations is a better description of the prevailing mood of the informal sector participants. Such aspirations even hold for a substantial proportion of workers whose goal is to start their own enterprise.

On Linkages/Relationships

Studies carried out in a number of cities show that the informal sector relies primarily on domestic resources for all types of its supply needs (trade goods, raw materials, capital equipment, skills, labour). Of particular significance is the sector's role in economizing capital and foreign exchange through re-use of second-hand goods and machinery and recycled scraps as raw materials. Although direct sale to consumers with low and middle income is the chief source of demand for the informal sector goods and services, subcontracting (*i.e.* orders from large enterprises) is widely prevalent among the informal sector manufacturing enterprises (ISMEs). Thus the signs of dependence upon the formal sector are of a substantial nature. But what is not so clearly understood is if this reliance on the formal sector leads to exploitation of informal enterprises. However, exploitation of the informal sector's own labour appears to be more potent: long working hours, relatively low wages, poor working conditions, no job security—all point to this impression.

On Future Outlook

Most studies suggest the presence of two distinct groups in the formal sector with different economic prospects: one group is comprised of workers reflecting such marginal characteristics as low income, low savings, little skills and experience and little hope for the future and another group reflects some dynamic characteristics as above average income, regular savings and investment, forward-looking attitudes, and continued confidence in respective businesses and self-employment. The overall trend in the accumulated evidence, however, casts doubt on the proposition that marginalization or proletarianization is the major feature of the informal sector.

II. Education and Training: A Priority in Action Programmes

The recent trend in informal sector study and research is to formulate action programmes as interventionist policies for realization of the potentials of the sector based on which the original optimism about the sector was articulated. These programmes or policies can be approached through these inter-related approaches:

1. enterprise development approach;
2. human resource development approach;
3. basic needs development approach.

In the first approach, identification of dynamic enterprises and entrepreneurs have been in focus so that their prospects can further be strengthened by supportive policies. The human resource development approach has been based primarily on the evidence on skill acquisition or apprenticeship system in the sector. The third, strong rationale for pursuing interventionist policies towards the informal sector can be targeted from the perspective of meeting the basic needs of the workers of the sector. It is somewhat awkward that while the informal sector has been seen as a producer or supplier of basic needs of the urban dwellers, there has been little attention to the basic needs of these workers. Admittedly, efforts have been made to protect their employment, particularly by ILO, but their:

1. education and training needs;
2. shelter or housing needs;
3. health needs; and
4. other basic needs such as food, clothing etc., have not had much discussion.

Increasingly, education and training cut across all the three approaches that we have outlined above, *i.e.* enterprise development, human resource development and meeting basic needs. Indeed, on a priori basis education and training seems to be the most desirable area of policy intervention for improvement of the overall situation in the informal sector since it has the potential of contributing to:

1. enhancing productivity and thereby raising income;
2. upgrading of skills and thereby raising quality of informal sector goods and services;

3. increasing the awareness and consciousness of rights and privileges so that crude labour exploitation will not be possible;

4. improvement of quality of life through access to knowledge and information.

III. Is Training Needed, Wanted and Feasible?

Although it does not require a lot of research to demonstrate how training could improve the lot of the informal sector workers as we have argued above, unfortunately it is not clear if the workers themselves see education and training in the above light. This disappointment is evident in Fluitman (1989) who on the basis of a comprehensive review of the possibility of mounting training programmes for work in the informal sector observes:

"Training comes to mind quickly as a possible area of intervention in the informal sector. Alas, it is not always evident that training is needed, wanted and feasible. It is not always obvious *who* should be trained (first) and *how* it should be done. It often goes unrecognized that many informal sector worker have been able to acquire skills without 'external' aid—a fact which should have a bearing on providing additional training opportunities". (Fluitman, 1989:XV); emphasis added.

My own observation and findings are not dissimilar to those of Fluitman. However, my interpretation of the observed facts of the above nature is somewhat different from those who would use Fluitman's statement for adopting a non-interventionist approach to the issue of training programmes for the informal sector workers. Although I do not think that Fluitman believes in a very laissez-faire approach, there are many who tend to consider that this is the ideal approach to the informal sector for preserving its strength and dynamism.

My own research on the informal sector in Dhaka and Bangkok show that owners as well as workers consider capital as the single most important constraint to their growth and development[1]. Other study results that I have seen also corroborates this. Indeed there is simply not enough evidence to suggest that these workers *need* training or they *want* training. My Bangkok study (Amin, 1988a) was an investigation of the nature and extent of technology adaptation among the informal sector manufacturing enterprises[2]. This is the subsector for which training requirement would appear to be most important. But even in this subsector while 61 per cent of respondents report that training is imparted to a workforce having no previous training, about a quarter of them (26 per cent) also stated that such training is offered not because of non-availability of institutional training. This indirectly conveys the message that non-availability of institutional training for imparting training. In other words, they tend to believe that this is their own job and they will have to offer the required training. Some related data on skill acquisition in the workshop subsector of Bangkok's informal sector is summarized in Table—23.1.

Do we have more direct data? Considering this question, I decided to pursue a case study approach among some informal sector enterprises in Bangkok just for reporting the experience to the participants of this course. What did we find? Let me respond to this by presenting the case study results of 14 workers with whom we briefly talked on their training needs just the other weekend.

Brief Conversation with 14 Bangkok Informal Sector Workers on their Training Needs (Conducted during the Weekend of 9-10 June, 1990)

Case I A recycling enterprise in Rangsit

Owner's Wife Age 31.
She has never been trained.
She does not need to be trained because she considers herself too old to be trained; she does not have enough time also for training. She also thinks that training would not increase her income.

Table—23.1: Evidence on Skill Acquisition among the Informal Sector Manufacturing Enterprises in Bangkok.

	Index/Measure/ Variable	*Enterprise Group* *Metal work*	*Leather work*	*Wood work*	*Elect./ Electr.*	*Printing*	*Total sample*
1.	Enterprises reporting imparting of training to workforce having no previous training	53.5	76.5	72.7	41.7	70.6	61.0
2.	Number of persons being trained per establishment (mean)	1.1	1.0	1.4	0.7	...	1.1
3.	Time required for training:						
(i)	Mean (month)	6.7	1.8	2.9	4.3	4.1	4.0
(ii)	Distribution (per cent)						
—	<3 months	55.0	79.3	41.7	50.0	64.7	60.9
—	4-6 months	12.5	13.8	41.7	50.0	64.7	60.9
—	7-12 months	25.0	0.0	25.0	16.7	5.9	14.5
—	1 year +	10.00	6.9	8.3	8.3	11.8	9.1
4	Training is imparted because no institutional training is available (per cent of enterprises imparting training)	34.8	28.6	22.2	n.a.	18.2	25.8
5.	Most trained workers remain with the enterprise after completion of training for:						
(i)	indefinite period (over 5 years)	17.4	7.7	0.0	20.0	16.7	12.9
(ii)	3-5 years	13.0	7.7	22.2	0.0	16.7	12.9
(iii)	1-3 years	52.2	76.9	44.4	80.0	41.7	56.6
(iv)	Under 1 year	17.4	7.7	33.3	0.0	25.0	17.7

Source: Amin (1988a)

She has problems in keeping accounts and she solves it by asking someone having the accounting expertise (*e.g.* from a revenue official who is known to her).
She has no problem in doing paper work, (*e.g.* filling in different application forms).
Raw materials used in the workshop come from rejected items of factories in Bangkok.

Case II An apprentice in the same recycling enterprise.
Age 19.
He has been working in the workshop for 1 year.
He was trained here from the senior worker who has already retired.
He does not need to be trained because he will work here temporarily.
He intends to go back to do rice farming at Ubonrajthani (his home town) which he used to do before coming to Bangkok to work in this workshop.

Case III A worker in a furniture making enterprise in Rangsit.
Age 33.
He has been a furniture maker for ten years in this workshop. Two years ago, he retired to work with his elder brother but came back to work in this shop again five months ago.
He does not need to be trained because the demand for quality products is not very high. The products are sold in Rangsit and other provinces; not in Bangkok, where people need high quality furniture.
He would like to be self employed but lacks capital.

Case IV Another worker in the same furniture making Enterprise.
Age 22.
He has been working in the shop for the last two years.

He was trained in the shop by the senior worker who has already left the enterprise and returned to rural home.
He does not need to be trained because he would like to go back to Korat (his home town) to do rice farming.

Case V A fried fish-ball seller in Rangsit.
Age wife: 46.
Husband: 39.
She has been selling fried fish-balls in Rangsit for two years.
He would like to change her occupation because price of raw materials in the market is always rising, so she gets less profit but needs more working capital.
Her husband was a barber but now he would like to go abroad for work.
They, themselves, do not need to be trained but they want their son and daughter to be trained. They can afford expenses if they are not too high. The content of training they need for their children is vocational training programme such as, barber, hair dressing.

Case VI A rickshaw driver in Rangsit.
Age 19.
He has been a rickshaw driver for three years.
He rents the rickshaw.
He does not need to be trained because he feels comfortable, in being a rickshaw driver and he does not want to change his occupation.

Case VII A Noodle Soup Seller in Rangsit.
Age 20.
She trained herself to cook noodle soup.
She sells on credit to workers in factories nearby from 10.00 a.m. to 2.00 p.m. everyday.
She is interested in getting training but she has not enough time to go to the training center

because she has to take care of her son too. She would like to participate if the trainer comes to her workplace.

She wants to know about nutrition.

She would like to expand her business but she does not have enough capital.

Case VIII A Metal Worker (exhaust pipe of motorcycle) in Rangsit.

Age 25.

He has been working in this workshop for last five years.

He was trained from his former workplace.

During his 2 work in this workshop, he has to be a trainer for other workers as well.

He needs to be trained because he wants to know about the system of engine that relates to his work. Moreover, he wants to know about market demand. He is free on Sunday. Training center for him can any anywhere in Bangkok. He wants to do something new but now he has no idea what he wants to do. He has no problem of capital.

Case IX A silk producing microenterprise in Sukumvit Soi 36.

Owner Age 40.

His enterprise runs very well, especially in respect of labour relations.

He wants skilled labour for weaving because his production is for export.

The skilled workers received training in weaving work when they were in their respective home town such as in the Northeast where weaving is an occupation during the off-season *i.e.* when they are free from rice farming.

Most of the thread roller operators, have engaged in household work before.

Case X A thread-roller operator in the same enterprise.
Age 18.
She has been working here for two years; before that she used to do household work.
The owner taught her the skilled of thread rolling.
She does not need to be trained because she would like to change the occupation to work in an office.

Case XI A weaver at Sukumvit, Soi 36.
Age 30.
She has been a weaver for 15 years.
She already has weaving skills. She wants to be trained for special or new technique.
She can leave her work for training because she works on a sub-contract basis with the owner.
It is very convenient for her if training will be arranged on Sundays in Bangkok.

Case XII A steel worker (steel gate manufacturing) in Sukumvit Soi 36.
Age 26.
Employee.
Length of present job: 7 months.
He said this type of job (beating and bending steel bars to the desired shape) requires no training.
To become a Lathe Machine Operator (an upper level job in the enterprise) training is required.
In this case, the bender has to practice steel bending and beating until he has enough skill before getting training to operate lathe machines.
He is not willing to have any training programme outside if he has to pay for it. He does not have time also to attend.

Case XIII Street vendor (selling ready-made clothes) near Ambassador Hotel.
Age 22.

She has worked for two months.
She was trained how to sell by the former seller.
She does not have enough time to participate in training because she works from 7.30 a.m. to 8.00 p.m.
She wants to have her own business but she has not enough capital.

Case XIV A food seller near Ambassador Hotel.
Age 24.
She has been working as a food seller for three years.
At first, she hired someone to cook and she used to observe and follow.
Now she can cook by herself.
She needs to be trained both in cooking and management.
She can leave her work for training and afford the expenses.
She does not think of changing occupation, but she wants to open a bakery.

I would draw two lessons from these responses:

1. A very few informal sector workers will be motivated *on their own* for education and training in the prevailing circumstances of their work environment.

2. Neither a common training programme will be appropriate nor a custom-tailored programme will be feasible in view of the difference in individual perceptions and circumstances.

But where do we go from here? Should we leave the informal sector workers with their present state of affairs? I do not think that will be appropriate. They will not be short of examples where 'external' prodding has been necessary to change things for the better. Our own education or for that matter all formal education has flourished through the provision of lots of subsidies and other form of incentives. Farmers did not introduce fertilizer or the so-called water-seed-fertilizer technology without 'external' proddings or incentives. If we trace the history of formal education, and farmers' adoption of modern technology, we shall certainly discover that not many came forward for learning or adoption on their own. It is only at the stage of a certain level of development when the results of education and training or adoption of modern practices become very clear that people start realizing their needs. Thus I would argue that 'external' intervention in the form of education and training should not be set aside just because the informal sector workers can not articulate the 'need' or 'want' of training.

The above position of course we are taking in consideration of the extreme response or possibility when the value of training is not appreciated. But if we look at our case study evidence a little more carefully, it will become clear that it is not that they do not value training. How else to interpret the response of that fried fish-ball seller in Rangsit (Case V) in which the man (39) and his wife (46) say that they do not need training but would like to send their sons and daughters for training if such a facility is available. Thus even for those who say that they do not need or want training, the response is likely to be a reflection of very individual situation like the case cited above as Case II, where the guy is working in the informal sector temporarily during time off from farming.

In view of the above diversity, is a training programme for the informal sector workers feasible? I would think it is. The approach really should not and need not be very specific to individual needs and circumstances. The programme should be launched on the basis of broad understanding of the informal sector situation and, as happens for the formal sector education and training, the informal sector workers would adapt and respond to these created facilities according to their needs and circumstances. One reason why many programmes for the poor do not succeed is that outsiders tend to think that they are very different people. However I should stress that a broad understanding of the sector and its composition and the people working there and their characteristics is absolutely necessary. A guideline is provided in the following section that would provide this understanding and facilitate identification of training needs according to the nature of the activity and workers characteristics.

IV. Informal Sector Definition Composition, and Workers Characteristics and Corresponding Training Needs

For consideration of any training programme for the informal sector, it is essential that we know the sector's composition by the nature of activity as well as by the employment and work status of the workers. Additionally, we should know about the workers' personal characteristics, particularly about their age, sex, education, skill level. A brief introduction to this has already been made by way of introduction at the outset of the paper (section I). What follows below is intended to provide a more clear picture with the aid of illustrative materials.

Definition or What Comprises the Informal Sector Conceptually

As already stated, the official non-status can be considered as an acceptable conceptual definition. The enterprise and employment characteristics listed in Table—23.2 capture the characteristics that follow from such fluid legal status.

Empirically

The empirical definition is illustrated through a flow chart (Chart I) which may have to be modified according to the specific situation of a city or country.

I should hasten to add that no one approach to defining the informal sector will be satisfactory to all because of difference in circumstances as well as in the intellectual inclinations and experiences of appliers of a definition. Some subjective judgement is bound to enter in the actual application of a definition. From this point of view, I have found it useful keeping in mind the various other names that have been used to describe the activities which we now call the informal sector (see Table—23.3). Turning to this would also help to make a judgement where there is unclarity. For example, if you are uncertain if an enterprise or activity should be included in the informal sector you can ask yourself: will this be found in the western world since someone has called the informal sector as 'non-westernized sector'? (Hackennburg, 1980).

Chart 1: Decision model for identifying informal sector enterprises in Dhaka city

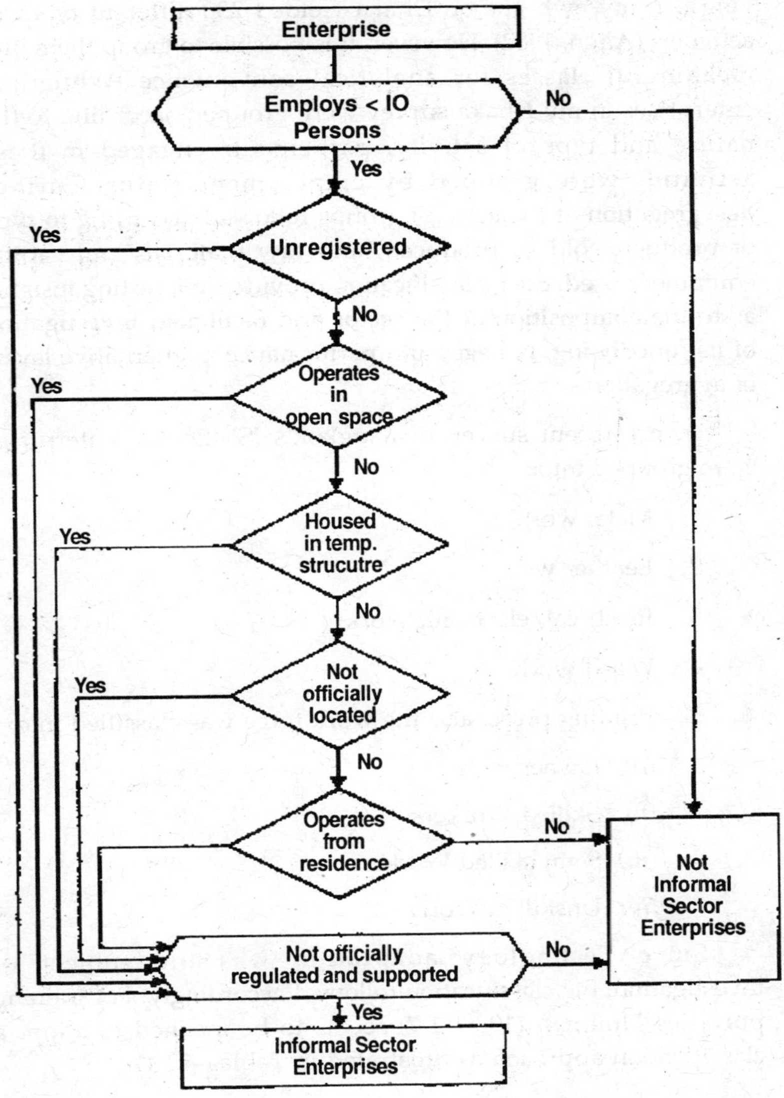

Source: Amin (1982: 58)

Composition

Census of informal sector activities is bound to generate a long list: my own one on Dhaka yielded 230 different types of activities (Amin, 1982). However, it is possible to group them into meaningful classes for analytical convenience. While 437 enterprises in my Dhaka survey were grouped according to the nature and type of activity, participants engaged in these activities were grouped by employment status. Further desegregation of the activity groups followed according to type of products sold or produced, and raw materials and capital equipment used. Such classification provided interesting insights as to the composition of the sector and facilitated investigation of its functioning, linkages and performance at alternative levels of aggregation.

In my recent survey of Bangkok's ISMEs, the enterprises were grouped into:

1. Metal work
2. Leather work
3. Electrical/electronic work
4. Wood work
5. Printing press; and the work force was classified into:
    (i) Owner
    (ii) Skilled Workers
    (iii) Semi-skilled Workers
    (iv) Unskilled Workers.

Since Technology adaptation was the subject of investigation, the classification followed accordingly. For training purposes Fluitman (1989: 4-7) seems to be inclined to adopt a classification approach as illustrated in Table—23.4).

Table—23.2: Distinguishing Characteristics of Informal Sector People, Activity and Habitat

Employment *Characteristics of the people engaged in the informal sector*	*Enterprise* *Characteristics of the activities in the informal sector*	*Settlement* *Characteristics of the informal sector habitat*
1. Low wages	1. Easy of entry	1. Absence of official authorization
2. Little job security	2. Reliance on indigenous resources	2. Illegal subdivision/rental of land
3. Absence of official protection/recognition	3. Family ownership of enterprises	3. Unauthorized building
4. Absence of trade union organisation	4. Small-scale of operation	4. Locally available/scrap construction materials
5. Non coverage by social security system	5. Labour-intensive and adapted technology	5. Absence or restrictive standards and regulations
6. Non coverage by minimum wage legislation	6. Skills acquired outside the formal school system	6. Low cost
7. No fringe benefits	7. Unregulated and competitive markets	7. Non-availability of mortgage or any other subsidized finance

Source: Amin (1988b: 14)

Table—23.3: The Urban Informal Sector by Some Other Names

Term	*Author*
Trade-service sector	Reynolds (1969)
Informal income opportunities	Hart (1971)
Unenumerated sector	Weeks (1971)
Informal sector	Hart (1971)
Intermediate sector	Child (1973)
	Steel (1976)
Community of the poor	Rempel (1974)
	Gutkind (1976)
Unstructured Sector	Emmerij (1974)
Family-Enterprise Sector	Peattie (1974)
	Majumdar (1976)
Lower-circuit of urban economy	Santos (1976)
Unorganized sector	Joshi (1976)
	Harriss (1978)
Irregular sector	Standing (1977)
Petty community production	Moser (1978)
Casual work	Bromley and Gurry (1979)
Non-plan activities	Sarin (1979)
Non-Westernized sector	Hackenberg (1980)
Urban subsistence sector	Cole and Sanders (1985)

Source: Amin (1988b: 6)

Characteristics

Apart from classification of the informal sector enterprises and workers according to their composition by enterprise type or employment status as described above, it is also important to look at the workforce characteristics *i.e.* their

1. age characteristics
2. sex characteristics
3. migratory characteristics and
4. educational characteristics

Table—23.4: Categories of the Informal Sector Enterprises and their Work and Training Needs

Informal secior categories	*Nature of training needs*	*Remarks*
1	2	3
A. Enterprise categories		
1. The craft subsector (*e.g.* artisans, handicrafts, home-based work of women)	Marketing and accounting skills	Rationale being that owner-artisan may have advanced on the basis of technical (sometimes even inherited), rather than business skills
2. The workshop subsector (*e.g.* metal workshops, furniture making enterprises electric/electronic repairing printing press)	Adaptation and modernization of technology and production processes	Should be structured around on-the-job activities for absorbing in the prevailing work mode
3. Commerce and services (*e.g.* petty trading, shop-keeping, repair services, etc.)	Marketing and management	Lack of capital and credit, not training, is seen as a major obstacle

(Contd.)

Table—23.4 (Contd.)

1	2	3
B. Workforce categories		
1. Entrepreneurs (Owners of small establishments, often also the principal workers,	Managerial and marketing skills; also technical skills depending on the nature of the enterprise	Establishing access to credit, capital, demand sources for products and services and replacing out-moded technologies
2. Establishment workers (wage-earning employees, apprentices, unpaid family,	1. Complementing and strengthening technical skills in respective area of specialization	Should complement rather than replace the prevailing apprenticeship system and indigenous work techniques
	2. Entrepreneurship development for those who have already set their minds on becoming self-employed or owner of an enterprise	

Table—23.5: Some Characteristics of the Informal Sector in the Four Major Cities in Asian Countries

Indicator	*Dhaka*	*Jakarta*	*Bangkok*	*Davao City Philippines*
1. Age Characteristics				
(i) Less than 25	46.7	28.9	45.8	5.4
(ii) 25-44	48.5	55.8	46.2	66.0
(iii) 45 and above	5.8	15.5	8.0	28.6
2. Sex characteristics				
(i) Male	99.6	90.0	47.1	66.0
(ii) Female	0.4	10.0	52.9	34.0
3. Length of stay in the city				
(i) Less than 5 years	44.3	29.3	5.1	7.7
(ii) 5-10 years	26.0	23.6	7.2	22.3
(iii) 10 years and above	29.7	47.1	87.7	70.1
4. Educational characteristics				
(i) No schooling	31.2	10.9	13.2	27.6
(ii) Primary	52.0	53.0	50.9	14.3
(iii) Secondary and above	16.6	36.2	25.9	58.1
5. Mode of skill acquisition				
(i) Formal sources	11.1	10.4	21.9	7.4
(ii) Informal sources	88.9	89.6	78.1	92.6

Sources: Data are obtained from Amin (1982) for Dhaka; Liong (1989) and Noir (1978) for Jakarta; Ashakul and Ashakul (1985), ILO-ARTEP (1988) and Amin (1988a) for Bangkok; and Martinez (1989) for Davao City.

Table—23.6: Classification of Informal Sector Workers by their Characteristics and their Training Needs

Classification based on workforce characteristics	*Nature of training needs*	*Remarks*
1	2	3
A. Age categories		
1. Young	Providing institutional training specifically for informal sector should be considered	Training is very important Proper incentive and support will be needed
2. Prime working age group	On-the-job training in related workline Entrepreneurship development	Extension services may be one mechanism
3. Old	Training and management	Many may be illiterate
	Some literacy and numeracy training	Could be difficult
B. Sex characteristics		
1. Male	According to the respective line of work	Imposes no constraints in particular line of training
2. Female	In addition to training in respective line of skills and work, training in family and health care should be considered	Could be sensitive in some cultures

(Contd.)

Table—23.6 (Contd.)

1	2	3
C. Migratory characteristics		
1. Recent migrants	Training is necessary to adopt to the urban environment and establish contact for business purposes	Vulnerable tc explotation if no community support is in place
2. Circular migrants	Training needs are not clear	Advantage of taking the training to rural areas
3. Long-term residents	Training in specialized skills and technique	Could be used as trainers
D. Educational characteristics		
1. Illiterate	Training in literacy and numeracy; adult education programme apart from training in respective line of work	should be a priority item
2. Primary school dropouts and those with primary level of education	Institutionalized training still may not be possible	Should not be difficult to organise difficult to
	On the job training may be the solution	
3. Secondary and higher secondary graduates	Institutionalized training as relevant for the informal sector could be feasible	Entrepreneurship development with this group could be productive

Our research has shown substantial difference among the workers in terms of each of these variables. Some impressions on this difference may be formed from data provided in Table—23.5. Based on these data we are inclined to offer the following classification by workforce characteristics analogous to the classification provided in Table—23.4.

NOTES

1. As would probably be expected this response is much higher in Dhaka which only illustrates the relative capital scarcity in the Bangladesh economy compared to Thailand.

2. This can also be called the workshop subsector as a World Bank study classifies the informal sector from a perspective of training requirements (Fluitman, 1989: 6).

REFERENCES

Amin, ATMN (1982). "An Analysis of Labour Force and Industrial Organisation of the Informal Sector in Dhaka City", Unpublished Ph. D. Thesis, University of Manitoba, Canada.

Amin, ATMN (1988a). "Technology Adaptation in Bangkok's Informal Sector", Working Paper No. 203, Geneva: World Employment Programme, ILO.

Amin, ATMN (1988b). "Labour Administration for the Urban Informal Sector", A Training Course Manual, Bangkok: Human Settlements Development Division, Asian Institute of Technology.

Ashakul, T. and Ashakul, C. (1986). "BMR Study on Urban Poor", Bangkok: National Economic and Social Development Board.

Fluitman, F. (1989). Training for Work in the Informal Sector, Geneva: ILO.

ILO-ARTEP (1988). "Urban Self-Employment in Thailand: A Study of Two Districts in Metropolitan Bangkok", Bangkok: National Economic and Social Development Board.

Liong, J.T. (1989). "Housing for the Urban Informal Sector Based on Affordability, Willingness to Pay and Type of Activity: A Case Study of Jakarta", M.Sc. Thesis, Bangkok: Human Settlements Development Division, Asian Institute of Technology.

Moir, H. (1978). "Urbanization and Employment Programme: The Jakarta Informal Sector", Geneva: ILO.

Martinez, E. (1989). "Locational Linkage and Labour Utilisation Patterns Among Informal Sector Enterprises in Davao City, Philippines", M.Sc. Thesis, Bangkok: Human Settlements Development Division, Asian Institute of Technology.

24

Promotion and Training Issues in the Informal Sector in the Context of Rapid Population Change

W.J. House
and
K. Paramanathan

1. Introduction

Self-employment—emcompassing own-account workers and employers (working proprietors of unincorporated enterprises)—has been increasing focus of attention in many countries. With slower growth, economic crisis, unemployment and the pursuit of structural adjustment accompanied by a disillusionment with centralized planning and the public sector as instruments for promoting growth and full employment, hopes are raised for self-employment as a means of injecting new vitality into economies while creating employment, income and wealth. There is a growing ascendancy of free market philosophies emphasizing private initiative and enterprise as the mainspring of economic progress. This new wave in the 1980s and beyond represents a reversal—perhaps temporary or enduring—in the long-term trend where non-agricultural self-employment has declined with modernization and development and the urban labour force has become increasingly occupied in regular protected wage employment. The implications of this tendency for the structure and nature of employment may be substantial.

What is the rationale for a strategy which relies heavily on stimulating self-employment opportunities in rural areas and in the urban informal sector? The main reason offered in many countries for promoting small-scale enterprises is that the demand for otherwise surplus labour, a consequence of high fertility, rapid growth of population and the labour force, and rising rural-to-urban migration for employment opportunities, is increased, which raises the income of the poorest groups in society. This is a result of the employment that the self-employed (own-account workers and working proprietors) create for themselves and for others (causal and regular wage employees, apprentices and unpaid family workers). However, small enterprises must be shown to employ both labour and capital more efficiently than larger units, given their real social costs, so that national output grows faster from their encouragement.

What is the justification for such heavy reliance on the promotion of those attached to the informal sector and the small-scale enterprise sector, of which some of the latter may belong to the formal sector in the sense that they are registered, licensed, housed in permanent buildings and use a more capital-intense technology than those found in the informal sector? And what general evidence is there that reliance on informal sector expansion will generate higher economic growth, via more appropriate technologies and an improved distribution of income, from employment expansion and income generation for poor and vulnerable groups of the population? What general lessons can be learned by Pacific Island country planners from the experiences of various policies and programmes to promote self-employment and the informal sector around the world?

The purpose of our paper is to attempt to bring some evidence to bear on some of these questions, without pretending that we can provide complete and adequate answers. The main purpose of our presentation is to stimulate discussion of the issues, identify some consensus in approaches to the problems, and to, hopefully, induce participants to identify policy-relevant strategies for their own country situations.

2. The Demographic and Employment Challenge Facing the Countries of the Pacific[1]

The Demographic Setting

Demographic conditions and likely developments in the Pacific will fuel a rapid increase in social service demand in the near future. Most of the countries share certain demographic attributes: young populations, high-fertility rates, low mortality and a highly mobile population and labour force. In the Federated States of Micronesia, (FSM), Marshall Islands, Solomon Islands, and Vanuatu, more than 40 per cent of the population is under 15 years of age. Elsewhere, more than a third of the population is under 15 years of age (See Table—24.1). The large number of young people relative to the size of the total population generates great demand for primary health care and schooling, and will, eventually, lead to a tremendous demand for income generating employment opportunities in the labour market.

Most of these nations are experiencing high-fertility with current total fertility rates clustering in the range of 4-5.5 births per woman. Only in Fiji does the fertility rate begin to approach the lower level of comparable low-middle income nations. A combination of high fertility rates and falling mortality levels characterizes the early stages of the demographic transition in which they now find themselves. Demand for health care, education, and other social services rises rapidly during the early stages of the transition due to the large number of births, the greater number of elderly, and the burgeoning population at the lower age distributions.

Emigration

Emigration has traditionally been an important demographic safety-valve for small nations, and the South Pacific is no exception. No other region in the world has such relatively easy access to the labour markets of three of the world's most advanced economies—the United States, Australia and New Zealand. Those countries that have most actively exported manpower—Tonga, Western Samoa and Fiji, have both the

Table—24.1: Demographic Indicators in the Pacific*

	Population under 15 (thousands)	*Population under 15 (% of total)*	*Population density (per sq km)*	*Population growth (%)*	*Working-age population (15-64) (% of total)*	*Total fertility rate (births per woman)*	*Life expectancy (years)*
Fiji	744	37	41	1.1	60	3.1	63
FSM	101	43	143	3.0	54	5.3**	64
Kiribati	75	40	93	1.8	57	4.2	60
Marshall Islands	46	51	254	4.2	46	7.2	62
Solomon Islands	335	46	12	2.9	52	5.6	61
Tonga	100	37	139	0.8	59	4.0	66
Vanuatu	151	44	13	2.8	54	5.6	65
Western Samoa	160	39	55	1.0	56	4.6	64

*Or most recent estimate

**Not including yap State

Source: World Bank (1993), Table—4.1.

lowest rates of absolute population growth and the highest social indicators in the region. In Tonga and Western Samoa, remittances from overseas migrants finance practically as much consumption as does agriculture, the largest productive sector. Although a wide range of individuals migrate from the Pacific, those most likely to leave have secondary or post-secondary education and tend to come from the upper-income, urban population.

Labour Force Indicators

Formal job creation in the Pacific has been slow and disappointing, characterized by a heavy reliance on public sector employment, with a low rate of female labour participation and a heavy reliance on agriculture to generate jobs (Table—24.2).

During the decade ending in 1986, labour force growth was insufficient to keep pace with the growing population of graduates and school leavers. The growth that did take place was, by and large, dominated by an expansion of the public sector. As growth in this sector slows, a key challenge will be to increase the relevance of social services to facilitate employment creation in the private sector. To identify appropriate training programmes for those embarking on self-employment opportunities, particularly in the formal sector, remains a key public policy issue.

Manpower demand projections have been made for a number of South Pacific economies. These projections are subject to a considerable margin of error but generally suggest that the capacity to generate employment will be closely linked to the level of private investment and growth, two key indicators of the level of social services required.

In the past, skill gaps in the public sector—of which there are many—have been used as an indicator of the demand for specialized training. Forecasting demand for skills based on public sector requirements is no longer appropriate, since fiscal constraints will limit growth in public sector employment. Education planners will need to pay more careful heed to the needs of the private sector in setting curricula and providing specialized training, especially for employment outside of the formal sector.

Table—24.2: Workforce Indicators, 1986

	Economically active labour force ('000)	*Share of labour force in total pop. (%)*	*Share of labour force in public sector (%)*	*Share of women in labour force (%)*	*Share of labour force in agriculture (%)*	*Share of government in non-agricultural labour force (%)*	*Labour force growth rate (1976-1986) (% p.a.)*
Fiji	241	33	16	21	48	49	3.2
FSM	31	30	24	28	47	–	3.5
Kiribati	33	47	n.a	46	33	35	4.6
Marshall Islands	11	27	58	27	21	25	5.7
Solomon Islands	39	12	7	25	46	43	5.5
Tonga	24	24	27	21	49	48	1.3
Vanuatu	65	44	7	47	74	32	3.1
Western Samoa	46	27	15	19	64	42	1.8

Source: World Bank (1993).

As the private sector becomes more important in the growth process, manpower demand may well exhibit initial signs of sluggishness. This is due to the small size of the private sector in most Pacific countries and the need to adjust from a public sector dominated labour market to one in which private sector skills and orientation are required. As private sector activity increases, manpower demand may recover as well. Even if private sector demand for labour becomes sluggish in the transition phase to higher growth, the promotion of human capital must continue if long-term development is to be realized.

The number of government employees relative to the size of the total population is relatively high and unsustainable over the long term. In the past, the public sector has provided a livelihood to more than two-thirds of all persons with post-secondary education. In addition, remuneration of civil servants is high, with average public sector salaries being four-six times per capita income, compared with developed country standards where the range is 1.5—2.5 times average per capita incomes. In a world dominated by structural adjustment, curtailment in public spending and retrenchment of public sector employees, future sources of employment growth must be sought outside the public sector.

The Provision of Education

A competitive, export-oriented economic environment demands that workers be able to perform new and multiple skills. These, in turn, invoke a requirement that future workers need to be taught the basic cognitive skills of reading, writing and arithmetic necessary to learn specific skills. In many studies around the world it has been consistently found that the rate of return to primary education is greater than the return to higher levels of education (Psacharopoulos, 1985). In economies experiencing dramatic changes, including unanticipated shifts in markets, climate and technology, a broad base of general skills through basic education is more critical for success than is specialized education. General education is likely to pay for itself in the long run, enhances receptivity to knowledge and new techniques, and improves the cost effectiveness of later training.[2]

This does not imply that post-secondary education can be ignored; but that improvements in post-secondary education need to be based on a sound primary and secondary education, while education of an elite group without mass education is unlikely to engender sustained economic growth over the long run.

In all Pacific countries except for Vanuatu, there is virtually universal enrolment at the beginning of primary education. Enrolment is usually not compulsory in most countries, however, either because there is no policy or because it is not enforced, and up to 15 per cent of the children drop out before the end of primary school. In areas with rapidly growing populations (*e.g.* Majuro in the Marshall Islands), children have had to be turned away from primary school because of insufficient numbers of teachers and schools. Only in Fiji and Tonga is compulsory primary education effectively enforced.

The quality of educational services in the Pacific is seriously deficient, measured in terms of literacy levels and secondary school achievement indicators. Low quality education contributes to high drop-out rates and raises the unit costs of providing a given amount of training.

The curricula of primary and secondary education are not sufficiently related to the social and economic activities in which most of the students will eventually find employment. Consequently, the vocational flavour of primary and secondary education is very weak in these countries, despite the fact that most school leavers return to village life and small-scale agriculture. Few schools provide any useful instruction in the scientific underpinnings of agriculture or its business aspects, beyond the typical school garden.

Vocational education has not been emphasized by most governments in the past, and strategies adopted for skills training have had a mixed record. Governments have tried to integrate vocational training into regular secondary systems. Fiji, for example, has 25 multicraft centres with an enrolment of about 700. Kiribati has a specialized vocational school. Specialized agricultural and marine schools at the secondary level exist in a number of Pacific countries. Most teacher and nurse training institutions take students after Form 5 or later, but there are three institutions (in Tonga, Vanuatu and Kiribati) which take students after Forms 3 and 4. While the supply of vocational training opportunities is not negligible, it lags well behind demand and is poorly integrated into private sector training programmes. Training for self-employment in the informal sector is in its infancy.

The Growth of the Labour Force

In this respect the island countries share in the world-wide global problem. As one commentary succinctly stated the dilemma:

"The economies of the less developed countries are about to face perhaps the greatest challenge in their histories: generating a sufficient number of jobs at reasonable wages to 'absorb' their rapidly growing populations into productive employment. In terms of absolute magnitude, this challenge has no precedent in human history. In some respects, the challenge is also unprecedented in terms of its nature, given, on the one hand, the limited availability of natural resources (especially land) in many countries and, on the other hand, the widespread availability of advanced technology" (Bloom; Freeman, 1986, p. 381).

What forms and kinds of training for self-employment can serve to promote labour absorption in order to the great bulk of new entrants to the labour market, particularly in the context of the Pacific?

The great challenge to human resource and employment planners in the Pacific is clearly portrayed in Table—24.3. The labour force is growing much more rapidly in most of the Pacific Island countries than the rate at which formal sector employment has been growing in the recent past. The residual group of job-seekers need training in order to seek productive, income-generating opportunities outside of the formal sector, many as self-employed entrepreneurs in the non-agricultural informal sector.

Table—24.3: Projected Annual Growth of the Labour Force and Recent Expansion of Formal Sector Employment

	Growth in labour force p.a	*Growth in formal employment p.a.*
Fiji	12000	4000
Solomon Islands	7500	550
Tonga	530	340
Kiribati	980	?
Tuvalu	73	50
Western Samoa	1260	919

Source: World Bank (1993) and various country papers of the ILO/UNDP/AIDAB project "Employment promotion manpower planning and labour administration in the Pacific".

3. Training for Employment in the Informal Sector

The Rationale for Promoting Self-Employment and Small-Scale Enterprises[3]

What is the justification for heavy reliance on the promotion of those attached to the informal sector and the small-scale enterprise sector (of which some of the latter may belong to the formal sector in the sense that they are registered, licensed, housed in permanent buildings and use a more capital-intensive technology than those found in the informal sector?). And what general evidence is there that reliance on informal sector expansion will generate higher economic growth, via more appropriate technologies and an improved distribution of income, from employment expansion and income generation for poor and vulnerable groups of the population? What general lessons can be learned by Pacific Island planners from the experiences of various policies and programmes to promote self-employment and the informal sector around the world? It is thus useful to briefly review findings with respect to analysis of micro enterprises, as well as interventions in other countries and regions, as an introduction to our analysis of the situation in the Pacific.

The main reason offered for promoting small-scale (micro) enterprises as against larger enterprises is that the demand for unskilled and otherwise surplus or underutilized labour is increased, which promotes income and employment growth amongst the poor and so reduces poverty. To be accepted, proponents of this policy must also show that aggregate output will not fall as a result, since this might offset the promised income redistribution effect. The most convincing evidence would be if small enterprises employ both labour and capital more efficiently than larger production units, given their real social or opportunity costs, so that national output would rise as well as being distributed more equally (Little; Mazumdar, Page, 1987, p. 5). The static case for promoting such small units is that they use factors of production more efficiently, given their social costs. However, if they use both more labour and more capital to produce a unit of output then their promotion cannot be justified on efficiency grounds.

Even if small enterprises are more socially efficient and they employ more labour per unit of output, additional evidence on the extent of their competitiveness with the output of larger enterprises should be examined before their promotion can be justified economically. If their products do not compete with those of larger enterprises, then a reduction in the costs of production of small-scale units would lead to only a limited increase in their sales as demand would not switch from the output of larger to smaller units. A greater increase in their markets and a rise in the demand for labour by micro enterprises would result from a reallocation of the pattern of overall demand in favour of their products. This might be accomplished by a redistribution of income, if indeed it is established that their goods and services are purchased largely by the poor.[4]

Alternatively, in some productive sectors, the output of micro and large enterprises may be highly competitive such that a small change in the relative costs of production would lead consumers to switch their demand towards the more labour-intensive small plants, so that the demand for labour would be correspondingly increased.

To know whether there is much to be gained by a policy of favouring small-scale enterprises (or ceasing to disfavour them) requires disaggregated inquiry into the nature of markets because the degree of competitiveness between small-scale enterprises and large-scale enterprises will vary a great deal with the production sector... many of the failures of targeted approaches to aiding small enterprises, including the training of handicraft workers, seem to be attributable to a failure to ask whether an increased output—of products or of skilled workers—would find a market (Little; Mazumdar; Page, 1987, p. 6).

From their empirical study of narrowly-defined manufacturing sectors in India, Little, Mazumdar and Page (1987, pp. 313-314) found that the employment size of an enterprise is a very poor indicator of its capital intensity and productivity as well as of total factor productivity and technical efficiency. They found that many small enterprises with less than ten workers were not the most labour intensive, while their capital productivity and technical efficiency were very rarely the highest among size classes in their industry. They found that differences in labour intensity between industries were much greater than differences existing between enterprises within an industry. Therefore, they conclude that policies should be favoured which alter the patterns of demand in favour of labour-intensive industries. To this end, measures to promote exports, farm output, particularly that of small farmers who have been found to be more efficient, and income-redistribution would help to raise the overall rate of growth of employment.

In addition, they argue that banks should be permitted to charge higher rates of interest for loans to small firms, since they are both more risky and more costly to administer. On the other hand, the authors claim that while very small manufacturing firms with less than ten workers should not be relied upon for the efficient employment of factors of production, they must also not be discriminated against. The overall objective of supply-side intervention in favour of such small firms must be to identify individual winners and to provide them with the necessary inducements. Positive intervention is more likely to be successful at a stage when evidence already exists of some initial individual success. While these findings are based on Indian data, they likely have broader relevance, and are at least a basis for plausible hypotheses.

By its very nature, self-employment income, particularly that arising from the informal sector, is notoriously difficult to define conceptually and to measure correctly. The self-employed receive the rewards of their labour, either in kind or from the profits of the sale of their output. Differentiating between the returns to labour, land, capital and entrepreneurship is an almost impossible task (van Ginneken, 1988, p. 94).

General Policy Lessons from Programmes to Promote Self-Employment and the Informal Sector

The emergence of self-employment and wage employment in the urban informal sector in developing countries can be viewed as a reflection of the failure of development planning to create adequate job opportunities in the formal or modern sector (ILO, 1987, p. 9). Its growth might be viewed as a corrective response to the lack of employment creation in the capital-intensive sector so that the urban economy's human resources are utilized more fully. The co-existence of the dualistic formal and informal sectors is sometimes thought to reflect the prevalence of certain market imperfections and barriers to entry to the capital-intensive, high-productivity sector.

"The emergence of the informal sector can therefore be interpreted as a manifestation of the adjustment process. To the extent that this process is muted by market imperfections, it is evident that the object of research and action in this field should be to examine the pervasiveness of such imperfections and their consequences and, in the light of the findings, suggest remedial measures. The need for intervention cannot be overemphasized given the misallocation of resources that the process entails besides equity implications" (ILO, 1987, p. 10).

This short section examines some of the broad implications and general lessons derived from various programmes and policy interventions to promote urban self-employment and the growth of small-scale enterprises in various parts of the world. In turn, they can be used later as guidelines and standards against which to assess prevailing and proposed programmes and policies for the sector in the Pacific Islands countries.

Many of the most common constraints faced by would be self-employed entrepreneurs have been identified in numerous surveys of the informal sector conducted around the world in recent years. They include the lack of capital, both finance and physical equipment, technical know-how, lack of suitable working premises and the relatively high cost in both time and fees of becoming registered and licensed. Other related problems often mentioned include shortages of raw materials, difficulties of obtaining credit from financial institutions and the absence of institutional support. Once started they face problems relating to the limited size of the market, perhaps because of competition from other informal sector operators as well as from the formal sector, lack of working capital, inadequate sector operators as well as from the formal sector, lack of working capital, inadequate managerial and technical skills, including skilled workers, poor infrastructure, and insecurity of tenure because of the often negative attitude of the authorities.

In her review of over 20 micro-enterprise promotion programmes from various countries, Stearns (1985) used four important criteria to evaluate their impact: the degree of employment created; the extent to which incomes were raised; the level of financial self-sufficiency attained; and the number of people who benefited. She concludes that the most effective programme design is one which targets very poor entrepreneurial clients, emphasizes credit rather than business education, relies on client self-selection rather than programme staff for assessing credit worthiness, and initially extends very small loans with the proviso that larger sums will be forthcoming if repayment is full and prompt. A programme with these characteristics lends itself to institutionalization and helps to empower the poor via community-level organisations.

Programmes which create links between the informal and formal sectors are to be encouraged when, if institutionalized, they create greater opportunities for micro enterprises. More traditional programmes which stress business education as well as credit are found to be the least successful. They are expensive, teach very few clients, and do not raise incomes any more than programmes which alone focus on credit.

From his review of the USAID-funded Programme for Investment in the Small Capital Enterprise Sector project (PISCES), Ashe (1981, 1985) found that, within the category of small urban enterprises, there are distinct levels of potential beneficiaries that correspond closely with the most appropriate type of project assistance. At the lowest level (Level One) are persons not conceiving of themselves as entrepreneurs but undertaking some meagre activity—often petty trade—for mere subsistence. At Level Two are people with a good comprehension of business practices and with a viable going concern. They invest whatever limited resources they have in their business. At the highest level (Level Three) the entrepreneurs have better business skills, they understand their markets and can be flexible enough to expand when the occasion arises.

Marginal workers in Level One are often assisted by community-based programmes whose concern is with such basic services as health, education, nutrition and sanitation as well as with enterprise development and income generation. The process of creating new individual and group businesses is usually undertaken as part of an integrated community development effort which promotes collective solutions to problems. At level Two, programmes often attempt to create small informal groups of business owners from the community where loans are collectively guaranteed. Level Three micro-entrepreneurs have an acceptable inventory, a credit history and someone to co-sign a loan for them so that they can often be reached by innovative bank programmes.

The enterprise development programmes of PISCES provide credit and sometimes organisational and simple management assistance to already existing businesses. Group programmes are aimed at Level Two and individual programmes are aimed at Level Three clients. The emphasis on the solidarity group and loan pay back has several redeeming features. Funding from outside sources is assured by a low default rate which ensures the continuity of the loan fund. Group cohesion is reinforced by ensuring that the loan repayments are made on schedule.

Experiences in individual programmes aiming to reach slightly larger businesses were also encouraging. The projects directly administered by banks share three characteristics: a separate unit in the bank is established to serve micro-enterprises; simple procedures for administrating loans; and formalized contractual relationships with formalities held to a minimum. Ashe found that these businesses were able to grow without written records or formal management skills. Credit is often the binding constraint and by keeping loans small—from $200 to $1,000—and by ensuring frequent loan repayments and tight supervision, the projects avoided the high rates of default of so many other credit schemes.

In the most effective project, programme inputs reflect the plans and desires of the clients and stay close to the level of skills and knowledge existing in the community. Programmes following this precept tend to be simple and low cost, and closely involve the community groups in planning and execution. The following specific attributes were present in successful projects:

(i) ***Design:*** most projects were developed only after the problems of the poor were identified. Programme modifications were made via the daily interaction with the beneficiaries.

(ii) ***Staffing:*** field staff need not be trained in business while their most important skill is the ability to relate to the people in poor communities.

(iii) ***Outreach:*** to reach the target group project staff must obtain acceptance in the community for themselves and the programme.

(iv) ***Selection:*** to help the very needy, the most important selection criterion is the individual client's reputation for credit-worthiness among community residents before acceptance into the group.

(v) ***Loans:*** loans should be initially small and should be for a maximum of six months. Interest charges should fully cover loan costs while the pay back periods should reflect the cash flow cycle of the business, perhaps daily in the case of hawkers and vendors and monthly in other cases.

(vi) ***Job skills training:*** programmes should combine job skills training with business training and intensive follow-up.

(vii) ***Marketing:*** the demand for skills and products within local communities must be identified as a prerequisite to initiating training and enterprise promotion. Where potential markets lie outside the community, direct intervention may be required to establish marketing channels for client enterprises.

As he concludes that owners of urban micro-businesses can use small loans and other assistance productivity and effective mechanisms exist for delivering help. Donors need to find ways to work with a multitude of implementing agencies including small local and national non-governmental organisations, larger co-operatives, national development agencies, banks and government agencies.

Some of these conclusions are endorsed by Hill (1983) in his overview of A.T. International's role in the development of the small-scale enterprise sector, based on case-studies of urban informal sector promotion programmes in Brazil and the Philippines. Credit emerges as the service offered of greatest utility. Testing a first-time client with a very small loan enables the client to display his credit-worthiness while building his self-confidence and familiarity with the credit institution. Subsequent loans of increasingly larger amounts, dependent on the repayment of the last, keeps risks manageable and ensures that the credit is utilized effectively. Credit-worthiness was confirmed with realized repayment rates of over 90 per cent. Hills asserts that universal administration of management training is not cost-effective and believes that the most widely appreciated training comes in the form of practical tips on an informal, on-site basis, *e.g.* how to open a bank account, where to purchase supplies, how to avoid official harassment, etc. In terms of technical advice, it was revealed that training in equipment maintenance and repair is often lacking and should be an important aspects of programming.

Sethuraman (1985) assesses policies for the informal sector in Indonesia but some of the ingredients of his strategy for employment promotion have universal applicability. He accepts that, while the sector has been deprived of credit, training and technical advice, the availability of resources is not the only problem. The general policy environment, particularly in large urban centres, has not been conducive to the development of the informal sector. In addition, a suitable institutional network is required to communicate with, and channel assistance to, the sector. Activities should be promoted which display growth potential and scope for productivity increase through technological change, capital accumulation and skill development. In this case, policies should favour the promotion of manufacturing, construction and transport sectors, as opposed to trade and service activities where growth is largely involutionary via the multiplication of enterprises, rather than evolutionary or productivity enhancing.

Financial and trade policies at the macro level can significantly influence the evolution of opportunities in the urban small-scale enterprise sector. The allocation of investment within the formal sector is an important instrument for promoting or dampening employment generation in the informal sector. The strengthening of links to the formal sector is viewed as an important way to widen the market for informal sector goods and services. Tariff and exchange rate policies can significantly influence the extent to which the small-scale self-employed can acquire strategic imported raw materials and tools and equipment. Yet a weak aspect of government policy arises from the fact that no single agency is made responsible for the execution, monitoring the evaluation of the policy's impact.

Considerations in the Pacific

Self-employment provides an important entry point into the monetarized economy. It has the advantage of allowing the participants to start in a modest way, which enables long established social and economic links to the village to be retained at first. However, traditional patterns of obligations make it harder for self-employment to be financially successful, especially when the product or service is one which family members are likely to want to buy. It is difficult to insist on payment or refuse credit. It makes for special difficulties for indigenous managers, who cannot as easily fall back on the defence that the firm forbids them to make such gifts, since they have more discretion in their actions. To resist these perceived obligations raises the risk of being ostracized. However, if the venture is successful, good standing can be restored by making contributions to village events. The net impact of these social and cultural influences is to make self-employment much more risky. It increases the likelihood of failure, and the cost of failure if ostracism has been earned in the process. Offsetting this increased risk is the possibility of using unpaid family assistance in the early stages of operation, and of knowing that in the last resort one can return to the family for support if the venture fails. Some elaborate devices for resisting family or village claims have developed, however, such as minimizing holdings of cash and stocks on display and establishing self-denying ordinances (*e.g.* cash only transactions) covering transactions in the village stores.

One evaluation has found no reason to believe that, at an operative level, Pacific Island workers are not capable of being as productive as their western counterparts (Blandy; Richardson, n.d.). The impediments to higher productivity, in practice, are the limited ability to manage (where there do seem to be particular difficulties), the limited level of skill development, the absence of sufficient economies of scale in production and the dearth of sophisticated capital equipment. The small size of most local markets is a key barrier although newer technologies are improving the productivity prospects of small-scale production. It may also be the devotion to arduous work and standardized hours are not ingrained in people's values. This does not make them unproductive, provided leisure is properly valued as part of their standard of living.

Education and Training[5]

In the advanced Western societies there is now a good deal more questioning of the value of separating education and training into formal educational institutions divorced to a large extent from the world of work. This is particularly so with respect to secondary schooling and technical training. The idea of 'traineeships' for young people entering the labour market, of more on-the-job training interspersed by focused periods of formal instruction, has gained a strong foothold, formal education, by itself, is not well adapted to the learning of many of the most useful applied skills, is necessarily general and theoretical in focus, and has a distinct bias towards the literary white-collar, and potential professional in its value-system.

If development on the basis of village traditions is conceived of as a priority of economic policy, there seems to be a strong case for the learning of village traditions and skills as part of the core primary school curriculum in addition to the cognitive skills, literacy and numeracy, and modern work skills basic to modernization. Traditional skills are also important to people in the formal sector who need to move back to or to maintain customary obligations and ties with their traditional villages. Such traditional skills as what the plants are, what grows, how to grow it, how to cook it, how to catch crabs, how to weave, how to thatch, etc. are basically survival skills in village life. In addition, modern practical techniques of carpentry, mechanical repair, mental work, electrical maintenance, and so on are important. These basic traditional and modern vocational skills should be part of the primary school curriculum in the Pacific Islands.

The secondary school curriculum might also involve a better integration with on-the-job training, technical training and the world of work, although opportunity should be provided for the most academically gifted to graduate to tertiary education. Far more people with technical and vocational skills are needed, compared with what one might call people with 'political kills'. There is a widespread view that the private sector needs to be encouraged to undertake more training activities, even if this means shifting government resources from formal schooling to assisting on-the-job training programmes, apprenticeships and youth traineeships in industry.

A way in which this process could be helped (which would also reduce the need for government assistance) is to widen the differential in pay between trainees are skilled persons and to have pay scales which increase more with duration of service. In a labour market with such a wage structure, youth employment opportunities are expanded and the tendency for the teenage unemployment to grow in minimized. In addition, the returns to firm-specific skills acquisition are increased by low job turnover and firms and workers attain higher productivity and earnings (House, 1992).

In most Pacific Islands countries the pay differential for youth, or for a learner, is very small (say 10 per cent difference as an order of magnitude). Furthermore, although some employee benefits, such as holidays, increase with duration of service, very often the return to on-the-job experience is minimal. These features of the pay structure contribute to youth unemployment, provide little incentive for people to acquire more practical skills, and provide little incentive for employees to broaden the content of training.

The acquisition of job skills is expensive. The costs include the worker's time spent in learning (rather than in producing), the time of the teachers, the use of equipment for instruction purposes, and the costs of mistakes. The relative importance of each of these will vary with the form of training. Broadly, there are two main places where job skills are learned: formal education institutions and the workplace. It is important to be aware of the greater potential role of the workplace in providing education and job skills, especially for those likely to become self-employed entrepreneurs in the informal sector.

Formal apprenticeship do not play much of a role in the training of skilled workers in the Island countries. We believe that there is considerable scope to expand this form of education and training as a means of upgrading the level of skills available. Apprenticeships have a number of advantages as a vehicle for learning in both the formal and informal sectors.

One advantage is that the apprentice is able to combine the learning of skills with the earning of income. This opportunity ensures that people who do not have the resources to go for several years without an income in order to do full-time formal education courses still have the chance to acquire marketable skills. This can be important for young people who need or want to make some contribution to the material income of the family. It can also enable older people who have responsibility for themselves and dependents to move to new levels or areas of skill. We think it inappropriate to place age restrictions which limit access to apprenticeships for youth. Persons who may wish to enter the case economy with relevant skills are not just new entrants to the workforce, *i.e.* young people, but also adults who are currently engaged in the traditional or subsistence economy, or in the cash economy as unskilled workers.

A second advantage is that apprenticeships are not costly to the government. Most of the costs of firm-specific skill training will be met by the employer, in return for having a more productive worker, and by the worker who accepts a low nominal wage during the period of apprenticeship. The employer incurs costs through paying the apprentice more than the value of his production in the early years of the apprenticeship and by providing the skilled teachers' time to train the apprentice, together with any necessary equipment which is being used for training rather than for current output (and any raw materials consumed in the training process). The worker pays by accepting a lower wage than he or she could obtain by working in an unskilled job or in the traditional sector. In return the apprentice receives marketable skills and the prospect of higher earnings in the future.[6]

A third advantage is that training in firm-specific skills in automatically related to skills which are currently of use to employers and which are learned using equipment and methods viewed by employers as contemporary. For the economy as a whole, this instant relevance can be a drawback, as it may make the workforce less flexible in response to changes in the pattern of work skills required, and in technology. More broadly-based learning in general skills, perhaps enhancing the trainee's prospects of self-employment, helps to reduce such inflexibility; but then the apprentice must bear a greater burden of the cost. It is here that government subsidies to training may be considered. This is a particular advantage to economies which have only a small cash, hence taxable, sector. Such training would also encourage apprentices to graduate to self-employment status, given their ability to purchase the requisite site and equipment, which again might require support from government to ensure access to credit windows for aspiring entrepreneurs.

Through apprenticeship, fluctuations in the demand for skills will automatically be reflected in comparable variations in supply, though with a time lag. If activity in a particular area is high, employers will be keen to take on extra workers and help them to obtain the skills necessary to be fully useful. The first effect of an increase in the number of apprentices is to reduce the stock of skilled workers available for production, since skilled worker time must be diverted to increase the volume of training. But as the apprentices advance to the stage of being reasonably skilled, even if not yet fully trained, the net stock of skilled workers begins to increase. Should there be a move to increase the role of apprenticeship, aid agencies could be very helpful in bridging the gap until the net stock of skills begins to rise. If the demand for a particular skill is in decline, employers will cease to take on more apprentices, and with a short lag the supply of that skill will also fall. This automatic adjustment of supply to demand is in contrast to the outcomes of the formal education sector, where there may be little connection between the number of people completing specific courses and the demand for those skills.

Several requirements must be met before an extensive programme of skill formation on the job (such as an apprenticeship scheme) is likely to be successful. One is that the pay structure must be graded in a way which both encourages firms to train workers, and rewards workers for the skills they acquire. Pay should be low for trainees and significantly higher for skilled workers. Indenture contracts (such an apprenticeship), in combination with such pay ladders, also have advantages. It normally takes several years for a worker to acquire substantial skills on the job. It is thus necessary for there to be adequate security of employment for the employer and for the apprentice not to have to fear that the apprenticeship will be broken in mid-term.

Management and Entrepreneurial Training

A particular training problem frequently mentioned is in the area of management. The question of training and acquisition of skills applies just as much to managers as it does to operative workers. Management and marketing skills do not come naturally, and shortages of these can seriously hinder development: indeed, they appear to be doing so in each of the countries in question.

Entrepreneurial training for self-employment is a much more difficult area in which to design appropriate institutional structures. Since most people do not become managers or self-employed entrepreneurs immediately on entering the workforce, we do not judge formal apprenticeship to be suitable in this area. Nonetheless, the ideas underlying apprenticeship remain relevant. Management skills are largely learned on the job, are costly to acquire and require already skilled people to teach them. Where a shortage of management and entrepreneurial skills already exists, diversion of skilled people's time to training and being trained is particularly difficult. It is here that schemes such as AESOP scheme can be particularly valuable. Under this arrangement, experienced managers from other countries, such as Australia and New Zealand, work for a period with participating firms for rates of pay well below normal. They may either provide training directly, or stand in for existing managers who are involved in training. The commitment and effectiveness of AESOP experts has been widely acknowledged.

Two observations are worth making. One is that it is likely to suffer somewhat from the free-riding problem found with apprenticeships. That is, a firm which takes advantage of the scheme to upgrade its management may well find that they then become attractive as potential employees in other firms or as self-employed entrepreneurs. Such post-training mobility reduces the incentives to train in the first place (for the firm but not for the employee). This problem may be diminished by participation by trade associations and national training authorities, where these exist. They can also be diminished by the trained manager undertaking not to accept employment in a competing firm for a period of time after leaving a firm providing training. The second comment is that the scheme should not be confined to managerial and professional staff. It is equally applicable to the development of technical and trade skills, and could be a very useful complement to an extension of apprenticeship training for self-employment.

Encouragement of Entrepreneurship

Entrepreneurship is an ability which must be nurtured in a different way. It involves imagination, foresight, originality, ability to overcome risk-aversion and other attributes which cannot be learned in the classroom. Nonetheless, many entrepreneurs have failed because they lack management, marketing and other skills which could be learned. The Pacific Island countries each have development banks and programmes which are designed to assist entrepreneurs. Entrepreneurs may be assisted in a number of ways. *First,* entrepreneurial activities are risky. Unless the initiator is already quite wealthy, it is not appropriate to assist such ventures solely with loan finance. If the enterprise were to fail, the entrepreneur is left to pay the debt, with little or no means of doing so. This can be very destructive of risk taking. Instead, the financing institution should consider providing at least part of the finance as equity. While this is legally more complicated, it enables the development bank to spread the risk somewhat, and in return, participate in the benefits of success.

Second, entrepreneurs often need more than just money. In addition, they need skills and advice to complement their own talents. Thus the development bank should be prepared to work in partnership, especially in the early stages. This may involve providing direct advice, or directing the principal to where advice may be found. It should also involve financial supervision and the requirement for planning, both for their own sakes and as valuable disciplines. In these matters it is important that the advisers are themselves experienced in business, and are not solely public servants. Again it may be possible for voluntary organisations, NGOs and aid agencies to assist in the early stages of the establishment of such advisory services.

Third, it must be acceptable to let failures fail, as the former republics of the ex-Soviet Union are learning the hard way in their endeavours to privatize state-owned enterprises. Unless this is the case, the financial and personnel resources of the development banks will be devoted, increasingly, to trying to shore up ventures which do not have a future. Failure are a normal part of business life, and judging when to pull out and when to press on is an important business skill. Public servants are unlikely to have the opportunity to develop this skill, which is one reason why it is so important to employ experienced business people in such a scheme.

The ILO's Start/Improve Your Business is an interesting project which has operated in many locations around the world. The Start Your Business (SYB) package is designed to assist aspiring entrepreneurs organise ideas, resources and to formulate business planning strategies that facilitate consideration by financial institutions. The Improve Your Business (IYB) materials are intended to enhance existing entrepreneurs and strengthen their performance. Both SYB and IYB training packages include a workbook, a handbook, a video and audio tape and are available commercially in bookstores throughout Fiji. A manual focusing on the specific needs of women in the local business community is being edited for publication later in 1993.

The SYB/IYB Unit will conduct 12 Start Your Business and Improve Your Business participant workshops in addition to two SYB/IYB Training of Trainers workshops and two consultants workshops over the next two years. The effectiveness of this programme will be closely monitored and the materials modified, as necessary.

Funding for the first phase of the SYB/IYB project—the design and development of the SYB/IYB materials—came from the Australian International Development Assistance Bureau (AIDAB) in late 1989. The implementation of these materials, the second phase, is being funded by the United Nations Development Programme.

The Small Business Advisory Unit has premises in downtown Suva which is accessible to the general public. The Unit is staffed by one United Nations volunteer specialist, two business advisers, a secretary and a diver.

The Unit maintains a high public profile in the local print, radio and television media. A national and regional newsletter focusing on enterprise development is also planned for publication in 1993.

Another fundamental objective of the Small Business Advisory Unit is to complement and co-ordinate the business development efforts of other projects currently used by other government and non-governmental organisations by setting up a resource library and arranging for referrals so that those requesting assistance receive the most appropriate service available.

The long-term goal of the Fiji SYB/IYB project is to establish a network and to maintain a cadre of qualified management trainers who are capable of conducting enterprise development workshops, hence sustaining this programme and eventually reducing dependence upon donor organisations.

Extension of the SYB/IYB programme to other countries in the Pacific is under consideration.

4. Unresolved Training Issues for the Informal Sector[7]

Before we ask the pertinent question: "What kind of training should be given and how should it be provided?", we need to present a typology of work in the informal sector.

A Typology of Work in the Informal Sector

The single most common characteristio of the informal sector is the small size of establishments, often consisting of only one individual, with perhaps a couple of hired workers. Four categories of workers can be identified in the informal sector, each with different implications for training.

Entrepreneurs

Entrepreneurs tend to be the best educated category of informal sector workers. The owners of small establishments are often the principal workers in the enterprise, and when others are employed, they tend to be relatives. Most owner-operators buy raw materials locally, manage their own finances, and sell locally to different buyers. The major constraints they face are the lack of capital and of access to credit, and a limited demand for goods and services. In addition, few informal sector enterprises are covered by government regulations or benefits. The lack of managerial and marketing skills, along with low or outmoded technical skills, are usually the greatest training problems faced. These are followed by the need to locate information on better technology and production processes (Papola, 1981; Sethuraman, 1981). Instruction, however, must be fully adapted to the requirements of the owner of a very small business, and conveyed in ways which are practical for entrepreneurs who have limited resources and little free time available. This group generally has a level of education that suggests that they can benefit from formal and non-formal training.

Establishment Workers

Establishment workers are those employed by entrepreneurs. Wage-earnings employees, apprentices, and unpaid family workers make up the three or four additional workers, on average, that the owner-worker requires to meet market demand. They are usually employed on a regular, full-time basis, have relatively high skill levels, and they may have limited formal schooling. The availability of free time for training remains a problem with establishment workers, as with most others in the informal sector. On the other hand, with the exception of introducing new technology and managerial skills, apprenticeship and informal on-the-job training appear to provide substantial skill training.

Independent Workers

Another, often large, category is that of independent workers. While they may work for wages, they are basically self-employed. Rickshaw drivers, street vendors and hawkers, bicycle, clock, and shoe repairman, producers of earthenware and leather products, and laundry men and sweet cake bakers, are but a few of the multitude of individuals who perform daily tasks in the streets and alleys of large urban areas, along village roads and in the town squares of rural communities. They provide simple but essential services, independent but restricted by the generally low market value of their product or service. Papola (1981, p. 54) observes that "independent workers constitute the smallest units in the category of establishments and are the simplest forms of production units in the informal sector".

Workers in this category cannot easily be trained. Although many work from fixed locations, they are generally unorganised and difficult to count or keep track of. They have few resources and little time that they can give to training, and their working hours may be irregular. Many are so poor that they may be unable to afford even minimal extra expenses.

Better tools and equipment, and technologically more advanced ways of working, are desirable, but low-paid, labour-intensive work gives a competitive advantage in low-demand markets (LIM, 1978, pp. 75-81). The independent worker can compete, to a certain extent, because his physical labour is less costly than machinery or equipment. Independent workers are generally less educated than entrepreneurs or establishment workers in the informal economy or similar workers in the formal sector (Ettema, 1984, pp. 487-510; Waldorf; Waldorf, 1983, pp. 587-607; Papola, 1981). Many are in fact illiterate, which greatly restricts potential retraining and upgrading.

Casual Workers

Casual workers are the most disadvantaged category. Their jobs rely heavily on manual labour. Often little training is needed, and earnings are usually low, although some may earn more than their counterparts in the formal sector (Waldorf; Waldorf,

1983, pp. 587-607). Household workers make up the largest group, with gardeners, cleaners and sweepers also accounting for significant numbers. Construction labourers, watchmen, spinners and weavers fill other typical casual jobs. Casual workers are the least educated category. Most of them are illiterate and few have completed more than two or three years of schools. Work skills can usually be learned incidentally on the job. This fact, along with low pay and the lack of prospects associated with casual employment, suggests that if training is made available to causal workers, it probably should be directed to more skilled jobs that provide greater social and private returns.

Although these categories are useful for purposes of analysis and discussion, they are not exact or fixed. There is considerable movement of individuals between categories, as well as into and out of the informal sector.

An Alternative Classification

(i) The Craft Sub-Sector

In the craft sub-sector, production units are usually small, with work completed in home workshops by self-employed individuals, including a high production of women. Skills are basically learned on the job through an older worker teaching the novice over a relatively long period of time (King, 1977; Peil, 1979, pp. 3-22; Allen, 1982, pp. 123-137). The manipulative skills mainly taught usually take a long time to learn well. The greatest training need of the craft sub-sector appears to be the acquisition of marketing and accounting skills since the owner-artisan has usually advanced on the basis of technical, rather than business skills. Enterprises that produce quality products are also limited by their inability to expand their markets (Steel, 1979, pp. 271-284). In rural areas, it may be particularly beneficial to facilitate the establishment of marketing co-operatives.

(ii) The Worshop Sub-Sector

The workshop sub-sector produces a variety of products in addition to its services and repair activities. Its output may directly feed the modern sector through intermediate products.

Papola (1981, p. 65) observes that 'the only segment of the informal sector that can be expected to contribute significantly to income and employment growth is that of manufacturing units'. Relatively large amounts of income are generated in the workshop sector; an increase in output generates considerably more employment than in other activities, and growth is more 'autonomous' than in trade and commercial activities. Furthermore, there is some evidence to show that the major contribution to the urban economy and its growth has been made by units which are small but have technological and market characteristics of the formal sector units. Small manufacturing units are found to be the key segments of the 'informal' sector in this context, but in terms of technology, productivity and marketing characteristics they compare reasonably well with units in the formal sector. In fact, most of them are technologically and marketwise integrated with units in the organised sector (Papola, 1981, p. 124).

Any training scheme to address the workshop sub-sector should probably be structured around on-the-job activities, should co-ordinate learning with existing production processes and should introduce technologies and production processes that have a reasonable chance of being absorbed into the prevailing work mode. The World Bank (1980, p. 49) suggests that trainers "should be recruited from among the best local workers; and the community should be responsible for organising and running these training programmes".

(iii) Commerce and Services

The commercial and services sub-sector is usually large in developing countries. It is often integrated with other sub-sectors or with formal sector enterprise. For example, supporting services may be purchased from another establishment, or consumer goods may be purchased from a large, local supplier for resale (Sethuraman, 1981). The World Bank (1980, p. 99) observes that "for the literate rural dweller, the transition from daily marketing to the permanent status of an urban trader is the first step into the wider field of commerce and services". The overall growth rate of this sub-sector and its ability to absorb labour, however, are limited, since "trade and commerce activities have an induced rather than autonomous growth and, therefore, cannot be made to grow faster than warranted by the growth of other sectors" (Papola, 1981, p. 65). And even when these activities expand, the employment potential of commercial and service firms remains limited. Fewer workers are added for a given increase in output than in other economic activities. As previously suggested, lack of capital and credit restrictions remain major obstacles to the extension of activities. Training needs generally are in respect of marketing and management.

Training for Employment in the Informal Sector

In the less developed sectors of the economy, particularly in traditional societies, the greatest part of occupational training is acquired through informal means. The novice learns by observing and assisting other workers. The largely incidental and unorganised character of informal training distinguishes it from formal and non-formal programmes such as those offered through ministries of education or labour, or out-of-school by those individual firms and public and private agencies. To be sure, non-formal training may take place at the work site, but it is nevertheless a planned and organised form of training.

The amount of training obtained through informal means far exceeds that offered through formal or non-formal programmes. Blaug (1979, p. 396), for one, suggests "that the vast majority of the labour force throughout the Third World learn the skills they need for their livelihood not in the systems of formal and non-formal education, but informally...".

Probably to a greater extent than realized, formal education has a direct effect on the occupational success and mobility of individuals within the informal sector. Evidence suggests that those with basic literacy and numeracy fare better in the informal sector than those who lack these skills (House, 1984, 1987). Moreover, the lack of such skills often prevents the individual from taking advantage of the training opportunities available locally (Philips, 1978), and may constitute the single most tenacious barrier to occupational progress. Access to advanced skill training appears highly important to occupational mobility in the informal sector.

Although relatively few individuals may have access to formal on non-formal training, the skills learned through organised training programmes are often transferred to the informal sector. As McLaughlin (1979, p. 37) observes, "technical practice in the informal sector continues to be influenced profoundly by the infusion of skills and technology from the formal sector". And it is through this inflow of skills, often from formal sector workers who opt to move into the informal sector, that technical upgrading is achieved (ILO, 1979).

From a training policy point of view, it is not so clear how formal training should address informal sector training needs. Blaugh (1979, p. 397) cautions that 'at present, the best thing that could happen to informal education is that it be left alone, not the least because it appears to achieve a wide range of educational objectives more successfully than the formal system" One of the strengths of informal training is its unstructured and improvised character, which makes it flexible and adaptable to immediate employer needs. Hunter (1973, p. 282) suggests that 'since informal education is more specifically related to real needs and to locally felt demands, it may well be one of the most flexible and efficient forms of education there is...".

It is also difficult to formulate a training policy for the informal sector because there are no clear alternatives for financing the training. The cost of informal sector training is largely borne by the trainee and his family, notably through the payment of fees. In this sense, informal sector training is self-supporting. Direct, organised training interventions on a large scale would involve considerable resources that are not being supplied by governments. Furthermore, direct intervention may disrupt a system that now provides training at lower personal and social costs than can be achieved through other means.

Another problem is to provide training that is accessible to informal sector workers and that directly addresses their skill needs. Training may be inaccessible simply because of entry requirements. Workers in the informal sector are usually characterized by low levels of formal education are limited literacy and numeracy, and they may for that reason not be capable of successful participation in conventional training programmes.

Training may also be inaccessible because it cannot be afforded. Even token registration fees, when combined with transportation cost and expenses for instructional supplies, can be a real barrier to informal sector workers. In addition, the trainee is likely to be faced with high indirect (opportunity) costs. Work hours are usually long, often spent in piece work, and any time lost through training constitutes a real loss of earned income. And it is highly unlikely that employers will provide time off to pursue training. Although the employer in the modern sector may view additional training as a net gain because it leads to a better-qualified worker, the small entrepreneur will probably feel threatened: there is little guarantee that newly acquired skills will not result in demands for higher wages, the loss of the worker to a competitor, or the establishment of an independent business by the former employee (ILO, 1979a). Lacking the most rudimentary educational skills and faced with real economic and time constraints, informal sector employees may not enrol in training programmes organised for them. The ILO (1977, pp. 217-229), for example, found that in Chile programmes tended to have a high concentration of more prosperous workers; poorer candidates simply did not apply.

Courses for informal sector workers may offer instruction more suited to modern sector employment because this is what those who design the programme are most familiar with. In rural areas, in particular, the mismatch between organised skills training and indigenous production techniques may be marked. But even if training is relevant, employment may still be blocked. Entry into certain occupations may be tightly controlled through a small, well-knit network of social and personal relationships, and access to jobs may be jealously guarded. Training that is not conducted within this network may, in effect, place potential new entrants outside the power structure, and they may find it extremely difficult to gain access to jobs.

Approaches to Training for the Informal Sector

The following is a brief review of three approaches to training. Individually, they may not overcome the problems associated with training for work in the informal sector.

Collectively, however, they do point to promising practices, or ways to link training more closely to needs. Participants may wish to consider their relevance for training in the Pacific Island countries.

It is not surprising that apprenticeship constitutes a major way in which the young enter the informal sector. Few initial skills and little experience are needed. The apprentice merely has to locate a willing master, often a relative, pay the fees usually associated with such training, and be willing to undergo an extended period of training. At the start, Allen (1982, p. 128) observes, such apprentices act "as little more than errand boys or menial labour: going to the market, taking care of the shop, sweeping the floors, and being generally available'. In time, the apprentice will pick up skills by observing, be given simple tasks to perform, and eventually be expected to complete complex tasks, returning value to the master in the form of labour. If time permits, some formal instruction will be given, but basically the apprentice learns by observing and doing (Peil, 1979, pp. 3-22). The quality of training is only as good as the skills of the master and his willingness to teach the apprentice all he knows. Apprenticeship is a "relationship of exploitation", Allen (1982, p. 127) cautions, "in which the component of 'cheap labour'—as opposed to 'excellent training'—comes to dominate".

Nevertheless, because of its extensive use, and because of strong tradition, particularly in the craft and workshop sectors, skills probably can be best enhanced by working within the context of the indigenous apprenticeship system.

(i) *Making Services Available: the Extension Model*

McLaughlin (1979, p. 222) suggests that informal sector apprenticeship can be directly improved by providing more opportunity for technical upgrading. He observes, for example, that 'those artisans who had received specific trade training in an institution were more productive (*i.e.* had a higher output) and had higher earnings than artisans with only the usual apprenticeship training". One approach is to make technical assistance directly available to the employing establishment. This is an idea based on the agricultural extension model, in which assistance is provided to individual farmers either at the workplace or through a supporting centre. In an example reported by McLaughlin (1979, pp. 224-225), a truck was equipped with a complete mobile workshop used as an instructional centre. Through a schedule of regular visits, team members assisted small-scale mechanics, who had particularly difficult repair problems. Instruction focused on the problem at hand.

A variation of the extension model in the service centre. Working from a fixed location, a full range of services is provided. These may include: supplying or locating training; providing credit and financial services; assisting entrepreneurs with marketing and distribution; providing information on technical developments. Instead of being given in isolation, training is integrated with other services, thus providing co-ordinated support.

Applying the service centre concept exclusively to training, Thornton (1984) advocates a workforce productivity centre. A technical assistance unit of the centre helps entrepreneurs to assess their training needs and develop plans for training. A clearing house unit maintains a comprehensive, computerized catalogue of training materials, including those developed within the country and those available from outside sources. A training resource bank maintains a comprehensive list of individuals, firms, and public and private agencies prepared to conduct training within the country. In addition, a revolving, low-interest loan fund is available for financing to training activities.

The extension model in effect provides training specific to immediate work needs and assists individuals or small groups. Its effectiveness is largely based on the extent to which the individual problems of trainees are successfully addressed. A premium is thus placed on highly versatile and qualified staff capable of dealing with a range of complex problems. They may be hard to find, but they are crucial to the effectiveness of this approach to training.

In the case of the service centre, it may be preferable for staff to make referrals rather than supply direct technical assistance that can be provided better elsewhere. This can reduce the complexity of the assistance given. The staff's role is to facilitate the identification and use of existing resources by bringing them to the attention of firms.

(ii) Day Release

The release approach is a combination of regular on-the-job apprenticeship training and classroom instruction, with the week divided between work on the job and instruction at a vocational centre. The programme in Kumasi, Ghana, for example, has three stages. The first lasts about three months. The apprentice then returns to work full time. The second stage starts about nine months later and also lasts three months. The third stage consists of three months of training in the last year of apprenticeship. Formal instruction takes place two days a week and is roughly divided into 75 per cent practical and 25 per cent theoretical work. Each stage is more intensive than the one before. At the completion of training, the participant is eligible to take a trade examination.

The key to the programme is collaboration with the local vocational centre, whose staff and facilities are used. Members of the local Artisan's Co-operative Society also fully participate in instructional planning, helping to realize the "goal of delivering specially tailored supplementary training to an occupational group previously ignored by the educational establishment" (McLaughlin, 1979, p. 231).

In Jordan, the Vocational Training Corporation (VTC) conducts an apprenticeship training programme, combining formal instruction with on-the-job training. Trainees are placed with a variety of employers, including substantial numbers of small, informal sector enterprises. In the case of small employers, the trainee is assigned to a supervised work group at the job site, returning to a VTC centre from one to three times a week for formal instruction. In addition, the instructor or training officer makes regular visits to the workplace, monitoring the progress of trainees and providing technical assistance to the employers. Not only are employers helped through direct assistance but it is also possible to maintain a functional link between instruction in the centre and work. Two years of formal instruction in the centre, combined with practical on-the-job training, are followed by one full year of work experience. A Trade training Certificate is awarded upon completion of training (Herschbach *et al.*, 1985)

Both of these programmes combine elements of formal instruction with informal sector employment. This is an advantage to the extent that technical skills are transferred to the informal sector. Trainees, moreover, can move between the informal and formal sectors. On the other hand, the more disadvantaged elements of the population may avoid these programmes, because of educational, social or economic barriers.

Capable training officers and instructors are essential for successful training. They must supervise instruction, provide liaison with employers, negotiate agreements and monitor the progress of trainees. Members of the permanent instructional staff must have a variety of skills, because they will need to address a variety of skill requirements at the workplace.

(iii) Production Activities

Van Steenwyk (1985) advocates the use of production activities in structured vocational training programmes. Instruction is fully integrated with the production of items for sale in local markets, using indigenous or 'waste' materials and appropriate technology. Trainees are involved in all stages, including design and development, production, marketing, sales and accounting. In this way, they gain experience appropriate to the establishment of their own small shops or business. At the same time, training is more affordable, since trainees 'earn while they learn', thus offsetting the cost of training.

The major advantage of production activities is that they use adapted technology and local materials in the creation of products that prove competitive on the local market. The trainee is thus learning skills that will enable him to succeed in the context of the informal sector, not to mention the fact that the cost barrier to training is partially removed. These programmes are probably best run through volunteer and local agencies, because considerable flexibility is needed to adopt them to prevailing circumstances, and such flexibility cannot be achieved through government-run programmes.

As products are designed, produced and marketed, the necessary technical skills for each step are identified are can be built into the construction. This mechanism allows instruction to be adjusted to an on-going basis. Moreover, instruction is directly tied to its application. Because production centres have more control over the design of instruction and have wide arrays of practical activities to offer trainees, they can achieve a more satisfactory combination of theoretical and practical instruction than conventional on-the-job training.

Strong day-to-day, routine working relationships must be established between those who run the production centre, those who plan the instruction and work, those who market products and those who buy the products. Production centres should not compete with local businesses. Instead, they should produce goods or services not readily available in their communities. In addition to minimizing outside criticism, this approach offers greater potential for opening up new employment opportunities locally.

Again, instructors need a wide range of skills, because production often draws from different technical specialities and involves many different materials. It may be difficult to find instructors who have both broad practical experience and production management experience and skills.

Although trainees can perform many of the management tasks of production supervising instructors have greater responsibilities for management than those in programmes that do not involve production.

Lastly, working capital in the form of a revolving fund is needed to start a production centre. A loan gives greater assurance of proper management than an outright donation of capital.

5. Conclusion

Given the demographically-induced current and prospective employment problem in the Pacific, largely attributable to past and on-going rapid popuiation and labour force growth and the kind of economic structure which has evolved, policies and programmes which promote above-subsistence-level income and employment opportunities require the utmost priority. Despite past policy statements of good intentions towards small-scale, self-employed businessmen, at the practical level not much has been accomplished in the way of establishing positive inventives.

The most common constraints faced by small enterprises in the Pacific and elsewhere include a lack of access to working capital and credit, poor infrastructure and inadequate tools and equipment, inferior managerial and technical know-how, and the high cost of becoming registered and licensed. Once operational they face shortages of raw materials and skilled labour, limited markets because of intense competition in easy-to-enter lines of business, and insecurity of tenure because of the often negative attitude of the authorities, particularly those at the local level.

A general review of projects to overcome these constraints has concluded that the most effective programme design is one which targets very poor entrepreneurial clients, emphasizes credit rather than programme staff for assessing credit worthiness, and initially extends very small loans with the proviso that larger sums will be forthcoming if repayment is full and prompt. Such a programme lands itself to institutionalization and helps to empower the poor via community-level organisations (Stearns, 1985). Other experiences have shown that loans administered by banks, with an emphasis on group solidarity and loan pay back, have many positive features including a low default rate and the creation of a revolving fund of reloanable credit.

However, the availability of resources is not the only problem. Financial and trade policies at the macro-level can significantly influence the evolution of opportunities in the urban small-scale sector. Subsidization of investment and other incentives offered to the formal sector can dampen opportunities in the urban small-scale sector. The promotion of linkages between the two sectors can be an important way to widen the market for informal sector goods and services. Tariff and exchange rate policies can influence the extent to which the small-scale self employed can acquire strategic imported raw materials and tools and equipment.

Most of the surveys of the urban informal sector stress the heterogeneity of enterprises, as reflected in a wider dispersion of income, employment structure and technology. However, a significant number of entrepreneurs and their employees are able to realise incomes at least as high as could be received in the lower echelons of the formal sector, particularly where certain barriers to entry restrict competition. The findings confirm that not only does the informal sector provide employment at a much lower cost than similar activities in the formal sector, but that it provides incomes, basic needs and practical skills to a growing proportion of the urban labour force.

Evidence suggests that management may be a major obstacle to the expansion of small Pacific Island business apart from problems relating to capital scarcity, raw material supplies, skilled labour bottlenecks and limitations of market size. Legal barriers to self-employment have long been recognised as important and seven broad areas which constrain entry relate to licensing and registration, regulation of premises, labour laws, taxes, debt collection, lack of legal protection for product innovations, and foreign trade restrictions.

In the arena of non-financial promotional programmes many public and private institutions and agencies are involved, the major emphasis in some systems of education is on self-reliance and practical training, with the aim of ensuring that graduates at each level are capable of entering self-employment. However, the formal training system is criticized for contributing little in practice towards preparing students for self-employment. Unequal access to vocational and technical opportunities greatly hinders the chances of women starting their own businesses.

Meanwhile, most NGOs tend to be very target-specific in their promotional efforts and are able to reach only a limited number of potential beneficiaries. Training and extension services are frequently manned by inexperienced personnel with little exposure to the needs of small business. More emphasis must be given, therefore, to the preparation of appropriate curricula and materials in the training of small-scale enterprise trainer, as well as exposing students to practical problems. Co-ordination of various programmes is frequently lacking so that duplication is common. To transform policies into appropriate action, competent and committed personnel are needed but are believed to be not currently in place, especially in the public sector.

Very often, the general policy framework currently prevailing inhibits the expansion of self-employment. Governments need to divest themselves of direct involvement in promoting smaller enterprises and restrict interventions to creating essential infrastructure and to providing networks of information in which small entrepreneurs can prosper. For example, lending operations should be left to private financial institutions; industrial protection should be curtailed in order to promote a more competitive environment where the small business can thrive, all price controls on non-essential commodities should be removed and a flexible exchange rate should reflect a currency's value. Such reforms will facilitate the competitiveness of small-scale production in both domestic and foreign markets and allow greater access to imported raw materials and spare parts and perhaps to export markets. Furthermore, preferential treatment in gaining government contracts might be considered for those large businesses which are able to show that they extensively subcontract to smaller enterprises. A comprehensive review of all pertinent laws affecting small enterprises might be undertaken in order that those having negative consequences will be removed or revised.

Implementation of this comprehensive package of policy reform will create far-reaching new opportunities for self-employment and small-scale business expansion. In the foreseeable future the small-scale sector, in both rural and urban areas, must be relied upon to absorb into employment the greatest share of the rapidly growing labour force. Therefore, no time must be lost before an innovative 'enabling environment' is created. Any delay will have profound adverse consequences for decades to come.

NOTES

1. This section draws heavily on a recent World Bank Study (World Bank, 1993).
2. Locked; Jamison; Lau (1980) have confirmed from a review of country studies the extent to which productivity in agriculture is related to improvements in basic education.
3. This section draws on material in House, Ikiara; McCormick (1990).
4. Some of the case-studies presented in Baron and van Ginneken (1985) indeed confirm that informal sector production is efficient, labour intensive and purchased largely by the poor. The study of furniture-making in Kenya by House (1981, 1985) illustrates how the promotion of small-scale carpenters would enhance policies for employment growth and poverty reduction.
5. This section draws heavily on Blandy; Richardson, n.d.
6. If all the skills acquired by the apprentice are general or marketable elsewhere, increasing the graduate apprentice's mobility and his access to other labour market opportunities, the apprentice must pay the implicit costs of training, for the training firm has little to gain (House, 1992).
7. Here we draw heavily on a paper by Herschboch (1989).

REFERENCES

Allan, (1993). *Informal Sector Employment in Egypt*. Technical ILO/UNDP Comprehensive Employment Strategy Mission to Egypt, 1980. Geneva, ILO.

Aboagye, A.A. (1988). *The Informal Sector in Mogadishu: An Analysis of a Survey*. Addis, Abada, ILO/JASPA.

Allen, Hugh. (1977). *The Informal Urban Industrial Sector and Growth: Some Thoughts on a Modern Mythology*. Discussion Paper No. 259. University of Nairobi, Institute for Development Studies.

Allen, R. "Capitalist Development and the Educational Role in Nigerian Apprenticeship", in *Comparative Education*. Vol. 18, No. 2, 1982.

Ashe, J. (1981). *The PISCES Studies: Assisting the Smallest Economic Activities of the Urban Poor*. Washington, D.C., USAID.

Ashe, J. (1985). "Extending Credit and Technical Assistance to the Smallest Enterprises", in R. Bromley (ed.): *Planning for Small Enterprises in the Third World Cities*. Oxford, Pergamon Press.

Baron, C: Van Ginneken, W. (1985). *Appropriate Products, Employment and Technology*. London, Macmillan.

Blandy, R.; Richardson, S. (n.d.), "Pacific Island Labour Markets'. Mimeographed.

Blaug, M. "The Quality of Population in Developing Countries, with Particular Reference to Education and Training', in Hauser, P.M. (ed.): *World Population and Development*. New York, Syracuse University Press, 1979.

Cardova, E. (1986). "A Typical Employment Patterns: Significance and Repercussions", in *Social and Labour Bulletin*, Vol. 1, April.

Etterma, W. "Small-scale Industry in Malawi", in *The Journal of Modern African Studies*, Vol. 22, No. 3, 1984.

Herschboch, D.R. (1989). "Training and the Urban Informal Sector: Some Issues and Approaches" in F. Fluitman, *Training for Work in the Informal Sector*, ILO, Geneva.

Hill, D. (1983), "Overview", in M. Bear, H. Jakelen and M. Tiller: *Microenterprise Development in the Urban Informal Sector*, A.T. International Working Paper.

House, W.J. (1981a). "Redistribution, Consumer Demand and Employment in Kenyan Furniture Making", in *Journal of Development Studies*, July.

House, W.J. (1981b). "Nairobi's Informal Sector: An exploratory Study", in T. Killick (ed.): *Papers on the Kenyan Economy*, Nairobi, Heinemann.

25

Education Employment Linkages in the Informal Sector

Brahm Prakash

1. Importance of Informal Sector

As generation of additional employment met with growing resistance in the organized sector of the economy, the attention of planners and development analysts turned towards other sectors. Informal sector was 'discovered' as one such area which was see to be playing a crucial role in absorbing more and more additional labour. However, understanding about this sector was rather limited because there was hardly any information available about organisation of work in this sector. One had a little knowledge about skills that were required in this sector and even less about how one could go about providing these. It is therefore believed that an analysis of linkages between education and employment in the informal sector would provide useful insights for educational planning.

2. Difficulties in analyzing Informal Sector Activities

There are several methodological difficulties which come in the way of rigorous analysis of this sector. First of all, as already mentioned, it is the absence of empirical evidence. Even though ILO has generated a series of studies on informal sectors of several cities of the Third World, the total evidence is hardly sufficient to provide a detailed picture of the phenomenon and is certainly not in conformity with the magnitude of the problem.

Secondly, the informal sector tends to acquire different profiles in different settings. Whereas, there are common features like 'employment for livelihood' which are universal in their manifestation, other aspects like the economic sector, occupational category, wage level and working conditions in which this employment is created remain contingent upon the larger spatio—socio—economic—cultural context. Consequently comparability of one sector with the other becomes difficult. This has inhibited emergence of a concerted strategic intervention in the area.

Finally, whatever little evidence has been created, it deals primarily with the more overt and immediate economic issues of employment and earnings. It does not go deeper into questions of skill, training and the role of education therein. This particular deficiency has been a constraint on human resource economies in the informal sector.

3. A Profile in Informal Sector

In the early eighties a study of informal sector in the port city of Bombay was conducted by ILO-ICSW.[1] The empirical evidence generated in this study is useful to describe the profile of informal sector and the role of education therein.

Table—25.1: Formal/Informal Sector Wage Differential by Sex

		Formal sector	*Informal sector*	*Overall*
Male wage	M	367.96	234.74	329.9
Employees	SD	(196.13) n = 1371	(139.58) n = 539	(191.56) n = 1910
Female wage Employees		229.79 (143.9) n = 73	134.27 (85.44) n = 62	184.24 (128.61) n = 135
All wage		361.0 (196.13) n = 1455	224.67 224.67 n = 602	

Note: M = Mean, SD = Standard Deviation, N = Number of Cases

The study shows that most of the employees in the informal sector were relatively young (Mean age 31.4 years; Standard Deviation 11.25) and had joined the labour force only in the recent past (3-5 years ago). Though the pattern of jobs varied from location to location, they were mostly engaged in unskilled jobs, or were engaged in such jobs for which on-the-job training was provided within the same taking. It usually meant unpaid work during apprenticeship, and only a small payment thereafter even though conditions of work were arduous and difficult. Depending upon the neighbourhood one could have pre-dominance of tailoring activity or auto repairing, or welding. But, more importantly, there were so many types of small and odd jobs that the residual category of 'other jobs' over-shadowed any other category. This variety in some sense is the hall-mark of informal sector activities.

But in terms of industrial divisions the maximum concentration of employment was found in 'Personal Services' manufacturing and trading activities in that order. However, the scale of operations in all these activities were extremely small. Their predominance and relative shared varied from location to location and was more a function of the neighbourhood and market linkages with the rest of the urban economy.

Even though working conditions were difficult, wages were low (Rs. 11.50 per day in terms of 1978 prices, approximately then equivalent to US$1.50) and there was absence of inter-job mobility. The entry into informal sector market was relatively easy. Most of the employees did not have to wait for entering into the labour market. Equally important was the fact that information about jobs and recruitment was carried out with the help of friends, relatives and common acquaintance. This is one of the more important features which has been well recognized and documented in the informal sector literature.

4. Education in the Informal Sector

A high proportion of these employees (thirty-nine per cent) was illiterate. About twenty-eight per cent were educated up to the fourth standard and another twenty-eight per cent were

Table—25.2: Formal/Informal Sector Wage Differential by Education

		Mean Wages	
Level of education		*Formal sector*	*Informal sector*
Nil education	M	336.14	197.8
	SD	(194.46)	(131.9)
	N	n = 4496	n = 236
0-4th grade		364.4	239.6
		(185.9)	(146.5)
		n = 389	n = 166
5-8th		356.2	239.4
		(174.4)	(129.1)
		n = 432	n = 172
S.S.C. and above		469.28	303.41
		(267.78)	(172.22)
		n = 119	n = 22
Mean wages		361.0	224.7

Note: M = Mean, SD = Standard deviation, N = Number of cases

educated between fifth and eighth standard. In other words as many as 95 per cent were educated less than grade eight. These percentages were substantively more than those found in the formal sector. But the more interesting results is that whatever the educational levels, the informal sector yields similar income differentials for different levels of education as is the case in the formal sector. This identical 'valuing' of educational (in pro rate sense) is an interesting finding. It supports the contention that the informal sector is a continuation of the formal sector and largely prices 'characteristics in the same way except that it is marked by low skills, low productivity and excess supply of labour. This leads to low wages and high earning differentials between the formal and informal sector.

The second ıspect which needs to be noted is that whereas there is a significant earning difference between illiterates and the literates, it is not so when we compare those who have studied up to four years with those who have studied up to grade eight. But again it is significant for those who are SSC (grade 10) and above. In other words, there are clear cut thresholds of education which are priced differently by the market. It does not yield much premium for drop outs or those who have not completed their schooling upto a definite standard. The relevant data has been given in Tables—25.1 and 25.2. On the face of it, the earning differentials may not seem much, but as a proportion of their meagre earnings, these are certainly substantial.

NOTES

1. ILO-ICSW *The Urban Dean-End?* Pattern of Employment Among Slum Dwellers: Bombay, Somaiya, 1983.

26

Small-scale Enterprises: Development and the Role of Education and Training

Anthony Nforba Nchari

1. The Concept of the Small-scale Enterprises

During the last decade, most African governments and their counterparts in other third world countries have developed enormous interest in promoting small-scale enterprises as a vehicle for promoting industrialization and accelerating development in their respective economies. A number of efforts and measures have been put in place to enable the attainment of this goal. Cameroon, for instance, created the Center for Assistance to Small-and Medium-sized Enterprises (CAPME) and the Guarantee Fund to Small-and Medium-sized Enterprises (FOGAPE) as technical instruments to encourage private domestic initiatives. Some Governments and development-oriented NGOs in the industrialized countries as well as UN specialized agencies have been making significant contributions towards promoting small-scale enterprises in developing countries.

The definition of what constitutes a Small-scale enterprise (SSE) has logically been the starting point for the identification of enterprises that should belong to this category, for the purpose of their benefiting from promotional activities. However, no universally accepted definition has so far emerged. One study undertaken by the Georgia Institute of Technology, USA, identified more than 50 definitions in 75 countries (Neck and Nelson, 1977). The problem of an adequate and operational definition of the SSE stems from the fact that most definitions appear to be governed by the interest of the perceiver, the purpose of the definition and the stage of development of the environment in which the definition will be employed.

An overview of the wide range of definitions reveals the amount of capital invested, the number of persons employed, the production capacity, the type of enterprise and technology used are the most prevalent criteria. Mauritius, a country well-known for actively promoting Small-scale enterprises (SSE), defines SSE as one with a maximum capital of Rupees (Rs) 300,000 (equivalent of about $US17,250) and employing a maximum of 25 persons. Ethiopia emphasizes the size of capital as basis for classification setting 1,000,000 Ethiopian Birr (equivalent $US 500,000) as the ceiling to be considered small. In her capital-oriented definition, Cameroon merges both the Small-and Medium-scale Enterprises (SME) in search for a definition setting the upper limit of FCFA 500,000,000 (equivalent $US 2,000,000) to be considered as SME.

From these examples, one can draw the logical conclusion that the problem of defining the SSE, no matter the criteria used, arises when attempting to set an acceptable upper limit for the definition, given the fact that there is no lower limit. Whilst the Ministry of Labour officials would tend to emphasize the number of people employed as the most pertinent criteria, manufacturers tend to emphasize the type of technology used or the maximum levels of capital used for production. Traders use the ceiling limit in the sales volume as the best criteria whilst service personnel view the total number of customers as the best criteria for defining the SSE. A combination of criteria, as in the case of Mauritius (capital and employment), seems a more acceptable approach since it takes into account other relevant criteria. Even then, the problem of an adequate and operational definition of the SSE that is universally accepted cannot be resolved once and for all. This was the conclusion arrived at in a 1986 report on the Study on Small-and Medium Scale Enterprises in the EEC member countries.

Given the varying perceptions of the SSE due to different interests and levels of economic development, there would be little or no justification striving to achieve a universally accepted definition. Each definition is important and acceptable in a given context. It is essential for the SSE development promoter to operate within each given context in undertaken SSE promotional activities.

What seems clear is that no matter the definition, given the country and context one can identify sub-divisions within the SSE sector. In an attempt to identify such sub-divisions, SSE's can be classified into 3 broad categories namely *the-Upper, Middle, and Lower level SSE's*. In the developing world, the description *micro-producers* is increasingly being used to refer to the predominant lowest class SSE's., *i.e.* the heterogeneous group of the extremely poor small producers of goods and services (World Bank/Urban Edge, 1989.)

One general characteristic of the SSE is that the owner or manager performs most functions undertaking general administration, procurement, sales and finance activities. The SSE can be found in any area of business activity where enterprising people have spotted business opportunities. It can be anything from a shop, farm, carpentry, workshop, hair dressing saloon, a tailor's establishment, a restaurant, a small printing press to a small manufacturing concern.

Small-Scale Enterprises include the informal business sector *i.e.* unregistered enterprises operating in a variety of activity areas without permits or licences. This heterogeneous group of very small producers or traders existing outside the formal sector includes hawkers and young people involved in fishing, weaving and technical work and vehicle repairs. The absence of regulations and registration formalities that characterizes this sector, suggests the informal SSEs to be dominant in Sub-Saharan African countries. Comprehensive data is not availablr to support this claim. However, a World Bank study undertaken in one of these countries revealed that only 1 out of 70,000 small businesses was registered. In Cameroon the dominance of the informal SSE is readily observable in the towns.

II. Small-scale Enterprises and the Development of African Economies

Most Sub-Saharan African countries are currently facing serious economic problems demonstrated by the declining Gross National Product, rising levels of unemployment at an alarming rate, increasing external debt, a perpetual external trade imbalance vis-à-vis their industrialized trading partners and the overall substantial drop in the standard of living. Their greatest concern is getting out of this phenomenon that is popularly known in Cameroon as the 'Economic Crises'. It is now widely accepted that the promotion of Small-Scale Enterprises (SSE) is one of the most reliable approaches that would solve or at least alleviate the deteriorating African economic situation. The Lagos Plan of Action by the OAU Member States in 1982, which urges the creation of a network of small and medium scale industries, as well as actively promoting and encouraging the informal sector, is testimony of the recognition at the continental level of the important role of SSE in African Economic Development. But what is the possible contribution of SSE to economic development? Carr (1984) summarizes this possible contribution when pointing out that the characteristics of SSE's dovetail well with the socio-economic objectives of many of the developing countries. Generally, they are labour intensive, employment generating, capital saving and capable of operating on a decentralized basis in rural areas.

In countries concerned with the generation of thousands of new work places and with raising the incomes and quality of life of the poorer sections of the population, small-scale industrialization offers a far more appropriate alternative to industrialization strategies that emphasis large-scale, capital intensive and centralized industries, which until recently were favoured by development planners and practitioners.

Thus a major national benefit arising from promoting SSE's is job creation. Besides being labour intensive, the relative case of entry and small scale-size, *inter alia*, makes SSE's affordable to most people, thereby enhancing greater participation by the population in business ventures. It is the SSE that generates the majority of employment for the urban poor and offers self-employment opportunities for the millions of unemployed youths and retired civil servants. Even those in employment that required a secondary source of income to make up for low incomes from the primary source, are involved in setting up SSE's. During the recent years of economic crisis, small firms in the formal sector have provided a growing share of jobs and output in Africa. This is currently estimated at 50% of urban employment and as much as 1/5 of the GDP in many countries (Elkan, 1988). In evaluating the development that Cameroon went through during the two decades 1966-86, the Sixth Five-Year Development Plan (1986-91), reveals that with equal investment, the informal sector created more jobs than the formal sector. Over 3,000 handicrafts small businesses are established annually in Cameroon. A higher rate of small business creation would be expected for barbers, hairdressers, carpenters, motor mechanics and hawkers.

SSEs are the schools for entrepreneurs that Africa badly needs as entrepreneurs are seen as the critical agents in the economic development effort. Entrepreneurs are frequently defined as people with initiative who have the ability to identify and evaluate business opportunities and to marshal essential resources to take advantage of those opportunities. They are people with self-confidence, foresight, imagination, analytical ability and specific skills in communication, delegation and organization. Small-scale industry provides channels for people with these attributes to take advantage of opportunities and to move to great heights in business. Some of the larger industrial establishments in West Africa began in the informal sector notably in the metal working trades, tailoring, and furniture making (Elkan, 1988).

A basic requirement for the rapid growth of an economy is capital formation for injection into the economy. As schools for entrepreneurship, SSEs do not only provide the basis for the formation of human capital, but also contribute to the formation of material capital. This is achieved through the proprietors own funds, reinvested earnings, personal savings and borrowings from relatives and friends. In Cameroon, the 'Tontines' or 'Njangis' are significantly growing in importance as mutual aid assistance groups for capital formation and channeling business earnings to finance member enterprises. Agreed amounts are periodically contributed by each member of the Njang tontine association and the total collection is given to each member in rotation. The total membership ranges from 10-50 persons and total collections have been anything up to 120 million FCFA depending on the composition, class and ability of the membership as illustrated by the table below:

In the absence of any systematic study undertaken nationwide, estimates and groupings are based mainly on authors experience and contacts with some Njangi members.

Some of the Njangi's/Tontines for the big business group have grown so large that they could no longer efficiently function as informal groups and have had to be transformed into banks. The Banque Unie du Credit (BUC) and Credit Mutuel Camerounais (CREMUCAM), now operating in the cities of Douala, Yaounda and Baffoussam, have their origin as Tontines. CREMUCAM, a registered credit institution with FCFA 1,000 million as capital essentially finances member enterprises. It is understandable that with growing size problems such as management inefficiency set in. Haggleblade (1978) established the maximum limit for the efficient operation of Njangi after which inefficiency sets in to be between US$20,000 and US$40,000. However, the vast majority of Najangis in Cameroon remain small and provide the most important source of capital for SSE.

In contemporary Cameroon, when banks are facing serious liquidity problems, the Tontines/Njangis are apparently the most important source of financing SSEs and even some medium/large scale enterprises. A major limiting factor of the Njangi system has been that, unlike the banks, access to credit is limited only to members and not to the general public. However, given the crude estimates of 50 per cent of Cameroonians being members of Njangis, a significant-proportion of SSEs can be

Group capital formation for investment crude classification of per capita: monthly savings/deposits in Njangis/Tontines

Nr.	*Class (Income Group)*	*Range of monthly savings or deposits in FCFA*	*Range of total monthly collections for rotating Njangis with 12 members FCFA*
1.	Low income-very small scale farmers, businessmen, low salaried employees, Subsistence farmers	1,000-5,000	12,000-60,000
2.	Upper low Income Small-Scale farmers, businessmen, employees	6,000-25,000	72,000-300,000
3.	Low Middle Level Income (small scale entrepreneurs commercial farmers, junior employees in public private sectors)	26,000-200,000	312,000-588,000
4.	Upper Middle-Level (Medium scale entrepreneurs, commercial farmers, senior employees in the public and private sectors)	50,000-200,000	600,000-2,400,000
5.	High income group medium scale entrepreneurs, senior employees in private sector and parastatals	200,000-500,000	2,400,000-6,00,000
6.	Super class, big business owners, managers of large private enterprises and parastatals	500,000-10,000,000	6,000,000-120,000,000

estimated to have access to credit. The tontine practice is widely spread amongst the dynamic business-oriented Bamileke tribe noted for its dominance in business. The tontines have here proven to the important capital formation centers for financing member SSEs and have contributed significantly to Bamileke dominance in the business sector.

Small-scale industries have the important developmental role to play as centers for technical skills formation. Besides, they can play a very helpful role in any well-planned policy to promote the diffusion of manufacturing amongst regions, and within regions. This diffusion of manufacturing could significantly reduce rural-urban migration by providing employment. Cameroon in its Sixth Five-Year Development Plan (1986-1991) acknowledges that her industrial and economic develoment will be increasingly dependent on the promotion of small and medium-scale enterprises (SSEs), employment generation and the unquestionable role they play in linking up regions which have made them remarkably instrumental to regional development.

Another possible major contribution of SSEs to development is the earning of foreign exchange through exports. Increasing production of local goods and services by promoting local SSEs can also reduce imports and save on the badly needed foreign exchange. Besides, the dynamism and competition within the economy accelerated by the SSE promotion is likely to significantly contribute to a country's self-reliant development.

Problems of SSE's in Sub-Saharan African (SSA) Countries

A major problem facing SSEs in most SSA countries has, as aforementioned, been their inaccessibility to credit from the banks and other traditional lending institutions. Many have had to revert to money lenders and to be subjected to paying high rates of interest. Inaccessibility to credit seems a major factor militating against the expansion of SSEs. Some donor agencies have been attempting to assist in meeting the credit needs of SSEs.

The Ford Foundation in Nigeria, for example, has a programme designed to give grants to grassroots associations to provide revolving loans to individual member enterprises. The Foundation, through PAID has also been organizing training programmes and providing technical assistance to strengthen these grassroots associations. In Cameroon, the problem of credit to SSEs has, as aforementioned, to a large extent been minimized through the existence of Tontines/Njangis. Government efforts in a number of SSA's to reduce or solve the credit problem of SSEs, have included the creation of specific credit institutions. The Aid and Loan Guarantee Fund for SMEs (FOGAPE) was created by the Cameroon Government to cater for their credit needs. FOGAPE has so far not been successful in attaining its goals due to the long bureaucratic procedures and the fact that the SSES have been discriminated against in favour of their medium scale counterparts.

Another problem area is in the managerial sphere. Most of the small-scale entrepreneurs skills which to large extent is accountable for the slow progress in getting enterprises develop into flourishing business. Accounting records are hardly kept and when one is maintained, it is either insufficient or misleading and in both cases, does not reflect the true picture of the business. A large number of entrepreneurs and their personnel do not have adequate business oriented qualifications or experience. The lack of the marketing skills needed to get the products of SSEs to consumers and generate the needed income, also constitutes a serious problem. This is very visible in grassroots enterprises in Cameroon and Nigeria.

The problems in the managerial sphere can be solved by training and extension. But although there are quite a number of Management Development Institutions (MDI) offering a wide range of education and training programmes in the domain of business studies, the vast majority of their programmes are geared towards personnel with higher educational backgrounds. With the exception of The Gambia, having a highly developed system of extension through its Indigenous Business Advisory Service (IBAS) programme, SSEs in other African countries South of the Shara hardly have access to any form of extension. Political pronouncements are not sufficiently followed by corresponding policies and actions.

III. The Role of Education and Training

Many of the problems militating against the growth of the SSEs can be solved or ameliorated through education and training particularly those problems identified in the managerial and technical domains. The question is who should benefit and by which type of training? Two broad categories are identifiable, namely the *existing enterprises and potential entrepreneurs.* The overall objective of any education and training undertaken for the SSE's should be to raise the productivity of the entrepreneurs and employees. This should, ceteris paribus, lead to a significant increase in the production of goods and services in a quantitative and qualitative terms.

The Existing Enterprises

These are those entrepreneurs who are already actively engaged in business and have set up enterprises that fall under the category of the SSE. The training should be directed to the entrepreneurs themselves and their employees. In view of the fact that the required knowledge, skills and attitudes (KSA) of the entrepreneurs and staff would vary from enterprise to enterprise, depending on the educational backgrounds and the experiences of the entrepreneurs and the employees, it would be imperative to first undertake a Training needs analysis (TNA) for each enterprise, before designing and implementing the training programme. The TNA exercise would require an analysis of the tasks and functions being performed by the entrepreneurs and the employees, and a determination of the KSA gaps. The training programme designed will then be tailor-made.

For each enterprise the global problems of existing SSEs already mentioned included the inaccessibility to credit, the lack of managerial, accounting, record-keeping and marketing skills. The problem of inaccessibility to credit is a *structural one* that requires creating credit facilities or institutions that would provide the badly needed credit by the entrepreneurs and not necessarily training. Training would, however, be required where the entrepreneurs or employees lack the skills to manage the credit granted or are not aware of the sources of finance, as is often the case with group business. The rest of the problems mentioned above, viz managerial, accounting, record-keeping and marketing, require specific KSA and are thus amenable, in varying degrees, to education and training. Based on the KSA gaps identified in each of these areas, a training programme can be-designed and implemented after undertaking a TNA.

Given the large numbers of SSEs, it would be difficult and unrealistic to design training programmes specific to a particular SSE. However, since many of the problems and the required KSA are likely to cut across the target population of SSEs, it would be necessary to design and implement training programmes in critical areas that are a frequent and common need such as record-keeping. The design of a training programme in this domain, taking into account the global gaps of SSEs, and making it adaptable to the very specific needs of each SSES, would not be out of place.

Based on it experience in working with SSEs, the Pan African Institute for Development West Africa (PAID-WA), Buea, Cameroon has identified the following subject areas as essential, though in varying degrees, for SSE education and training:

- Basic record keeping/financial management
- Organizing and managing production
- Marketing
- Business communications
- Pricing and costing
- Small business relations with financial institutions
- Credit management, investment appraisal, income
- Generating activities/entrepreneurship, and
- SSE extension services.

Training could be organized as short courses ranging from 1-8 weeks in the classroom, or on-the job, through extension. It is essential that training is a practical as possible and should adequately address the identified SSE needs. Training, through extension, would require the trainer or extension agent to go to each SSE and give on the spot technical assistance. Extension services could include:

(a) Assistance in

- All aspects of management
- Record keeping
- Domestic and export marketing
- Materials procurement and stores management
- The choice of technology
- Explaining government regulations if any, and dealing with paper work relating to them.

(b) Advise on potential sources of finance

(c) Quality control and standardization, particularly to promote exports.

Such outreach programmes have, from experience, been more effective than even the practical classroom training, based on practical exercises. The training and visit system, which has been highly successful in the agricultural sector, can be modified for staff of SSEs in the industrial sector. For both types of training, trainers or extension agents with the relevant knowledge and skills would be required. Programmes requiring attitudinal change, such as poor attitude to clients by sales staff, are likely to be more difficult to design and deliver than those requiring knowledge and skills.

Training for Potential Entrepreneurs

Future or potential entrepreneurs here refers to all those who currently have no enterprises but have the intention of going into business. This category includes the millions of unemployed people in Sub-Saharan African countries, notably school leavers, university graduates and retired civil servants. It also includes all those already in employment but whose incomes are hardly able to sustain their families and they are consequently looking for additional income sources. This last category of the comparatively 'better off' is rapidly growing particularly in countries such as Sierra Leone, Zambia and Uganda where the currency has been significantly devalued and salaries have not been adjusted to meet the seemingly astronomical prices.

Given the virtual lack of business experience by the members of this category, the training approach has to be different from that applied to those already in business. Although the objective of the training should be to give the potential entrepreneurs adequate business management skills, emphasis should be on enabling them to minimize or avoid the bitter mistakes by successful entrepreneurs, whilst learning from those experiences

Model for the Training of Potential Entrepreneurs: An Incubator Approach

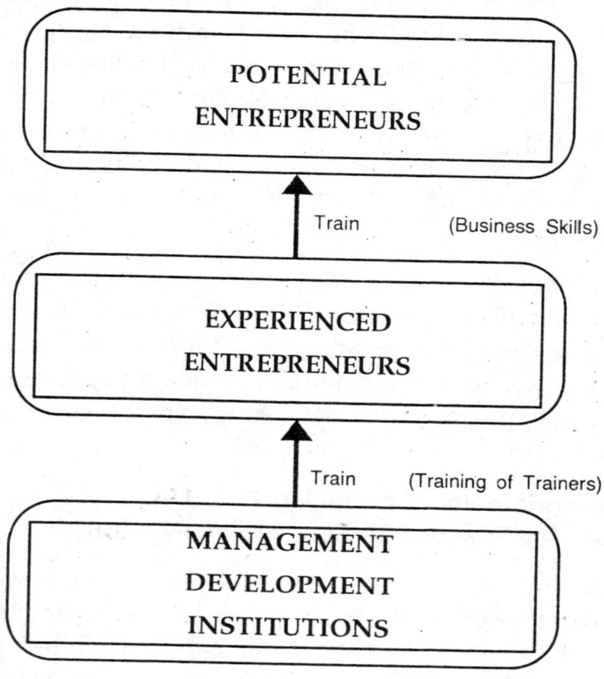

that contributed to their success. Successful entrepreneurs therefore, would seem to be the logical trainers, for any training programme designed for potential entrepreneurs. Successful entrepreneurs do not have the training skills required to undertake the training. Designing and implementing a Training of trainers (TOT) programme for the successful entrepreneurs, to give them training skills would solve the problem of their lacking these skills to successfully undertake training.

Many management development institutions (MDIs) and other relevant institutions are in a competent position to organise the proposed TOT selected for successful entrepreneurs. This thought is illustrated in the figure below.

An important pre-condition for the success of a programme designed to train potential entrepreneurs is the careful selection of participants to obtain the right candidates. During the interviewing criteria, such as a minimum level of literacy *e.g.* First School Leaving Certificate, demonstrated interest for business, seriousness of purpose demonstrated by some savings earmarked for setting up the business, the desire and ability to contribute to the costs of-training, practicability, can be used to select the right participants.

A training programme for potential entrepreneurs could be organized on a pilot basis and a TNA undertaken for the selected trainees. The TNA would be the basis, not only for formulating the training objectives and determining the content, but also for selecting the appropriate successful entrepreneurs who would be the trainers after the TOT programme.

IV. Appropriate Policy Formulation and Implementation: As Basis for Small-scale Enterprises Promotion

Small-scale enterprises cannot successfully perform their already recognized role as important instruments for accelerating economic development in Sub-Saharan African countries, if they are not backed by appropriate and adequate policies. Such policies will, however, be of little value, if they are not followed by their appropriate and adequate implementation.

Policies which facilitate lending to SSE by the traditional credit institutions or which create specific institutions to cater for their credit needs are likely to solve or reduce the credit problem by assisting SSEs to have access to the sources of credit. Although some African countries have formulated such policies and designed programmes to implement them, the results have been far from satisfactory. This has, to a large extent, been due to poor programme implementation. Cameroon is one such example. SSEs have rare obtained loans from FOGAPE as mentioned above. Although the current Sixth Five Year Development Plan (1986-1991) attended to this problem by reorganizing FOGAPE, the impact has so far been negligible.

Policies which enhance the availability and efficient use of inputs would also be of crucial importance. The regular supply of inputs avoids the occurrence of stock-outs and ensures the continuity of production. Subsidies and policies which ease large scale production or importation of in-puts are likely to reduce unit costs of inputs and make the SSE's more competitive. Many SSE countries are having serious foreign exchange problems and for these countries a policy preference, which favours the SSEs in the allocation of the limited foreign exchange will facilitate the procurement of the necessary imported inputs needed by SSEs. A major policy requirement here would be one favouring export-oriented SSEs.

Institutionalised government policies and programmes are also necessary in such areas as regulations limiting imports of products locally produced by SSEs in both the urban and rural areas, and increasing the range of marketing opportunities.

One key policy area, which is virtually absent in most SSA countries is in the domain of education and training. The noted exception are SSE's in the agricultural sector, which in most SSA countries are attended to by a large contingent of extension staff. The available management and technical training institutions hardly cater for the training needs of the SSEs. The continuous upgrading of-skills of SSE personnel as the basis for greater efficiency and increased production will only be achieved if relevant policies and accompanying programmes are put in place. The role of extension for regular technical assistance to the SSE has to be emphasized. The thousands of agricultural/ extension agents, attending to farmers in the villages of Cameroon, has been a major contributory factor to that country's, agricultural success story. The Ministry of commerce and industries may achieve a similar success story, only if relevant institutions are created to train and make available adequate extension agents in the SSE commericial and industrial sector. This would seem to be a major requirement for the attainment of Cameroon's goal of industrialization.

Summary and Concluding Remarks

Most SSA countries have recognized the fact that their desire for rapid economic development can be satisfied through the promotion of SSEs. The absence of a universally accepted definition of the SSE does not constitute a problem and should not deter any SSE promotional efforts as each SSA country can formulate her own definition based on her peculiarities and priorities. A number of problems have militated against efforts to promote SSEs. Paramount amongst these have been their inaccessibility to credit and the lack of skills in the managerial and technical domains. Education and training as the basis for knowledge and skills acquisition, have been virtually absent for the SSE sector. There is the urgent need to design and implement training programmes for both existing a potential entrepreneurs as an institutionalized and integral part of SSEs promotional efforts. A major requirement for SSE promotion is the formulation of appropriate and adequate policies favouring SSEs. These should aim at solving the major identified problems of SSEs.

All these measures would enable the SSEs to foster the development of the economies of SSA countries and would ultimately pull them out of the current economies crises. It is essential that SSA countries learn from the experiences of other countries. The role played by the SSE sector in such rapidly developing economies as Japan and the Republic of Korea should not go unnoticed by SSA countries. Their experiences provide useful lessons to SSA countries.

BIBLIOGRAPHY

Malcolm Harper and Tan Thiam Soon: *Small Enterprises in Developing Countries. Case Studies and Conclusions,* Intermediate Technology Publication Ltd. London, 1979.

The World Bank: *Employment and Development of Small-scale Enterprises,* The World Bank, Washington D.C, 1982.

Philip A. Neck and Robert E. Nelson: *Small Enterprise Development. Policies and Programmes,* ILO, Geneva, 1987.

Walter Elkan: *Entrepreneurs and Entrepreneurship in Africa in:* Research Observer Vol. 3, No. 2, The World Bank, Washington DC, 1988.

Marilyn Carr: *Developing Small-scale Enterprises in India. An Integrated Approach.* Intermediate Technology Publications Ltd., London, 1984.

Ministry of Plan and Regional Development. *Sixth Five-Year Economic, Social and Cultural Development Plan: 1986-1991,* Yaounde, Imprimerie National, 1986.

Mauritius Employers Federation: *Starting and Managing a Small Business in Mauritius,* Mauritius Employers Federation, 1958.

Anthony Nforba Nchari: *Cooperatives as Decentralized Socio-Economic Institution-the Case of Cameroon:* In Decentralization Policies and Socio-economic Development in Sub-Saharan Africa (Round table Discussion Paper). EDI of the World Bank, 1990.

S. Haggblade: *Africanization from below-The Evolution of Cameroon Savings Societies into Western Style Banks.* In rural Africana New Series 1978.

The World Bank: *Small Business Seek help as Development Swirls in:* The Urban Edge Vol. 13. No. 1 The John Hopkins University Press, Baltimore USA Jan./Feb. 1969.

27

Vocational Education

Françoise Caillods

Background

Based on the common assumption that there was a strong relationship between education and economic/social development, many countries, including countries of south and south east Asia, gave a high priority to education in the 1960s and early 1970s. The original concern with shortages of educated manpower per se rapidly shifted to one targeted unscientific and technical personnel, since it was felt that the lack of such personnel could seriously hamper the countries' industrialization and economic development policy. Labour market analyses pointed to the serious shortages of high level specialists but it was soon felt that the lack of middle level manpower could constitute another bottleneck for development. Consequently several developing countries have diversified their secondary education systems and/or created specialized training institutions to meet their middle-level manpower needs.

Between 1970 and 1980, enrolments in technical and vocational education in the world increased from 15.7 to 24.3 million, at an annual growth rate of 4.5% - higher than that of general secondary education which during the same period equalled 3.9%. In Asia the share of vocational technical schools in the enrolments of secondary education equals 8% on average but it varies a great deal between countries, from 1.4% in Malaysia in 1982 to 9.7% in Indonesia, 14.8% in Japan, 18.1% in Republic of Korea, and 20.9% in Thailand (UNESCO, 1984).

The policy which favours provision of vocational technical and agricultural education within schools has been regularly criticized since Philip Foster wrote his famous article on "The vocational school fallacy in development planning" in 1965. According to Foster, vocational schools are expensive and they produce students who are no more employable than those from academic schools. In the present context of rapid technical changes and increased competition within and between countries, vocational and technical schools are more than ever accused of being costly, non-responsive to labour market requirements and generally inefficient. More and more people suggest that the formal educational system should concentrate on providing a good general education and leave the responsibility of vocational training to enterprises. Opponents to the suggestion of leaving the responsibility of vocational training to enterprises however recall the fact that developing countries normally have a weak industrial base: there are not enough "good" enterprises to recruit and train apprentices. Also, experience shows that enterprises particularly small and medium size enterprises, can be reluctant in training their employees. They tend to offer only very narrow job-specific skill training, as they don't want their employees to be poached by others. Finally, switching to on-the-job training would not cater for the needs of rural areas, the urban informal sector and women. Other possible strategies include training outside the school system in vocational centres linked with industry or with the Ministry of Labour. Alternance training which combines school training (for theoretical teaching), with on-the-job training for the teaching of practical skills is also very much spoken of.

Terminology

A wide spectrum of activities is often regrouped under the title of technical, vocational education and training, ranging from a few work-oriented programmes in academic schools and pre-vocational education—also called diversified secondary education—to vocational courses aiming at training skilled workers and technicians to job-readiness training. In certain countries the use of the term vocational education is restricted to the training of skilled workers, while technical education refers to the training of technicians at the upper-secondary level (middle-level technician) or at post-secondary level (upper-level technician). In other countries the terms are used indiscriminately, mainly to refer to the training of skilled workers. This confusion does not help to clarify the debate since not only are we not talking of the same thing, but there is a certain tendency to generalize conclusion from one particular training mode to another; from pre-vocational diversified education to vocational education, from vocational education to technical education, etc.

In the context of our discussion, the following definitions have been adopted:

- pre-vocational education and diversified education: all programmes which include some "practical" subjects in the curriculum of general (academic) secondary schools;
- vocational education and training: all programmes in-school or out-of-school, that prepare for a specific trade, *i.e.* training of skilled workers and employees;
- technical schools: all educational programmes that are concerned with the transmission of knowledge on a technology and specific techniques. Such programmes, which prepare technicians, are normally organized in schools at upper secondary or post secondary level with a much broader scientific and technical content.

This lecture will be devoted to vocational education and training. It will analyse in particular the pros and cons of offering vocational education in the formal system.

Objectives of Vocational Education and Training

Vocational education and training programmes often have several objectives.

1. *Economic Objective: Raising Productivity*

The first and foremost objective of a system of vocational education is to train skilled workers and middle level manpower for industry, commerce or services. To use their capital and technology in an efficient way enterprises need competent personnel: vocational programmes would provide them with personnel having the relevant skills and attitudes.

Vocational education and training programmes would contribute as well in developing an industrial culture in the country, thus promoting economic development.

2. *Employment Objectives*

These original aims have been enlarged, however, and vocational education and training programmes in a growing number of countries are expected to alleviate the unemployment problem and to improve pupils' and trainees' chances of finding a job. The assumption is that it is possible to equip young school leavers with certain skills which will make them more easily employable on a highly competitive labour market. It is implicitly assumed that it is the lack of skilled manpower which is hampering the economic growth.

Another objective is to encourage positive attitudes towards manual work and to prepare school leavers or trainees to settle on their own account.

3. *Economic Objective: Reducing Educational Expenditures*

By preparing pupils to enter the world of work, vocational education would contribute to reducing excess demand for higher education. Although vocational education is expensive, it is less costly than higher education. Expanding vocational education would help reducing the overall educational expenditures.

4. *Pedagogical Objective*

By making the curriculum less abstract and more concrete, vocationalization of education would facilitate pupil's understanding and their cognitive and non cognitive achievement. By making it more relevant to employment it would encourage their motivation.

5. *Equity Objective*

For the reasons mentioned above, vocational education would facilitate the schooling of low achievers, who do not succeed in highly theoretical academically oriented streams, and subsequently contribute to their finding a job.

Vocational education would also make it easier for women to find a skilled job.

Assessing Vocational Education

The World Bank recently reviewed a large number of vocational education and training systems in developing countries. They concluded that "training systems are often too large, poorly financed, inflexible and of low quality". "Vocational education and training is cost effective when it provides training for productive employment, actively seeking to balance the supply of trained persons to employment demand, and investing in the quality of training" (Middleton, Ziderman and Adams 1990). Indeed, vocational education has not always achieved the various objectives above.

Productivity Objective

Employers often complain that vocational school graduates are not directly employable and/or that they have been badly trained. Some employers actually prefer to recruit graduates from academic schools and train them on-the-job, rather than recruit vocational schools leavers.

- The former suffer from the bad image of their schools, which "is enrolling low achievers".
- Vocational education is accused of being rigid and non responsive to labour market requirements. School-and vocational centers—tend to train according to their training capacity rather than according to the needs of the labour market. This is due to fact that new equipment is expensive and that when teachers have been recruited in one specialization it is not easy to get rid of them or to retrain them if the need arises.

- Vocational education is not always of good quality. Most teachers are recruited just after they graduate from teacher training and few of them have a real industrial experience. The best teachers desert as soon as they have an opportunity for a better paid job in the private sector.
- Equipment and raw materials are not always available in sufficient quantity. Many vocational programmes have too small recurrent budgets and these have been cut further as a result of the crisis which has hit certain countries severally.

Employment Objectives

Vocational schools have not succeeded in alleviating the unemployment problem. The rate of unemployment of vocational school graduates is high in certain countries. This is often the result of a bad economic situation. When enterprises do not recruit, or when fewer jobs are created than people come out of school, unemployment increases. There are countries, however, where the rate of unemployment of vocational school leavers is even higher than that of academic school leavers (due to employers attitudes as mentioned above).

Vocational schools have not succeeded in training large numbers of self-employed either. Even when they have done so, it is at a very high cost.

Reducing Educational Expenditures

Vocational education has not succeeded in discouraging people from entering higher education. Thus educational expenditures have continued to rise. The unit cost of vocational education is quite high as well, on average 2.5 times that of academic secondary education (although not necessarily much higher than that of vocationalized general secondary plus training in a vocational center).

Equity Objective

Vocational and training programmes mav have made a contribution to opening access to skilled employment for women and children from lower socio-economic background. Poor children are indeed often over-represented in their enrolments. When vocational courses are not terminal, they may have helped in opening the way to further studies to such children. When vocational courses are terminal, *i.e.* do not lead to further studies, however, they have been accused of reproducing existing social structure and inequalities.

What should one conclude in front of such gloomy results? Should one conclude, as some have done, that existing vocational schools should be closed?

Obviously each country has to evaluate its own vocational and training system first, by means of employer surveys and tracer studies undertaken on a regular basis. It is often better to build on an existing system, if it is not doing too badly, rather than create an entirely new system altogether. Various measures can be taken to improve the functioning and performance of existing school and vocational centers:

- diversify the clientele, so as to increase the enrolment and reduce the per capita cost;
- diversity the source of finance, including obtaining support from enterprises;
- improve the quality of education through reformed curricula and stronger management;
- increase the flexibility of training through the regroupment of specializations taught and / or through the introduction of alternance training;
- bring vocational education closer to the production sectors through such measures as: exchange of teachers, organization of internships for pupils in enterprises, increased institutional links and consultations regarding skills requirements, curriculum, etc.

In fact, when organizing—or reorganizing—a vocational training system, the following questions have to be raised:

1. *What are its main objectives?*

The structure and organization of the vocational education and training system will be quite different, according to the emphasis laid on different objectives.

2. *Who should organize it?*

The State, the enterprises, a federation of industry, the private sector (private schools), a combination of the above?

In many developed countries, vocational training was originally organized by enterprises (apprenticeship and on-the-job training). State direct intervention was justified later by the fact that enterprises were under-investing in training (*e.g.* in France). Trade Unions, who wanted to see their workers' qualifications better recognized and certified, pressed in this direction. State vocational schools became also a way of providing secondary education to low achievers, and pupils from lower socio-economic backgrounds. In most developed countries State vocational schools exist along with private schools, various non-formal programmes and training in enterprises.

In developing countries, it is often argued that the State should organize vocational education and training when, and only when, the private sector (whether enterprises, or other private bodies) under-invest in this area. Many of the criticisms regarding training run by enterprises disappear when the training is organized by a federation of industry; the latter programmes are more likely to be broader in scope, include theoretical courses and cater for the needs of small enterprises and special groups (women and rural areas).

3. *Who should finance it?*

- the State: directly or indirectly (through sponsorships and/or levy-grant mechanisms)
- the enterprises (as main beneficiaries)
- the schools or training centers, selling their own product;
- the trainees (through fees).

This question is different from the previous one since a state school or programme may very well be financed by enterprises and training in enterprise can be financed by the State, through tax exemption for example.

It is generally argued that the beneficiaries (enterprises and trainees) should finance their own training. Again the State should intervene only when there is under investment in vocational education and training, and/or when the society benefits from the education and training organized more than beneficiaries actually do (in economic terms when there are externalities). It can be the case if the programmes allow the education of children from under-privileged groups, if it helps fostering an industrial culture in the country, etc.

Payroll taxes are often used to finance in-service and pre-service training; enterprises get their money back if they organize their own programmes. Such schemes can be quite successful and contribute to financing existing schools and training centers. They can however work as a disincentive for enterprise to use labour-intensive technologies. Certain firms have started this way to "informalize" their labour force through subcontracting of informal enterprises.

Levy-grant mechanisms have been introduced in several countries in an attempt to get a higher proportion of enterprises undertaking serious training schemes. Results have been mixes as large scale modern firms—often multinationals, who were doing significant amounts of training anyway—have best utilized the provision. Medium-and small-scale enterprises, on the other hand, have not always expanded their training provision.

As for fees, given the difficulty of attracting good pupils in vocational schools or centers, they should probably be kept low so as not to discourage pupils or adults from enrolling even further.

4. When should it be organized: pre-employment or in-service?

The debate concerns primarily pre-employment training: to what extent is it over-expanded, and how specialized should it be? In the first stages of development and industrialization, most occupations do not require very specialized training before employment. When the countries move to another stage of development and when industry start using more sophisticated techniques, then the situation becomes different. Technical schools in particular are then required.

The importance of in-service training is recognized by everybody: such training is essential to ensure labour productivity, occupational mobility, and labour flexibility. Given the difficulty of making accurate manpower projections, and the rapid technical change, the need for continuous education, recycling and in-service training is high. Obviously, it is easier to organize in-service training if pre-service education and training was of good quality. Good basic education and a good science and technology education at the secondary level is often what is primarily required.

5. How specialized should vocational education and training be?

With the arrival of new technologies which lead to the gradual disappearance of former trades, there is a tendency to "vocationalize" general academic education and to "generalize" vocational education. Specializations have been regrouped and theoretical courses reinforced. Vocational courses should not become too academically-oriented and theoretical however, without losing there specificities and professional "ethos" (Castro 1988).

Another tendency aiming at making formal vocational education more relevant to the needs of the world of work is to establish closer linkages with industry: (organize internships in enterprises; staff exchanges; passing contracts; counselling small enterprises, etc.).

6. Who should certify the training?

The question arises mainly when education and training occurs outside the school system: in private "independent" schools, in non-formal education, and in enterprises. The emphasis should be on mechanisms that progressively open access to national certification (such as trade tests) regardless of the provenance of the trainees. The opportunity for trainees and workers to test their skills and achievement against a national trade testing system is likely to contribute to increased quality in private schools, and to increased concern with standards and professionalism. Firms often resist certification since it may lead to workers asking for a pay increase (or their leaving the company). The State has thus a role to play here, as it can contribute to better training practices everywhere.

According to the answers given to the questions, above, according to the country's level of development and skill requirements, the organization and structure of the vocational education and training system will look different. In any case no single system can be used everywhere. What works well in Singapore, Hong Kong or Japan may not work well in Vietnam, Korea or India. Countries have to take into consideration their level of development, their types of skill requirements, but also their history, their industrial tradition and culture, before they define their strategy in terms of vocational education and training.

BIBLIOGRAPHY

C. De Moura Castro, 1988, The Soul of Vocational Schools: Training as a Religious Experience, *International Review of Education*, Vol. 34, nº 2.

P. Foster (1965), The Vocational School Fallacy in Development Planning in A. Anderson and M.J. Bowman (eds) *Education and Economic Development;* Aldine Publishing Company, Chicago.

J. Middleton, A. Ziderman, and A. Adams (1990) *Making Vocational Training Effective,* Finance and Development, March.

B. Salomé, J. Charmes, 1988. *In-service Training: Five Asian Experiences,* OECD Development Centre.

J. Tilak, 1988, Vocational Education in South Asia: Problems and Prospects, *International Review of Education,* Vol. 54, nº 2.

UNESCO, 1984, Data Sheet, Regional Office for Education in Asia and the Pacific, Bangkok.

28

Vocationalization of Secondary Education

Maureen Woodhall

1. Introduction

For more than a hundred years there have been proposals to reform the education system in many countries by giving greater emphasis to technical and practical skills, rather than theoretical instruction, and there have been repeated attempts to "vocationalize" the curricula of academic schools, in the belief that this would prepare pupils better for employment. In nineteenth century British politicians advocated setting up technical schools, on the German model, on the grounds that this was the best way to prepare children for work in the rapidly expanding industrial sector. Yet a hundred years later British schools are still criticized for failing to prepare pupils for the world of work and recent initiatives such as the Technical and Vocational Education Initiative (TVEI) and the Certificate of Pre-Vocational Education (CPVE) have been introduced in an attempt to reduce the so-called "mismatch" between education and employment by increasing vocational and pre-vocational preparation at the secondary level. But this is still highly controversial in Britain, and a number of critics have attacked the whole notion of "vocationalizing" secondary education.

In Africa there have been repeated attempts to increase the provision of agricultural and technical education, which have also been attacked by critics. In 1965 Philip Foster examined the history of secondary education in Ghana in the nineteenth and twentieth century and showed that proposals to shift the emphasis of education from general, academic studies towards practical training in technical and agricultural skills had been a feature of every official report on education in the Gold Coast from 1847 to the granting of independence to Ghana in 1957. Nevertheless, he claimed that none of these proposals had been successfully implemented and he attacked the whole notion that imposing a technical or agricultural bias in African schools would solve the problem of unemployment as a fallacy, which he described as "The Vocational School Fallacy" (Foster 1965).

In India, also, there have been recommendations for more than a hundred years to "diversity" the school curriculum by introducing vocational education at the secondary stage. The 1985 Report of the National Working Group on "Vocationalization of Education" quoted Wood's Despatch of 1854, the Indian Education Commission of 1882 and successive Secondary Education Commissions, all of which had called for increased emphasis on vocational education, the creation of "diversified" or "multi-purpose" schools, which could provide technical and vocational, as well as general, academic education.

Elsewhere in the world the same pressures have been widespread and a review of World Bank lending in the past twenty years has shown that half of all education projects have included a component which aimed to "diversity" or "vocationalize" the secondary school curriculum. Yet the recent World Bank study designed to evaluate these projects (the Diversified Secondary Education Curricula or DiSCuS Study) was highly critical, and questioned the underlying rationale for vocationalizing secondary education, questioned the benefits, and concluded:

"Paradoxically, it seems that the lower the overall level of a country's development, the weaker the case for introducing a diversified curriculum. The more developed the country, the more it may be able to afford diversification. This policy conclusion is exactly the opposite of what actually happens: The poorer the country, the greater the pressure for making the secondary school curriculum 'more relevant to the world of work' (Psacharopoulos and Loxley, 1985, p. 228)

This lecture will try to examine why the whole concept of vocationalizing secondary education is so controversial, and will summarize:

- the arguments put forward for a greater vocational bias in secondary schools
- the arguments of the critics, including both Foster's "vocational school fallacy" argument and more recent critics
- some of the evidence about the effects of previous attempts to vocationalize or diversity the secondary school curriculum, including the World Bank's DiSCuS study.

Finally, we will link the continuing debate about vocationalizing secondary schools to the alternative theories of the labour market, examined in Module 3, and consider some of the implications for implementing educational reforms designed to improve the links between education and employment.

2. The Rationale for Vocationalizing Secondary Education

The arguments put forward for "vocationalization" or "diversification" of secondary schools can be summarized under four heads:

2.1 *Employment Objectives*

Diversified secondary schools, which provide vocational education (including technical, commercial, and agricultural streams) as well as general, academic education, will improve pupils' chances of finding jobs, by giving them useful, practical skills, and encouraging positive attitudes towards practical work. Vocational education will therefore increase the supply of technically trained manpower and reduce unemployment caused by unreal expectations.

2.2 *Economic Efficiency Objectives*

By improving the links between education and employment, diversified secondary schools will offer a higher rate of return than academic schools and will reduce the "excess demand" for higher education which is caused by academic schools over-emphasizing qualifications that simply prepare pupils for entry to post-secondary education.

2.3 *Quality Objectives*

By making education more relevant to the world of work vocationalization will improve pupils' motivation, increase their knowledge and lead to gains in cognitive and non-cognitive skills.

2.4 *Equity Objectives*

Diversified secondary schools will improve opportunities for pupils from poor families, who are often denied access to academic schools, and therefore vocationalization will lead to a more equitable distribution of resources.

More specifically, the World Bank's DiSCuS study attempted to test the following nine hypotheses:

- Diversification favour the recruitment of students from lower-income families and thus provides more equitable access to schooling.
- Diversification enhances cognitive achievement in the field of vocational course work and later on the job.
- Diversification creates a desire for further training and instills occupational aspirations better suited to national economic needs.
- Diversification diminishes the private demand for post-secondary education especially at the university level.
- Diversification increases the motivation to seek work at the end of secondary schooling.
- Diversification leads to employment in the field of vocational specialization at school.
- Diversification enables graduates to earn more than they would after other forms of schooling.
- Graduates of diversified schools have a shorter period of unemployment while seeking work after graduation than do graduates of other secondary schools.

- Investment in diversification has a higher social rate of return than in either vocational or academic education along.

3. Arguments Against Vocationalization

Critics of vocationalization argue that it is expecting too much of the education system to suggest that curriculum reforms, by themselves, can reduce unemployment, and they also argue that attempts to vocationalize schools have proved expensive, inefficient and have failed to achieve most of their objectives. Like the arguments in favour of vocationalization, the arguments of critics fall under four heads.

3.1 Employment

Vocational schools do not necessarily increase the likelihood that school-leavers will find a job, since employers may prefer to train workers on the job, or may regard school leavers from vocational streams as "inferior" to pupils with academic schooling. Moreover, if vocational streams in diversified secondary schools prepare for a narrow range of jobs, then school-leavers will emerge with less flexibility, so that in a rapidly changing labour market job-specific vocational education may actually reduce, rather than increase chances of finding work.

3.2 Cost of Economic Efficiency

Because vocational education requires specialized equipment and tools, it is much more expensive than general education, and on cost-benefit grounds it is often cheaper and more effective to provide vocational education and training on-the-job, rather than in secondary schools.

3.3 Quality

Because of the difficulty of recruiting teachers with technical skills the quality of vocational education is often poor and pupils may leave school without adequate general of vocational skills.

3.4 Equity

In many countries vocational streams in secondary schools are regarded as leading to "dead-end", rather than high-status jobs. The result is that pupils from high socio-economic backgrounds tend to choose academic streams, which are more likely to lead to university or other post-secondary education, while pupils from poor families are concentrated in low-status "technical" or "vocational" streams.

4. Evidence on the Effects of Vocationalization of Secondary Education

Many evaluations of attempts to introduce or increase vocationalizaiton or diversification of secondary schools have pointed to problems of implementation and have suggested that many of the supposed benefits of vocationalizaiton have not been forthcoming.

A review of 79 World Bank projects between 1963 and 1978 (Haddad 1979) concluded:

(a) many projects were successful in meeting *quantitative* manpower targets

(b) there was no evidence of changes in pupils' attitudes towards practical or manual work, and in the majority of projects pupils still preferred academic fields to vocational training.

(c) With very few exceptions the general quality of education did not appear to improve, and attempts to broaden the curriculum were hindered by implementation problems.

(d) There were serious doubts about the cost-effectiveness of diversification projects.

In the light of these rather pessimistic conclusions, the World Bank carried out a more detailed evaluation of secondary school diversification in Colombia and Tanzania (Psacharopoulos and Loxley 1985). On the basis of detailed comparisons of different types of school, including comparisons of costs and pupil achievement (as measured by special tests) in academic and vocational streams, and by tracer studies which examined the subsequent employment and earnings of school leavers, the study attempted to evaluate diversification of secondary education in terms of:

- access to schooling of different socio-economic groups
- cognitive achievement in both academic and vocational subjects
- differences in pupils' ambitions, motivations, attitudes and aspirations regarding occupational choice and further education
- post-school experiences in further education and employment
- cost-effectiveness of different types of school or "streams" within schools.

Once again, the results were very pessimistic about the result of diversification in Colombia and Tanzania. In particular:

(a) Curriculum diversification is expensive and its cost-effectiveness very questionable. In some cases improvements in vocational skills were achieved at the expense of general skills; in other cases there was an unambiguous increase in pupil achievement, but at high cost.

(b) Vocational education in diversified schools did not increase either the chances of employment or the earnings of school leavers.

(c) The rate of return to vocational streams is often lower than to academic streams.

(d) Vocational education did not reduce the private demand for higher education, and those who had taken specific vocational courses (such as agriculture or technical subjects) were just as likely to change subject fields those who had followed academic courses.

Such results have been widely interpreted as undermining the case for vocationalization or diversification of secondary schools. On the other hand, critics have argued that it is too soon to evaluate the effects of the experiments, and that a tracer study which follows school leavers for only one or two years is too short.

5. Links between the Vocationalization Debate and alternative theories of the labour market

Much of the controversy about vocationalization is linked with the alternative theories of the labour market, discussed in Module 3. Those who advocate detailed forecasts of manpower requirements are likely to support training in specific vocational skills in secondary schools. On the other hand, those who believe in a flexible, competitive labour market, in which wages and salaries change in response to changes in demand and supply, and there is a high degree of substitutability between labour and capital, and between different categories of labour, are more likely to favour general education, which prepares school leavers for a wide range of jobs. So, for example Blaug (1985) argues that "The old battle cry for vocational job-specific education, which at first glance might seem to be the rallying ground of economists, is actually the very opposite of what is implied by the 'new' economics of education".

If education is no more than a screening device, then the content of vocational courses is of little significance, and cheaper academic courses are to be preferred to more costly technical subjects, which require specialized equipment and staff. On the other hand, this theory would suggest that employers will be very interested in the effects of different types of education on motivation and attitudes, even if they prefer to give on the job training in specific skills (Blaug 1973). In fact a recent survey of employers in the United Kingdom showed that "academic achievement" and "personal qualities" are far more important for many employers than other criteria, and that "general skills" are more important than "specific skills" (Table 1)

Table 28.1: Employers' selection criteria: United Kingdom Survey

Level	*Selected Criteria skills*	*Specific skills*	*General achievement*	*Academic potential*	*Personai appearance*	*Personal qualities*	*Personal*
Graduate and above	8* A	423 (0%)	830 (24%)	67 (48%)	50 (4%)	349 (3%)	(20%)
HND etc.	B	8 (10%)	384 (26%)	691 (46%)	35 (2%)	103 (7%)	276 (18%)
School leaver at 18+	C	64 (3%)	402 (21%)	575 (30%)	327 (17%)	134 (7%)	420 (22%)
School leaver + 16	D	116 (6%)	238 (12%)	358 (18%)	313 (15%)	249 (12%)	749 (37%)
YTS Trainee	E	8 (0%)	153 (11%)	309 (22%)	62 (4%)	268 (19%)	582 (42%)
Weighted Column Totals		204	1600	2763	804	804	2376

Note: *criterion weighted by number of recruits to which it applies. The percentage in brackets shows the relative importance of each criterion at a given level.

Source: J. Wellington *et.al. Skills for the Future* The University of Sheffield 1987, p. 69.

If labour markets are highly segmented, then one way in which this segmentation occurs, according to radical theorists, is the segmentation of schooling, with children of high socio-economic backgrounds choosing academic education, leading to high status jobs, and children of poor, unskilled parents choosing low status "vocational" streams which actually limit, rather than widen occupational choice. However the hypothesis that diversified secondary schools will increase equality of opportunity for different social groups is not supported by the evidence in many countries.

Conclusion

Despite all the criticisms of previous attempts to vocationalize secondary education, the world wide pressure for improved links between education and employment continues. Both theoretical work on the labour market and empirical research on diversified schools support the argument that vocational education at the secondary level should be as broad-based as possible, and should aim to increase flexibility and to prepare pupils for a wide range of jobs or for self employment, rather than being too job-specific. In other words, the concept of "vocationalizing education" should not be rejected, but should be reassessed in the light of information about how labour markets actually operate in different countries or regions, including how employers choose workers and whether they prefer general or specific skills, and also in the light of information about the relative costs and effectiveness of different types of secondary education.

REFERENCES

Blaug, M. (1973) *Education and the Employment Problem in Developing Countries*, Geneva: ILO.

———(1985) "Where are we now in the Economics of Education?", *Economics of Education Review*, Vol. 4 (1).

Foster, P.J. (1965) "The Vocational School Fallacy in Development Planning" in C.A. Anderson and M.J. Bowman (eds.) *Education and Economic Development*, Chicago: Aldine.

Haddad, W. (1979) "Diversified Secondary Curriculum Study: A Review of World Bank Experience", Washington D.C: World Bank, Education Department.

Psacharopoulos, G. and Loxley, W. (1985) *Diversified Secondary Education and Development: Evidence from Colombia and Tanzania.*, Baltimore: Johns Hopkins, for the World Bank.

29

Education and Productive Work

Wim Hoppers

Education with Production (EWP) as a concept refers to a situation whereby productive work is an integral part of a programme of general education. Although essentially EWP can also serve to broaden courses in vocational training or constitute a basis for workers' education in places of work, it mostly refers to the integration of production into the curriculum of primary and secondary schools. The common understanding of the productive work is that it concerns the actual production of goods and services that are useful to the school or the surrounding community (Gustafsson 1987). The activities take place either on the school premises or in farms and factories outside the school's control.

EWP considers the involvement of all pupils in production as central to the learning process. It has a cognitive dimension in that pupils are to develop a broad range of practical skills, get acquainted with relevant aspects of the world of work and learn about the application of science and technology in processes of production. EWP also has an important affective dimension as it aims to develop in interest in and respect for (manual) work, instill desirable social values and habits, and bring the school closer to the realities of everyday life. In poorer countries production is also meant to contribute towards the running costs of educational institutions and serve equity by increasing access for larger numbers of youth. Beyond these aims a central concern in EWP is that the integration of learning and working is a basis for altering the nature of education and contribute towards the development of a new society.

EWP already has a long history. While it is closely related to polytechnical education, the concept is not exclusively Marxist. It has been applied in educational experiments in 19th century Europe and is currently finding acceptance in countries as far apart in geographical and ideological terms as Vietnam, Lesotho and Panama.

1. EWP and Vocational Education

In its widest meaning of work-oriented education, vocational education incorporates EWP. With its emphasis on broad cognitive, moral and social objectives, EWP is not meant to train pupils in job-specific skills or improve their changes in the labour market but rather to enhance the overall value of general education as a preparation for life. Thus EWP can be regarded as a variant of prevocational studies, laying a sound foundation for subsequent specialist vocational training (Atutov 1986). It has a distinct method in that its benefits are not merely gained through practice periods in supplementary craft subjects or excursions to places of work, but through the actual involvement in all stages of the production process and correlating these to other subject areas in the curriculum.

EWP is not identical to "work experience programmes", which have multiplied rapidly during the last decade, particularly in Westarn countries. Although their aims very a good deal they generally stem from a pragmatic concern about the articulation between schools and the labour market, and the resulting need to help youth learn more about employment opportunities and develop social life skills necessary to obtain and hold a job (Jennings 1987a). The programmes rarely make work a central vehicle for learning or the manipulation of its organization and methods an experimental ground for social and economic transformation.

2. Traditions of EWP

EWP has it roots in traditions originating in different parts of the world. In different degrees these have influenced contemporary advocates of production in schools. Particularly in developing countries a practice of eclecticism has made that interpretation may exist side by side or receive attention at different times.

EWP has been strongly influenced by the concept of polytechnical education with its emphasis on the need for a direct interchange between theory and practice. Productive work would help to understand the basic theories underlying technology and engineering, guarantee a close connection between schools and the world of work and provide an introduction to the main trades (Pfeifer and Wald 1987). The combination of education and work in socialist countries also led to other policy variants such as post-revolutionary practice of engaging all students in some form of labour in factories and farms in direct contact with workers and peasants and the establishment of half work study centres especially in economically backward areas, for example those in China (Thögersen 1987).

The fate of the work component has depended much on the dynamics in individual socialists countries. One trend has been to shift the emphasis of production practice from places of work to farms and workshops within the schools (Soviet Union, Cuba) or to specially designed polytechnical centres (German Democratic Republic). The educational requirements have thus led to a degree of institutional separation even where integration with work was the aim (Lauglo 1983). There are also debates as to how far a broad-based labour education can be reconciled with a new interest in vocationalization, as in China and Soviet Union (Atutov 1986).

In Western educational thought education and work have tended to ramain rather separate domains, each with its distinct organization and functions. There has been a trend to relate learning much more to the immediate environment and create opportunities for the development of a wider variety of skills and aptitudes. The more recent depression in the labour market justified a more explicit attention to the world of work itself. But the various programmes have generally stopped short of blurring the boundaries between schooling and work and they have not interfered with the conventional philosophy and organization that underlie learning in schools.

Educational reforms in many developing countries have been a reaction to the traditions of Western, especially European education. A strong motivation for allocating a central place of productive work in schools was that it symbolized a link with the traditional local communities in contrast with the academic and urban features of the imported colonial system. In line with populist traditions physical work came also to be seen as a valuable instrument for personal development: a source of moral fibre, self-reliance and civic virtue (Lauglo and Lillis 1988). Populist sentiments were often mixed with direct inspiration from socialist thinking, especially the moral aspects of labour education and the linkages between theory and practice. Above all a central attraction of EWP was the very output of production which could help expand education through a reduction of unit costs. Indeed, interest in the economic aspects of school production has been closely associated with the changing fortunes of national development.

In countries where the EWP tradition has been strongest, such as India and Tanzania, a national philosophy emerged incorporating the above elements. Basic education, as developed by Gandhi, emphasized traditional village crafts (especially spinning) as a method for character building, instilling basic skills and attitudes of self-reliance and mobilizing youth for rural reconstruction. Although during the 1960s the idea was abandoned, later it inspired a modern revival in the form of socially useful productive work. This has become an attempt to reconcile the Gandhian concept with the requirements of current socio-economic developments.

In the case of Tanzania's education for self-reliance the aims are similar to those in India. Education is to serve the needs of the majority living and working in rural areas and should help to transform the inherited colonial structures. Productive work or self-reliance activities in schools became the embodiment of the new philosophy. Pupils should not be exempted from the activities of the local community, and through involvement in work develop socialist attitudes and habits, contribute to the unkeep of the school and increase the national income. Self-reliance activities and classwork are meant to feed each other, so that academic work becomes practical, and productive work becomes educative. Schools, therefore, should become economic communities as well as social and educational communities (Nyerere 1968). Like in many other developing countries production takes place on the school's premises, mostly in the form of agricultural work. Some attention is given to handicrafts like woodwork or basketry.

In the last two decades EWP has been accepted as educational policy not only in Africa's avowedly socialist countries, such as Ethoipia and Mozambique, but also in countries with a more mixed economy like Zambia and Zimbabwe. Here the concerns are more diverse. In Zambia all educational institutions were to establish production units since 1975. But while originally there was greater emphasis on production as an enhancement of general learning, current interest stems much more from its perceived potential to substitute for parts of government's subsidies in education (especially non-salary recurrent costs) and to prepare youth for a future of self-development. In Zimbabwe the ideological inspiration is stronger, but EWP is limited to only a handful of schools while mainstream attention is on more pragmatic efforts to vocationalize the rapidly expanding secondary system.

Diverse considerations have also guided EWP programmes in the Commonwealth Caribbean. Although the hope of ensuring a greater balance between academic and practical work as well as a degree of self-sufficiency for the institution has been a general objective, attention to wider social objectives varied in accordance with the political environment in which EWP was introduced. New attitudes and values, linked to the school's role in creating a new society were prominent in Jamaica under the Manley government and in Grenada under Maurice Bishop (Jennings 1987b).

3. The Practice of EWP

An important weakness of education with production is that while much has been written about its nature, underlying philosophy and relevance, the literature investigating actual processes and outcomes is relatively scant, notably with respect to EWP in developing countries (King 1985a). A picture that emerges from available reports is one of many problems and constraints in implementation, and of only limited success against more failures. This is especially pronounced in educational systems where EWP has not received consistent political protection, has not been introduced throughout the system and/or has not enjoyed the internal technical support necessary to help sort out the many practical aspects or organization and management, resource mobilization, curriculum development, teacher education and school community relations.

Often EWP programmes, even if well conceptualized, were not given much time to develop adequately before being officially abandoned or substantially modified. Jamica is a case in point. Where protection has been more continuous, as in China and India, over time reinterpretations of the combination of learning and working have led to severe criticisms of existing policies. The credibility of the concept suffered in consequence, even though the critique may have been more related to the needs for adjustment to new socio-economic circumstances than to failure of old policies to achieve their objectives.

In quite a few countries the philosophhy of EWP has had to compete with other concepts of education which were more in line with the ralities of socio-economic structrue. Where EWP has been introduced in single institutions or existed as a separate educational channel alongside conventional schools there have been many reports about parental resistance to manual labour, partly becuase such work tended to be associated with the drudgery of village life from which schools were perceived to be an escape, partly because mainstream academic education was clearly more highly rewarded in society. However, in many developing countries the widespread depression in the formal economy may well improve the standing of EWP programmes.

There has been evidence all long of individual institutions succeding in many of their objectives, including the development of practical skills and positive attitudes towards work and a substantial degree of self-reliance. Progress appears to be related to high quality teaching, inspiring leadership, a shared believe in the value of combining work and study and a collective pride in the institution's outstanding features. This very achievement, however, also made them a subject of local political controversy. Examples have been Swaneng Hill Secondary School in Botswana, Jose Marti Secondary School in Jamaica, and the Mayflower School in Nigeria (Van Rensburg 1974; Jennings 1987b; Solarin 1972). The contradictions between EWP and the prevailing social and economic structures have led many scholars to be sceptical about the feasibility of EWP in non-socialist countries or denounce it as retarding development (for example Zachariah 1988).

Implementation problems are very conspicuous in countries were EWP has been introduced throughout the system of general education. Available studies point to weaknesses in the conceptualization of EWP, lack of clear policy guidelines, lack of management and technical skills in the schools, lack of adequate curriculum materials insufficient support for procurement of tools and materials and for the marketing of produce, and difficulties in working out suitable assessment procedures. Such problems greatly affected the process of EWP, particularly the integration of production into the curriculum, the production of useful and good quality items, the involvement of pupils in decision making and the interaction with the local community. As result these problems have compounded the external factors affecting EWP and made that such programmes scored low on their pedagogical as well as their social and economic objectives (Sinclair 1976, 1977; Komba and Temu 1987; Jennings 1987b), Where, however, in a systematic manner efforts are made to communicate effectively with headmasters, teachers and community leaders, there is evidence that more can be achieved: for example through the Rural Education and Agriculture Programme (REAP) in Belize, the Self Help Action Plan for Education (SHAPE) in Zambia, the Polytechnical Education Support Programme (PESP) in Tanzania and the "Nouvelle Ecole" programme in Benin.

4. Issues in EWP

Despite the problems and constraints EWP remains strong in socialist countries and is highly popular among governments in the developing world. In more countries it has become an attractive way to reform education along lines that appear consistent with indigenous culture, while at the same time helping to reduce the costs of education and prepare youth for self-reliance. Therefore the prospects for EWP look good. But research shows that there are basic issues that need urgent attention. One concerns the expectations of what EWP is to achieve, and this is related to the role of EWP in different socio-economic and political structures. In countries that are not socialist or aim to develop socialist structures EWP is given a task to contribute significantly towards personal and ultimately towards social transformation; but not towards accommodation to existing realities. There is an underlying assumption here that schools have a degree of autonomy in their interaction with society, potentially exerting a strong influence on the development of skills, attitudes and values that are not congruent with prevailing practices. This challenge puts a heavy burden on the organizers to secure sufficient protection for such programmes as well as resources for their implementation. Furthermore, even if curricular objectives are achieved, school leavers may not necessarily have an advantage in the employment market. Thus consideration may need to be given to arranging follow-up assistance with non-educational inputs; a consequence drawn by only a few programmes, such as in Botswana through the Brigades and in Zimbabwe through school leaver cooperatives (Gustafsson 1987).

A second issue concern how to combine education and work without one undermining the benefits of the other. As was noted there is a trend to establish clear institutional boundaries between "normal production" and production for educational and training purposes. Even when supervized by the school and question remains how far the production process can be compromised before it loses its meaning as a genuine learning experience. Scholars have pointed to the inherent contradictions between conventional learning through school subjects with their distinct structures, sequencing of concepts and controlled instructional settings, and learning through (production) practice which follows the tenets of experiential learning and is by definition less amenable to manipulation (Lauglo and Lillis 1988; Atutov 1986). More experimentation is needed to achieve an optimal balance and degree of integration.

A final issue related to the nature of productive work to be carried out by pupils. To what extent should it be in line with local activities or introduce pupils to varieties of work of which they have less direct knowledge? What concessions should be made to availability of resources and access to markets? In countries in the North as well as in the South there is a tendency to involve pupils in lower and intermediate grades in handicrafts, agricultural activities or needlework (King 1985a; Pfeifer and Wald 1987). Sometimes this choice is influenced by philosophical or educational considerations, other times by expediency. Sex role stereo-typing in the allocation of practical work has remained a persistent phenomenon and has further limited and educative value of work (Jennings 1987b). Some burning questions in this regard are: what exposure can be reconciled with local resources and social tolerance, what place is there for commerce and service activities, and in what ways can the advantages of low technology handicrafts be combined with an introduction to more advanced technologies, including computer aided ones? Further interchange between theorists and practitioners should help to clarify these and other concerns in education with production.

BIBLIOGRAPHY

Atutov P.R. 1986, Polytechnical Education and the Comprehensive Development of the School Child's Personality. *Sov. Educ.* 29(1): 7-21.

Gustafsson I. 1987, *Schools and the Transformation of Work; A Comparative Study of Four Productive Work Programmes in Southern Africa*. Institute of International Education, Stockholm.

Jennings Z. 1987a, *Work Experience Programmes in Commonwealth Secondary Schools*. Commonwealth Secretariat, London.

Jennings Z. 1987b, The Effectiveness of Programmes Linking Education with Productive Work in the Commonwealth Caribbean. In: Drooglever Fortuyn E., Hoppers W., Morgan M. (eds.) 1987 *Paving Pathways to Work; Comparative Perspectives on the Transition from School to Work* CESO, The Hague.

King K. 1985a, *The Planning of Technical and Vocational Educaiton and Training*. Occasional Paper No. 72 IIEP, Paris.

King K. 1985b, The Environments of Education with Production: School, Training Institutions and Productive Enterprises, *Educ. with Prod.* 4(1): 75.

Komba D. and Temu E.B. 1987, *State of the Art Review of Evaluation of "Education and Self-reliance" Implementation*. Univ. of Dar-es-Salaam.

Lauglo J. 1983, Concepts of "General Education" and "Vocational Education" Curricula for Post-Compulsory Schooling in Western Industrialized Countries; When Shall the Twain Meet? *Comp. Educ.* 19(3): 285-303.

Lauglo J. and Lillis K. (eds.) 1988 *Vocationalizing Education*. Pergamon, London.

Nyerere J. 1968, *Freedom and Socialism*. Oxford Univ. Press, Oxford.

Pfeifer R. and Wald H. 1987, *Polytechnical Education; Issues and Trends*. Information File 8. International Bureau of Education, Geneva.

Price R.G. 1984, Labour and Education. *Comp. Educ.* 20(1): 81-91.

Sinclair M.E. 1976, *Gandhian Basic Education*. Joint UNECSO-Unicef Programme of Educational Assistance, Notes, Comments 12. UNESCO, Paris.

Sinclair M.E. 1977, Introducing Work-experience Programmes in Third World Schools *Prospects* 7(3): 362-78.

Solarin T. 1972, The Mayflower School in Nigeria. In Ponsioen J.A. (e.d) 1972 *Educational Innovations in Africa; Policies and Administration*. Institute of Social Studies, The Hague.

Thögersen S. 1988, Education and Production in China after Mao; Some Social and Political Aspects. Paper Presented at Conference of Nordic Assoc, for Educ. in Dev. Countries, As, Norway, June.

Van Rensburg P. 1974, *Report from Swaneng Hill: Education and Employment in an African Country* Dag Hammerskjöld Foundation, Uppsala.

Zachariah M. 1988, Continuity Between School Curriculum and vocation: Manual Labour's Ineffective Role. *Int, Rev. Educ.* 34(2): 207-23.

30

Education and Productive Work: Some General Considerations

J. Jayshri Jalali

1. Introduction

1.1 Education-work interface and the need to integrate education with productive work

The major problem today both in the developed and the developing worlds is the mismatch between the demand for and supply of skilled labour. This problem is imbeded in the relationship between education and work since centuries. It leads to unrealistic employment expectations, often underutilization of human resources, slow down economic growth of countries and check the developing countries from becoming self-sufficient economies.

For countries of Asia and the Pacific based both on agriculture and highly developed industrial economies; and yet having substantial work oriented school curriculum have still failed to meet the required match between demand for the supply of skilled labour. According to UNESCO "Work needs to be incorporated at all levels of school education ... because it inculcates in the four essential values". These are:

(*a*) It teaches him/her the dignity of human labour;

(*b*) It makes him/her more responsive to social functions/ obligations;

(*c*) It developes in him/her innate talents, creativity and enterprise and helps to bring out a team spirit in his/ her own ethics;

(*d*) It helps him/her appreciate the traditional link between man and nature contributing to the development of societies based upon democracy.

The stages through which this school programme can be introduced is as given below:

(*a*) Either integrating work experience/productive work in the educational process; or

(*b*) Taking education to work situations.

Stage I—Introduction of work education as separate subjects in schools.

Stage II—Introduction of work experience/productive work as optional subjects in the general secondary schools.

Stage III—Introduction of work experience/productive work as compulsory subjects in all general secondary schools.

Stage IV—Introduction of work experience/productive work at senior secondary level.

Stage V—Introduction of work experience/productive work as a life long process.[1]

2. Evolution of the Concept

Ancient and medieval theories of education based as they would of feudal modes of production adopted a strategy which divorced intellectual training from manual work. The feudal system started the process of differentiated training systems such as training for craftsman, military training, and education of princes.[2]

The relationship is less complicated in the developed world because of the evolutionary. process through which this relationship grew. The factory system changed the nature of jobs and in this education played an important role in pre-induction training for factory workers. The emphasis on education also changed from generating knowledge to that inculcating performing skills. It trained workers to adjust to the new social environment in the factories. Education also played an important role in bringing together the different social groups living in a new urban milieu.[3]

2.1 The European Concept

In Western societies, the link between 'instruction' and 'manual work' dates back to the Renaissance movement. Reformers like Thomas More, T. Campanella and others regarded participation in productive work as an essential feature of an 'ideal society'. John Bellers had proposed a 'College of Industry' which should teach children useful sciences, different trades and manual work. Jean Jacques Rousseau preached 'labour instruction'. Pestalozzi had felt that elementary education should combine intellectual training with a knowledge of crafts. Robert Owen had devoted a lot of his time to manual training.[4] The philosophies of these thinkers have expressed themselves in favour of 'work experience' as a part of academic curriculum in Western schools.

In English comprehensive schools, housecraft, mothercraft, needlework, nursing and such subjects are taught between the years twelve and sixteen with a view to teach certain basis skills required in the day to day living of the child.

2.2 The Soviet Concept

The Soviet system of polytechnical education incorporated the ideas of Marx, Lenin and Makarenko, according to which education is directly linked with production. Education is training of citizens to produce a socialist state and has to take into account the productive forces. Makarenko wrote, "Pedagogy is the most dialectical, mobile, complex and diversified of sciences". Participation in community activities was important. Thus the Soviet child has to work for the material production of his society which includes agriculture, transport, industry, construction, communication and such areas. This 'Socially useful labour' consists of two components, namely:

(a) Productive work in a branch of material production such as is mentioned above, and

(b) Work in non-productive fields such as education, public health, housing and communal services, transport, public administration, co-operative and social organizations, banking and insurance and communication.

The activities either separately or jointly form an essential component of the 'labour lessons' curriculum in the daily school routine.[5]

2.3 The Indian Experience

In India agrarian mode of production in ancient and medieval times carried an epistomo-logical belief that "thinking emasculates work and work pollutes thinking".[6] Initially the change came out of trade transactions between India, Arab countries and China. The changes in the modes of production also occured due to the arrival of the Portuguese, Dutch, French and the British in India. The changes continued during the colonial period when education was being used as an instrument for discrimination among the Indians—the academic courses being meant for the native intelligentsia which avoided manual work and the non-academic technical courses incorporating manual and practical work for the lower echelon of the Society.

3. Nationalist Response and Government of India's Efforts Till 1986

During the early colonial period Indian nationalist educators made attempts on 'Linking education with work' at the school level and conducted experiments. However it was Gandhi ("Harijan"–31 July 1937–Nai Talim) who made the most intensive appeal in 1937 that basic education should be the basis of a combination of theory and practical manual work based on the local needs of the environment. It should be productive in nature and the crafts made by school children, would in the long run pay for the maintenance of this system. The Zakir Hussain Committee accepted this as its principle and suggested crafts like spinning, weaving, carpentry, agriculture, food processing, gardening, leather work, and any other work which suits the local and geographical conditions to be integrated in the curriculum. The Kher Committee in 1938 agreed that this Basic Education need to be for the primary stage.

The Mudaliar Commission of 1952-53 while accepting one craft in its core curriculum out of spinning, weaving, wood work, needle work, gardening, tailoring, sewing, embroidery and modelling and envisage steps like agriculture etc. For diversification at the secondary level. The Kothari Commission in 1966 had stated "Whereas Basic Education was concerned primarily with traditional crafts and the village employment patterns".

India has now reached a level of scientific and technological development and recommended that work experience should be "oriented to industry" and simple technology should be introduced in fair proportion in rural schools. In such schools, where school workshops cannot be provided suitable tools and materials, these may be manufactured at low cost and made available to the pupils. In the same way, steps should be taken to introduce gardening in as many urban schools as possible to provide experience in farm work to at least to the secondary stage of education of urban pupils.

Work experience has now become known as 'Socially useful productive work' in the higher secondary curriculum. The Ishwari Bhai Patel Committee, the Adishesiah Committee in the late seventies also recommended work experience to be incorporated in the school curriculum.

REFERENCES

1. UNESCO, ROEAP, Linking Education With Work in General Schools, Regional Profile, Bangkok.
2. Aldo Visalbergi, on Education and Division of Labour in the Developed World; *Learning and Working*. Paris. UNESCO. 1979, p. 32.

3. Jalali. Jayshree "Secondary Education and Work—A Third World Dilemma" *Progressive Educational/Herald, Number,* October 1. Hyderabad, 1987.

4. UNESCO, *Polytechnical Education in the USSR.,* Paris, UNESCO, 1963, pp. 21-22.

5. Jayshree Roy. A Comparative Study of Secondary Education in India and in the USSR with Special Reference to the Concept of Work Experience. M.Ed. Dissertation, CIE. University of Delhi, Dated 20th May, 1981.

6. Moonis Raza, Braham Prakash, Education and Work, *Amity* New Delhi, ISCUS, 1986.

31

Education and Productive Work: Examples of Concrete Cases in India

K. Sudha Rao

1. Objectives of Socially Useful Productive Work (SUPW)

The rationale for introducing work education in general education at the school level has already been elaborated in the previous session. The following paragraphs would high-light the findings of a national level study conducted by NIEPA to analyze the present status of this programme in India and also a case study of "Earn while you learn" scheme in Madhya Pradesh as an example of programme implementation in India. For the purpose of this analysis the performance has been compared with the stated objectives of the programme. The stated objectives of the SUPW programme are:

- to prepare for practicing and performing manual work;
- to acquaint with world of work, and to develop respect for manual work;
- to inculcate positive attitude, team work and socially desirable values such as self reliance, dignity of labour, tolerance, co-operation, sympathy and helpfulness;
- to help in understanding the principles involved in various forms of work;

- to lead to participate in productive work; 'Earn while you learn' scheme;
- to lead to the development of vocational preparedness.

At the primary level the programme was thought to be introduced in the form of hand work, at the middle level in the form of projects, at the secondary level–work experience and at the senior secondary level it is implemented in the form of projects and participation in services which would contribute to the development of desirable social qualities in the child. The criterion set for selecting the objectives are:

(a) it should be educative

(b) it should be productive

(c) it should be socially useful

The work education programmes centers around six areas of human needs, namely, food, health and hygiene, clothing, shelter, culture and recreation and social service. Although the activities will differ from school to school, depending upon its needs and resources, the programme of essential activities is compulsory for all children and the programme of productive work and services under work practice would result in production of goods or services which are saleable or consumeable at home or in the school or outside. Decentralized planning for the work education programme has been considered to be the best strategy. Teaching-learning process has been divided into three phases; study of the work through observation and inquiry; experimentation with materials, tools and techniques and work practice. The first two are concerned with preparation for actual participation in productive work and service, and the third leading to production.

Before analyzing the case study of Earn while you learn scheme in Madhya Pradesh, let us briefly look at the present status of SUPW/LE in India.

2. State of the Art

Socially useful productive work/work experience programme has been introduced in all the schools at primary, middle, secondary and high secondary levels in India. It has been given the status of full fledged/compulsory subject at the school level. In some States, it is an examination subject (*e.g.* Rajasthan, Madhya Pradesh, West Bengal, Mizoram, etc.) whereas in others only internal evaluation is conducted for this subject. The school curriculum outlines the suggested programme of activities to be performed by the students in primary, middle and secondary schools. Instruction of SUPW is imparted by the specialized teachers, it is only during their absence a stop gap arrangement is made by assigning it to the subject teachers. The various agencies that are involved in training these teachers are: National Council for Educational Research and Training (NCERT), and their counterparts in the States (SCERT), Directorates of Education etc. In addition, wherever the education department has been able to establish proper linkages with the production centers and other agencies, the training programmes are also organized by these agencies. B.Ed. and M.Ed. courses have been revised to incorporate training related to work education in their curriculum. We have one week intensive courses organized by NCERT, where in the craft performance is emphasized.

Financing of SUPW is done by the States. The States do get funds from private sources. Other inputs like raw material and expertise are given by the students, parents and other production centers. Majority of the states provide Rs. 200 to Rs. 500 per annum as contingency for purchasing raw materials. Jammu & Kashmir provides Rs. 500–Rs. 1000 per annum. Karnataka provide Rs. 4000 per annum, per school for appointment of part-time teachers, purchase of equipments, raw material, conveyance, etc.

Developing linkages with other agencies, other than education, is an individual phenomena. Except in Madhya Pradesh, it is the individual institutions that are establishing relationships with neighbouring agencies for its effective implementation. It is only in Madhya Pradesh at the headquarters level itself the State has established linkages with other sector.

Produced goods are generally distributed amongst the students, parents and teachers depending upon who provides the raw materials. Wherever the large scale productions are there, they are sold in the annual fares or exhibitions of the school. But in such cases invariably school provides the raw material. In Madhya Pradesh and Kerala where large scale goods are produced are purchased by the education department itself. In the majority of the schools the products are only handicraft articles. Wherever agriculture products are there it is used in the annual feasts by the school itself.

Coming to the attitudinal that part of it, it appears that the established dichotomy of the superiority of mental work over the manual work is persisting; parents feel that school is meant for white collar academic activity and not a place for doing manual work. Hence they consider it as waste of time. Though they feel that is good for children's attitudes, the type of activities introduced are found to be of no use. Teachers are of the opinion that the activity is good but when it comes to practice, they prefer to be academic teachers. Principals are not very happy with the programme because its serious implementation means additional responsibility and inefficient implementation would bring bad reputation.

It is obvious from the responses that wherever the leadership is good the programme is successful. Invariably in all the schools run by voluntary agencies, and other missionaries the programme is highly successful.

States are facing a number of problems in introducing the SUPW/work education programme. Some of them are:

- Lack of awareness of the parents, teachers, students and community about the objectives of the programme.
- Financial input is too meager to introduce any large scale activity leading to production.
- Lack of availability of trained teachers.
- Management difficulties.
- Lack of instructional material, teacher guides, training guides etc.

In general, as it stands today, the programme has not been able to contribute to either self employment of students or to the rural development. This does not mean that there are no cases of successful implementation. Rajasthan has implemented activities that are of daily use to the students. As a result student response is very high. Similar is the case in Maharashtra and Kerala. A detailed case study of one such state which has introduced the programme in a successful manner is given in the following paragraphs.

3. 'Earn While You Learn Scheme': A Case Study of Madhya Pradesh

'Earn while your learn' scheme was introduced at six centers in 1978 on an experimental basis in Madhya Padesh. Success achieved in these centres encouraged the planners and administrators to ramify the programme to as many as 413 centres in the State. The major objectives set for the scheme are as under:

(a) Rejuvenating craft teaching

(b) Developing productive skill

(c) Utilizaiton of leisure in productive work

(d) Developing dignity towards labour

(e) Helping retention in schools.

The state took precautionary measures to overcome those problems that posed hindrances to the success of the work education programme in India. The SUPW/work experience programme did not achieve success (except in few institutions here and there) because of three major problems (a) lack of supply of raw material to the institution; (b) lack of trained teachers; and (c) lack of motivation.

To overcome these the State established linkages with small scale industries, Khadi and Village Industries, Handicrafts Board etc. which would supply raw materials to the educational institutions. The products from the institutions are purchased by the education department itself. It is with those in view, th activities introduced in the institutions are: making of tatpattis (jute mats), chalks, sealing wax, uniforms and dolls. The motivation of teachers, students and institutional heads was restored by making provision for remuneration to all these. The third problem was overcome by arranging a massive teachers' training programme during summer vacations.

A brief look, therefore, at the school product which reflect this production capability of schools and its distribution over the years, on the one hand, and at the participation of students in different activities on the other hand, suggests that what was considered not to be possible, till now, is not something that is impossible. The number of students involved in the programme and the list of parents are show in Tables 31.1 and 31.2.

Table—31.1: Showing the Number of Students' Participation in the Production of Tatpatti and Chalk Sticks and Uniforms at the State Level

Year	*Tatpatti*	*Chalk sticks*	*School uniforms*	*Total*
1978-79	924	100	-	1,024
1979-80	1,358	148	-	156
1980-81	1,696	300	-	1,996
1981-82	3,045	304	-	3,349
1982-83	3,600	98	-	3,698
1983-84	2,252	n.a	400	2,652
1984-85	1,732	n.a	4,134	5,866
1985-86	n.a	n.a	n.a	n.a
Total	**14,607**	**950**	**4,534**	**20,091**

The participation number and the number of goods produced by students in school hours reveals that student participation continuously increased from 1978-79 (924) to 1982-83 (3,600) in the activity of making of tatpattis but then started decreasing. Where as in the uniform making it is increasing. Similarly the

Table—31.2: Production of Tatpattis, Chalks and School Uniforms at the State Level

Year	*No. of tatpattis*	*Cost in lakhs (Rs.)*	*No. of chalks*	*Cost in lakhs (Rs. 0)*	*No. of uniforms(a)*	*Cost in lakhs (Rs.)*
1978-79	23,100	7.97	25,000	0.38		
1979-80	24,200	11.80	37,000	0.55		
1980-81	41,482	14.81	75,200	1.13		
1981-82	72,447	24.99	75,300	1.13		
1982-83	87,547	28.66	12,403	0.25	4,000	1.40
1983 84	52,857	18.50	-	-	5,06,000	114.00
1984-85	6,670	5.00	-	-	10,00,000	215.00
1985-86	-	-	-	-		
Total	**3,08,303**	**11.73**	**2,24,938**	**3.4**	**15,10,000**	**330.40**

Note: Rs. 1 lakh = Rs. 1,00,000.
(a) Started in 1983.
Source: UN Shahane 'Earn while you learn' scheme in Madhya Pradesh.

products are also affected. In 1978-79 the number of tatpattis produced were 23,100 and it is 87,547 in 1982-83. But again the drop could be noticed in 1983-84 (52,857) and 1984-85 (6,670). Production of school uniforms and the number participating is continuously increasing since its introduction in 1983-84.

A survey conducted in Gwalior district also revealed similar findings as far as the products and the participation are concerned.

Responses of the non participating students revealed that the reasons for their non-participation are: (a) their parents did not permit them; (b) though willing, they were not given the opportunity to work; (c) they did not like manual labour; (d) they considered the activity as a hindrance in regular studies; (e) the items being produced are not of their choice and (f) the remuneration is too low.

Results in the annual examination revealed that amongst the participating students 11 per cent scored 60 per cent and above, 50 per cent scored 45-59 per cent and the rest scored 33 per cent to 44 per cent.

Except for the difficulties faced in the way of operationalisation of the programme in general, the programme is found to be successful in achieving the stated objectives. As regards the objective of rejuvenating the craft teaching the scheme has undeniably succeeded. The scheme has actually reanimated the craft teaching which had almost lost its meaning. In the area of development of productive skill, the success of the scheme is indicated by the quality of products, lack of wastage of goods and the remarkable reduction in the time taken to produce these items. Leisure time utilization is another success of this scheme. And finally the scheme is also successful in reducing the dropouts and increasing the attendance rates.

Only objective to which the study is not able to depict positive responses is the developing dignity towards labour.

Concluding Remarks

Above paragraphs are indicative of merits and demerits of the programme and also the reasons for its success and failure. If we are to achieve only success then we need to rectify the demerits and overcome those problems that are causal to failure.

REFERENCES

"The Third Dimension of Education" C.B.S.E. New Delhi.

"Work Experience in School Education" N.C.E.R.T., New Delhi, 1986.

Shahane V.S. "An Evaluative Study of the Earn While You Learn Scheme of Madhya Pradesh" Dissertation submitted to NIEPA, New Delhi 1986.

"Earn While You Learn" (mimeo) Circula[illegible] Directorate of Public Instruction M.P. Bhopal, 1986.

32

Diversification of Post-Secondary Education in Relation to Employment: The International Context

Bikas C. Sanyal

1. Objectives of the Analysis

It has been mentioned before that the post-secondary education system is often very diversified with many sub-levels and a large range of institutions. This diversity yields different types of qualified manpower. The objective of the present session is:

(a) to acquaint the participants with the rationale for diversity and the different forms which such diversification may take in programmes of post-secondary education in general;

(b) to examine the diversity of the higher education system in the international context, and;

(c) to analyze its consequences on the education-employment relationship.

2. The Rationale for Diversification and the Forms it may Take

While formal institutions play the dominant role in higher education in general, they are by no means the only places where individuals may pursue explicit training objectives. A whole range of other educational programmes playing a great variety of roles have developed outside the formal system, which are the result of the growing awareness that the formal institutions of higher education are no longer capable of satisfying the whole range of increasingly diversified educational needs. These needs are the direct outcome of both the rapid pace of economic, technological and social change in contemporary society and a gradual broadening of developmental objectives. More specifically, diversification has taken place for the following reasons:[1]

(a) Educational objectives have become more diversified. (While educational objectives in the past were mainly cultural and a desire for knowledge for its own sake, today education must in addition satisfy the manpower needs of the economy, and be made available to all segments of society to achieve the objective of democratization. Education has to provide the means to gain a livelihood to all citizens).

(b) Diversity of 'new' client groups has also caused diversification. (One may mention here adult learners, disadvantaged and handicapped persons, unemployed youth, employees who need post-experience and refresher courses, and out of school youth).

(c) Widening of the process of resource mobilization, allocation and utilization has resulted in the diversification of higher education. (Resource mobilization now covers government sources (at different levels, *e.g.* national, provincial and local), private foundations, enterprises, students own funding, voluntary agencies and international organisations. Different sources have different types of allocation mechanisms and modes of utilization of resources).

(d) New modes of programme delivery and management have emerged to meet specific educational objectives, thus contributing to diversification. (These include open universities, workers' colleges, sandwich courses, television and radio universities, etc.)

(*e*) Underlying institutional diversification (to respond to local and regional needs, the needs of enterprises, etc.) has also been responsible for diversity in higher education. (This has taken the form of providing specific services to the community or interested groups. Co-operative programmes between institutions of higher education and industries also fall in this category).

These different reasons have given rise to different types of diversification, of which there are five major forms in higher education:

(*a*) Structure, *e.g.* part time/full time, single/full course, open admission, etc.

(*b*) Content: balance between theory and practice, more work experience, skill formation, orientation, new types of disciplines.

(*c*) Organisational methods: open university, university-industry co-operation, etc.

(*d*) Controlling authority: state, private, government sponsored, regional, local etc., and

(*e*) Duration of studies.

There may be various other forms depending on the country.

3. Examples of Diversification in the International Context

In this respect the industrial sectors of the economy have played a significant role, especially in higher education. This is more common in industrialized countries because of the availability of training infrastructures, the incapability of formal institutions to provide the necessary skills in a short period of time, the need for job specific training and to relate training more closely to the needs of the job. Some examples of the different forms prevalent in different countries are given below:[2]

The increasing need for workers to participate in management, the growing tendency of companies to meet their employment needs by upgrading the work force within the company rather than depending on the external labour market, and the specific types of skills needed by different industries have been the motivating factors for the organisation of adult education in the Federal Republic of Germany; as a result, about 40 per cent of all the firms employing 50 employees or more had provision for such education as early as 1974. Training could take place, depending on the purpose, either 'on the job' in the firm or 'off the job' with paid educational leave.

The chronically high level of unemployment in Sweden has encouraged the development of recurrent education among youth there, in addition to the stimulus provided by experiments in 'industrial democracy' for increasing workers' participation in decision-making on the conditions of work. Swedish universities have formally recognized work experience as a criterion for admission, in place of upper secondary school certificate, for those aged twenty-five and above. A joint project between the University of Lund and the regional trades union has formalized an education-employment linkage whereby course content and teaching are adopted to trade union needs and the union supports research relevant to its interests.

In the United Kingdom, recurrent education has developed against a background of skill obsolescence, lagging productivity, high unemployment among youth, shifts in occupational distribution and changing labour/management relations. The Employment and Training Act of 1973 gave rise to courses making education more responsive to the world of work. In the mid-seventies, around two-thirds of the total labour force was covered by the Industrial Training Boards, responsible for this training. In addition to the ITB's, there was also a programme of Training Within Industries (TWI), offering short courses under the direct responsibility of the Government. Medium and long-term 'off the job' recurrent education was provided in the Training Opportunities Scheme (TOPS). These programmes became so popular that between 1973-1976, the number of courses nearly doubled. Flexible hours, compressed work courses and part-time employment enable the workers to undertake such training more easily.

More recently in the United Kingdom there has been a considerable increase in programmes, financed by the Manpower

Services Commission (MSC), which provides vocational education and training linked with work experience, both for unemployed school leavers and older unemployed.

For school-leavers, the Youth Training Scheme (YTS), now provides a guarantee of two years' vocational training and organised work experience for all 16-18 year olds who cannot find employment.

For older workers there are a variety of government programmes offering opportunities for retraining, such as the MSC's Job Training Scheme (JTS) and the updating of skills, such as the Department of Education and Science PICKUP programme, which offers "professional, industrial and commercial; updating". The most recent innovation is the Open College, launched in 1987, which offers work related courses on television, and gives employers the opportunity to sponsor programmes which are tailor-made for their own training requirements. The Open College hopes to attract 50,000 students in its first year.[3]

Open developments in the United Kingdom include programmes to update industrial managers and researchers in modern techniques, *e.g.* a programme entitled 'Integrated graduate development programme', initiated in 1980 with initial financing from the Department of Education and Science, with courses jointly designed and managed by industrialists and academics and run on a repeated modular/residential basis, located at six university or polytechnic centres around the Kingdom. The flexibility of the course allows highly senior officials to attend it. The emphasis is laid on empirical practicality and to specific industrial needs. Several major companies work together in supporting a particular course. The local joint management committee consists of members from industry, academic and research councils, which provides a bridge between industry and academic. Financing of the programme is gradually being shifted to industry. The programme has benefitted several hundred managers, with post graduate qualifications and the industry with quickly trained manpower.

Another example in the same country is the Austin Rover course for Directors held at Warwick University with a duration of 18 months. The course, financed partly by the MSC Commission addresses a wide range of issues related to high technology and their implication for manufacture, production and design of products and strategic planning. Organisation of the course follows the same pattern as above emphasizing the benefit of industry, academic co-operation.[4]

In the United States, in 1975, 7.500 of the largest private employers spend over US$2 billion on employee education; of this total, internal company courses accounted for US$1.6 billion, excluding the cost of employees' wages and salaries while they were learning, and the rent and other overhead expenses. In all, 45,000 people were engaged on a full-time basis, as instructors, programme developers, administrators and evaluators. The type and scope of the training today varies from industry to industry, but the core of the programmes is active student involvement through simulation exercises and end-of-course critical evaluation, individually-oriented course content, duration and instructional method, the increased use of programmed materials, advanced instructional technologies and the appreciation of the student's sensibilities, behaviour and attitude. The Fund for the Improvement of Post-Secondary Education, a Federal Government fund, has been established to relate education to work with the objective of providing more avenues for routing out-of-school adults back into education and through education to work. The Fund works in co-operation with voluntary agencies, educational associations and institutions for higher education.

In Eastern European and many developing countries, there are similar programmes for the training of the work force. In some of them, investment in such training will exceed investment in formal education.

Discussions on diversity of higher education would remain incomplete if we did not include two innovations that are being implemented in the United Kingdom and in the United States, respectively, the 'Open University' and 'Co-operative Education'. The Open University was established in 1969 with the primary objective of giving to those who would not otherwise have access to it, the opportunity to pursue higher education. Provision was made for 'open entry' admission of mature students (21 years and upwards) as part-time, non-residential students who would work at home in their spare time. The instruction can lead to a degree (BA Ordinary or Masters), but other, non-degree programmes, are also available. 'Foundations courses' are provided to most students, but those who have the regular qualifications for following a particular programme are exempt. Instruction takes different forms. A variety of correspondence units and television and radio broadcasts provide students with information and guidance in a standard package. The packages are prepared by a course team composed of regional and central academic staff, the BBC, and educational technologists. In addition to working at home, students can attend, on a voluntary basis, 'study centres' located throughout the country, usually in other educational institutions. These centres are the focal points for the under-graduate students' meeting with their tutor/counsellors, who take the role of a general educational adviser at the local level throughout the student's educational course. Tutor-marked assignments by correspondence are the major means of improving upon the students' work. Computer-marked assignments complement these. Degrees are awarded to students who have achieved a given number of credits in the programme. In addition to continuous assessment through assignments, every course has a final examination for the degree. Since the Open University was established, such distance learning systems are spreading over many countries in the developing world centred around the correspondence courses already in existence. This new avenue is providing many individuals with a chance to upgrade their social roles as well as to pursue higher education for its own sake.

The American programme, 'Co-operative Education', is an academic strategy that integrates on-campus classroom study with off-campus work experience. Although the term is more common in the United States, such programmes are prevalent in many other countries. Students in co-operative education alternate between periods of study in their colleges and universities and periods of employment in business, government and non-profit-making organisations. Employment areas are directly related to academic areas. Depending on the situation, such work experience is given due academic credit and may be remunerated (*e.g.*, USA, United Kingdom) a honorary (Federal Republic of Germany). The main characteristic of these programmes is that they are organised from and within the education system as an attempt to develop a closer relationship between the education system and the world of work.

4. Consequences on Education-Employment Relationships

Diversification of education has its advantages and disadvantages when one analyses the relationship between education and employment. We shall discuss both.

4.1 Benefits

The following is a partial list of benefits that can be derived from diversification of post-secondary education:

(*a*) Diversification provides job-specific skills and education can be more relevant to the needs of the job.

(*b*) Latest development in science and technology can be interpreted in the flexible structure of a diversified system.

(*c*) Flexibility in some programmes allows for quick updating of highly senior official's knowledge base in the context of fast technological change.

(*d*) Diversification obliges the formal system of education compete with new types of delivery systems and make it more responsive to the needs of the world of work.

(*e*) Industry organised training programmes seldom would produce unemployment graduates because of their very nature.

(*f*) Diversification allows better match between education and employment through continuous updating of educational programmes with employment needs as discussed in some of the programmes mentioned above.

4.2 Some Problems of Diversity

While diversification of the education system has a lot of advantages, as indicated above, it also has certain disadvantages. These are:

(a) Problem of co-ordination. A large network of delivery systems needs proper monitoring and co-ordination to safeguard quality, achieve economies of scale and increase mobilization in case of structural changes in manpower needs.

(b) Training carried out by enterprises or by the sectoral ministries tends to be excessively narrow and job specific. Mobility among workers is restricted.

(c) Diversity creates the problem of converting educational output to occupational needs.

However, the advantages of such diversity appear to outweigh the disadvantages which can be overcome by a proper monitoring mechanism.

NOTES

1. See UNESCO/IIEP *Educational Planning in the Context of Current Development Problems*, Vol. 1, Paris. 1983 pp. 38-40.

2. Sanyal B.C. 'Alternative Structures of Higher Education and the World of Work', *International Review of Education*, Vol. XXVIII, 1982.

3. I am grateful to Ms. M. Woodhall of the University of London. Institute of Education for Updating my Information on the Subject in the United Kingdom.

4. Reiff, Hans: Training Qualified Manpower: The Joint Role of Higher Education and Enterprises, IIEP, Paris, June 1986.

33

Diversification of Post-Secondary Education in Relation to Employment with Special Reference to India

G.D. Sharma

1. An Overview

In this paper we deal with diversification in post-secondary education in India through:

1. Courses of studies: formal system
   - (a) Introduction of new courses of studies and specialization, in general, professional universities
   - (b) Restructuring of undergraduate courses; and
   - (c) Diversification in professional education.
2. Modes of delivery: formal system
   - (a) Correspondence courses
   - (b) Open university system.

3. Institutions for Training of Skilled Manpower: Non-Formal System

In the end we attempt to conceptualize the problem and indicate the planning imperatives for the country. Process of diversification of post secondary education in India in the formal system of education started in the 1950s. It was in response to the felt needs of planned process of development, which focussed on agriculture and industrial development. Diversification here was in the form of introduction of new courses and specialization in these courses. After 1975-76 diversification took the form of redesigning undergraduate courses. This was in response to the changing needs of industrial and modern development as well as inability of the formal system of education to produce required type of manpower, as the existing system produced a prototype of manpower which had difficulty in finding employment. Recently, *i.e.*, in 1985-86 the need for diversification was further reiterated to meet the changing demands of development, particularly for building a science and technology base and development of human capabilities to contribute to the national developmental process. Here focus is on: redesigning of courses, flexibility in course combinations and developing wider capability among people through open learning system.

Under non-formal system, where both public and private efforts were involved, the diversification was mainly in response to the needs of skilled and semi professional persons in the job market. This type of diversification mainly started in late 1950s and it continues till now.

2. Diversification Through Introduction of New Courses: Formal System

Within the formal system, the diversification in general education took place in the development of arts, social sciences, commerce, science and education branches. On industrial side—it occurred through the establishment of industrial training institutes for skilled workers; polytechnics for the semi-professional and engineering colleges and institutes of technology for the professionals. On the agriculture side—agriculture colleges, agricultural universities and agricultural technology university had been set up. On the side of business operations—institutes of management were established. For tackling the problems of human health at the skilled and semi professional level nursing and compoundering training institutions and at the professional level medical colleges were set up.

Veterinary colleges were set up for dealing with the problems of animal health. On the side of fine arts and culture, fine arts and music colleges and arts and music university as well as oriental learning colleges/institutes came into existence. Within these broad disciplines further diversification took place in the form of specialization. In economic subjects like, industrial, agricultural and urban economics and economics of education become separate branches. Similarly in agricultural science, plant breeding, high yielding variety seeds, and tissue culture became new subjects. Similar examples can be cited for almost all other broader disciplines. These diversifications have been mainly effected through development in the state of art and knowledge and to some extent on the basis of needs for development.

The type of diversification in post-secondary education, as stated above, mainly started in 1950s and continues till date. However, by mid 1970s a good number of institutions were already offering new courses of studies and specialization. This trend continues even today. This may be seen in Table—33.1.

However, during early 70s signs of graduate unemployment became visible. Nearly 20-27 per cent of the graduates were not finding placement. Although this situation was mainly attributed to the slow rate of growth of economy, yet it was observed that the system of higher education was producing a prototype of manpower, whereas developing economy required wider capabilities among people and hence for many jobs suitable persons were not available. There was a mismatch between types of capabilities demanded and the types of capabilities developed among students by the education system.

This argument is supported by the fact that of the 2.4 million students enrolled in higher education in 1975-76 nearly 80 per cent were pursuing arts, science and commerce studies (See Table—33.2). Indicating thereby that the system was generating older type of capabilities among most of the prospective educated work force, whereas the world of work required variety of capabilities.

Hence during mid seventies questions were raised regarding relevance of general graduate education and the need was expressed foı redesigning and diversifying under-graduate programmes.

Table—33.1: Number of Institutions by Courses of Studies—India

Institutions/Years	*1950-51*	*1975-76*	*1984-85*
1	**2**	**3**	**4**
Colleges			
Arts, Sciences and Commerce	246	3,085	3,925
Technical and Professional	102	412	608
(a) Engineering/Technology	33	109	215
(b) Medicine Pharmacy/Ayurveda/ Nursing/Dentistry/Homeopathy	39	224	304
(c) Agriculture	20	56	61
(d) Veterinary Science	10	23	28
Law	19	132	192
Physical Education and Edn.	60	330	412
Oriental learning	73	271	276
Music/Fine Arts	14	42	65
Total	514	4,272	5,498
Universities			
General universities	27	77	97
Engineering/Technology	1	2	3
Ayurveda— (Indian Medicine)	-	2	4
Agriculture universities	-	21	24
Open universities	-	-	1
Deemed universities			
General	-	5	7
Technology	-	1	1
Agricultural/Rural development	-	2	2
Sciences	-	1	1
Mines	-	1	1
Architecture	-	-	1
Veterinary Sciences	-	-	1

(Contd.)

1	2	3	4
Education	-	-	1
Total	-	10	15
Professional Institutes			
IIT	-	5	5
IIM	–5	5	
Vocational institutes	-		
Industrial training institutes	29	365(a)	356(b)
Polytechnics	62	327	389

Note: *(a)* UGC Annual Report, Educational Statistics at a glance, AIU, 1976 based Ministry of Education, Govt. of India and IAMR, Third Survey of Technical Manpower, 1976.

(b) The data are for 1973.

Table—33.2: Distribution of Students Enrolled in Higher Education by Field of Studies

	1975-76 *Percentage*	*1984-85(a)* *Percentage*
Arts	44.5	40.0
Science	19.1	19.7
Commerce	17.1	21.0
Education	3.2	2.4
Engineering and Technology	4.0	4.5
Medicine	4.3	3.8
Agriculture	1.2	1.3
Veterinary Science	0.3	0.3
Law	5.8	6.0
Other	0.5	0.6
Total	100	100
Number in millions	2.4	3.55

(a) In order to get clear picture of the extent of diversification, the data need to be collected and presented by courses of studies within a broad discipline.

It may be mentioned that during this very period questions of relevance of higher education system, particularly within reference to third world countries were also raised at the UNESCO level. It was felt that traditional subject combination, contents of the courses and methodology of teaching hardly develop the desired capabilities among the students, so as to enable them to respond to the emerging needs of developing economy and the society. As economy becomes more industrialized and society becomes more complex the knowledge and skills required to deal with the situations also change. Hence for enabling students to acquire the desired capabilities, contents of courses and their combinations need to be diversified and made more flexible.

3. Diversification Through Restructuring of Courses: General Education

In response to this need the University Grants Commission of India initiated a scheme of restructuring of undergraduate programme in 1977. However, this scheme was not implemented by many universities. Only a couple of universities came forward to implement it. In 1983 the revised guidelines were formulated and further stress was laid on the implementation of this scheme. Since then nearly 30 out of 80 affiliating universities have attempted redesigning of courses and these redesigned courses have been implemented in nearly 159 out of 5,400 colleges.

The scheme of restructuring of courses focusses on: *(a)* social value formation through foundation courses on science and society, contemporary problems of Indian development, freedom struggle, national integration, etc.; *(b)* developing required knowledge—through different courses combinations like—Physics, Mathematics and Computer Sciences/Electronics; Economics, insurance, business entrepreneurship, etc.; and *(c)* developing abilities to apply knowledge—through applied courses under different disciplines. Under this scheme the diversification was introduced in the form of foundation, core and applied courses with a built in flexibility in subject combinations. The scheme also provides for introduction of courses for developing vocational skills in certain areas related to regional and national needs.

The applied and job-oriented courses, so far implemented by the universities and colleges may be briefly narrated here. The courses for B.Sc, degree programme relate to: Agriculture and Rural Development—with five course options. Applied Physical and Chemical Science—with seven options, Applied biological sciences—with nine options.

That for Arts degree programmes these courses relate to: Rural Development—with seven options; Business and Public Management and Co-operatives—with eight options. Financial Management—with three options. Health and Home Economics—with seven options; Mass media and Communication—with seven options, Arts and Culture—with two options, Commerce degree courses—with seven options.

The job oriented courses relate to: Agriculture and animal husbandry—with six options, Marine Sciences—with seven options, Rural Development with—with four options, Business operations—with five options, Public Management—with four options, Financial Management—with five options, Industrial Operations—with four options, Small Scale and Household industries—with two options; Science and Technology—with ten options, Computer Sciences—with two options, Health and Nutrition—with four options. Home Economics—with three options, Mass Media—with two options. Thus through job-oriented courses attempt is being made to develop skills which are likely, to be demanded in job situations.

However, implementation of these courses, owing to built in limitations of the system, lack of training and orientation of teachers in this new approach and resources required for the same, has been very limited. Hence diversification in enrolment of students has also been marginal. The New Education Policy, 1986 and Programme of Action has laid to further stress on implementation of this scheme.

4. Diversification in Professional Education

Besides, diversification in general degree programmes, the need for diversification in professional degree programme in Engineering and Technology is also strongly felt. The present programmes of professional education based on traditional pattern have tended to develop older type capabilities in certain areas leaving many new and developing areas unattended. Therefore, to meet the needs of new industries, the diversification in professional education is also contemplated. Recent review of IITs and Engineering education has laid a stress on introduction of new areas of studies in professional education.

5. Diversification through New Modes

5.1 Correspondence Courses

Distance education through correspondence courses, more on the lines of traditional graduate and post-graduate programmes, in arts, commerce and education started in the late 60s and early 70s. This was mainly in response to the needs of persons who were either employed or who could not attend regular day scholar programmes or could not get admission in universities and colleges. This mode catered for the educational demand of not only participating but also prospective work force as well as household population. Correspondence courses in liberal arts programmes tended to develop, more or less, older type of capabilities among students. Since the degrees awarded under this programme provided opportunities for further promotions and the scope for better job opportunities, many persons enrolled for correspondence courses. As on the date nearly 23 universities are offering graduate and post-graduate programmes through correspondence courses and are enrolling nearly 400 thousand students.

6. Open Learning Systems

Diversification through open learning system is of greater implication for developing human capabilities in a variety of areas and among wider groups of population. The formal university and collegiate system tends to impart knowledge, skills and values to, by and large, prospective work force, whereas open learning systems tends to impart and upgrade knowledge, skill and values to household population, prospective and employed work force in different vocations or walks of life. This system implies: *(a)* introduction of variety of courses (in modular form) catering to the knowledge and skill up-gradibility needs of persons in different walks of life; *(b)* built-in flexibility in options of courses with or without evaluation and certification. This concept of open learning in a formal system pertains to: open university system and informal way it relates to radio, TV and print media. This kind of diversification has come in response to the realization that the modern production and distribution process as well as social interaction require continuous knowledge and skill upgrading (both in broader and specialized areas) and this could be provided more effectively through open learning systems.

7. Open University System

The first open university in India was set up at Andhra Pradesh in 1982. Recently in 1986, at the national level, Indira Gandhi National Open University has been set up. The later one is attempting to cater to the wider needs of population in work force, population at home and prospective work force through various programmes. Some of the programmes launched by Indira Gandhi National Open University pertain to rural development, business management teachers' proficiency, science and society as well as a structured graduate degree programme. Such programmes are available to people irrespective of their previous formal educational attainments.

8. Television

A television programme has been launched by the UGC for general awareness in science, social science and arts. These programmes are regularly telecast for the benefit of students and community at large.

9. Institutions of Training for Skilled Manpower: Informal System

In response to immediate labour market needs, several skill formation institutions with private/public efforts have been set up in 1950s and these continue to grow till today. Most important among them are: institutions for training in secretarial practices, company secretaryship, agriculture, forestry, fisheries, maintenance and repairs of TV, electronic goods etc. Very recently institutions offering computer programming courses have also been started with private/public efforts. Private institutions are totally financed by the students/trainees. Detailed data on number of such institutions and students enrolled in them are hard to come by. However some data collected by IAMR, indicate that as on 1980-81, there were 4,393 institutions offering various skill oriented courses. These institutions enrolled 3.99 thousand students (see Table—33.3).

Table—33.3: Distribution of Technical and Vocational Education Programme Institutes and their Enrolment for the Year 1981-82

1. Industrial/Technical/Arts and Crafts schools	2,296	2,35,793
2. Agriculture and Forestry schools	78	6,707
3. Nursing, ANM and HV schools	639	33,306
4. Pharmacy schools	101	4,545
5. Other Para-medical schools	129	4,059
6. Schools for Music and Fine Arts, etc.	386	49,648
7. Other schools	754	65,299
Total	**4,393**	**3,99,357**

IAMR, New Delhi, 1981-82.

10. Conceptualization of Problem and Planning Imperatives

It may be pertinent to conceptualize this process of diversification so as to draw some conclusions for linking the post-secondary education with world of work and for planning the system to meet the needs of modern development.

Diversification through addition of new courses or through specialization is an easier task and it mainly depends on development of knowledge and the amount of resources allocated to the education system. However, diversification through restructuring of courses, *i.e.*, diffusing among the mass, which over a period of time gathers around a few selected subjects, is most difficult task, as this effort encounters opposition from faculty and other institutional forces. How and why this happens may be seen in the following analysis.

The development of education system particularly higher education in most parts of the world (other than those parts where there is a built in relationship between the world of work and the education either through centralized planning or through market mechanism) is mainly influenced by development in academic fields, the momentum of growth of the system and to some extent by the signals of market forces. In such systems education and world of work are likely to move somewhat separately. Although there is a resemblance of relationship between education and planned process of economic development, as broad policy statements and plan decisions are always brought to bear on educational policy and its planning, yet as these decisions remain at a very broad level, many subtle and crucial aspects pertaining to implementation are left out. In such situation there is always a gap—more than the desired one—between the social and economic development and the educational development. This gap is further strengthened by the system own momentum of growth which in turn is influenced by the past trend and built-in structural limitations namely regulations, procedures, financial mechanism, faculty orientation and decision making processes. Therefore, in the absence of rigorous planning, supported by resources and institutional mechanism, the interaction of policy and plan decisions with institutional forces create a state of nebulousness. In this state the policy implementation always falls short of expectations. This invariably causes a gap between the education and the world of work.

Therefore, establishment of closer linkage between education and the world of work, particularly through diversification of higher education involves:

(a) development of relevant contents of courses based on the changing needs of economy and society;

(b) modularization of courses;

(c) combination of courses cutting across the disciplines;

(d) flexibility in course options;

(*e*) orientation of teachers;

(*f*) introduction of new forms and modes of teaching-learning strategies and their evaluation;

(*g*) proper mechanism of resource allocation, flow and utilization; and

(*h*) introduction of proper planning and management practices.

The implementation of these aspects requires: First: Identification of the need areas for establishing closer linkage between the world of work and education. This depends on capability of policy makers to perceive and conceptualize policy options and their implications. In the absence of this capability there is always a long gestation period between the response of policy and the needs of the employment market.

Second: Operationalization of policy through highly scientific and detailed planning, proper resource input and institutional mechanism of implementation of policy. A weak planning invariably results in state of nebulousness in implementation.

Third: Promotion of forces which facilitate the implementation as well as development of a mechanism to sort out operational problems which quite often surface in the process of implementation. An inadequate care of these forces and the absence of a mechanism to sort out problems, thwarts the implementation.

Fourth: Assessment of impact, feed back and necessary changes in plan as well as the process of implementation.

All these demand a greater understanding of institutional and socio-economic forces as well as development of rigorous planning and implementation processes, in much more minute details than quite often demonstrated under a broad macro theory of planned development.

34

Need for Pupil/Student Flow Regulation

Gabriele Göttelmann-Duret

Many developing countries have to cope with two major problems when trying to balance the demand for and supply of qualified manpower:

(i) *'Over-production' of graduates,* given the limited prospects for finding corresponding employment in the modern economic sector and

(ii) *A lack of qualified scientific and technical manpower because certain branches,* especially secondary science courses and certain post-secondary technology studies, *do not attract enough able and motivated young people.*

In order to overcome these problems educational planners and policy makers have to find adequate ways and means of improving the regulation of pupil and student flows.

I. Regulating Access to Higher Levels of the Educational System

In many developing countries undergoing extraordinary growth of primary schooling the existing systems of selection have hardly succeed in braking exponential enrolment growth in secondary and post-secondary education.

- Stopping the 'diploma race' has proved to be difficult, indeed. In the 1970s critics of the 'diploma disease' (1) suggested the *'de-liking' of diplomas from access to modern sector employment* as a possible way of limiting excessive enrolment growth in secondary and post-secondary courses of the academic type. They were hoping, then, that employers, especially the public sector (as the largest modern sector employer in most developing countries) could play a strategic role in the fight against 'over-schooling' by applying their own selection and training devices and procedures, independently of school diplomas and examinations. In practice, however, educational certificates have never ceased to be employed for job allocation, and a majority of people tend to believe that in spite of many negative facets, educational credentials constitute 'the least unfair' device for selection and recruitment.

- A number of countries have been trying to reduce pupil flows toward higher levels of the educational system by *restricting admission to upper secondary schools and, in certain cases, to lower secondary schools*) in the public sector. But such initiatives have often entailed increasing enrolment in the private sector. According to certain authors (2) the expansion of private secondary education could be kept under control by subjecting institutions in the sector to general admission and entrance examination regulations; private institutions would be all the more ready to accept regulations of their selection procedures to the extent that they receive public subsidies in return. This type of strategy may, however, run up against strong pupil and parent opposition to any restriction of access to secondary and post-secondary levels because the latter are the only pathways to employment and to a decent standard of living. In such a context educational planners and policy makers have to identify and act upon the various factors affecting individual demand and educational choice that are amenable to their influence.

- The decision to go on to post-compulsory education at any given level or cycle (3) seems to be influenced (among other factors) by certain *structural features of the educational system*, the age at which choices occur, the multiplicity of choices and their more or less reversible nature. Early diversification of educational streams or tracks—*i.e.* into general, technical, vocational courses of variable duration—right after completion of primary school for example, obviously tends to limit the proportion of pupils who are either able or willing to complete the longer secondary courses. This is all the more so to the extent that some of the tracks/streams emphasize the terminal (job-related) nature of the course and that decent jobs are available even for those who have not completed longer secondary or post-secondary programmes. Many developing countries (especially in Africa), however, are characterised by high levels of unemployment and under-employment and cannot afford to develop the generally expensive technical secondary courses while the needs for basic education are still far from being satisfied.

- *Admission policies*, especially admission requirements to higher education, constitute another institutional factor affecting pupil/student choices. The precise effects of various admittance procedures to different cycles and different subjects is still a field open to investigation. But at any rate careful thought should be given to possibilities of breaking up the 'automatic' nature of immediate transfer between cycles and encouraging students to consider taking a break before returning to school or college. This suggest the need to maintain a flexible policy towards late entry to higher education.

- The consideration of *cost* seems to be particularly important when a pupil is making the decision about whether to leave school at the minimum age or not. Studies in developing and in developed countries suggest that enrolment growth rates in secondary/upper secondary schools tend to decline as a consequence of increases in school fees. There is some danger, however, that if increases in fees are uniform relatively bright but poor students may have to terminate their education and be replaced by less able students from high income families. To avoid this eventuality *increases in user fees* should be *discriminatory*.

Within certain limits the above-mentioned strategies can help restrict the growing student flows towards secondary and higher education; but they can hardly ever reverse 'strong trends' characterising the demand for education in a given country. In most developing countries the demand for education at the higher levels will continue to be high as long as there is a strong relationship between the educational cycle which provides a diploma and the level of jobs for which that diploma either qualifies a person or allows him to compete. Where the pool of eligible primary school leavers grows inexorably larger every year and where the political pressure on governments to expand the capacity of the system is high, educational planners and policy makers will have to cope with a quantum increase in enrolments at secondary and higher education levels—even if the mentioned flow regulation mechanisms prove successful to a certain extent. In a context of austerity *new ways and means of education*—in particular distance courses at secondary and post-secondary levels—are required to satisfy the non compressible demand for education without a commensurate increase in total cost or a serious decline in educational quality. (The Malawi Correspondence College is an interesting example in this respect).

II. Attracting Students Flows Towards Certain Sectors

Quite a number of countries are facing a serious shortage of science and technology trained manpower while at the same time unemployment among graduates in the social sciences and 'humanities' is growing. In such circumstances, educational planners have to develop appropriate strategies to attract more students to those study fields and courses which can help overcome the stated manpower shortages.

- Formal *information and guidance systems* can bring young people in touch with the realities of educational choices, and their occupational consequences. However, substantial resources are necessary to create and develop effective school guidance services. In poor countries such services are generally not well developed. Even when a rather well functioning guidance tool is available one should not over-emphasise the persuasive role capable of being played by improved information systems. Added information may influence a very small minority of pupils/students who are less confident of their choice; but it is by no means evident that it will help overcome significant problems of adjustment between pupil/student wishes and the employment market.

- Some governments have used special *financial incentives* such as bursaries to 'guide' a greater number of pupils/ students towards specific branches (especially scientific or technical ones) at upper secondary and post-secondary levels; they seem to have all the more succeeded in attracting the more able students to the extent that they have made parallel efforts to enhance the reputation of the branches or courses concerned (in improving their quality and/or adopting severe selection criteria and procedures for admission).

- Certain groups of pupils and students (pupils in remote areas; older and married students, etc.), are particularly susceptible to geographic proximity when making their educational choices. *Location* can thus become a policy instrument which might form part of a system of inducements that helps channelling more young people towards certain courses or branches.

- *Admission policies* have direct and indirect effects on student choices and student flows. Certain countries have succeeded in attracting more students towards less popular courses by adopting special selection and recruitment procedures for these courses: in selecting candidates for post-secondary courses in Agriculture and Technology on the basis of internal school-based assessment—without the necessity to sit the national university entrance examination—the Indonesian government *e.g.* has been able to increase the number of secondary school leavers with decent achievement levels enrolling in these courses; strict selection of secondary schools benefiting from the privilege of participating in this scheme and systematic comparison of university performances of the relevant recruited students with their schools' assessment contributed to the success of this initiative (4).

- Policy action aimed at *overcoming sex stereotyping* may also have to play a significant role: Frequently few active attempts are made to persuade girls to consider subjects such as science and technology. Policy solutions which could be envisaged to increase their enrolment in these subjects might include quotas for girls or even the setting up of separate schools for girls offering such traditionally 'less feminine' courses. The Girls' Science Schools in Nigeria constitute a rather successful example in this respect.

Concluding Remarks

With a view to enhancing the flow regulation capacities of educational systems it will in particular be necessary to monitor:

- student choices and the factors affecting them;
- the results of any changes in the structure of the educational system and in admission policies;
- labour market changes and hirers' recruitment policies.

References Books for Additional Reading

Bhaskara Rao, Digumarti (1994). *Scientific Aptitude*. New Delhi: Ashish Publishing House.

Bhaskara Rao, Digumarti (1995). *Animal Kingdom*. New Delhi: Discovery Publishing House.

Bhaskara Rao, Digumarti (1995). *Batracology*. New Delhi: Discovery Publishing House.

Bhaskara Rao, Digumarti (1996). *Scientific Attitude vis-a-vis Scientific Aptitude*. New Delhi: Discovery Publishing House.

Bhaskara Rao, Digumarti, ed. (1996). *Encyclopedia of Education For All*. 5 Vols. New Delhi: APH Publishing Corporation.

Vol. I Education For All: The World Conference.

Vol. II Education For All: The EPA-9 Summit.

Vol. III Education For All: Quality Education For All.

Vol. IV Education For All: Planning and Monitoring.

Vol. V Education For All: The Indian Scenario.

Bhaskara Rao, Digumarti, ed. (1996). *Global Perceptions on Peace Education*, 3 Vols. New Delhi: Discovery Publishing House.

Bhaskara Rao, Digumarti, ed. (1996). *National Policy on Education*, 2 Vols. New Delhi: Anmol Publications Pvt. Ltd.

Bhaskara Rao, Digumarti, ed. (1997). *Care the Child*, 2 Vols. New Delhi: Discovery Publishing House.

Bhaskara Rao, Digumarti, ed. (1997). *Education for the 21st Century*. New Delhi: Discovery Publishing House.

Bhaskara Rao, Digumarti, ed. (1997). *Reflections on Scientific Attitude*. New Delhi: Discovery Publishing House.

Bhaskara Rao, Digumarti (1997). *Scientific Attitude*. New Delhi: Discovery Publishing House.

Bhaskara Rao, Digumarti, ed. (1997). *Success Story of a Primary Education Project*. New Delhi: APH Publishing Corporation.

Bhaskara Rao, Digumarti, ed. (1997). *World Food Summit*. New Delhi: Discovery Publishing House.

Bhaskara Rao, Digumarti, ed. (1998). *Adolescence Education*. New Delhi: Discovery Publishing House.

Bhaskara Rao, Digumarti, ed. (1998). *Community and School Nutrition Education*. New Delhi: Discovery Publishing House.

Bhaskara Rao, Digumarti, ed. (1998). *District Primary Education Programme*. New Delhi: Discovery Publishing House.

Bhaskara Rao, Digumarti, ed. (1998). *Earth Summit*, 2 Vols. New Delhi: Discovery Publishing House.

Bhaskara Rao, Digumarti, ed. (1998). *National Policy on Education: Towards an Enlightened and Humane Society*. New Delhi: Discovery Publishing House.

Bhaskara Rao, Digumarti, ed. (1998). *Reforming School Education*. New Delhi: Discovery Publishing House.

Bhaskara Rao, Digumarti, ed. (1998). *Teacher Education in India*. New Delhi: Discovery Publishing House.

Bhaskara Rao, Digumarti, ed. (1998). *World Summit for Social Development*. New Delhi: Discovery Publishing House.

Bhaskara Rao, Digumarti, ed. (2000). *Education For All: Achieving the Goal*. 3 Vols. New Delhi: APH Publishing Corporation.

Vol. I The Global Consensus.

Vol. II Mid-Decade Review Reports of Regional Seminars.

Vol. III Issues and Trends.

Bhaskara Rao, Digumarti, ed. (2000). *International Encyclopedia of AIDS*, 11 Vols in 13 Parts. New Delhi: Discovery Publishing House.

Vol. 1 Introduction to HIV/AIDS.

Vol. 2 HIV/AIDS—Issues and Challenges, 2 Parts.

Vol. 3 HIV/AIDS—Socio Economic Realities.

Vol. 4 HIV/AIDS Law Ethics and Human Rights, 2 Parts.

Vol. 5 AIDS and NGOs.

Vol. 6 AIDS and Home Care.

Vol. 7 STD Case Management.

Vol. 8 HIV Prevention and Care—Teaching Modules for Nurses and Midwives.

Vol. 9 HIV/AIDS Prevention Education for Educational Institutions.

Vol. 10 Instructional Modules for AIDS Education.

Vol. 11 School Health Education to Prevent AIDS and STD—A Package for Curriculum Planners.

Bhaskara Rao, Digumarti, ed. (2000). *International Encyclopedia of Science and Technology Education*. 11 Vo'umes. New Delhi: Discovery Publishing House.

Vol. 1 Science and Technology Education.

Vol. 2 Science Education in Developing Countries.

Vol. 3 Organisational Structure of Science.

Vol. 4 Science Education in Asia and the Pacific.

Vol. 5 Science and Technology Education for All.

Vol. 6 Values, Ethics, Talent and Girls in Science and Technology Education.

Vol. 7 Popularization of Science and Technology Education.

Vol. 8 Science, Power and Society.

Vol. 9 Information Technology.

Vol. 10 Teacher Training in Science and Technology Education.

Vol. 11 Science, Technology and Society: A Curriculum Framework.

Bhaskara Rao, Digumarti, ed. (2001). *Distance Education in Different Countries*. New Delhi: APH Publishing Corporation.

Bhaskara Rao, Digumarti, ed. (2001). *Decentralised Management of Education (Management of Education in Panchayati Raj and Municipal Bodies)*. New Delhi: Discovery Publishing House.

Bhaskara Rao, Digumarti, ed. (2001). *Electrochemistry for Environmental Protection*. New Delhi: Discovery Publishing House.

Bhaskara Rao, Digumarti, ed. (2001). *Global Educational Studies*. New Delhi: Discovery Publishing House.

Bhaskara Rao, Digumarti, ed. (2001). *Global Synthesis of Educational Assessment*. New Delhi: Discovery Publishing House.

Bhaskara Rao, Digumarti, ed. (2001). *International Encyclopedia of Human Rights*, 7 Volumes in 13 Parts. New Delhi: Discovery Publishing House.

Vol. 1 International Instruments of Human Rights, 2 Parts.

Vol. 2 Regional Instruments of Human Rights.

Vol. 3 Human Rights and The United Nations, 2 Parts.

Vol. 4 Fact Files of Human Rights, 2 Parts.

Vol. 5 Study Stories of Human Rights, 3 Parts.

Vol. 6 International Meetings on Human Rights, 2 Parts.

Vol. 7 Professional Training in Human Rights.